Management for Professionals

More information about this series at
http://www.springer.com/series/10101

Jan vom Brocke • Theresa Schmiedel
Editors

BPM – Driving Innovation in a Digital World

Springer

Editors
Jan vom Brocke
Institute of Information Systems
University of Liechtenstein
Vaduz
Liechtenstein

Theresa Schmiedel
Institute of Information Systems
University of Liechtenstein
Vaduz
Liechtenstein

ISSN 2192-8096 ISSN 2192-810X (electronic)
Management for Professionals
ISBN 978-3-319-38530-3 ISBN 978-3-319-14430-6 (eBook)
DOI 10.1007/978-3-319-14430-6

Springer Cham Heidelberg New York Dordrecht London

Softcover reprint of the hardcover 1st edition 2015

Printed on acid-free paper

Springer International Publishing AG Switzerland is part of Springer Science+Business Media (www.springer.com)

Foreword

Business Process Management (BPM) has proven largely successful in increasing the competitiveness of a large variety of organizations by fostering the efficiency of operations within and between organizations around the globe. In this book, we show how BPM can also contribute extensively to the innovativeness of organizations in leveraging new technology of the digital age. Consequently, BPM can contribute to one of the most important challenges of our modern economies and societies, which is to sustain wealth by means of new business models. In featuring the views of global thought leaders, we showcase not only the potential of BPM but also the need of the discipline to further develop in order to take on this new role.

This book has been initiated in the context of the European BPM Round Table that took place in Vaduz, Liechtenstein, in May 2014 on the theme, "Business Process Management—Driving Innovation in a Digital World" (www.bpm-roundtable2014.eu). The idea of a BPM Round Table at a European level emerged from several local BPM Round Tables that were established in Europe over the last years. The first European BPM Round Table took place in Eindhoven in 2012 with the objective to broadly exchange knowledge and experience between experts from business, administration, and science.

We would like to express our gratitude for having had the opportunity to host the 2nd European BPM Round Table in Liechtenstein and would like to particularly thank Wil van der Aalst and Hajo Reijers for suggesting Vaduz as the venue for the event. In addition, we are also deeply thankful for the large support we received from the Eindhoven University of Technology and the European Institute of Innovation and Technology for its realization. Also, the strong sponsorship from industry has been instrumental in the successful organization of the European BPM Round Table in Liechtenstein: The Hilti AG contributed as a platinum sponsor, Camelot ITLab and Swarovski as gold sponsors, Ivoclar Vivadent and mbpi as silver sponsors, and Hoval as bronze sponsors. We, therefore, cordially thank all company representatives for contributing to the success of the event.

Further, we extend our thanks to the University of Liechtenstein for the additional funds that were provided in order to host the event. We would also like to thank the organizing team, especially Nadine Reuter and Nicole Thöny, as well as the whole team of the Institute of Information Systems for their excellent work in preparing the conference and making every guest feel comfortable during their visit at our University.

Finally, our special thanks go to the authors of this book. The contributions in this book are essentially based on the insightful talks the authors gave at the Round Table in Liechtenstein. In addition, the book also includes further authors who we invited from beyond the framework of the event. We would like to cordially thank all contributors for their efforts in bringing their work, experience, and ideas to paper. All chapters have undergone a thorough review process and we are very grateful for the effort both reviewers and authors have made in making our vision of this BPM book focusing on innovation in a digital world come true. They all share the spirit that it is important to emphasize the strong contribution BPM can make to the economy and society, and that it is the right time to demonstrate BPM's contribution by means of this book.

Companies are advised to focus on their capabilities to manage business processes as a means to increase their agility in mastering innovation and transformation efforts. The book shows that a rich body of knowledge is available that can be applied right away. The book also addresses researchers, for these to engage in further developing this body of knowledge to better account for the new role of BPM as a driver and facilitator of innovation.

We are confident that the research underlying this book and the discussions of the topics at the European BPM Round Table in Liechtenstein are inspirational for driving innovations in the context of BPM. It has been a pleasure and privilege to work with all the people involved and we hope that a lot of positive developments will emerge from this work.

Vaduz, Liechtenstein

Jan vom Brocke
Theresa Schmiedel

Preface

Innovation can be regarded as the *idea-to-execution process*, i.e., the conversion of emerging insights, opportunities, and creative designs into new products, services, processes, or entire new business models. However, unlike most transactional processes such as purchasing, sales, or payroll, the transformational process of innovation has been underexplored by the business process management (BPM) community. Beyond support for internal idea management processes, corporations have been short on improving the productivity and scale of their innovation value chain consisting of processes such as open innovation, design-led innovation, or co-innovation.

Adding a process-centered mind- and toolset to innovation promises all the BPM benefits organizations have harvested for over two decades. In particular, a well-orchestrated and where possible IT-supported innovation process will be more efficient, predictable, and less risky while at the same time protecting the pockets of creativity along such processes. As such, BPM has the potential to accelerate innovation processes and to reduce the failure rate of innovation, leading to a much needed increase in innovation activities.

Innovation processes are of course less predictable than highly repetitive transactional processes. Nevertheless, by now BPM has grown in terms of maturity when it comes to case management, exception handling, cloud, and social processes. As such, BPM seems sufficiently equipped to approach the challenges related to innovation process management (IPM) as its next significant unit of analysis.

In contrast to the view of adding BPM to innovation, there is also tremendous potential in *enriching BPM approaches with innovation methodologies*. Currently, the typical process life cycle starts by capturing the actual process via a series of interviews, observations, or more recently process mining. Subsequent activities are then dedicated to identifying process issues and their root causes and to creating solutions, which overcome these. This inside-out approach can be characterized as being reactive and problem driven.

Such an approach was more than sufficient in the *age of automation* which was centered on streamlining processes by eliminating waste (lean), variation (Six Sigma), and manual labor (workflow), leading ultimately to cost-resilient processes.

However, in the *age of digitization*, cost resilience is no longer sufficient. Digital solutions have shifted the focus from corporate digital capital as materialized in compliance-driven IT systems to customer-centered mobile apps and solutions and by this are much more revenue sensitive.

As a series of recent examples, most prominently Kodak, have shown, high levels of cost efficiency are necessary but not sufficient for survival. In the current economic environment, competition emerges quickly in the form of technology-savvy disruptors able to provide superior value propositions based on light asset models. Thus, organizations have to strive for revenue resilience in addition to cost resilience when designing future-proofed processes.

Consequently, the BPM body of knowledge is in desperate need to be complemented by a more opportunity-driven, proactive approach to process design. Instead of questions such as "How do we reduce re-work, bottlenecks, or waiting time in our processes?", such an opportunity-driven approach answers questions such as "In which of our processes do Google Glasses create substantial gains?" or "Where in our landscape of processes could mobile, social, or location-based services lead to new revenue streams?"

The coexistence of demands for cost and revenue resilience, i.e., the need to simultaneously address process issues and to capitalize on new digital process design opportunities, is called "*Ambidextrous BPM*." Ambidextrous BPM demands two different types of capabilities, i.e., the continuation of the exploitative strength of traditional BPM needs to be combined with the explorative potential of a design-intensive approach sensing external opportunities and converting these quickly into improved processes.

Adding BPM to innovation and innovation to BPM will ultimately lead to a new class of (process-aware) information systems, which can be labeled "*(process) innovation systems*." After understanding, modeling, analyzing, and proposing reference models for most of the transactional processes, the speed, disruptive potential, and opportunities of the digital age now require making transformational processes the focus of our investigations.

This book can be seen as an important step toward such process innovation systems. I very much like to congratulate the editors and authors for presenting such an impressive scope of ideas for how to address the challenging but very rewarding marriage of BPM and innovation.

Brisbane, Australia — Michael Rosemann

Contents

Part I

Introduction

Business Process Management: Potentials and Challenges of Driving Innovation

Theresa Schmiedel and Jan vom Brocke

Abstract

Business process management (BPM) is fundamental for organizational competitiveness. In the last decades, BPM has evolved from a technology-focused into a holistic and principle-oriented discipline concerned with efficient and effective business processes. However, the emerging digital age requires rethinking the role of BPM in organizations. On the one hand, we identify opportunities of BPM as a driver of innovation that institutionalizes digital technologies in business processes. On the other hand, we also recognize opportunities to, in turn, innovate BPM. Overall, we identify both opportunities and challenges of BPM when it comes to innovation in the digital age. Based on these insights, we provide an outlook on the chapters of this book which may guide both the research and practice of BPM in driving innovation in a digital world.

1 Introduction

Information technology (IT) plays a vital role in driving innovation in today's digital world, and Business Process Management (BPM) is key in leveraging these potentials. Many new technologies, such as mobile and real-time technologies, the Internet of Things, big data analytics, and social media, have come to the fore in recent years, which seems to accelerate the speed of business innovation and transformation. While such new technologies represent important triggers of innovation, only the incorporation of IT into business processes allows

T. Schmiedel (✉) • J. vom Brocke
Institute of Information Systems, University of Liechtenstein, Fürst-Franz-Josef-Str. 21, 9490 Vaduz, Liechtenstein
e-mail: theresa.schmiedel@uni.li; jan.vom.brocke@uni.li

J. vom Brocke, T. Schmiedel (eds.), *BPM – Driving Innovation in a Digital World*, Management for Professionals, DOI 10.1007/978-3-319-14430-6_1

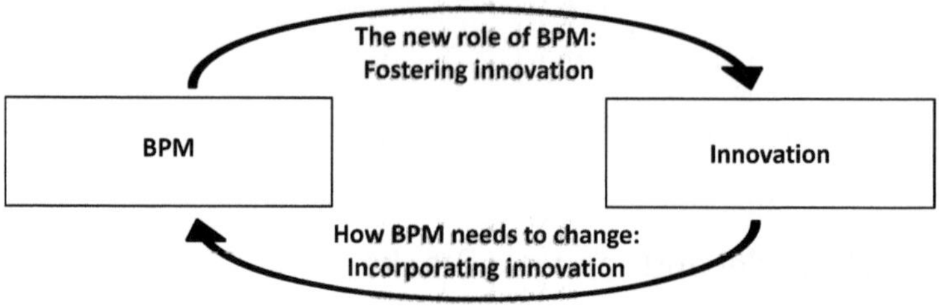

Fig. 1 BPM and innovation

organizations to be innovative and remain competitive. Thus, business process management (BPM) can be considered a key driver for innovation.

Against this background, the purpose of the present chapter is to analyze the role of BPM in driving innovation in a digital world in greater detail. In doing so, we follow a comprehensive (Rosemann & vom Brocke, 2015) and principle-oriented (vom Brocke, Schmiedel, et al., 2014) understanding of BPM. Our socio-technical cognition of BPM builds on a growing consensus among both researchers and practitioners that BPM is comprised of more than just methods and systems supportive of operational excellence. BPM is also instrumental for innovating and transforming businesses through strategy-, governance-, people- and culture-oriented factors (Rosemann & vom Brocke, 2015).

The remainder of this chapter is organized as follows: As a next stage, we provide some background information on business innovation in general and about innovation in the digital age in particular. We then examine the role of BPM in business innovation, looking into two complementary facets: the potentials of BPM in driving innovation and the challenges for BPM in taking on and demonstrating this new role. Particularly, we look into the potentials of BPM's new role in fostering innovation and into the challenges of changing BPM where necessary to incorporate required innovation (Fig. 1). Finally, we provide a brief outlook on the chapters of this book.

2 The Need for Innovation

Innovation is a concept that seems to enter more and more business- and management-related discussions. While one could at times gain the impression that innovation has become a buzzword or hyped concept in both research and practice, there is strong consensus that innovation is and always has been a key driving force of competitiveness and welfare.

In fact, the wealth of a society strongly depends on the innovative capacity of its people and organizations. Particularly in regions that witness production- and service-oriented jobs moving to other parts in the world, innovation is considered to be a continuous requirement for sustaining welfare in a changing industrial environment. Such regions comprise North America, Europe, and Australia, but other regions such as Asia and South America will face a similar situation very soon. In essence, innovation is essential for all areas of the world to sustain and further develop living conditions, both from an economic and a societal perspective.

Considering the rapidly changing business environment and technological developments in recent years, the innovative capacity of BPM gains increasing importance. In this context, it can appear challenging for organizations, however, to recognize such external changes, not as a threat to established business habits, but, rather, as an opportunity that ultimately allows fostering the success of organizations.

Over the last couple of decades, research and practice have developed BPM into a discipline that has proven to drive the competitiveness of organizations (Hammer, 2010). BPM is concerned with the design, implementation, and monitoring of efficient and effective business processes (Smith & Fingar, 2004; vom Brocke & Rosemann, 2015). Since processes, i.e., operations in and across organizational functions, are at the core of every organization, the relevance of BPM for companies of all kinds of industries, private, and public organizations has been recognized worldwide.

We can distinguish between two abstract modes of managing business processes: On the one hand, BPM concentrates on running business, i.e., it ensures both process compliance through performance monitoring and also continuous workflow improvement with the overall objective to maintain operational excellence (Schmiedel, vom Brocke & Uhl, 2015). On the other hand, BPM engages in changing and disruptively innovating business, realizing superior ways to provide products and services utilizing new technologies.

Having recognized the relevance of innovation in general and with regard to BPM in particular, we next look more deeply into the meaning of innovation, since it seems to be a rather broad term that can refer to various aspects.

3 The Power of Process Innovation

Innovations have been distinguished in many ways. To illustrate this we exemplarily look at three dimensions of innovation with two particular types of innovation each and pay special attention to the power of process innovation as one example that, naturally, stands out in the context of BPM.

One dimension refers to the **origin** of innovations. In this regard, there are two typical sources (Chesborough, Vanhaverbeke, & West, 2006).

- **Closed innovation:** Innovations that stem from the research and development activities of companies and institutions, i.e. from a specific group of people who are employed in order to innovate.

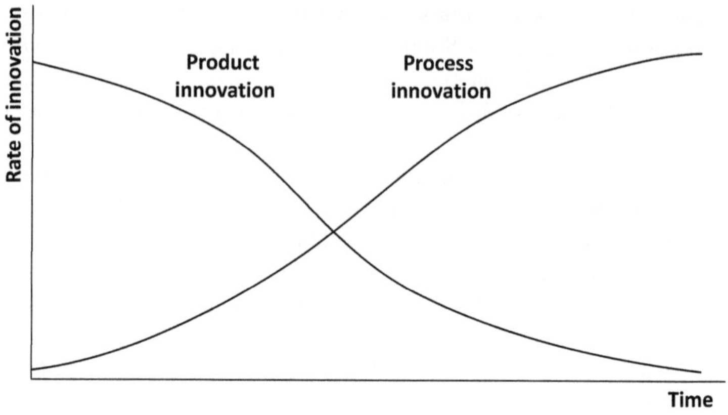

Fig. 2 Product vs. process innovation

- **Open innovation:** Innovations that are developed through open innovation processes, e.g., through involving the crowd, namely people from outside the organization (e.g., MyStarbucksIdea.com or Dell's IdeaStorm.com).

Further, we can distinguish innovations based on their **impact**. Innovations with a very broad impact are based on disruptive technologies which completely change the way people interact and do business; also referred to as "game changing" innovations. Whereas innovations which "only" influence a particular industry are more focused in their impact on society.

- **Specific innovations:** Innovations that have an impact only within a limited scope, e.g. within a very specific market (e.g. iPods in the music market).
- **Disruptive innovations:** Innovations that have a substantive influence on many or even all parts of the economy (e.g. the Internet).

Distinguishing innovations based on their **form**, two key types of innovation are typically differentiated as depicted in Fig. 2 (Fichman, Dos Santos, & Zheng, 2014; Utterback & Abernathy, 1975).

- **Product innovation:** Innovations that focus on the development and diffusion of new products (which often contain some form of new technology), i.e. innovations as seen from the producer perspective.
- **Process innovation:** Innovations that focus on the adoption of such products (which often requires some form of new behavioral pattern) through individuals or organizations, i.e. innovations as seen from the user perspective.

While the importance of product innovations is undisputed, the innovation of processes seems to be a key differentiator of our times, mostly through the use of new technology. Take for example, Nespresso, PayPal, or iTunes. These are largely successful businesses built around products that seem to have been out there forever, namely, coffee, money and music. It is a very old need which is addressed but it is fulfilled in a highly innovative way, namely by process.

Process Innovations are particularly appealing, since they

- directly affect people's experience,
- often do not need heavy engineering,
- can take place with a given technology,
- can be deployed globally.

In comparing the development of product and process innovation over time, smartphones serve as a good example to illustrate the shift in the rate of innovation across time. Smartphones represent a product innovation combining various functionalities such as the ones of mobile phones, web browsers, or navigation systems. When the first smartphones entered the market, the rate of this product innovation was very high. Meanwhile, however, this product innovation has led to countless process innovations in both private and business life, ranging from individual assistance (e.g. on health care) to corporate app stores innovating sales processes for instance. Even though smartphones as such are not highly innovative any more, they still enable manifold process innovations in all kinds of application areas. New technologies of our times represent the foundation for further process innovation in the digital age (see the chapter by Sandy Kemsley (2015)).

4 Potentials of Our Digital Age

Most of today's innovations are driven by IT. New technologies including mobile and real-time technologies, the Internet of Things, big data analytics, and social media clearly illustrate the enormous impact of IT on society in terms of enabling competitiveness and welfare (vom Brocke, Debortoli, Müller, & Reuter, 2014). Further, examining such technologies gives an indication how strongly IT generally shapes our times. The digital age is increasingly characterized by usage of the Internet through anyone and anything at anytime and anywhere:

- **Anyone and Anything:** Addressing the question on who represents the digital age, we can observe that large parts of modern societies are experts in using IT in their daily business. Looking at new generations growing up with the Internet, i.e. so-called digital natives, their expertise with IT is even more advanced, working with the Internet comes ever more naturally to them and is increasingly taken for granted. Not only people are online today, however, as nearly anything can be connected to the Internet, including cars, houses, clothes, tools, and machines. It has been reported that since 2013 more "things" are on the Internet than people (Mclaughlin, 2013). The possible connection of anyone and anything to the Internet is a key characteristic of the digital age.

- **Anywhere:** Another key characteristic of the digital age refers to the ubiquity of the Internet. Technically it is possible to realize a comprehensive network coverage that enables Internet access around the globe. Internet providers for such services are omnipresent and Internet-to-go use is growing as it becomes more and more affordable. Being able to go online anywhere can fundamentally change social and economic processes. Potentially, ubiquitous Internet access might increase efficiency as waiting and travelling times can be used effectively. For example, HomePlus has innovated the retail market in South Korea by placing QR-code-based shopping experiences in local underground transport, which can now be seen in many places around the world.
- **Anytime:** Another characteristic of the digital age relates to the fact that data is not only available anywhere (irrespective of location) but also anytime (irrespective of time). Particularly, it also relates to the idea of real-time availability of data. The possibility to receive up-to-date information at any point in time is key for essential innovations in many business processes. Integrating multiple kinds of real-time data, analytics today already enables the prediction of events like the spread of the flu or the occurrence of traffic jams much better than conventional methods could have managed. It is intriguing to think how such data integration will innovate our professional and private lives in the near future, and first studies are available to report on specific use cases in business (vom Brocke, Debortoli, et al., 2014).

The implications of these characteristics may become clearer when looking into some scenarios: The car of the future will not only optimize routing based on real-time traffic information, but it will be able to avoid accidents through information from other cars in its proximity. The house of the future will be able to do smart energy management based on weather information and based on the location of the people inside the building. Clothes of the future will manage the personal state of health, eventually suggesting to the wearer to drink a glass of water or to rest for a few minutes based on body data taken from the skin (vom Brocke, Riedl, & Léger, 2013).

In industry, such innovations of the digital age will significantly change business. Apart from new possibilities in designing and managing internal organizational processes, new customer services will be available that could not have been offered before. At the same time, it is obvious that the mere technological action opportunities will not result in value creating innovations right away. It is rather about new business processes that can be afforded through the technology, and BPM plays a key role in leveraging the manifold opportunities. In the next section, we further examine the role of BPM in driving such innovations.

5 The New Role of BPM

Considering BPM as a source of innovation, we can generally distinguish between the modes of running and changing business. Based on this differentiation, BPM can drive innovation in two ways: (1) through managing processes which yield product innovations (running processes) and (2) through managing the redesign of processes which yields process innovations (changing processes).

(1) **Focusing on the management of creative processes to foster product innovations**. Some organizational processes aim at generating innovations, such as processes in the research & development department of a company. The primary focus of these processes lies in identifying innovations of products and services that generate additional business value. In such processes, for instance, creativity plays an important role (Seidel, 2011), and the management of these processes includes designing, implementing, and monitoring creative and administrative work to enable overall smooth procedures and to maintain operational excellence.

    Traditionally, organizations consider processes that generate innovations as the heart of their business. Working on product innovations has typically been driven, for example, by engineers in a secured environment inside the company. In recent years, however, open innovation has proven beneficial in more and more cases (Chesborough et al., 2006). Involving people from outside the organization in innovating products and services often makes use of open innovation platforms such as the one from the coffee brand Starbucks, where customers suggest new recipes for drinks and food, among other ideas.

    The growing trend to involve customers in innovation processes seems to be fostered by the possibilities that the various IT-supported collaboration systems of the digital age offer. Online platforms, social media, and mobile apps, for example, are increasingly used to technologically support collective efforts to develop new products and services, also referred to as crowd sourcing (Leimeister, Huber, Bretschneider, & Krcmar, 2009). Thus, managing processes which yield innovations today truly refers to both internally and externally grounded processes.

(2) **Incorporating new technologies into organizational processes to foster process innovations**. Apart from managing innovation processes, BPM also allows for managing process innovations, i.e. redesigning business processes to increase competitiveness. Establishing innovations in organizational processes can refer to various aspects, including the redesign of process steps through integrating IT products such as smart phones and tablets or IT services such as mobile apps.

Generally, we can distinguish between two triggers of process innovation. On the one hand, both internal and external requirements from involved stakeholders can lead to the redesign of business processes. On the other hand, the possibilities of new technologies can trigger process innovation. While stakeholder requirements have always been triggers for change and innovation, new technologies of the digital age represent a key source of numerous affordances for process innovations today.

In fact, fundamental business transformations are often driven by incorporating IT into business processes. Examples are wide-ranging, including globally integrated ERP systems that allow for harmonized processes, mobile phone apps that allow for new sales processes, and big data analytics that allow for real-time process decisions based on data available from products in use.

Overall, we can observe distinct ways in which BPM can serve as a source of innovation. In the next section, we look into how BPM needs to change in order to account for its new role and examine how BPM as a management approach may need to be innovated in order to further drive innovation.

6 How BPM Needs to Change

As a discipline, BPM builds on an established pool of methods and models that have proven successful in improving the competiveness of organizations in various forms. However, we might observe a shift in one of the core institutional logics that BPM professionals draw from: turning from a logic of automation to a logic of innovation (Tumbas, Schmiedel, & vom Brocke, 2015). With regard to established BPM methods, we need to recognize that such methods have been designed for the application areas of their times. Originally, BPM essentially focused on well- (or semi-) structured processes, while driving innovation today calls for management practices suitable for processes of diverse natures.

Therefore, it is highly relevant to develop methods and models that account for different types of application areas. In developing such methods and models, it will be important to particularly leverage the potential of new technologies to prove that they successfully drive innovation in a digital age. Considering how far BPM requires innovation, we can again distinguish between the two modes (1) running and (2) changing business.

(1) **Considering the nature of processes in context-aware BPM**. Regarding the continuous management of organizational processes, extant BPM models and methods seem to focus on structured and standardizable processes. However, knowledge-intensive and dynamic business processes tend to be neglected. It seems to be important, though, to examine how far existing models and methods are applicable to all kinds of processes.

For example, one might reflect whether all processes should be modeled and, if so, whether all processes should be modeled in the same way. New technologies of the digital age, for example, meanwhile allow for real-time mining of business processes based on the digital traces that single process steps leave or based on text mining possibilities (Günther, Rinderle-Ma, Reichert, Van der Aalst, & Recker, 2008). Such analytical possibilities enable new ways of modeling as-is processes.

Generally, we can observe a lack of distinction between existing types of organizational processes for applying suitable methods and models. Research has shown, for instance, that we need to address creative processes differently than we have addressed routinized processes in the past (Seidel, 2011). Such considerations are necessary in order to consider the nature of processes when managing them. Identifying dimensions that distinguish business processes and that require a distinct approach for their management will be particularly important in order to realize context-aware BPM in both research and practice.

(2) **Leveraging the potentials of digital technologies in a holistic approach towards process innovation**. The digital age offers manifold opportunities to innovate business processes. In order to do so, it will be important to first identify value-creating potentials (vom Brocke, Debortoli, et al., 2014). In particular, reflecting on the possibilities that anything may be connected anywhere and anytime may be supportive in finding relevant innovation ideas. For example, monitoring and analyzing process performances based on digital processes enables real-time deviance mining, i.e. the identification of best and worst process performances (see the chapters by Recker (2015) and by Dumas and Maggi (2015)).

Once required process changes are identified, research has found that BPM needs to follow a comprehensive approach in order to successfully manage such changes (vom Brocke, Petry, & Gonser, 2012). Beyond modeling and IT-related factors, BPM should consider various other factors in developing dynamic capabilities of process transformation. Prior research has shown that such factors include capabilities, such as strategic alignment, governance, people, and culture (Rosemann & de Bruin, 2005), that need specific consideration in management (Müller, Schmiedel, Gorbacheva, & vom Brocke, 2014; Schmiedel, vom Brocke, & Recker, 2013).

Looking beyond the two modes of running and changing business, recent research has suggested essential principles for BPM that also apply for leveraging and shaping BPM as a driver for innovation (vom Brocke, Schmiedel, et al., 2014). In the following, we will further outline how (3) drawing from essential BPM principles helps to build up innovation capabilities in an organization.

(3) **Building up innovation capabilities following essential BPM principles.** Managing innovation through BPM and building up long-term innovation capabilities in an organization can be guided by essential principles of BPM (vom Brocke, Schmiedel, et al., 2014). Such principles include, for example, the "principle of purpose", which emphasizes the need that BPM contributes to strategic value creation. This is an important aspect to consider when managing for innovation, because innovation may well be enabled by technology, but it

ultimately needs to deliver business value, and from a number of projects there is evidence that value-orientation is often neglected throughout IT projects.

Another example relates to the "principle of continuity" which suggest that BPM is a permanent practice—and which also implies that innovations should constantly be considered in organizations and not only when reasons for change have piled up. In the digital world in particular, the "principle of technology appropriation" is another highly relevant principle. It suggests that BPM makes opportune use of technology, which is fundamental in an innovation context. An overview of the principles is also given at www.bpm-principles.org. While the identified principles of good BPM are generally relevant for managing extant processes, they are particularly important to consider when changing business processes and incorporating innovations in the organization.

In the next section, we present an overview of the chapters in this book, outlining how they further inform researchers and practitioners on driving innovation in the field of BPM.

7 Contributions of This Book

The chapters of this book provide a broad overview of the various facets of BPM when it comes to driving innovation in today's digital world. The authors of these contributions show how BPM plays a key role in establishing and maintaining organizational competitiveness and ultimately societal welfare.

The book is structured into five parts. **Part I** gives a general **introduction** on innovation in the context of BPM. The overview on potentials and challenges of innovation in this chapter is followed by two further chapters. Charles Møller reports on "*Business Process Innovation as an Enabler of Proactive Value Chains*". He outlines the importance of agile and resilient value chains and discusses how process innovation supports the transformation of value chains, using the example of a Danish research and innovation program in manufacturing. Richard Welke presents "*Thinking Tri-laterally About Business Processes, Services and Business Models: An Innovation Perspective*". He outlines the close connection of business models (as purpose of a service), services, and processes (as sequence of tasks in a service) and illustrates a fresh perspective on process innovation based on bottom up, top down, or middle out viewpoints.

Following up on this introduction, **Part II** gives insights on **driving innovation through emerging technologies**. Four chapters outline the important role of new technologies including mobile, social, and cloud technologies, in realizing innovative ideas in the context of BPM. Sandy Kemsley provides an overview on "*Emerging Technologies in BPM*". She explores the role of new technologies in the context of BPM, outlining how mobile, cloud, social, and analytical technologies initiate change in the nature of work and what the implications of intelligent processes are. Peter Trkman and Monika Klun report on "*Leveraging Social Media for Process Innovation. A Conceptual Framework*". They illustrate how social media can be used in various phases of business process life cycles to support, for example, the modeling, execution, monitoring and improvement of organizational processes. Bernd Schenk outlines "*The Role of Enterprise Systems in Process Innovation*". He highlights how enterprise systems can function as enabler, trigger, and enforcer in organizational innovations and illustrates this by the opportunities of cloud computing for the integration of enterprise systems in process innovations. Jens Ohlsson, Peter Händel, Shengnan Han, and Richard Welch report on "*Process Innovation with Disruptive Technology in Auto Insurance: Lessons Learned from a Smartphone-Based Insurance Telematics Initiative*". They present the potentials of behavioral-based insurance and emphasize the need for process changes in organizations to leverage the potentials of insurance telematics.

Based on these insights into emerging technologies, **Part III** focuses on **driving innovation through advanced process analytics**. Four chapters present latest findings on the role of analyzing extant data for realizing innovations in a process context. Wil van der Aalst reports on "*Extracting Event Data from Databases to Unleash Process Mining*". He introduces an approach to create event logs from underlying databases as a fundamental prerequisite for the application of process-mining techniques when information systems do not explicitly record events. Jan Recker gives insights on "*Evidence-Based Business Process Management: Using Digital Opportunities to Drive Organizational Innovation*". He illustrates how digital capabilities enable organizations to innovate based on facts rather than fiction and outlines how research can play a key role as an innovation support service. Marlon Dumas and Fabrizio Maria Maggi give insights on "*Enabling Process Innovation via Deviance Mining and Predictive Monitoring*". They show how analyzing process execution logs offline can detect deviant behavior that leads to performance changes and how process analytics at runtime can predict the influence of certain activities on probable process outcomes. Peter Loos, Peter Fettke, Jürgen Walter, Tom Thaler, and Peyman Ardalani outline the "*Identification of Business Process Models in a Digital World*". They introduce a comprehensive seven-phase method for the inductive development of reference models and present an application scenario of specific techniques that allow to automatically derive reference models.

Following the elaborations on process analytics, **Part IV** sheds light on **driving innovation through new generation process modeling**. Three chapters give an overview of latest developments in documenting business processes in organizations. Jörg Becker presents "*Designing Process Modeling Tools to Facilitate Semantic Standardization: Increasing the Speed of Innovation in a Digital World*". He outlines five design principles for process modeling tools which support the development of harmonized process models and illustrates a prototypical implementation. Mikael Lind and Sandra Haraldson provide details on "*(Air)port Innovations as Ecosystem Innovations*". They show how business process modeling can be used to facilitate digital innovations in ecosystems with multi-actor collaborations and illustrate key innovations in the case of Future Airports. Monika Malinova and Jan Mendling report on "*Leveraging Innovation Based on Effective Process Map Design: Insights from the Case of a European Insurance Company*".

They use a specific case to illustrate how companies benefit from systematic process map design and how this relates to process innovation.

Complementing the previous technical and methodological aspects, **Part V** gives insights into **driving innovation through organizational capabilities**. Four chapters elaborate on the importance of factors including strategy, governance, and culture in innovating in a BPM context. César A.L. Oliveira, Ricardo M.F. Lima, and Hajo A. Reijers present "*Implementing a Digital Strategy Through Business Process Management*". They outline how informing employees about strategic corporate goals during workflow execution increases strategic alignment and offers innovative possibilities for the implementation of strategic change. Stefan Sackmann and Kai Kittel elaborate on "*Flexible Workflows and Compliance: A Solvable Contradiction?!*". They introduce an innovative approach and its prototypical implementation to solve the trade-off between flexible and compliant workflows by allowing a workflow to be changed according to requirements during run-time. Amy Van Looy reports "*On the Importance of Non-technical Process Capabilities to Support Digital Innovations*". She suggests a process capability framework that recognizes the importance of non-technical capabilities relating to process-oriented management, structure, and culture. Janina Kettenbohrer, Mirko Kloppenburg, and Daniel Beimborn provide insights into "*Driving Process Innovation: The Application of a Role-Based Governance Model at Lufthansa Technik*". They elaborate on effective governance models that support decision-making in process improvement and innovation, and apply a role-based governance model to an exemplary process at Lufthansa Technik.

Overall, the book illustrates several distinct facets of BPM that are important for driving innovation in a digital world. The various viewpoints show, on the one hand, that BPM bears huge potential to foster such innovations, and, on the other hand, that BPM also faces challenges, which call for advancing both BPM research and practice towards examining how to further develop BPM as a discipline. We hope you find the chapters of this book inspiring food for thought and action.

References

Chesborough, H., Vanhaverbeke, W., & West, J. (2006). *Open innovation: Researching a new paradigm*. Oxford: Oxford University Press.

Dumas, M., & Maggi, F. M. (2015). Enabling process innovation via deviance mining and predictive monitoring. In J. vom Brocke & T. Schmiedel (Eds.), *Business process management: Driving innovation in digital world*. Berlin: Springer.

Fichman, R. G., Dos Santos, B. L., & Zheng, Z. (2014). Digital innovation as a fundamental and powerful concept in the information systems curriculum. *Management Information Systems Quarterly, 38*(2), 329–354.

Günther, C., Rinderle-Ma, S., Reichert, M., Van der Aalst, W. M. P., & Recker, J. (2008). Using process mining to learn from process changes in evolutionary systems. *International Journal of Business Process Integration and Management, 3*(1), 61–78.

Hammer, M. (2010). What is business process management? In J. vom Brocke & M. Rosemann (Eds.), *Handbook on business process management: Introduction, methods and information systems* (Vol. 1, pp. 3–16). Berlin: Springer.

Kemsley, S. (2015). Emerging technologies in BPM. In J. vom Brocke & T. Schmiedel (Eds.), *Business process management: Driving innovation in a digital world.* Berlin: Springer.

Leimeister, J. M., Huber, M., Bretschneider, U., & Krcmar, H. (2009). Leveraging crowdsourcing: Activation-supporting components for IT-based ideas competition. *Journal of Management Information Systems, 26*(1), 197–224.

Mclaughlin, D. (2013, June 17). More mobile devices than people by the end of 2013 – Is your business prepared? *Cisco Blog.*

Müller, O., Schmiedel, T., Gorbacheva, E., & vom Brocke, J. (2014). Toward a typology of business process management professionals: Identifying patterns of competences through latent semantic analysis. *Enterprise Information Systems, 8*, 1–31.

Recker, J. (2015). Evidence-based business process management: Using digital opportunities to drive organizational innovation. In J. vom Brocke & T. Schmiedel (Eds.), *Business process management: Driving innovation in a digital world.* Berlin: Springer.

Rosemann, M., & de Bruin, T. (2005, February). Application of a holistic model for determining BPM maturity. *BPTrends*, 1–21.

Rosemann, M., & vom Brocke, J. (2015). The six core elements of business process management. In J. vom Brocke & M. Rosemann (Eds.), *Handbook on business process management. Introduction, methods and information systems* (Vol. 1, pp. 105–124). Berlin: Springer.

Schmiedel, T., vom Brocke, J., & Uhl, A. (2015). Operational excellence. In A. Uhl & L. Gollenia (Eds.), *Digital enterprise transformation* (pp. 207–230). Farnham: Gower.

Schmiedel, T., vom Brocke, J., & Recker, J. (2013). Which cultural values matter to business process management? Results from a global Delphi study. *Business Process Management Journal, 19*(2), 292–317.

Seidel, S. (2011). Toward a theory of managing creativity-intensive processes: A creative industries study. *Information Systems and e-Business Management, 9*(4), 407–446.

Smith, H., & Fingar, P. (2004, July). Process management maturity models. *BPTrends*, 1–5.

Tumbas, S., Schmiedel, T., & vom Brocke, J. (2015). Characterizing multiple institutional logics for innovation with digital technologies. *Proceedings of the 48th Annual Hawaii International Conference on System Sciences (HICSS)*, Kauai, Hawaii.

Utterback, J. M., & Abernathy, W. (1975). A dynamic model of product and process innovation. *Omega, 33*(4), 639–655.

vom Brocke, J., Debortoli, S., Müller, O., & Reuter, N. (2014). How in-memory technology can create business value: Insights from the Hilti case. *Communications of the Association for Information Systems, 34*(1), 151–167.

vom Brocke, J., Petry, M., & Gonser, T. (2012). Business process management. In A. Uhl & L. Gollenia (Eds.), *The handbook of business transformation management*. Gower: Farnham.

vom Brocke, J., Riedl, R., & Léger, P.-M. (2013). Application strategies for neuroscience in information systems design science research. *Journal of Computer Information Systems, 53*(3), 1–13.

vom Brocke, J., & Rosemann, M. (Eds.). (2015). *Handbook on business process management* (2nd ed.). Berlin: Springer.

vom Brocke, J., Schmiedel, T., Recker, J., Trkman, P., Mertens, W., & Viaene, S. (2014). Ten principles of good business process management. *Business Process Management Journal, 20* (4), 530–548.

Business Process Innovation as an Enabler of Proactive Value Chains

Charles Møller

Abstract

Proactive value chains are an emerging business practice rooted in advanced process management and underlying technologies and organizations. The paper presents a recently inaugurated research and innovation program in manufacturing, and proposes business process innovation as an enabler of proactive value chains. Finally the paper discusses the role of business process innovation in the transformation of the manufacturing value chains.

1 Introduction

In many Western countries there is a deep concern that their manufacturing industry is losing ground to the newly industrialized countries. In Denmark, 25 % of the jobs in industry have disappeared in the last decade. At the same time, however, it has been realized that access to manufacturing is vital to preserve innovation capabilities. Consequently a national strategy towards re-industrialization is needed. MADE (Manufacturing Academy of Denmark) is a national initiative with international collaborations aimed at restoring the competitiveness of Danish industry.

The role of national companies in global value chains is largely determined by extrinsic variables. Differences in national framework conditions, such as salary levels, taxes, workforce skills and infrastructure, determine the footprint of global value chains. As a small welfare nation it is difficult to compete with regard to salaries or technology alone. Therefore a national strategy for manufacturing needs to be rooted in supporting local organizations with the creation of unique

C. Møller (✉)
Center for Industrial Production, Department of Business and Management, Aalborg University, Fibigerstræde 10, 9220 Aalborg, Denmark
e-mail: charles@business.aau.dk

J. vom Brocke, T. Schmiedel (eds.), *BPM – Driving Innovation in a Digital World*, Management for Professionals, DOI 10.1007/978-3-319-14430-6_2

competencies for industrial leadership. Following this thinking, we investigate how business process innovation approaches can be developed and deployed in the creation of proactive value chains, and outline this transformation.

The research and innovation program on Proactive Value Chains reflects an emerging business practice focusing on agile and resilient organizations (Hugos, 2009). These organizations are sometimes referred to as adaptive organizations, sense-and-respond organizations or real-time enterprise (Hugos, 2004). Operations and supply chain management have predominantly focused on reactive planning of inventories, whereas contemporary practices put more emphasis on the execution of business processes and real-time event management.

An example from a food supply chain is the ability to track and trace individual items across the entire supply chain. This capability can be used to respond to unforeseen events and to evade problems, such as the containment of non-conforming supplies before impacting consumers.

This requires real-time visibility in the supply chain but also advanced management of the business processes. Standard IT systems can support real-time enterprises, but organizations do usually not have the transformative capacity to absorb and leverage the technology into proactive capabilities, also referred to as sense and respond. In order to develop sense-and-response capabilities, enterprises need an integrated model-based infrastructure. Many of the required process technologies and methods such as process mining and business analytics have been researched and developed extensively, while others are emerging. One of the challenges is the integration of the new technologies and tools into the existing ERP and manufacturing systems, and in particular the adoption of the new practices by the organizations.

The aim of the program is to provide Danish industries with methodologies to transform advanced process technologies into proactive supply chain capabilities. The envisioned solutions build on breakthrough enterprise systems solutions, accompanied by radically new management and development approaches. This research will address how new process technologies and methods for proactive decision-making can enable new levels of intelligence in global supply chains by providing inter-organizational process analytics.

The aim of this paper is to present the idea and challenges of proactive value chains in the context of the MADE initiative and to identify an appropriate research approach. The planned approach is based on business process innovation in an experimental setting. The paper is organized as follows. First we present an overview of the national MADE initiative, and MADE is positioned in relation to other similar national initiatives in the manufacturing area. Second, the specific research program on proactive value chains is outlined, and the research challenges are proposed and discussed. Third, it is discussed how the advanced process technologies may contribute to address these issues. Finally, the findings are summarized and conclusions made.

2 The Danish MADE Initiative

Since the financial crunch in 2008, more than one fifth of the jobs in Danish industry disappeared. Even after the recovery, jobs have continuously 'evaporated' from Danish soil. MADE is a national initiative designed to reverse this trend.

In the Danish public debate, the future of manufacturing has predominantly been seen as an endeavor that belonged to low-wage countries like China. Industrial manufacturing is considered to be an archaic and polluting activity and we are not able to compete with Chinese salaries is the general tenor. Rather, countries like Denmark should focus on high value added activities such as innovation, product development and marketing.

However, in the recent years it has been realized that this strategy is not viable due to the close links between manufacturing and product development. Also the close relationship between manufacturing jobs and related jobs in the service industry causes worries. It is estimated that for every 100 jobs created in industry, an additional 35 jobs are created in related businesses. This emphasized the importance of the retaining jobs in industry. In summary, it is now accepted that manufacturing is a sector that should proactively be kept in Denmark, and it should actively be developed and strengthen in order to create growth and wealth for the future.

The creation of manufacturing jobs in a national context is a not an easy task. It is politically possible to redesign the framework conditions for doing business in Denmark in such a way that the investments in Denmark (FDI) increase, thus, improving the job situation. An analysis of the framework conditions, such as the salary rate, reveals that competing on cost alone is not feasible for a Western welfare society and therefore likely to fail. So the challenge is to find an approach where the value created in Denmark and by Danish companies exceeds the high cost of manufacturing in Denmark.

The road towards more Danish manufacturing jobs requires that industry become smarter, faster and more innovative in order to regain competitiveness. In "Manufacturing 2025", a collaborative study published in 2010 by the Danish branch of Manufuture, Manufuture.dk, five future scenarios where industry can compete were identified (Johansen, Madsen, Jensen, & Vestergaard, 2010):

- The highly competent manufacturing company
  - Danish manufacturing companies must strive to be among the best at exploiting new technologies developed by other countries and at developing new products
- The industrial power center
  - The industrial power center consolidates and coordinates competences and resources across businesses, industries, universities and knowledge centers to take up the challenge presented by the technological leadership of large international manufacturers

- The innovation factory
  - The innovation factory cultivates and optimizes the interplay between design and manufacturing competences in order to develop 'intelligent products' for customers and accelerate the time-to-market. Advanced manufacturing methods such as prototyping and ramp-up are applied to support and accelerate the innovation process
- The flexible value chain integrator
  - The central idea of the model is to build a network of suppliers supported by global, flexible value-chain integrators that understand how to integrate with international original equipment manufacturers (OEMs) with regard to business and delivery
- The virtual business
  - Virtual business connects the best global competences in virtual networks in order to quickly and effectively exploit more business opportunities and pool its resources of business creation, innovation, distribution, and production

These five scenarios were the key input of a process leading to the formulation of a joint Danish national society for manufacturing: "Manufacturing Academy of Denmark" or MADE, presently consisting of 26 manufacturing companies, 5 universities and 2 technological services, and the confederation of Danish industries.

MADE has the ambition to drive a re-industrialization of Denmark by co-developing manufacturing insight and new knowledge. Initially, MADE is provided with seed funding provided by the Danish government, industry and universities in an action program called "MADE platform for future manufacturing".

In many western countries, a similar debate has been around and in the US a major program on advanced manufacturing was launched last year (Holdren, Lander, Press, & Savitz, 2011) and the German government established the "Industrie 4.0" program (Kagermann, Wahlster, & Helbig, 2013). Manufacturing is also an issue in the European context where, e.g., the "Factory of the Future" program within the "Horizon 2020" framework program addresses these issues (Factories of the Future, 2014).

The concept of "Industrie 4.0" refers to a potential fourth generation of industrialization, where the first three industrial revolutions came about as a result of mechanization, electricity and IT. The fourth industrial revolution is enabled by the introduction of the Internet of Things and Services into the manufacturing environment. In the future, businesses will establish global networks that incorporate their machinery, warehousing systems and production facilities in the shape of Cyber-Physical Systems (Lee, 2008).

A shared view in these programs is a consistent emphasis on technology and on digital manufacturing and smart factories in particular. Topics like new materials, sensors and advanced robotics predominantly define these programs.

The MADE approach takes a more holistic approach to manufacturing and nine interrelated programs have been defined in the initial research framework: platform

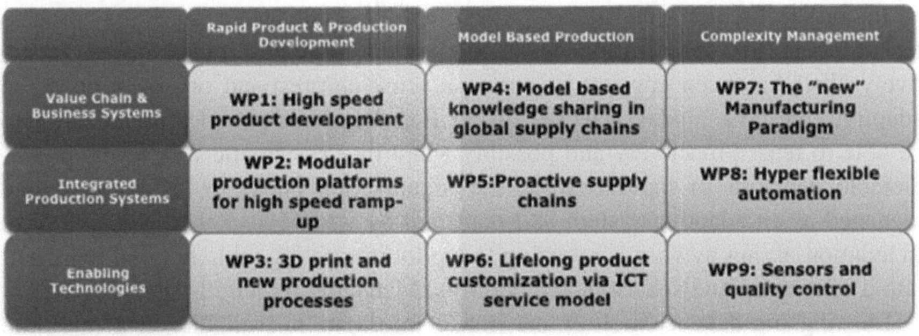

Fig. 1 MADE platform for future manufacturing

for future manufacturing. These work packages (WPs) and their coordination are illustrated in the following Fig. 1 (Manufacturing Academy of Denmark, 2014):

The platform focuses on three business functionalities: Rapid Product and Production Development, Model Based Production, and Complexity Management. These are key enablers for realizing the potential for innovation, agility and sustainability and consequently are of significant competitive importance to Danish industry. These business functionalities will be investigated from three different viewpoints: Value Chains and Business Systems, Integrated production systems, and Enabling Technologies.

The following sections will focus on a specific work package within the MADE platform: proactive supply chains or rather proactive value chains in the larger context.

3 Proactive Value Chains

Compared to "Industrie 4.0" MADE extend the smart factory into value chains and business systems. The aim of work package 5 is to provide Danish industries with methodologies and approaches to transform advanced business process technologies into proactive value and supply chain capabilities. The envisioned solutions build on breakthrough enterprise systems solutions, accompanied by radically new management and development approaches. The research will address how new process technologies and methods for proactive decision-making can enable new levels of intelligence in global supply chains by providing inter-organizational process analytics.

Proactive supply chains reflect an emerging business practice. Operations and supply chain management has predominantly focused on reactive planning of inventories, whereas contemporary practices put more emphasis on the execution of business processes and real-time events. An example from a food supply chain is the ability to track and trace individual items across the entire supply chain. This capability can be used to respond to unforeseen events and evade problems by, for example, early containment of non-conformant supplies.

In order for an enterprise to leverage the advanced business process technologies, the organization needs to develop strategies for managing proactively. This has been conceptualized as a sense-and-respond organization or an adaptive enterprise model (Haeckel, 2013). For a large and complex organization to be able to react proactively and possibly adapt in a systematic way to the unpredictable demands of rapid change, the organization needs to be designed and managed as an adaptive system and managed by wire (Haeckel & Nolan, 1993). In aviation, flying by wire is referring to a pilot interacting with a digital representation of the airplane's sensors and controls. Managing by wire is similar.

Existing big-data technology can make information available on a real-time basis and at the same time enable prediction of future events, and thus enable real-time sense-and-respond capabilities.

An example of this kind of problem is a discrete manufacturing supply chain where demand disturbances are known to cause the bullwhip effect, affecting the required capacity throughout the supply chain. A proactive strategy could be to monitor the demand patterns for exceptional variation and to create strategies for containing the disturbances within the existing supply chain capacity (see Fig. 2).

Many of the required process technologies and methods such as process mining and analytics have been researched and developed extensively (Grigori et al., 2004). Even business activity monitoring or complex event processing are available as off the shelves solutions (Luckham, 2011). Modern standard IT systems support many of the real-time enterprise concepts, but organizations usually do not have the transformative capacity to leverage the new technologies. A major challenge is the integration of the new technologies and tools into the existing ERP and manufacturing systems landscape, and the adoption of new practices in the companies (Butner, 2010). This includes the challenge of transforming supply chain visibility into management capabilities and providing business cases for adopting new advanced process technologies into the production and supply chain (Siurdyban & Møller, 2012). This extends from the supply chain to the entire value chain, including the development of new products and processes (Møller, Chaudhry, & Jørgensen, 2008).

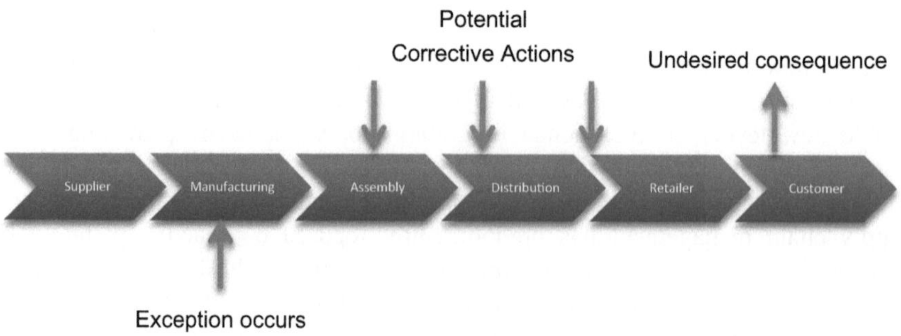

Fig. 2 Value chains are global processes with time/place lag between cause and effect

Table 1 Smart process manufacturing business transformations (Smart Process Manufacturing Engineering Virtual Organization Steering Committee, 2009)

From	To	Results
Investment in facilities	Investment in knowledge-embedded facilities	Investment and management of facilities and knowledge are equally important
Reactive	Proactive	Economic optimization is achieved by anticipation and decision, understanding probability, risk and impact
Response	Prevention	Sensing, modeling and analysis are used to predict events and operations are controlled to mitigate the impact
Compliance	Performance	Zero-incident EH&S is part of the performance culture
Tactical	Strategic	Requirements become opportunities, optimizing total enterprise operation
Local	Global	Every decision must be made in the context of a globally competitive environment

Another example is within a food chain where quality variation in raw material measured up front is used to calibrate the entire supply chain to accommodate for variations in final goods production.

In these cases the information is already available, the technology for collecting and processing the data in real-time is known. However the existing organization and business processes becomes a barrier for improvements. Thus a more profound process innovation approach is needed for designing a responsive supply chain.

Finally, the transformation of new requirements and capabilities into global supply chains and the exchange of knowledge need to be revisited in the digital manufacturing context. The transformation has been defined in the "Smart Process Manufacturing: an Operations and Technology Roadmap" as in Table 1.

An example of such a process is virtual commissioning in a mechatronic production system, where the operating characteristics of new production technology can be simulated at the design time and ramp-up problems avoided (Reinhart & Wünsch, 2007).

In the ideal world there would be digital models and a complete tool chain from the point of conceptualizing new value chain concepts to implemented solutions. The speed and agility with which an organization is able to mobilize an eco-system of vendors and partners, and integrate their technology and knowledge in the development of new products and processes is of paramount importance. However, in the real world this is hampered by organizational boundaries and a lack of systems integration.

The outcome of the proactive value chain program is a number of documented pilot cases that are intended to serve as demonstrator models, with the aim of illustrating potentials such as substantial reduction in non-conformance costs.

Furthermore, for wider use, the methodologies should be translated into applicable roadmaps and software tools.

3.1 Proactive Value Chains in a Process Innovation Perspective

Digital and flexible manufacturing has been around for many years. In the past, the concept was referred to as Computer Integrated Manufacturing (CIM) and even though the original idea was innovative, the implementations were less successful—partly due to immature technology. However, the research resulting from exploring the CIM concept was very important. Models and frameworks, like the CIMOSA or GERAM architecture, emerged out of very large-scale research. This provide a systematic and consistent architecture on which we can build the proactive value chains (Bernus, Nemes, & Schmidt, 2003).

The real-time enterprise concept has also been around for several years (Fingar & Bellini, 2004). In general the availability of data is never an issue. The usability of data on the other hand hinders the concepts from flourishing in the factories. Interoperability is consistently an issue.

Visibility in the value chain is a prerequisite for a proactive reaction. However the integration of information in the value chain is a barrier for proactive management. Consider a typical systems landscape with Manufacturing Execution Systems (MES), Enterprise Resource Planning (ERP) systems and Data Warehouses (DW) as illustrated in Fig. 3 below. The data processing, from the time an event occurs in manufacturing (for example a measurement of quality data) until management is able to make sense of the event and its consequences, requires the aggregation on information through several systems layers as illustrated below. Even though the information is available, the time delay from the events that are generated until these are aggregated into actionable management information is considerable. In extreme cases it takes months until management is able to make sense of the situation, and by that time the product is delivered and the window for corrective actions is closed. This time lag forces decision making to be reactive. We want to be able to make decisions based on real time data, which can be done using, e.g., in-memory database technologies.

To sum up and to frame the research challenges of proactive value chains: we state the premise that required process technologies and methods are already available. We can conceptualize proactive value chains from a business process perspective as the management of integrated processes on three levels:

- Managing the process of end-to-end system engineering from conceptualizing the product or service to the decommissioning
- Managing the end-to-end supply chain from supplier to customer
- Managing the end-to-end process information from sensors on the shop floor to the board room and back

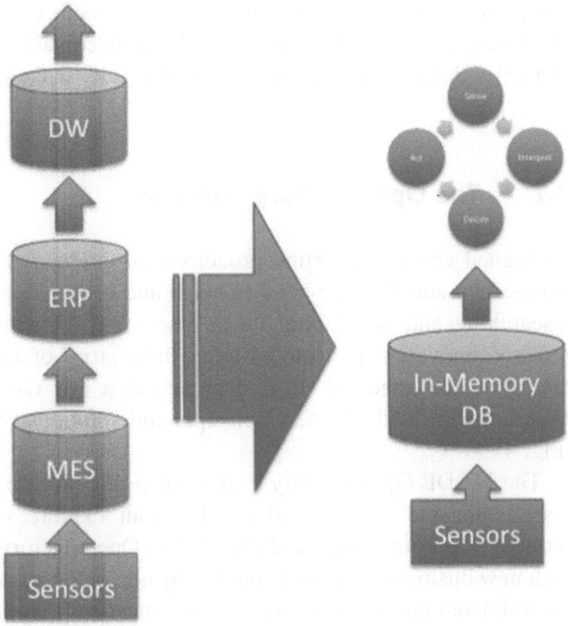

Fig. 3 Towards real-time capabilities

This research agenda is aligned with "Industrie 4.0" that further emphasizes "New social infrastructures in the workplace" and "Cyber-Physical Systems technology" as research areas. These are dealt with elsewhere in the MADE program. However the technological transformation can be summarized as in Table 2.

Achieving the benefits from a new process-innovation-based approach to digital manufacturing is a long-term endeavor and will involve a gradual experimental learning process involving technology, systems and management processes. For a

Table 2 Smart process manufacturing technical transformations (Smart Process Manufacturing Engineering Virtual Organization Steering Committee, 2009)

From	To	Results
One-off models in operations	Models integrated into operations	There must be pervasive, coordinated, consistent and managed applications of models
Dispersed intelligence	Distributed intelligence	Data, information, knowledge, models and expertise are available and used to make decisions at the right time and place
Unintelligent systems	Self-aware systems	There must be autonomous systems that understand their role and performance in the enterprise and systems that take action to optimize performance
Proprietary systems	Interoperable systems	Systems must communicate through standard protocols for information sharing, capability and best-in-class components
Unpredictable industry	Predictable Industry	Operations within defined operating envelopes must be performed with predictable impacts

company it will be key to ensure that the value of existing manufacturing systems is preserved. At the same time, it will be necessary to come up with migration strategies that deliver benefits and productivity from an early stage.

3.2 The Open Factory Concept

As argued above, we define proactive value chains from a process management perspective and thus we need to stage and orchestrate an innovation platform for researching and developing these processes. A central mechanism for business process innovation is a model-based laboratory of the digital factory. The open factory, as outlined below, is designed as a low risk prototype environment for experimenting with the new concepts and solutions for the proactive value chain (Fig. 4).

The MADE Open Factory is also a meeting place between companies, vendors, researchers and students where they can explore ideas in an unconventional settings. The core function of the MADE Open Factory is the ability to experiment with new business processes enabled by advanced process technology. The outputs are validated concepts that can be advanced further as pilots in the participating companies. Central ideas in the MADE Open Factory have previously been described as the process innovation laboratory (Møller, 2007).

Initially, three cases are planned: (1) A discrete manufacturing case, aimed at containing the effects of demand variation in the supply chain; (2) a case in the windmill industry, aimed at containing the effects of production variability; and (3) a case in the food supply chain, aimed at configuring the quality variation in raw

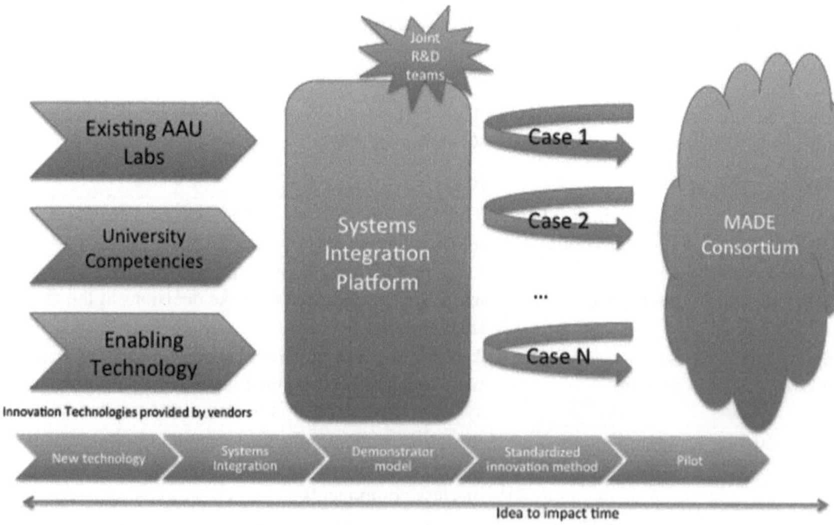

Fig. 4 MADE open factory concepts

material measured up front, are used to calibrate the entire supply chain to accommodate for the variations in final goods production.

Further, an inquiry into the valuation of the benefits from integration is already in progress and a study and an experiment with design thinking as a methodology for process innovation are also being investigated, including an approach where students are engaged as a resource into the ecosystem of an enterprise.

The MADE program will run from 2014 to 2018 and besides the Danish consortium of manufacturing companies and vendors, SAP Service Innovation and the University of Liechtenstein, as an international partner, will also contribute to the research.

4 Discussion and Conclusion

This paper has now presented and discussed a research agenda for developing manufacturing industry in Western developed countries. It is argued that business process innovation has the potential to contribute to manufacturing competitiveness in several ways and, potentially, with more effect than simple automation technology.

Applying the business process perspective on manufacturing has several implications (see also chapter by Welke (2015)). First of all, it puts the end customer in focus. Traditionally, manufacturing is centered on balancing inventories. Business process management deals with managing end-to-end business processes. Second, business process management provides the components needed to build the integrated processes using existing and verified methods. Third, the new technologies, like Internet of Things, require that manufacturing broaden its perspective: from the factory floor towards the entire life cycle of a product or service. This is where business process innovation becomes a central enabler of the business transformation outlined in Table 1 shown previously. Although the roadmaps are being explored in various programs around the globe, there are transformational challenges where nations and companies without huge budgets may succeed. The journey towards the future will be an evolutionary process (Kagermann et al., 2013):

- Current basic technologies and experience will have to be adapted to the specific requirements of manufacturing engineering, and innovative solutions for new locations and new markets will have to be explored
- Achieving the benefits from digital manufacturing is a long-term endeavor and will involve a gradual experimental learning process involving technology, systems and management processes
- For a company it will be key to ensure that the value of existing manufacturing systems is preserved
- At the same time, it will be necessary to come up with migration strategies that deliver benefits and productivity from an early stage.

The concept of a proactive value chain and the MADE research is in its very early stage. The close engagement between researchers and companies will likely result in new and different perspective that will impact the research focus—but that is part of the fun, and a source of innovation.

References

Bernus, P., Nemes, L., & Schmidt, G. (2003). *Handbook on enterprise architecture*. Berlin: Springer. Retrieved from http://www.google.dk/books?id=LTR93xiadtEC&pgis=1

Butner, K. (2010). The smarter supply chain of the future. *Strategy & Leadership, 38*(1), 22–31. doi:10.1108/10878571011009859.

Factories of the Future. (2014). Retrieved February 1, 2014, from http://www.effra.eu/

Fingar, P., & Bellini, J. (2004). *The real-time enterprise: Competing on time with the revolutionary business S-Ex machine* (p. 222). Meghan Kiffer Press. Retrieved from http://www.amazon.com/The-Real-Time-Enterprise-Competing-Revolutionary/dp/0929652304

Grigori, D., Casati, F., Castellanos, M., Dayal, U., Sayal, M., & Shan, M.-C. (2004). Business process intelligence. *Computers in Industry, 53*(3), 321–343. doi:10.1016/j.compind.2003.10.007.

Haeckel, S. H. (2013). *Adaptive enterprise: Creating and leading sense-and-respond organizations (Google eBook)* (p. 295). Harvard Business Press. Retrieved from http://books.google.com/books?id=pkrFugJBAn4C&pgis=1

Haeckel, S. H., & Nolan, R. L. (1993). Managing by wire. *Harvard Business Review, 71*, 122–132.

Holdren, J. P., Lander, E., Press, W., & Savitz, M. (2011). *Report to the president on ensuring American leadership in advanced manufacturing* (p. 56). Retrieved from http://www.whitehouse.gov/sites/default/files/microsites/ostp/pcast-advanced-manufacturing-june2011.pdf

Hugos, M. H. (2004). *Building the real-time enterprise: An executive briefing* (p. 224). Wiley. Retrieved from http://www.amazon.com/Building-Real-Time-Enterprise-Executive-Briefing/dp/0471678295

Hugos, M. H. (2009). *Business agility: Sustainable prosperity in a relentlessly competitive world* (1st ed.). Wiley. Retrieved from http://www.amazon.com/Business-Agility-Sustainable-Relentlessly-Competitive-ebook/dp/B001VLXNII/ref=sr_sp-btf_title_1_7?s=digital-text&ie=UTF8&qid=1394847288&sr=1-7

Johansen, J., Madsen, O., Jensen, H. V., & Vestergaard, A. (2010). *Manufacturing 2025: Future scenarios for Danish manufacturing companies* (p. 36). Aalborg: Center for Industrial Production and Department of Mechanical and Manufacturing Engineering. Retrieved from http://www.en.manufuture.dk/activities/production-2025/

Kagermann, H., Wahlster, W., & Helbig, J. (2013). *Securing the future of German manufacturing industry: Recommendations for implementing the strategic initiative INDUSTRIE 4.0: Final report of the Industrie 4.0 working group* (p. 84). Retrieved from http://www.plattform-i40.de/sites/default/files/Report_Industrie4.0_engl_1.pdf

Lee, E. A. (2008). Cyber physical systems: Design challenges. *2008 11th IEEE International Symposium on Object and Component-Oriented Real-Time Distributed Computing (ISORC)* (pp. 363–369). doi:10.1109/ISORC.2008.25

Luckham, D. C. (2011). *Event processing for business: Organizing the real-time enterprise*. Wiley. Retrieved from http://www.amazon.co.uk/Event-Processing-Business-Organizing-Enterprise-ebook/dp/B005YO4XUU

Manufacturing Academy of Denmark. (2014). Retrieved February 1, 2014, from http://made.dk

Møller, C. (2007). Process innovation laboratory: A new approach to business process innovation based on enterprise information systems. *Enterprise Information Systems, 1*(1), 113–128. doi:10.1080/17517570601092143.

Møller, C., Chaudhry, S. S., & Jørgensen, B. (2008). Complex service design: A virtual enterprise architecture for logistics service. *Information Systems Frontiers, 10*(5), 503–518. doi:10.1007/s10796-008-9106-3.

Reinhart, G., & Wünsch, G. (2007). Economic application of virtual commissioning to mechatronic production systems. *Production Engineering, 1*(4), 371–379. doi:10.1007/s11740-007-0066-0.

Siurdyban, A., & Møller, C. (2012). Towards intelligent supply chains. *International Journal of Information Systems and Supply Chain Management, 5*(1), 1–19. doi:10.4018/jisscm.2012010101.

Smart Process Manufacturing Engineering Virtual Organization Steering Committee. (2009). *Smart process manufacturing an operations and technology roadmap* (p. 61). https://smartmanufacturingcoalition.org/sites/default/files/spm_-_an_operations_and_technology_roadmap.pdf

Welke, R. J. (2015). Thinking tri-laterally about business processes, services and business models: An innovation perspective. In J. vom Brocke & T. Schmiedel (Eds.), *Business process management: Driving innovation in a digital world*. Berlin: Springer.

Thinking Tri-laterally About Business Processes, Services and Business Models: An Innovation Perspective

Richard J. Welke

Abstract

We propose a new, integrated "way of thinking" about processes, services and business models. The starting point of this paper is that "getting things done" is the set of services the organization employs. These services are often broken, ineffective and/or misaligned with client/users needs. Any attempt to pre-emptively or reactively respond to market change or internal transformations must invariably rely on some of these (broken) services while, at the same time creating new ones that, in turn, make use of pre-existing services as building blocks. It is argued that services (both internal- and external-facing) are two things: a business process (the "how" of a service), and a mini-business in its own right (the "why" of the service). Each service has clients (the "who") that, through choice or mandate, solve some, or all, of a problem they have. In short, a service (and its underlying process) represents a "value proposition" to the service consumer (client) that enables them to "get their job done." A service is, in effect, a mini-business or "business within a business" and therefore is implicitly governed by a business model of the process/service owner, the "CEO" of that business. Adopting this perspective affords a fresh way to view "process" innovation. It can be top-down by considering its business model. Or middle-out, where a specific service for an internal or external client is examined for innovation potential. Or bottom up, where the business process that delivers the service is modified and, in so doing, alters the characteristics of the service being delivered to the client.

R.J. Welke (✉)
Center for Process Innovation, Georgia State University, PO Box 5029, Atlanta, GA 30302, USA
e-mail: rwelke@ceprin.org

J. vom Brocke, T. Schmiedel (eds.), *BPM – Driving Innovation in a Digital World*, Management for Professionals, DOI 10.1007/978-3-319-14430-6_3

1 Services and Processes

1.1 Service Architectures and Composition

Many alternative "fundamental" building blocks of an organization have been proposed and justified to serve various needs. Robert Anthony's seminal book (Anthony, 1965) provides an early framework. Porter's equally seminal framework is certainly one of the more widely cited and used (Porter, 1998). Another is Steven Alter's "Work Systems" framework (Alter, 2008).

This paper adopts a different perspective; one that's most closely aligned with what is termed the "service oriented enterprise" (SOE; Khoshafian, 2007) and its variations, e.g., value-stream architecture (Whittle & Myrick, 2004) and a substantial refinement and extension of the "Think Service—Act Process" work of Welke (2005). The basic premise of these is that any purposeful (teleological) system, such as an organization is, from an execution perspective (how it does what it does), a collection of services of varying levels of scope and specificity (granularity). Larger, so-called end-to-end services that fulfill customer needs are at one end of the granularity spectrum, while rather narrow services such as an order-approval, database request, or an ERP-based shipping receipt event entry are at the other end. Larger services of the "end-to-end" variety are typically composed of (and rely on) lower level (more granular) services.

Creating or adapting the larger, end-to-end services is, in SOE thinking, a matter of composing or re-composing lower-level, available services. Don't have what you need to achieve the service offering in mind? Then create a new one, modify or extend an existing one, or find an alternative service provider that has what you want. Just like your customers' do.

To take a classic example of this, consider Virgin Mobile (Sawhney, Wolcott, & Arroniz, 2011). It offers a mobile phone voice and data service to its targeted customers (primarily teens and young adults) consistent with its youthful, innovative brand.

To offer this service (sign-up to on-going voice/data provisioning) it could have created all the secondary, tertiary and lower level services associated with payments, accounting, network connectivity, etc. Instead, it has chosen to wire together (compose) existing services from other service providers to achieve the bulk of its "end-to-end" service offering to its customers, and to differentiate its offering by selecting a very few bespoke services that distinctively meet their clients needs, thereby offering a unique value proposition to its mobile customers.

In general, an organizational service architecture, with decreasing levels of granularity, might appear as shown in Fig. 1 below.

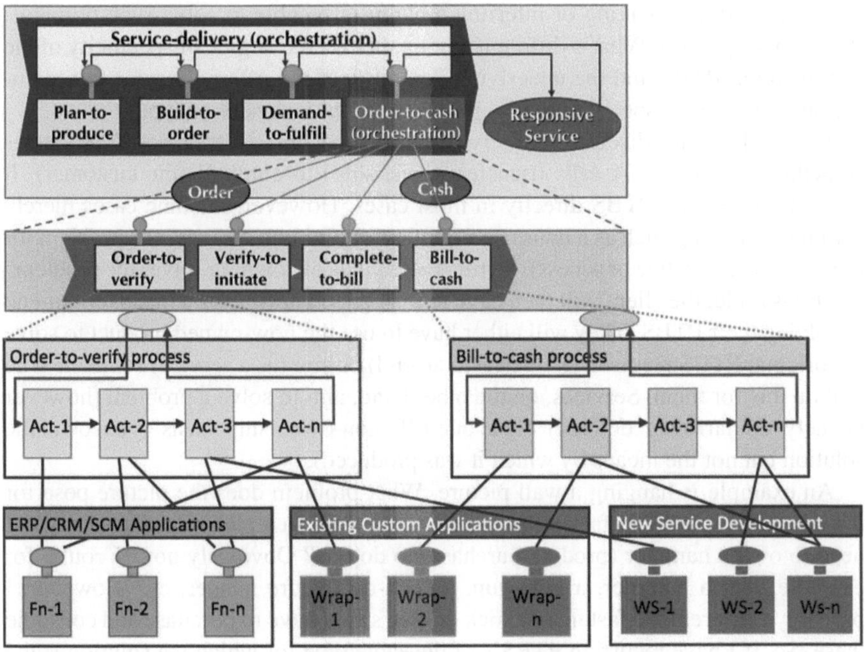

Fig. 1 A service-oriented enterprise view

1.2 Service Types

The word "service" invariably evokes different notions of what the term means and what it embraces.

For some, such as those in information technology, it could mean a very well-defined interface definition that, when correctly invoked and initiated, returns a pre-specified set of values based upon an equally well-defined set of input values. This interface is defined by a "service definition" and the means by which it gets from input to result (a method).

Or, it could mean an outsourcing service arrangement, where the invocation, results, and other aspects are governed by a contract that includes an SLO (service level objectives) and related SLA (agreement, typically with penalties).

At the other end of the spectrum are services designed to respond to prospective users (clients) with vaguely defined/formalized needs that nevertheless have a problem they wish to have solved. One example of this might be a client that wants a "killer" design for a product or service, or an associated marketing campaign to increase awareness of same, based upon some as-not-yet-well articulated objectives and needs. Or, it could be an internal client whose problem is to find out what the current accounts receivable aging's are by arrear days and customer.

What's common among all of these examples is a client with a problem-to-be-solved (PTBS) seeking a service (and service provider) and the discovered/offered/

mandated services making or inferring a claim to be able to solve such problems (Christensen, 1997). What's different among them is the degree of specificity of the clients initial PTBS and the underlying flexibility of the offered service to accommodate this lack of specificity. This gives rise to various service types.

Invariably, in any discussion of services, the idea of "products' arises. A product is something that entity A sells (transfers ownership) to entity B (the customer). It doesn't "solve" the PTBS directly in most cases. However, in some cases merely owning something such as a house or a Bentley automobile "solves" the problem for the client (e.g. prestige or access). Setting these kinds of "owning solves the problem" solutions aside, the client will then have to treat the ownership as a means-to-an-end to solving their PTBS. They will either have to use the now-owned product to solve the original PTBS themselves (means to an end) or hire (as a service) someone who will do this for them. Services, on the other hand, aim to solve a problem (however vaguely or narrowly defined) on a one-off, non-ownership basis (you own the solution but not the means by which it was produced).

An example is hanging a wall picture. What problem does the picture pose for the consumer? Answer: fasten the picture to the wall in a particular location. Do I need to own a hammer (product purchase) to do this? Obviously not. "I could, for example, rent a hammer, a glue gun, a stick-on picture hanger, etc. However, I probably can't rent the fastener or stick of glue so I'd have to purchase and consume these. So, if I have recurring PTBS's of the same type for which the solution is the same (fasten something to a surface using focused force) then I might want to invoke "me" as the service provider to solve the PTBS (and possibly save something regarding time, cost, convenience, etc.)" with "I could rent a hammer or a glue gun (service) but I would still have to invoke another service (me or a professional) to solve the actual PTBS – hang a picture.

Services, on the other hand, are solutions to a current problem. They are sometimes (in the marketing literature) referred to as "value co-creation" (Vargo, Maglio, & Akaka, 2008). In short, that means that the consumer (invoker of the service) and service provider interact (generally, over time) to define an acceptable solution to the service consumer while at the same time providing value to the service provider in terms of payments, knowledge, brand enhancement, etc.).

1.3 Service Typology

There are many other ways to "classify" services including: the organizational area served by the services, it's granularity, its mode or channel of delivery (e.g. web-based, walk-in bricks-and-mortar, etc.), its alignment to generic functional areas of an organization (marketing, accounting, etc.) or a typology of the customer's problem to be solved. None of the latter classification schemes are particularly generic, but do serve the purpose of "key wording" a specific, pre-defined service definition or offering. A somewhat comprehensive attempt at this is Kalakota and Robinson (2003).

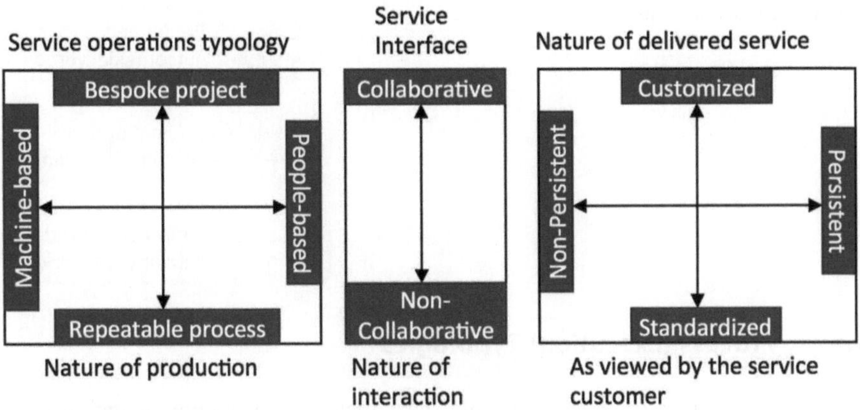

Fig. 2 Generic service typology

An alternative approach is to take a client/provider interaction view. This can be done from several perspectives: the service consumer, the service provider, and the interface between the two. Some common dimensions appearing in the literature adopting this view are given in Fig. 2. We note from the diagram above, is that services can be classified from either the client or provider perspective (with the preferred interface type defined by either).

Instead, what we note from the diagram above, is that services can be classified from either the client or provider perspective (with the interface type defined by either).

We adopt the perspective that a service is, in the first instance, something sought by a client (so-called "outside in" thinking) and therefore should be defined in terms of the nature of their problem to be solved. How, operationally, the provider chooses to respond to this need (services operation typology) is up to them.

What we can derive from this is a service definition and delivery "n-tuple" to the customer based on: <customized, standardized>, <persistent, non-persistent>, <collaborative, non-collaborative > as our high-level choices for the nature of the service provided, and thus the manner in which the underlying service execution mechanism (business process) functions and is prosecuted.

Stated somewhat differently, we observe the client interaction continuum as one characterized by the degree of a priori specificity in the result to be delivered:

1. Is it tailored to their specific needs, or is it providing a pre-defined result
2. What is the level of interaction needed to achieve the result they're seeking, within the limits of results possible

Is it a one-size fits all solution, a configurable solution, or one that's tailored (mass customized) to their specific need? This leads to the simplified classification of service types, based upon how the customer's problem is solved, shown in Fig. 3.

Fig. 3 Basic service types

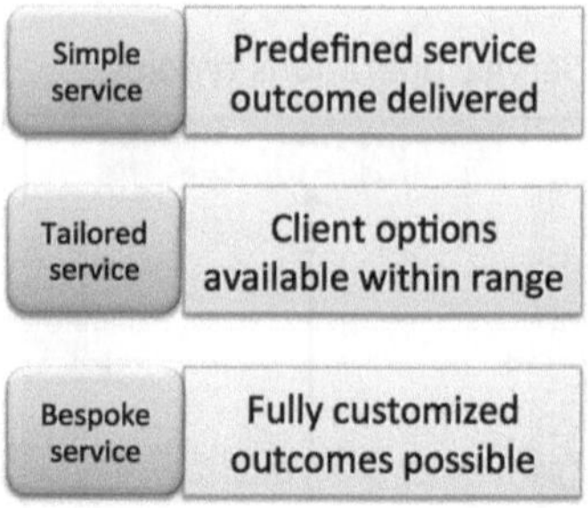

1.4 Process (Execution) Typologies

From the execution (process) side one must match the behavior of the process execution to the type of service it is offering. Or, more precisely, the nature of the process execution (how it receives inputs and delivers results) gives rise to the service attributes above.

Again, there are many process typologies and, not unsurprisingly, they tend to focus on the same attributes as their (dual) service typologies, namely: type of result produced, functional area they belong to. For example, an oft-cited process typology is the MIT/NIST "Process Handbook" project (Malone, Crowston, & Herman, 2003). It enumerates processes as shown in Table 1. The APQC process classification framework (AQPC, 2014) is a different classification system that's more aligned with SOE (service) thinking than named process categories.

Here we're interested in more generic (abstract) execution typologies. For this, we find the Business Process Management System (BPMS) literature more helpful. In this domain it's generally acknowledged that, in broad terms, process execution types tend to fall into standard, fully pre-specified and modeled processes, more flexible "case" management approaches, and fully adaptive (emergent) adaptive case management (Swenson, 2010) and "HIM" (Human Interaction Management; Harrison-Broninski, 2005) approaches.

These are summarized in Fig. 4.

2 Service-Process Duality and Alignment

2.1 Service-Process Duality

In various branches of science it's common to look at a problem through complimentary lens. For example, a difficult "inventory problem" solution can also be looked at as a mixed integer-programming problem. Or either of these perspectives on the problem might be re-stated as a dynamic programming or systems dynamics simulation problem. A reason for doing so (aside from solution method awareness) is that what becomes an intractable problem in one representation may be more readily solved using a method (and its techniques and tools) from another solution

Table 1 Example processes from the process handbook

Account management	Customer acquisition	Manuf. capability development	Program management
Advance planning & schedule	Customer inquiry	Market research & analysis	Promotions
Advertising	Customer requirements	Market test	Property tracking/ accounting
Assembly	Customer self-service	Materials procurement	Proposal preparation
Asset management	Customer/product profitability	Materials storage	Publicity management
Benefits administration	Demand planning	Order dispatch & fulfillment	Real estate management
Branch operations	Distribution/VAR management	Order management	Recruitment
Budget control	Facilities management	Organizational learning	Returns & depot repair
Build to order	Financial planning	Payroll processing	Returns management
Call center service	Financial close/ consolidation	Performance management	Quality control
Capacity reservation	Hiring/orientation	Physical inventory	Sales channel management
Capital expenditures	Installation management	Planning & resource allocation	Sales commission planning
Check request processing	Integrated logistics	Post-sales service	Sales cycle management
Collateral fulfillment	Internal audit	Problem resolution management	Sales planning
Collections	Inventory management	Process design	Service agreement management
Commissions processing	Investor relations	Procurement	Service fulfillment
Compensation	Invoicing	Product data management	Service provisioning
Component fabrication	IT service management	Product design & development	Shipping
Corporate communications	Knowledge management	Product/brand management	...
Credit request/ authorization	Manufacturing	Production scheduling	Zero-based budgeting

perspective. These restatements of the problem through the lens of a different perspective are commonly referred to as "duals" of the original scenario or problem statement (Wagner, 1975).

To "make the case" for service and process being "duals" of one another, we need to examine this from both the service and process perspective. Can and should a service also be viewed as a process, and conversely?

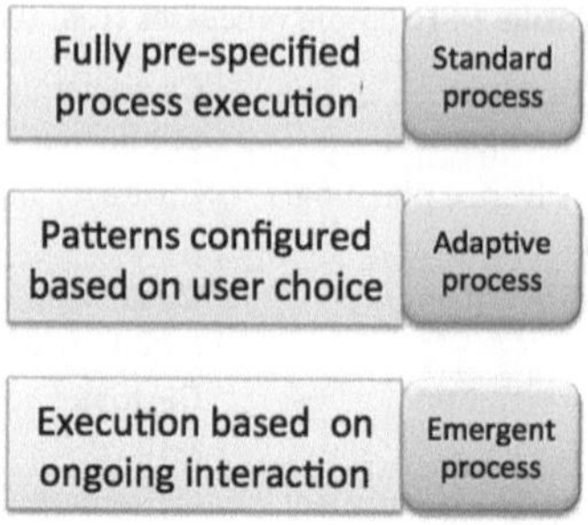

Fig. 4 Process execution types

2.1.1 Service to Process Duality

A service, regardless of type, is initiated by a customer, either directly or indirectly (e.g., some form of pull request based on time or another external event), and in turn delivers an outcome that hopefully provides the customer with a solution to the problem they invoked the service to help solve. How this is accomplished may be a "black box" to the customer, or some shade of gray to white transparency, depending upon their degree of engagement in shaping the need and form of solution as well as the "visibility" of the underlying service execution. Seen from the service provider's perspective, once a service is initiated, a series of actions are set in motion to refine and then respond to the initial customer's request. This "series of actions" we assert, is generically referred to as a (business) process. In other words, a process, whether it's fully pre-defined or ad-hoc, is how the provider of the service to the customer attempts to deliver the solution sought by them.

2.1.2 Process to Service Duality

Similarly, an existing (business) process can be seen as a set of activities (and associated tasks, events, gateway branches, roles and other representational artifacts that represent how the process operates) undertaken by an organization to "solve" a customer's problem. The service definition (customer, problem to be solved, etc.) is the process' raison d'être. However (and this is a big "however") boundaries around processes and the names arbitrarily given to the contents within such a boundary (as in, say the MIT process framework) may not have well-defined customers, problems to be solved or solutions provided. In many cases, where arbitrary boundaries of a process are defined, it's generally possible to modify the boundaries so that the preceding is true—having a specified customer as the process initiator, their defined PTBS, etc. We'll refer to these as "servitized" processes. That is, the business process is well aligned with its customer, their PTBS and a solution to the customer's problem (the process result or outcome) in the form of a service the customer invokes.

A reasonable question to ask at this point is "why?" as in "why bother to adjust process boundaries to align them with customer service needs?" Why not, instead, stick with current organizational labels such as "accounts receivable process," or "complaint handling," "requisitions," "project planning," "compliance" or a myriad other labels often used to (vaguely) reference and define business processes? While a more detailed answer must await a subsequent section, the short answer is that without a service-to-process alignment the customer isn't clearly defined, the problem being solved and tendered isn't defined and thus any justifications for improving or innovating the process itself can only be done through the lens of the actions taken and not the value of their result to the end-user (customer). This myopia, in turn, leads to so-called process improvements, but rarely to process innovation.

2.2 Service-Process Alignment

2.2.1 Forms of Service-Process Alignments

From the preceding we can now postulate that the service-process duality assertion manifests itself as a design consideration. That is, if we align the three broad categories of process execution types with the three types of service interfaces that can be offered we get the model shown in Fig. 5.

As stated before, this is not a highly nuanced model of either process execution types (or their underlying technology architecture) or of service offering types, but it illustrates the basic idea.

Regardless of the categories on either side, it implies that as we change the nature of the service behavior in going from "here's what you get," to "we'll figure out and then do what you need done" you change the basic nature of how the underlying process organized, designed and executed. Conversely, if you decide on a particular approach to how processes are to be executed (a high-level, service-process design choice), you constrain the flexibility of the service offering to its client.

2.2.2 Service-Process Alignment Implications

There are a number of implications that can be drawn from the preceding alignment model. Below is a short list of some of these:

1. Deciding how one wishes a service to behave, whether stated in terms of degrees of collaboration and co-creation of value, or in terms of the "market of one" tailoring of the delivered result to the clients needs, is a design decision that in

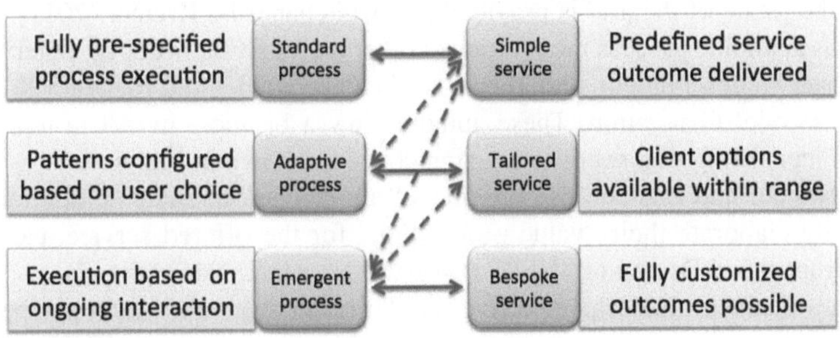

Fig. 5 Service-process alignments

turn directly affects the type of process execution approach taken. And, conversely.
2. Nearly all processes begin life as emergent (or ad hoc) processes in order to understand the actual client needs. These are nowadays referred to as “adaptive case management” processes. As time passes and these needs are better understood, the process execution becomes more rigidified (to allow for such things as repeatability, efficiency, oversight, regulatory compliance, etc.). But, at the same time, the agility of the process (and its service’s ability to adjust to changing customer needs, diminishes).
3. Hybrid models are possible in that one can have an emergent approach to the service interface, but that process can in turn draw upon internal and external services that are, in fact, “simple” services with standardized process executions.

We next turn our attention to the final aspect to be considered in this proposed integration of ideas, namely business models.

3 Service Business Models

We begin here with the assertion that any service, whether it’s consumed internally (by organization members or processes) or externally (by a customer), represents a ‘mini-business.” And, as such, it has an implied business model—its raison d’être. And therefore, invoking the by the service-process duality argument, any business process or the service(s) it defines has an implied business model as well. Normally, and to the extent a business model is developed at all, it is applied to the major value streams of an organization, i.e., the principal, revenue-producing products and services. However, there’s no reason why this thinking can’t be scaled to suit any service within the organization. As we will try to demonstrate, there are several good reasons why this point of view should be applied.

There has been a great deal of discussion in both the professional and academic literature over the past decade regarding what is meant by a business model, how best to capture it, and whom its customers are. There are many excellent frameworks and summaries on business models, including an “older” but integrative summary on business models provided by Al-Debei and Avison (2010). A summary of the current the “state of the art” is provided in a whitepaper by Krcmar (2011). Of the numerous available process model frameworks, we adopt the work by Osterwalder, et.al. (Osterwalder, Pigneur, and Tucci (2005), Osterwalder and Pigneur (2010)) on Business Model Generation. These authors view a business model in terms of a “canvas” consisting of a set of interacting concepts shown in Fig. 6.

Osterwalder and Pigneur also provide a “sub-canvas” to enable practitioners to more fully elaborate their “value proposition” for the offered service, called the Value Proposition Design or “VPD” (Osterwalder, et.al. 2015) (Fig. 7):

From a business model perspective, on the client side (outside-in perspective), each customer consuming the service has a problem-to-be-solved (PTBS), directly related to their job-to-be-done (JTBD), that governs the service he/she elects. From a

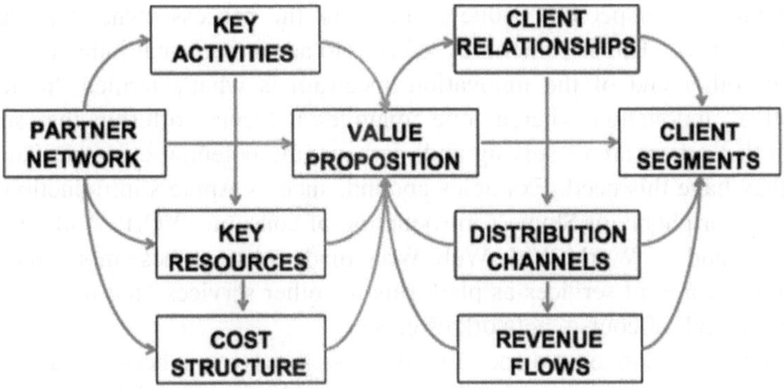

Fig. 6 Business model concept associations

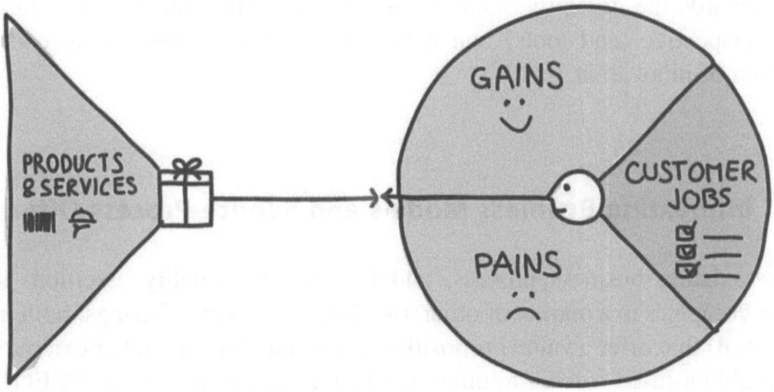

Fig. 7 Value proposition customer-facing elaboration

provider perspective, you're offering to the internal (to the organization) or external (revenue-generating customer) your service and underlying business process, a solution response to this customer's PTBS; that is your "job-to-be-done" (JTBD). You differentiate yourself by a superior value proposition delivery and execution that successfully differentiates, in the minds of your internal or external customers, your service/process approach to their job-to-be-done.

4 Business Model–Service–Process Innovation

The term "innovation" has many meanings and interpretations. At one end of the spectrum it has been used to refer to a multiple times improvement in one or more characteristics of a pre-defined result or offering. For example a 3× reduction in cost, a 5× improvement in reliability, a 10× improvement in cycle-time or a 4× improvement in customer satisfaction. In short, an improvement in one or more dimensions associated with the delivery of the same solution, as seen either from the consumers' perspective (value metrics) or the process owner's perspective (process metrics). This is sometimes referred to as "incremental innovation."

At the other end of the innovation spectrum is what's termed "radical" or "disruptive" innovation wherein one imagines a service offering that solves a problem that others aren't solving and, perhaps, the potential customer isn't even aware they have this need. Examples abound, such as Apple's introduction of the iPod and smartphone, or Skype's introduction of consumer VOIP. And, of course, the Internet and the World Wide Web. What made many of these more compelling is that they represent services as platforms for other services (and thus additional innovation) and, of course, network effects.

Both ends of the innovation continuum, as well as steps in between, are applicable to services and processes (and their associated business models). It depends on the perspective and tools you bring to the innovation/improvement task. If one begins with questioning and re-thinking the value proposition being offered, one moves towards the disruptive end. If on the other hand, one brings a Lean/Six-Sigma perspective (and tools) one moves towards the improvement end of the continuum of innovation.

4.1 Innovating Business Models and Service-Process Offerings

Any pre-existing business process, and (through the duality assertion) service offering, competes in a market of other, overlapping service offerings (both internal and external) that offer a value proposition to the internal external or external client with a problem-to-be-solved. In other words, the process owner (the "CEO" of the service-process offering he/she is responsible for) is in competition with other value propositions that offer to (partially or completely) address the customers' problem-to-be-solved.

As a process owner, your first (and arguably primary) job is to define what the value proposition(s) are for the service-process you're internally (organizational customer) or externally (customer facing) offering and responsible for. And then do a competitive assessment of your service offering's value proposition relative to its peers. An appropriately formulated Google search can easily identify a range of offerings for a particular PTBS that "compete" with an organization's internal and external service offering(s).

The key issues here are:

1. What is your value proposition relative to an internal/external customer's PTBS?
2. On what basis do you differentiate your offering from those of others (e.g., scope of solution, client perceived transaction cost, cycle time, support. . .)?
3. How should you differentiate your offering so as to dominate those of others that offer a similar (perceived) value proposition to the customers you're seeking to attract or retain?

Given answers to the above, how should you redesign, configure and implement the underlying business process to compete with external offerings? Or, going beyond these "improvement" dimensions, how do you "head to where the puck is going" and expand your addressed PTBS, or define and respond to the "under served," and/or disrupt your view of delivery before competitors do this for you? While an organizationally mandated "sole source" requirement for internal offerings (only) may exist now, such protection is, at best, short-lived.

The value proposition, expressed or implied, is an obvious starting point for any innovation efforts. Who is the current customer? What is the problem they're using your service (and underlying business process) to solve; or alternatively, what job are they trying to get done? Once this is established, then one can begin to ask "unfreezing" questions such as: how might we be able to solve more of their problem or complete more of their work? What do they do before they use our service? What must they then do after using it to complete their work or solve their problem?

This is precisely the type of questions that slowly revolutionized the travel industry. Airlines, for example, once viewed their service as providing seat reservations. But this is but part of the PTBS—hotels are needed, transportation may be needed, meals, entertainment, and so forth. In short, the original value proposition greatly expanded from booking a seat to putting all the pieces together to solve the problem of having a pre-planned trip. To do this they not only used some of their own internally managed services, but employed external services from others. But to the travelling public, they represented a "one-stop" shop.

Alternatively, external providers now do many employee services that were once provided internally, by the organization. Why? Because the internal service (e.g., employee benefits, legal services, small item purchasing, employee travel) fail to adequately solve the employee or employers PTBS. And, at some point, the gap grew large enough that rather than innovate the internal service they began using services that had already been innovated. Even many previous "core" services of organizations, such as customer support, manufacturing and logistics have met similar fates. The old adage, "innovate or die" applies with equal force to company's internal- and external-facing services and underlying processes.

4.2 Innovating with Service Composition

While one can think about developing new service offerings (and thus new processes to support these services), in reality many organizations use a combination of internally existing services, along with externally available services to "wire together" new service offerings. What the end-customer sees is a new service offering from that organization. Under the covers, there's a business process (typically supported by a BPMS or equivalent) that orchestrates these services, while putting an organizational face on the end result. We previously noted Virgin Mobile as one that has done this masterfully. But many other examples abound. Travel services, such as Priceline or Kayak. Or, financial information services such

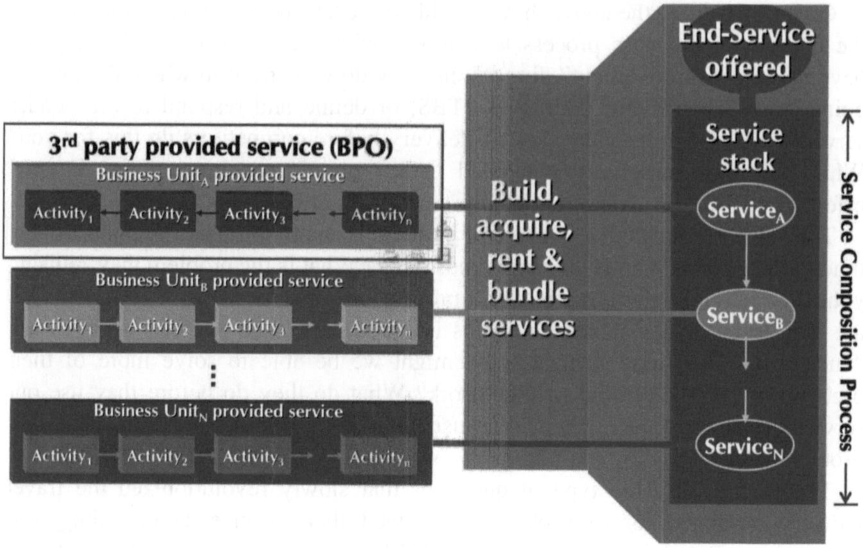

Fig. 8 Innovating with service composition

as Yodlee (who, in turn, sell their composition services to yet other financial organizations such as Fidelity on a "white label" basis).

The basic pattern for this looks like (Fig. 8):

4.3 Process Innovation and Improvement

The line between improvement and innovation blurs when focusing primarily on the process itself. For sure, one can sometimes dramatically change process characteristics such as resources consumed, availability of the service, cost, reliability, cycle time and consistency/quality of the results. These are metrics that may or may not have meaning to the consumer of the process, although they often have value to the process owner (in terms of the metrics they are evaluated on for purposes of performance evaluations). If you're truly focused on "innovation" then as an innovator you will need to go beyond process-owner metrics of improvement (and associated process improvement techniques and tools) and attempt to grasp what the consumer of the process-supported service actually needs, now and in the future, to solve their PTBS and get their "job" done. As already noted, there are many methods and techniques that address various aspects of process improvement, as well as questions one can reasonably ask regarding the process to stimulate thinking. An older such compendium is provided in Tom Davenport's book on "Process Innovation" (Davenport, 1993). A list of thoughtful questions the author often uses to stimulate discussion at this level comes from "The 7 R's of Process Innovation" (Shapiro, 2002).

5 Summary and Conclusions

5.1 Business Model–Service–Process Connection

This paper argues for a tri-partite view of business model-service-process thinking and innovation. The directional view adopted: process → service → business model (bottom up), or business model → service → process (top-down), or starting with the service (middle out) depends upon whether the object of interest is that of a customer trying to solve a problem, or a process owner seeking to rationalize (and improve or innovate) the process they're responsible for.

From an inside-out (or process first) perspective, it is argued that any business process presents itself to its consumer as a business service that attempts to solve the customers' problem. That "service," in turn, exists for the purpose of meeting and satisfying a customer's need; that is, to solve a problem they have (PTBS) and, by invocation, to get their job to-be done (JTBD) in solving their problem. Moreover, the service can appear to its consumer as a progression from rigid (a one size fits all solution) to highly tailored (a customized or "bespoke" solution adaptively tailored to each customer). And, these presentments (solution approach alternatives) are a function of the underlying process execution type chosen.

The organization has an evolving collection of such services (and underlying processes), with a presumed clientele drawn from either internal or external customers. Regardless of demand origin (internal or external) there are competitors to the offered service. For example, the organization could provide its own payroll service, but there are external competitors such as (in the US) ADP or PayCom (and, in large organizations, competing internal units) that solve the same problem (i.e., how to reimburse individuals for the time they spent on adding value to current or future organizational offerings or: Contribution-to-Compensation). If it's internal service competition, then the solution could be "shared services" (single internal provider). If it's external competitors, then the issue becomes one of service differentiation, based upon characteristics that matter to the client. In the end however, it's all market competitors and client perceptions of the best fit between service offerings and their perceived job to be done.

Conversely, an organization, with an existing client base, may be interested in better differentiating its offerings to external customers so as to gain or retain market share, and/or rationalize the processes they perform internally, by defining both their customer and business value and whether or not an internally delivered solution is competitive (viable).

Either way, a business model of a service and its underlying process helps to sort out the intent and competitive positioning of any service being contemplated or offered.

5.2 Interaction Effects

Regardless of the directionality of the business model, service and process taken, there are significant interactions that should be proactively managed. If one adopts an outside in (client first) perspective, then it is argued that a business model of the proposed service offering should precede its detailed definition. And the service definition should precede a choice of the process execution type and finally its process execution model.

Conversely, if a specific business process is under improvement scrutiny whatever reason (e.g., cost reduction, lean and/or six-sigma related process improvements), it should be cross-defined as an offered service, and then when so-defined, the service should be examined through the lens of its implied business model, by making that business model explicit.

In summary, a business model, service or business process, whether proposed or existing implies the existence of the other two. Each provides a unique and equally important perspective on the offering that offers both comprehensive definition and critique, and presents valuable insights into improvement and innovation opportunities that are not afforded by any single perspective.

5.3 Conclusions

This paper argues that business models, service definitions and business process models are, in effect, different perspectives on the same underling phenomenon. While these three concepts have hitherto been treated separately in both the literature and in practice, this paper asserts that they are, in fact, different views of the same artifact, with each contributing complimentary insights that the other perspectives diminish or set aside.

Working between the three perspectives can create more challenges than a single perspective view. However, the natural complementarity of these three perspectives suggests that ignoring this trifecta may have business consequences and/or process execution consequences. Conversely, more adequately accounting for all three views can lead to a far greater emphasis on innovation as well as improved implementation outcomes by more fully taking into account both the intended client of the solution offered, the market of competitive offerings as well as the alignment of the process that delivers this value, through the service, to the market of customers for it.

References

Al-Debei, M. M., & Avison, D. (2010). Developing a unified framework of the business model concept. *European Journal of Information Systems, 19*(3), 359–376.

Alter, S. (2008). Service system fundamentals: Work system, value chain, and life cycle. *IBM Systems Journal, 47*(1), 71–85.

Anthony, R. N. (1965). *Planning and control systems: A framework for analysis* (180 pp.). Boston, MA: Harvard Business Press.
APQC. (2014). *Process classification framework (Version 6.1.1)* (p. 25). Houston, TX: APQC. free PDF downloaded from http://www.apqc.org/pcf.
Christensen, C. M. (1997). *The innovator's dilemma: When new technologies cause great firms to fail*. Boston, MA: Harvard Business Press.
Davenport, T. H. (1993). *Process innovation: Reengineering work through information technology*. Boston, MA: Harvard Business School Press. ISBN 0-87584-366-2.
Harrison-Broninski, K. (2005). *Human interactions: The heart and soul of business process management*. Tampa, FL: Meghan-Kiffer Press.
Kalakota, R., & Robinson, M. (2003). *Services blueprint: Roadmap for execution*. Boston, MA: Addison-Wesley.
Khoshafian, S. (2007). *Service oriented enterprises*. Boca Raton, FL: Auerbach Publications.
Krcmar, H. (2011). *Business model research: State of the art and research agenda*. Working paper of Technische Universitat Munchen, Chair for Information Systems, Munich, Germany.
Malone, T. W., Crowston, K., & Herman, G. A. (2003). *Organizing business knowledge: The MIT process handbook*. Cambridge, MA: MIT Press.
Osterwalder, A., & Pigneur, Y. (2010). *Business model generation: A handbook for visionaries, game changers, and challengers*. John Wiley and Sons, 1st edition, Hoboken, NJ, USA.
Osterwalder, A., & Pigneur, Y. (2013). *Value proposition designer*. TBD (in press).
Osterwalder, A., Pigneur, Y., & Tucci, C. L. (2005). Clarifying business models: Origins, present, and future of the concept. *Communications of the Association for Information Systems, 16*(1), 1–25.
Osterwalder, A., Pigneur, Y., Bernarda, G., & Smith, A. (2015). *Value proposition design: How to create products and services customers Want* (1st ed.). Hoboken, NJ: Wiley.
Porter, M. E. (1998). *Competitive advantage: Creating and sustaining superior performance*. New York, NY: Free Press.
Sawhney, M., Wolcott, R. C., & Arroniz, I. (2011). The 12 different ways for companies to innovate. *Sloan Management Review*, *47*(3), 28–34.
Shapiro, S. (2002). The 7Rs of process innovation. *The 24/7 Innovation Thought Leadership Series* (3 p.). Retrieved from www.24-7Innovation.com
Swenson, K. D. (2010). *Mastering the unpredictable: How adaptive case management will revolutionize the way that knowledge workers get things done*. Tampa, FL: Meghan-Kiffer Press.
Vargo, S. L., Maglio, P. P., & Akaka, M. A. (2008). On value and value co-creation: A service systems and service logic perspective. *European Management Journal, 26*(3), 145–152.
Wagner, H. M. (1975). *Principles of operations research: With applications to managerial decisions*. Englewood Cliffs, NJ: Prentice-Hall.
Welke, R. J. (2005). *Think service, act process: Meeting today's demand for innovation and agility* (37 p.). HowDoUPress. ISBN: 978-0-9835439-1-6.
Whittle, R., & Myrick, C. (2004). *Enterprise business architecture: The formal link between strategy and results*. Boca Raton, FL: CRC Press.

Part II

Driving Innovation Through Emerging Technologies

Emerging Technologies in BPM

Sandy Kemsley

Abstract

Business process management (BPM) has always been about productivity improvements. But new aspects need to be considered in BPM today, including knowledge work, transparency, and customer-orientation. Many emerging technologies are being integrated into BPM in order to account for these new aspects. Two categories of innovations and technologies can be distinguished: those that change the way people and organizations work, and those that create more intelligent processes. This chapter explores emerging technologies and how they apply to BPM.

1 Introduction

Business process management (BPM), from its early roots in workflow and enterprise application integration (EAI) technologies, has always been about making businesses more efficient through automation. Productivity improvements are still a cornerstone of many BPM implementations, but there are now many other factors: different styles of work, such as dynamic, goal-driven knowledge work; collaboration with remote and mobile participants, including those outside an organization; greater transparency and insights into processes for both internal workers and external customers or business partners; and the ability to optimize processes as a competitive differentiator (Hammer, 2010; Rosemann & vom Brocke, 2010; vom Brocke et al., 2014).

Many emerging technologies are being integrated into BPM in order to achieve these new goals, falling into two main categories: those innovations and technologies that change the way that people and organizations work, and those

S. Kemsley (✉)
Kemsley Design Ltd., 50 Camden Street, Toronto, ON, Canada M5V 3N1
e-mail: sandy@kemsleydesign.com

J. vom Brocke, T. Schmiedel (eds.), *BPM – Driving Innovation in a Digital World*,
Management for Professionals, DOI 10.1007/978-3-319-14430-6_4

that create more intelligent processes. In the first category, social collaboration and adaptive processes provide functionality to create more dynamic, customer-focused processes, but can create challenges in the cultural and organizational changes required to implement them (Schmiedel, vom Brocke, & Recker, 2013). Intelligent process technology, particularly simulation and predictive analytics, offers new ways to optimize processes during runtime (vom Brocke, Debortoli, Müller, & Reuter, 2014).

This chapter will explore emerging technologies and how they apply to BPM, showing how these new capabilities can make processes more engaging, more adaptable, more transparent, and smarter (also see chapters by Trkman and Klun (2015), Schenk (2015), and Ohlsson, Händel, Han, and Welch (2015)).

2 Emerging Technologies

There are a variety of newer technologies that are reaching commercial viability, although few have achieved mainstream adoption. Not specific to BPM, these are transforming both consumer and enterprise software; these are described next to provide context for the following sections on BPM technologies.

2.1 Mobile and Cloud

Mobile and cloud, although they can be implemented independently, are often related since many mobile solutions also depend on public cloud infrastructure. On the surface, mobile and cloud are just deployment platforms: mobile is the platform for the end user, while cloud is the platform for serving the end-user functionality. Both, however, are transformative technologies since they expose and democratize access to information.

Mobile applications allow access to information and functionality in ways never before possible. Mobile has become mainstream for consumer applications—finding when the next bus is coming while you are walking to the station, or using your phone to pay at your favorite coffee shop—but is also making inroads with remote and mobile enterprise workers. A healthcare worker working with patients in their homes can gather patient information on a mobile device, removing the need to re-enter data when they return to their office, and receive immediate feedback on potential drug interactions and suggested next steps. An industrial site inspector can input inspection data directly, triggering maintenance requests. Enterprise mobile applications can improve efficiency and quality by capturing information at the point of collection, provide real-time context through information lookup and automated decisioning, and trigger follow-up actions and notifications.

Enterprise cloud applications, whether accessed via a mobile device or a traditional computer, allow anyone to participate from anywhere: employees from home or remote corporate offices, or business partners and customers from their own location. Since cloud applications typically do not require licensing and installation on the user's computer or mobile device, anyone who is permitted access can participate. Information is stored in the cloud, hence accessible regardless of the user's location, and easy shared between users.

2.2 Social Collaboration and Distributed Co-creation

Enterprise social collaboration typically takes one of two forms: either it is focused on social interaction that strengthens weak ties within a large or geographically dispersed organization, or it is focused on goal-oriented social production. Although social interaction is important to build networks within and across organizations, distributed co-creation is the ultimate goal of enterprise social interaction: many people, in different locations and with a variety of skills, working together to create content or other work product. For maximum benefit, the social aspect is integrated directly into the core business applications that people are using, so that the collaboration has a direct business purpose. This trend towards social collaboration as a feature of enterprise applications, rather than a separate tool, is accelerating the acceptance of collaboration within enterprises.

Two essential characteristics of social co-creation are tied to its unpredictability: it is typically goal-driven rather than prescriptive, and collaboration occurs on demand rather than with predetermined participants.

Note that social collaboration often relies on cloud infrastructure, since there may be participants from a number of different organizations.

2.3 Events, Big Data and Analytics

Information-filled events are generated by a wide variety devices and systems: computers, mobile phones, vehicles, industrial equipment, sensors, security systems, building automation systems, and even social networks such as Twitter. The result is a flood of data that may contain valuable information, if that information can be detected.

Information gleaned from events may allow for real-time pre-emptive problem detection and resolution, by finding correlated sequences of events and applying predictive analytics to determine that a problem is likely to occur in the future, then applying automated decisioning or user alerts to avoid the problem.

Aggregated events from a longer period of time can be analyzed to detect patterns of behavior, allowing business operations to be introspected and optimized.

A variety of data-focused technologies are combined to achieve these goals, including complex event processing, pattern analysis and detection, big data processing, predictive analytics and automated decisioning.

3 The Changing Nature of Work

The nature of work is changing: routine work is becoming highly automated, leaving the complex and unpredictable knowledge work for people. These knowledge workers apply their skills not just to perform individual tasks assigned to them, but also to decide which tasks to perform, in what order, and by whom, in order to accomplish a goal (Müller, Schmiedel, Gorbacheva, & vom Brocke, 2014). The following sections give insights into how emerging technologies change the way people and organizations work.

3.1 Social BPM

Consumer social software, first identified in the early 2000s, has a defining characteristic of harnessing collective intelligence by allowing user-created content and collaboration. This raised user expectations for enterprise software: today's workers expect to be able to configure their own environment to suit their working style, to collaborate with others at any point where they see fit, and to combine information from multiple internal and external sources in order to accomplish their tasks. Furthermore, management experts recognized the benefits of distributing co-creation across the value chain, so that ideas from workers at all levels are captured to provide a more accurate picture. This led to the development of social business applications that allow for emergent structure and processes rather than imposing pre-determined taxonomies and procedures, but with business-related purposes:

- Enabling social interaction that strengthens weak ties within a large and/or geographically diverse organization. For example, an internal social network that allows employees to create profile pages can be used for locating others with specific skills and interests for research and project collaboration, although that collaboration does not necessarily happen within the social application itself.
- Enabling goal-oriented social production. For example, a wiki used to document internal operational procedures can be updated directly by any worker with information on specific areas of the procedures.

Increasingly, these functions are integrated directly into the line of business applications that workers use every day, and BPM systems are proving to be an ideal platform for this integration: social in the flow of work, rather than in an ancillary collaboration application.

Social functionality manifests in a number of ways in BPM systems:

- Collaborative process discovery, where people from a variety of technical and non-technical perspectives contribute to process design. A centralized process model repository preserves institutional memory, and web-based tools facilitate collaboration across business units and with other organizations. As the community forms around the collaborative process discovery tools, new uses will be discovered for process discovery and management, and workers from different areas will more easily lend their expertise to projects that bear some similarity to their own. This creates a network effect—where something becomes more valuable as more people use it—causing an exponential increase in potential performance improvement.

- Runtime collaboration, where a user can add collaborators to his assigned task by expanding the visibility of that task to others based on his tacit knowledge of their skills and experience, then collecting their responses and decisions as part of the task history. As well as completing the work more effectively, this captures a record of the collaboration, including who was involved in decision-making on each process instance.
- Activity stream user interfaces, to improve visibility and opt-in participation across a broader range of people and devices. Users define their own subscriptions and alerts to fine-tune the flood of information, allowing for better identification and management of their important tasks; for example, they may "watch" a particular class of process instances, and receive updates whenever they are created or specific milestones are reached. Typically, a process event within a stream will include a direct link to the process instance, allowing for the recipient to easily click through in order to participate. The short message nature of the event stream simplifies the information into an easily-digestible update, and allows the stream to be formatted for a mobile device, allowing process monitoring via event streams by anyone on the monitoring platform of their choice.

Collaboration has always been present in how work is done: the difference now is that systems now support and track that collaboration, making it a measurable contributor to work improvement rather than a hidden factor.

3.2 Dynamic Processes

Dynamic processes allow the worker to modify a process, or even create a new process, to satisfy the current context or to integrate their knowledge into the process. Most often created as part of goal-directed social co-creation, dynamic processes can also be created by a worker purely for their own use.

In routine work, process models are pre-defined and the focus is on making processes more efficient. Each step in a process is either automated or assigned to a person as a specific task, leaving little room for creativity. Conversely, knowledge work is required for non-repeatable processes, where only the goals and general guidelines may be set in advance, and the worker dynamically decides the tasks required to complete the goals in response to current conditions. Most organizations have both routine work and knowledge work, often within the same processes.

In the spectrum between routine and unpredictable work, a business process may be pre-defined but allow the participants to modify the process during execution on a case-by-case basis. If a particular process instance requires additional steps, the user can define them for that instance without changing the underlying model on which new instances will be based. For example, it's often not feasible to model all the possible exception paths when something goes wrong in a process; instead, the tasks required to handle a particular exception are decided by the process participant at that point in time.

In addition to allowing for greater flexibility, dynamic process variations can be captured as feedback to process improvement, so that if a specific pattern of activities is always added during runtime, that could be added to the underlying process model, reducing the runtime effort for this task in the future.

3.3 Cultural Changes

Social and dynamic BPM capabilities require rethinking the concept of "control" within an organization: management no longer dictates every action that employees take, but everyone is given an appropriate level of control required to complete their tasks. Collaboration and dynamic process are not new within organizations, but they may be performed using unmanaged (and unmonitored) methods if overly-strict management control does not allow knowledge worker flexibility within the line of business systems. Providing flexibility allows knowledge workers to improve the quality of the work completed, based on their skills and experience.

More flexible work styles can also be challenging to less confident workers, who may not collaborate or dynamically change processes because they don't want to appear unknowledgeable. This can be overcome by a work environment where creative solutions are rewarded, encouraging workers to offer their own ideas.

In many cases, organizations can benefit from collaborate, dynamic business processes, but may have corporate cultures and incentive plans that discourage collaboration and creative problem-solving. It may be necessary to shift employee metrics from pure efficiency measures to those that capture contributions to problem-solving and social collaboration, and change extrinsic incentives and reward systems in order to guide worker behavior.

4 Smarter Processes

Improved intelligence in business processes is achieved through the combination of many different technologies, including orchestration, decisioning, simulation and analytics. Many of these technologies are not new to BPM, but the emergence of predictive process analytics gives rise to a fundamental shift towards self-adjusting and self-optimizing processes.

The time-oriented nature of processes enables forecasting future behavior and averting problems before they occur, both for individual process instances and in the aggregate. Using pre-determined process models, historical data from the executing and past processes, and simulation techniques to project forward from a point in time, predictive process analytics can predict if a process will meet its goals. While standard process analytics indicate that a deadline was missed, predictive process analytics indicate the probability of missing a deadline at some point in the future.

Once a potential future problem is identified, runtime simulation can compare "what-if" scenarios to determine optimal pre-emptive actions based on the current context of the process instance and historical data for similar instances. This allows process simulation—typically considered a design-time process optimization tool—to be repurposed for runtime predictions and optimization.

Next, if these processes are automated in a sufficiently dynamic BPM system, information can be fed back to allow the process to self-adjust through automated decisioning, or to alert a worker to take manual actions.

Finally, predictive process analytics can be used to dynamically optimize the process model relative to the process goals. This automates continuous process improvement through self-adjusting mechanisms.

5 Summary

The definition of BPM is constantly changing (see also introductory chapter (Schmiedel & vom Brocke, 2015)), driven by market forces and vendor offerings, and resulting in the continual introduction of new technologies into BPM products.

Social and dynamic BPM, although robustly implemented in many vendor products, are still considered emerging concepts because of the low penetration rate within customer organizations. These capabilities have broad cultural implications that may require changes in management style and organizational structures in order to succeed, creating significant barriers to adoption.

Self-adjusting processes based on predictive process analytics represent truly emerging BPM technology, with only a handful of BPM vendors offering these capabilities within their products.

These emerging BPM technologies go beyond the basic goals of efficiency and productivity to focus on optimizing processes during runtime: either through human collaboration and knowledge work, or via automated responses to changing conditions.

References

Hammer, M. (2010). What is business process management? In J. vom Brocke & M. Rosemann (Eds.), *Handbook on business process management: Introduction, methods and information systems* (Vol. 1, pp. 3–16). Berlin: Springer.

Müller, O., Schmiedel, T., Gorbacheva, E., & vom Brocke, J. (2014). Toward a typology of business process management professionals: Identifying patterns of competences through latent semantic analysis. *Enterprise Information Systems, 8*, 1–31.

Ohlsson, J., Händel, P., Han, S., & Welch, R. (2015). Process innovation with disruptive technology in auto insurance: Lessons learned from a smartphone-based insurance telematics initiative. In J. vom Brocke & T. Schmiedel (Eds.), *Business process management: Driving innovation in a digital world.* Berlin: Springer.

Rosemann, M., & vom Brocke, J. (2010). The six core elements of business process management. In J. vom Brocke & M. Rosemann (Eds.), *Handbook on business process management. Introduction, methods and information systems* (Vol. 1, pp. 109–124). Berlin: Springer.

Schenk, B. (2015). The role of enterprise systems in process innovation. In J. vom Brocke & T. Schmiedel (Eds.), *Business process management: Driving innovation in a digital world.* Berlin: Springer.

Schmiedel, T., & vom Brocke, J. (2015). Business process management: Potentials and challenges of driving innovation. In J. vom Brocke & T. Schmiedel (Eds.), *Business process management: Driving innovation in a digital world.* Berlin: Springer.

Schmiedel, T., vom Brocke, J., & Recker, J. (2013). Which cultural values matter to business process management? Results from a global Delphi study. *Business Process Management Journal, 19*(2), 292–317.

Trkman, P., & Klun, M. (2015). The match of business process management and social media – A conceptual framework. In J. vom Brocke & T. Schmiedel (Eds.), *Business process management: Driving innovation in a digital world.* Berlin: Springer.

vom Brocke, J., Debortoli, S., Müller, O., & Reuter, N. (2014). How in-memory technology can create business value: Insights from the Hilti case. *Communications of the Association for Information Systems, 34*(1), 151–167.

vom Brocke, J., Schmiedel, T., Recker, J., Trkman, P., Mertens, W., & Viaene, S. (2014). Ten principles of good business process management. *Business Process Management Journal, 20* (4), 530–548.

Leveraging Social Media for Process Innovation. A Conceptual Framework

Peter Trkman and Monika Klun

Abstract

Business processes management should not be a one-off activity and processes need to be continually modelled, executed, monitored and improved; stakeholders need to be aptly involved in each of these activities. Potentials for achieving this lie in social media, as an increasingly popular option in the digital world with which to involve the creativity and opinions of various stakeholders from both within and outside an organization. Yet, it is still not well researched how companies can harness the various benefits for using social media to better involve both employees and customers in various phases of the business process life cycle. We propose a conceptual framework that enables the classification of various types of social media use (e.g. within organization or with customers) and provide examples for each type.

1 Introduction

The business processes within the organization need to be continually modelled, executed, monitored and improved; stakeholders need to be properly involved in each of these activities. In fact, principles of involvement (the need to integrate all stakeholder groups) and continuity (continuous gains in efficiency and effectiveness) are among the 10 main principles of business process management (vom Brocke et al., 2014). Potential options for achieving both involvement and continuity are social media ('SM'), as an increasingly popular option in the digital world with which to involve the creativity and opinions of various stakeholders from both within and outside an organization (Kaplan & Haenlein, 2010; Kietzmann, Hermkens, McCarthy, & Silvestre, 2011). A rich exchange of ideas and information

P. Trkman (✉) • M. Klun
Faculty of Economics, University of Ljubljana, Kardeljeva pl. 17, 1000 Ljubljana, Slovenia
e-mail: peter.trkman@ef.uni-lj.si; monika.klun@ef.uni-lj.si

J. vom Brocke, T. Schmiedel (eds.), *BPM – Driving Innovation in a Digital World*,
Management for Professionals, DOI 10.1007/978-3-319-14430-6_5

can produce invaluable results, such as innovation and knowledge "spillovers" (Jerome, 2013). SM are a group of Internet-based applications that build on the ideological and technological foundations of Web 2.0, and that allow the creation and exchange of user generated content (Kaplan & Haenlein, 2010). They can be of different types: blogs, social networking sites (e.g. Facebook), collaborative projects (e.g. wikis), content communities (e.g. YouTube), virtual social worlds (e.g. Second Life) and virtual game worlds (e.g. World of Warcraft). Kane, Alavi, Labianca, and Borgatti (2014) define SM as information technologies that support interpersonal communication and collaboration using Internet-based platforms. We here understand SM to be a service that facilitates networking among employees and stakeholders, regardless whether this solely includes internal, or also encompasses external stakeholders.

Several authors have already discussed coupling strategies, benefits, and the requirements for successful implementation of SM (Bruno et al., 2011; Schmidt & Nurcan, 2009; Silva et al., 2010). Yet, as noted by Trkman and Trkman (2011) the purpose of SM needs to be clearly identified before the start of SM implementation. Therefore, the roles in which SM can be used in various phases of a business process life cycle need to be clearly understood. Accordingly, this paper attempts to provide a classification of potential SM uses in each phase of the business process life cycle: process modeling, process execution, process monitoring and process improvement. We argue that such an approach can help to better understand the possibilities of SM uses in BPM.

The structure of the paper is as follows: after a brief review of literature on SM and BPM, we outline the challenges accompanying the incorporation of SM into BPM. We then present the conceptual framework of the types of SM use in BPM, accompanied by examples from literature and personal experience. Finally, we present the types of uses according to each business process life cycle phase in greater detail and suggest ideas for future research.

2 Background

The possibilities of joining SM with BPM are manifold, as demonstrated by an increasing number of research contributions in this area. Bruno et al. (2011) introduce a new paradigm of the life cycle of business processes that enables agile business process management by applying social media in the business process life cycle. Whereas the traditional business process life cycle usually contains fixed flows, social software allow for an "a posteriori control of quality" (Bruno et al., 2011). Our paper builds on the research by Bruno et al. by adding to their paradigm and framing the different possibilities of SM use in a systematic framework, divided into four business process life cycle phases. Erol et al. (2010) identify the main advantages of using SM for BPM such as integration of users into BPM, lowered information pass-on threshold, absence of formal barriers and ease of use. Koschmider, Song, and Reijers (2010) discuss social networks and their proximity as a possibility of sharing and exchanging process models. Pereira, Vera, and Miller

(2011) present the increase of interest by firms in social and mobile technologies to tackle the challenges of traditionally static business processes, like the demand of users for "instant gratification, rich user experiences and rapid access to information".

There is abundant literature that deals with exploring and exploiting the potency that SM have as a part of the organization's marketing strategy (e.g. Evans, 2012; Heymann-Reder, 2011). Going beyond the scope of marketing and public relations, SM can be a tool for process development and improvement as well. Organizations are beginning to recognize the advantages of incorporating "collaboration into business processes" (Kemsley, 2010). Therefore we investigate the opportunities for BPM.

SM, especially web-based, represent a communication tool of choice for many organizations—the powerful and cost-effective means of communication can foster digital innovation to reach previously unknown proportions (Hawn, 2009). Social networking tools provide intensified collaboration among all stakeholders by providing a common network for interaction, thus engaging one of the main advantages of SM—making new acquaintances. The connection among rather unfamiliar individuals, termed weak ties by Granovetter (1983), surpasses the boundaries of the hierarchical structure and provides a horizontal flow of knowledge sharing and collaboration. Additionally the SM enable locating experts on a particular topic within the organization (Stieglitz, Schallenmüller, & Meske, 2013) or beyond. In turn they can function as "incubators" for collaboration (Jerome, 2013).

Schmidt and Nurcan (2009) present the five principles of SM tools that drive the creation of content and context:

- Self-organization: Along with the bottom-up approach it enables the classification, structuration and organization of information by entire communities of interacting users as opposed to pre-determined specialists.
- Continuous aggregation: Different sources contribute content, which is constantly aggregated and immediately made visible and effective.
- Egalitarianism: Absence of separation between content contributors and consumers as well as low input efforts mean lowered thresholds for contributing data and knowledge.
- Continuous assessment: The contributions are under constant and recursive assessment by all users, so errors can be identified and corrected immediately.
- Value of content and context: Apart from the content, the context is also of importance, as it can represent additional information, e.g. relationship.

Obviously, the use of SM per se will only bring certain benefits if it will be used solely for marketing and for "individual heroics by employees". A more structured approach towards its use is needed in order to explore the range of possible benefits. A good help in this regard is the body of knowledge relating to BPM which has always focused on defining, organizing and optimizing business processes, bringing about benefits such as reducing cost, increasing value, expediting execution and adding customer value (Dumas, La Rosa, Mendling, & Reijers, 2013; Rosemann & vom Brocke, 2015; Weske, 2007). The idea of BPM has traditionally been the standardization of processes, which could then yield continuous and uniform results. In order to enable decision making for the purpose of analyzing and designing business processes, rigorously structured process models were created and the science of modeling became increasingly sophisticated (Recker, 2010; Rosemann, 2006). SM present a tool that can enable the users to "step outside" the structured process and initiate an "ad hoc collaboration" (Kemsley, 2010). Therefore the potential benefits of SM for business processes need to be further explored.

3 The Challenges of SM for BPM

"Socializing" BPM with SM is difficult due to the innate nature and characteristics of both concepts. Often business processes are governed by strict regulations and thus poorly suited for collaboration, while SM require participatory involvement of network actors. Several barriers, such as fearing the loss of management control, lack of trust or understanding, or risks of data loss, may prevent organizations from (successfully) implementing SM in a business process life cycle (Kemsley, 2010).

BPM should combine the views of several stakeholders in order to define, analyze and (re)create business processes (Dumas et al., 2013). However, while most BPM efforts nominally start with the emphasis on customer needs, the customer "voice" is often lost during the execution of the project. Now, in the digital age, it is possible to include new stakeholders (e.g. co-workers, business partners or consumers) in various phases of business processes through the utilization of SM. SM use does not need to be limited to one organization since valuable innovation-related knowledge can be drawn from several different actors, organizations or even communities (Chesbrough, 2003). Any form of communication and collaboration entails knowledge sharing and brings with it a series of potential risks (Trkman & Desouza, 2012). These are especially important when it concerns obtaining knowledge from outside the organization. With SM, employees and stakeholders are given much more freedom of choice to collaborate and connect.

The use of SM can often seem unpredictable—new tools are developed at a rapid pace, users tend to migrate—in often unpredictable ways—to new tools, and the reasons for content contribution are highly diverse (Quan-Haase, 2007). Data put online can quickly go viral. A typical case of the "virulence" and unpredictability of SM is the *United Airlines breaks guitars* video clip which spread quickly and presumably caused the airline $180 million in loss due to reputation damages (Huffington Post, 2011). Yet, some risks apply to internal use of SM as well. As one of the authors of this article was told by a chief information officer of a large American company, the comments from internal SM, illustrating awareness about particular (undesirable) internal events or information, could be used as incriminating data in court proceedings. A further example entails the use of SM for sexual harassment (Bradley & McDonald, 2011).

A lack of responsiveness from users can undermine the successful implementation of SM. It can be brought about by unclear expectations (regarding both the purpose and use of SM as well as project execution) and also by a lack of motivation. Kolind (2013) suggests delegating professional leaders or "gurus" for guidance and encouragement. Trkman and Trkman (2011) argue in favor of a number of designated contributors to drive the initial content development. Incentives of various forms are another possibility.

An egalitarian and bottom-up creation approach without any formal guidelines or governing authority is the characteristic of general SM like Facebook, but can prove too passive for the business environment. Consequently, the original purpose of SM integration into the process may be diluted and could even cause counter-productive results. Some companies and organizations are already blocking the access to such sites (Frosch, 2007), but studies show that SM adapted to an organization setting can provide substantial benefits for organizations (Sena & Sena, 2008). Yet, any use of SM needs a clear ex-ante determination of purpose (Trkman & Trkman, 2011). In doing so our framework proposed in the next section can be an important help.

4 A Framework for Classification of SM Use in Business Processes Management

Often companies adopt technology or procedures in the hype phase just to follow others, but insufficient planning and vague goals lead to undesirable results, even financial loss (Fenn & Raskino, 2008; Trkman, Kovačič, & Popovič, 2011). A better understanding of the possibilities of SM use in BPM and the potential risks accompanying them can aid practitioners in their SM adoption. Our framework contributes to the understanding of the SM-BPM relationship. Firstly, it offers a classification of different possibilities of SM incorporation in BPM. Secondly, since the phase of the BP life cycle affects the purpose of SM, the framework analyzes the role of SM in different phases. Success stories and best practice examples are not uniformly applicable for all organizations and are often biased or embellished.

The business process life cycle has various versions—the number of phases differs depending on the granularity and scope (Weber, Sadiq, & Reichert, 2009; Wetzstein et al., 2007)—see the full review of business process (management) life cycles in Morais, Kazan, Pádua, and Costa (2014). Houy, Fettke, and Loos (2010) state that despite the varying numbers and names of steps, conceptually the differences between those steps are small. For the purpose of this paper we will use the four following phases, namely, process modeling, process execution, process monitoring, and process improvement as shown in Fig. 1.

Table 1 presents the overview of possible uses in these four phases, which are explored in more detail in the following section. SM can accommodate three purposes in the modeling phase: (1) increase awareness of all stakeholders regarding

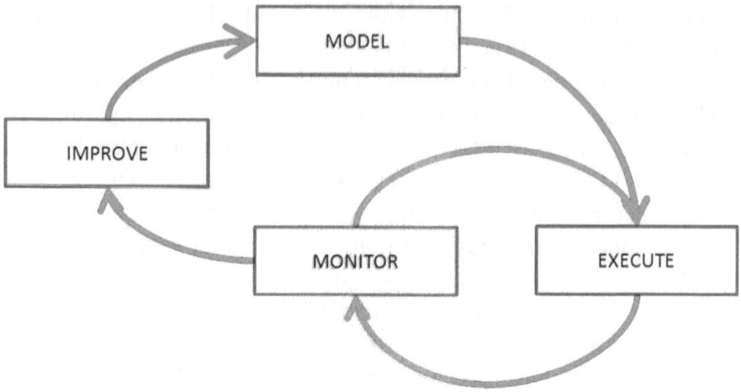

Fig. 1 Business process life cycle

process modeling and execution, (2) aggregate information, relevant for process modeling by different participants, (3) enable inclusion of more employees than just a few selected experts in the modeling group.

In the execution phase there are many possibilities for SM use: (1) enabling continuous support during process execution by connecting all stakeholders (especially for immediate coordination in unexpected situations), (2) coordination support for distribution of execution processes among geographically-dispersed co-workers, and (3) outsourcing certain activities in the process (e.g. "open innovation" platforms for outsourcing the "innovation" process).

The monitoring phase can benefit from including SM for (1) receiving the (quantitatively measured) data and feedback from all stakeholders of the network and (2) sharing the process performance results with co-workers and customers/end-users alike.

In the improvement phase SM (1) facilitate a platform for gathering suggestions for process optimization and feedback on those suggestions, (2) praise-based rewards for the top contributors of improvement ideas, (3) statistical analysis of SM data to provide possibilities for process improvement.

4.1 Modeling Phase for Internal Participants

The modeling of business processes provides a shared and comprehensive understanding of the business process (Aguilar-Saven, 2004). Involving more stakeholders in the modeling process can facilitate a more holistic perspective of the business process and its requirements. Typically processes are modeled by a closed group of business analysts, employees and process owners; in our experience often the individuals most in favor of process view and approach are included. While the model preparation phase is usually a product of collaboration, the final process model is mostly prepared by one person (Koschmider et al., 2010). While limiting the number of individuals on the modeling project seems prudent for

Table 1 A framework for classification of SM inclusion in business process life cycle

	Internal participants	External participants
Process modeling phase	Involving the employees in process modeling	Gathering data or providing feedback on process models from external stakeholders
Process execution phase	Supporting employees in process execution	Outsourcing process activities or providing users' support during execution
Process monitoring phase	Enabling real time visibility and feedback on process performance to employees	Enabling real time visibility and feedback on process performance to customers or suppliers
Process improvement phase	Gathering and evaluating ideas for process improvement from employees	Gathering and evaluating ideas for process improvement from stakeholders

coordination reasons, excluded employees, if not involved at a later stage, can develop negative predispositions towards the process approach (Rosemann, 2006).

Usually the model is presented to the entire organization for evaluation after the modeling is finished, but by using SM all employees, not just a handful, are given insight into the model creation. Employees are actively involved in preparing the process model by contributing the needed data or knowledge, resulting in a (better) process understanding and acceptance rate of the process model itself.

Giving departments insight into the procedures and processes of other departments enhances understanding and cooperation among them. SM tools can provide a clear overview of all activities and the means of participating in these activities. A typical example are IBM's internal network bluepages which enable communication and collaboration among all employees by providing job-specific tools and applications on the intranet (IBM-News, 2006).

In various forms, SM can facilitate a direct and active approach to modeling a business process for all participants of the network. An example of a hands-on approach would be using a wiki for modeling processes (see e.g. Ghidini, Rospocher, & Serafini, 2010; Trkman & Trkman, 2009). The modeling project leader develops the model on a wiki page and thus makes the modeling process transparent and accessible. Other users are included in the process itself, since they are aware of the project activities and are able to participate in them.

Obviously, just being given the possibility to use SM for process modeling does not mean employees will indeed do so; usually explicit top management engagement is necessary. An example of that is in a German commercial bank, where, as the bank's middle managers explained to one of the authors, most of the employees have 5 % of their work hours explicitly reserved for modeling processes.

4.2 Modeling Phase for External Participants

Organizations today strive to be customer-centric and try to engage end-customers on one hand and suppliers on the other, as much as possible (Aguilar-Saven, 2004; Murthy, Baratam, & Whelan, 2012). Existing knowledge about customer preferences gained from marketing research has an effect on process improvement and therefore also on (future) process modeling. Yet, even though the customer focus is advocated at the start of the process-modeling project, customers are then rarely included in the modeling itself. The lack of direct participation in the modeling process could be avoided by including SM.

Customers can even participate in the modeling of processes in which they are directly involved and sometimes attain a better or at least a different view on them, for example by contributing the knowledge about desired output(s), flow and prerequisites of the process (Wagner & Majchrzak, 2007). SM provide a common platform for communication and collaboration. Even more, SM encompass tools to connect, present and share data or artifacts (video, pictures or other forms of non-textual content). Collaboration in the preparation of the outline of the model provides improvement suggestions that would otherwise be acquired in the analysis phase.

A typical example is a pharmaceutical company which included its supplier in the modeling process (Trkman, Mertens, Viaene, & Gemmel, 2015). Both parties gained a deeper understanding of the process execution and aim. The involvement of the supplier enabled the joint modelling and consequently improvement of processes by both companies.

4.3 Execution Phase for Internal Participants

Using SM in the execution of the process enables easy coordination and distribution of the execution across any number of co-workers, in any particular department or location. Due to the low costs of connecting collaborators and an online "meeting room", project teams need not be limited in size. Physical proximity and time difference are less of an issue, since the ubiquity of the network allows for constant, close collaboration e.g. connection to other teams in their subsidiaries.

Numerous instances of collaboration among coworkers facilitated by SM can be found. One possible example is employees using Yammer to get advice from colleagues when additional information about a process (or an activity in the process) is required. An organization can use SM to encourage both interdepartmental and cross-departmental collaboration. Xerox for instance developed an internal support system based on technicians providing other technicians with solutions to technical issues (Moore, 1999). All employees have access and contributing rights, the most affluent contributors being ranked as top users.

The use of SM in execution of business processes can bring about organizational changes as well. New, less hierarchical models of organizing have started to appear instead of traditional organizational forms, especially in highly dynamic environments

(Majchrzak, Jarvenpaa, & Hollingshead, 2007). Kolind and Bøtter (2012) describe a new managerial philosophy, where companies no longer have employees, but partners, and the goal is not profit, but creating value.

4.4 Execution Phase for External Participants

In the execution phase, SM can be applied for two purposes: either to facilitate communication or to distribute process execution onto customers. An example of the former is the airline company TAP, which used Facebook to communicate with passengers during a natural disaster. When the Eyjafjallajökull volcano erupted in May 2010 flights were cancelled at most European airports. With a mass of stranded passengers, the customer service call centers were overwhelmed. TAP was able to reach a much wider audience via Facebook instead of one customer at a time via the call center (Vaz Vieira & Jaklic, 2013).

On the other hand, organizations can use SM to form platforms on which they can present their innovation "demands". In turn "suppliers" can access these sites and contribute innovation ideas. An example thereof is the *connect + develop* site of Proctor and Gamble; a networking base for outsourcing process development (Proctor&Gamble, 2014). Among other inventions, the site enabled expedited development of their pulsating toothbrush, which was only an idea at the time and would have needed up to 5 more years in development. After partnering with a Japanese manufacturer, found through their open innovation site, the joint research and development effort resulted in the product being on the market in a single year.

Yet, the use of SM in the execution phase is in no way limited to the product development process. Some companies also include SM in some internal processes, such as recruitment. One way of using SM in the recruitment efforts is for companies to inspect popular sites, such as Facebook, for additional information about the candidate. In such processes SM are applied as an evaluation device, rather than an actual networking tool, therefore examples of such SM use will not be included in the framework. Further examples of using SM in the recruitment process are connections and referrals through existing employees or other stakeholders.

4.5 Monitoring Phase for Internal Participants

In the monitoring phase, the execution of the process is assessed. Such monitoring typically makes use of key performance indicators such as cycle time, rejection rate, inventory, order waiting time, etc. Qualitative measures such as opinion surveys are also used to monitor the performance. All participants should have access to the monitored data, and thus, in some way receive feedback about the business process they are participating in or business processes throughout the organization in general (Schmidt & Nurcan, 2009).

The acquired feedback during the monitoring phase gives information on the appropriateness of a process and its execution. Gathering the data required for the analysis can be time-consuming and fragmentary. Achieving a high response rate with surveys and similar data gathering tools can be challenging. The already existing involvement of users in SM can simplify data contribution. Including SM in the monitoring process provides stakeholders throughout the organization with a chance to contribute and also become acquainted with the results simultaneously.

Employees that are more aware of the processes can have a more holistic view of the workflow and a wider understanding of the interdependency of process activities. Their feedback is thus also more significant and in-depth. Additionally, due to an increased understanding of the processes, individuals are more willing to accept potential changes (Manfreda, Kovačič, Štemberger, & Trkman, 2014).

SM can also act as a quality assurance tool since they provide clear feedback on the success rate and capacities of processes. A company thus presents their rates of successful process execution, support activities (e.g. which items currently in production) or capacities (e.g. number of laboratory vials still available).

4.6 Monitoring Phase for External Participants

One possibility of incorporating SM in the monitoring phase is also to make acquired data publicly accessible. Organizations can use SM to collect information from a variety of stakeholders and present the findings via SM as well. Customer engagement of this kind is more than just marketing, since the customers affect the process. SM can facilitate customer communities where customers can give immediate feedback and see real-time information.

Such openness of the organization seems risky and can be met with initial resistance by the management. An example of such resistance was seen when Amazon introduced customers' comments and allowed critics to be visible online. As controversial as this seemed to some managers in the organization, customer reviews brought competitive advantage to Amazon and grew to be a standard feature on most retail web sites (Ante, 2009).

4.7 Improvement Phase for Internal Stakeholders

All processes need to be continuously improved due to ever changing technological development, organizational changes and market demands. SM allow employees to help improve the processes by contributing their opinions and suggestions for adaptation.

All this should not be a one-off activity without a clearly defined procedure on how to do it. One of the authors was told about the case of a company, where a large number of improvement suggestions from employees was be gathered, but due to an overwhelming amount and unclear procedures for "processing" the ideas, it resulted in little improvement and a very high level of employee dissatisfaction.

By connecting all employees on a common platform, companies can find potential experts who might not have been known to them before or had not participated previously due to a high information-pass-on threshold. Such individuals provide insightful recommendations that can prove valuable in the improvement phase.

Yet, the use of SM for process improvement is not limited to just gathering and analyzing ideas. The statistical analysis of available data, flows and other SM measures enable the evaluation of alternative process designs. These measures offer better information for process designers, especially during the process design task (Busch & Fettke, 2011; Hassan, 2009).

4.8 Improvement Phase for External Stakeholders

Of course, also external stakeholders can contribute to optimizing processes. By doing so, the company can bring the customers closer to the process. The external stakeholders are in this case not only limited to customers, but extend to business partners as well, acting as "internal" customers (Weske, 2013). SM are flexible, targeted to user needs, often designed by users themselves and allow many types of content to evolve through a wide variety of collaborative processes (Von Krogh, 2012).

SM can be used to involve active participation in the process improvement phase, since customers and business partners can submit and assess improvement and innovation suggestions. Some companies enable customers to decide on change prioritization, i.e. voting on which suggestions are most important to them and should be implemented next.

The open innovation site of the coffee shop chain Starbucks ("My Starbucks Idea") is an example of such an open innovation approach; its idea was to receive innovation suggestions from its customers (Starbucks, 2013). The latter provide the company with either product, experience or involvement ideas that are rated by customers and those most endorsed are put into practice, thus realizing exactly what the customers desired the most.

5 Conclusion

SM can provide an excellent way of bridging the gap between the potential rigidness of well-structured and optimized business processes and the often changing environment of a digital world. Incorporating SM into BPM provides flexibility by enabling communication and collaboration among a wide-spread net of employees and external stakeholders. The challenge of making the BPM and SM "marriage" last is to identify the needs of BPM in a sufficiently structured way, while at the same time using SM to infuse flexibility in all phases of a business process life cycle. This would counteract the model-reality divide, which is a common complaint in BPM practice (Erol et al., 2010). A combination of BPM and SM should thus bring flexibility to structure, but also structure the flexibility.

Yet, as with any new technology and concept, many companies adopt SM without a clear overview of their potential in their particular case. The types of SM use differ according to the stakeholders included and the business process life cycle phase. Therefore we suggested a framework that can be used as a guideline for organizations considering implementing SM in BPM. The framework showcases how practitioners can use SM for internal and external stakeholder integration and provides a more structured approach to including SM in BPM.

Of course our paper has several limitations. We acknowledge that the choice of categories for the conceptual framework is partly arbitrary and gives a limited perspective regarding the possibilities of SM use in BPM. Each of the types is illustrated with brief examples from the existing body of knowledge or personal experience of the authors. Further research could determine whether there are other variables that could provide an addition to the framework. Additionally, the classification of examples into a particular phase of BP life cycle can sometimes be dubious, since many examples exhibit a fusion of the characteristics of several phases.

Further research possibilities include a case study of particular uses of SM in a corporate setting from a process-oriented perspective. Thus the necessary prerequisites and critical success factors of the adoption of SM into BPM could be identified, along with an in-depth examination of particular types of SM used in organizations (e.g. Yammer). A more in-depth examination and validation of the framework could be done with focus groups and Delphi studies with both practitioners and researchers.

Careful consideration of all of these issues can help the company to increase the likelihood that SM use will be carefully planned and successfully executed. As such, the use of SM would not only lead to some marginal gains in a company's reputation but to real improvement in business processes as well as employee and stakeholder satisfaction.

References

Aguilar-Saven, R. S. (2004). Business process modelling: Review and framework. *International Journal of Production Economics, 90*(2), 129–149.

Ante, S. E. (2009). Amazon: Turning consumer opinions into gold. *Bloomberg Businessweek Magazine*. Retrieved from http://www.businessweek.com/magazine/content/09_43/b4152047039565.htm

Bradley, A. J., & McDonald, M. P. (2011). *The social organization: How to use social media to tap the collective genius of your customers and employees*. Boston, MA: Harvard Business Press.

Bruno, G., Dengler, F., Jennings, B., Khalaf, R., Nurcan, S., Prilla, M., et al. (2011). Key challenges for enabling agile BPM with social software. *Journal of Software Maintenance and Evolution: Research and Practice, 23*(4), 297–326.

Busch, P., & Fettke, P. (2011). *Business process management under the microscope: The potential of social network analysis*. Paper presented at the 44th Hawaii International Conference on System Sciences (HICSS).

Chesbrough, H. W. (2003). *Open innovation: The new imperative for creating and profiting from technology*. Boston, MA: Harvard Business Press.

Dumas, M., La Rosa, M., Mendling, J., & Reijers, H. A. (2013). *Fundamentals of business process management*. Berlin: Springer.

Erol, S., Granitzer, M., Happ, S., Jantunen, S., Jennings, B., Johannesson, P., et al. (2010). Combining BPM and social software: Contradiction or chance? *Journal of Software Maintenance and Evolution: Research and Practice, 22*(6–7), 449–476.

Evans, D. (2012). *Social media marketing: An hour a day*. San Francisco, CA: Wiley.

Fenn, J., & Raskino, M. (2008). *Mastering the hype cycle: How to choose the right innovation at the right time*. Boston, MA: Harvard Business Press.

Frosch, D. (2007). Pentagon blocks 13 web sites from military computers. *New York Times*. Retrieved from http://www.nytimes.com/2007/05/15/washington/15block.html

Ghidini, C., Rospocher, M., & Serafini, L. (2010). *MoKi: A wiki-based conceptual modeling tool*. Paper presented at the ISWC Posters&Demos.

Granovetter, M. (1983). The strength of weak ties: A network theory revisited. *Sociological Theory, 1*(1), 201–233.

Hassan, N. R. (2009). Using social network analysis to measure IT-enabled business process performance. *Information Systems Management, 26*(1), 61–76.

Hawn, C. (2009). Take two aspirin and tweet me in the morning: How Twitter, Facebook, and other social media are reshaping health care. *Health Affairs, 28*(2), 361–368.

Heymann-Reder, D. (2011). *Social media marketing. Erfolgreiche Strategien für Sie und Ihr*. München: Unternehmen.

Houy, C., Fettke, P., & Loos, P. (2010). Empirical research in business process management–analysis of an emerging field of research. *Business Process Management Journal, 16*(4), 619–661.

Huffington Post. (2011). *'United breaks guitars': Did it really cost the airline $180 million?* Huff Post Business. Retrieved from http://www.huffingtonpost.com/2009/07/24/united-breaks-guitars-did_n_244357.html

IBM-News. (2006). IBM's intranet one of the world's top ten. Retrieved from http://www-03.ibm.com/press/us/en/pressrelease/19156.wss

Jerome, L. W. (2013). Innovation in social networks: Knowledge spillover is not enough. *Knowledge Management Research and Practice, 11*(4), 422–431.

Kane, G. C., Alavi, M., Labianca, G. J., & Borgatti, S. P. (2014). What's different about social media networks? A framework and research agenda. *MIS Quarterly, 38*(1), 275.

Kaplan, A. M., & Haenlein, M. (2010). Users of the world, unite! The challenges and opportunities of social media. *Business Horizons, 53*(1), 59–68.

Kemsley, S. (2010). Enterprise 2.0 meets business process management. In J. vom Brocke & M. Rosemann (Eds.), *Handbook on business process management* (Vol. 1, pp. 565–574). Berlin: Springer. http://link.springer.com/chapter/10.1007/978-3-642-00416-2_26

Kietzmann, J. H., Hermkens, K., McCarthy, I. P., & Silvestre, B. S. (2011). Social media? Get serious! Understanding the functional building blocks of social media. *Business Horizons, 54* (3), 241–251.

Kolind, L. (2013). *Why organisational charts don't work*. Retrieved from http://unboss.com/2013/why-organisational-charts-dont-work/

Kolind, L., & Bøtter, J. (2012). *Unboss*. JP/Politikens Forlagshus.

Koschmider, A., Song, M., & Reijers, H. A. (2010). Social software for business process modeling. *Journal of Information Technology, 25*(3), 308–322.

Majchrzak, A., Jarvenpaa, S. L., & Hollingshead, A. B. (2007). Coordinating expertise among emergent groups responding to disasters. *Organization Science, 18*(1), 147–161.

Manfreda, A., Kovačič, A., Štemberger, M. I., & Trkman, P. (2014). Absorptive capacity as a precondition for business process improvement. *Journal of Computer information Systems, 54* (2), 35–43.

Moore, C. (1999). *Best practices: Eureka! Xerox discovers way to grow community knowledge. And customer satisfaction.* KM World. Retrieved from http://www.kmworld.com/Articles/Editorial/Features/Best-Practices-Eureka!-Xerox-discovers-way-to-grow-community-knowledge.-.-And-customer-satisfaction-9140.aspx

Morais, R. M. D., Kazan, S., Pádua, S. D. D., & Costa, A. L. (2014). An analysis of BPM lifecycles: From a literature review to a framework proposal. *Business Process Management Journal, 20*(3), 412–432.

Murthy, N., Baratam, J. R., & Whelan S. (2012, December 10). Social media and business process management (BPM) enable customer centricity [White paper by Wipro Technologies]. Retrieved from http://www.wipro.com/Documents/Social%20MediaBPM-Whitepaper.pdf

Pereira, N., Vera, D., & Miller, H. G. (2011). Business process management and the social web. *IT Professional, 13*(6), 58–59.

Proctor&Gamble. (2014). *Connect + develop.* Retrieved from http://www.pgconnectdevelop.com/

Quan-Haase, A. (2007). University students' local and distant social ties: Using and integrating modes of communication on campus. *Information, Communication and Society, 10*(5), 671–693.

Recker, J. (2010). Continued use of process modeling grammars: The impact of individual difference factors. *European Journal of Information Systems, 19*(1), 76–92.

Rosemann, M. (2006). Potential pitfalls of process modeling: Part B. *Business Process Management Journal, 12*(3), 377–384.

Rosemann, M., & vom Brocke, J. (2015). The six core elements of business process management. In J. vom Brocke & M. Rosemann (Eds.), *Handbook on business process management* (Introduction, methods and information systems, Vol. 1, pp. 105–124). Berlin: Springer.

Schmidt, R., & Nurcan, S. (2009). *BPM and social software.* Paper presented at the Business Process Management Workshops.

Sena, J., & Sena, M. (2008). Corporate social networking. *Issues in Information Systems, 9*(2), 227–231.

Silva, A. R., Meziani, R., Magalhaes, R., Martinho, D., Aguiar, A., & Flores, N. (2010). *AGILIPO: Embedding social software features into business process tools.* Paper presented at the Business Process Management Workshops.

Starbucks. (2013). *My starbucks idea.* Retrieved December 10, 2013, from http://mystarbucksidea.force.com/

Stieglitz, S., Schallenmüller, S., & Meske, C. (2013). *Adoption of social media for internal usage in a global enterprise.* Paper presented at the Proceedings of the IEEE 27th International Conference on Advanced Information Networking and Applications (AINA), Barcelona, Spain.

Trkman, M., & Trkman, P. (2009). A wiki as intranet: A critical analysis using the Delone and McLean model. *Online Information Review, 33*(6), 1087–1102.

Trkman, M., & Trkman, P. (2011). *Getting business value from wikis.* Paper presented at the AMCIS 2011, Detroit, Michigan.

Trkman, P., & Desouza, K. C. (2012). Knowledge risks in organizational networks: an exploratory framework. *The Journal of Strategic Information Systems, 21*(1), 1–17.

Trkman, P., Kovačič, A., & Popovič, A. (2011). SOA adoption phases. *Business and Information Systems Engineering, 3*(4), 211–220.

Trkman, P., Mertens, W., Viaene, S., & Gemmel, P. (2015). From business process management to customer process management. *Business Process Management Journal, 21*(2). In press.

Vaz Vieira, A. R., & Jaklic, J. (2013). *Business process management and social networks: A case study in an airline organization.* Paper presented at the Active Citizenship by Knowledge Management & Innovation: Proceedings of the Management, Knowledge and Learning International Conference 2013.

vom Brocke, J., Schmiedel, T., Recker, J., Trkman, P., Mertens, W., & Viaene, S. (2014). Ten principles of good business process management. *Business Process Management Journal, 20*(4), 530–548.

Von Krogh, G. (2012). How does social software change knowledge management? Toward a strategic research agenda. *The Journal of Strategic Information Systems, 21*(2), 154–164.

Wagner, C., & Majchrzak, A. (2007). Enabling customer-centricity using wikis and the wiki way. *Journal of Management Information Systems, 23*(3), 17–43.

Weber, B., Sadiq, S., & Reichert, M. (2009). Beyond rigidity–dynamic process lifecycle support. *Computer Science-Research and Development, 23*(2), 47–65.

Weske, M. (2007). *Concepts, languages, architectures* (Vol. 14). Berlin: Springer.

Weske, M. (2013). Business process modeling and analysis – Online course. https://openhpi.de/

Wetzstein, B., Ma, Z., Filipowska, A., Kaczmarek, M., Bhiri, S., Losada, S., et al. (2007). *Semantic business process management: A lifecycle based requirements analysis.* Paper presented at the Semantic business process and product lifecycle management workshop at 3rd European semantic web conference.

The Role of Enterprise Systems in Process Innovation

Bernd Schenk

Abstract

Process innovation—redefining the way of doing business—is of paramount importance for the sustainable success of organizations. Innovation initiatives must relate to latest technological developments and opportunities these offer. The important role of enterprise systems in process innovation is neglected in many of these initiatives. This chapter highlights the different roles enterprise systems can play in an innovation scenario and analyzes the interrelation of technological innovation and enterprise systems as process management platforms. The ambiguity of opportunities offered by new technology is illustrated by the example of the cloud computing paradigm. The chapter closes with the description of a solution path for an improved integration of enterprise systems in process innovation initiatives.

1 Introduction

Many contributions have in the last years focused on the way in which IT triggers or enables innovation and the accompanying change (cf. Markus, 2004; Turedi & Zhu, 2012). The findings refer to data integration and business process support as the main benefits of enterprise systems and analyze their potential to rethink and redesign business processes in process innovation activities. Process innovation, as it concerns us in this chapter, focuses on the adoption of new IT in an organization, both in a material and conceptual form (Wang, 2009), and is usually distinguished from product innovation processes targeting new products for customers.

B. Schenk (✉)
Institute of Information Systems, University of Liechtenstein, Fürst-Franz-Josef-Str. 21, 9490 Vaduz, Liechtenstein
e-mail: bernd.schenk@uni.li

J. vom Brocke, T. Schmiedel (eds.), *BPM – Driving Innovation in a Digital World*, Management for Professionals, DOI 10.1007/978-3-319-14430-6_6

In search of process improvement, organizations analyze and evaluate emerging technologies, considering fields of application in their process landscape. Following this argumentation, one core area of process innovation must lie in the embedding of technology in an organization, i.e. its enterprise system.

An organization's enterprise system consists of many different applications that form *the* enterprise system of an organization in the sense of an individually designed solution integrating all business applications. Different parts of an enterprise system are in different phases of their application lifecycle. Today's understanding of an enterprise system must consider this specific complexity. Such a system type does not follow a clearly identifiable lifecycle, as pre-packaged, homogeneous solutions did earlier (Davenport, 1998; Shanks, Seddon, & Willcocks, 2003). With regard to innovation, new technologies and concepts are applied and integrated in enterprise systems continuously. Today's enterprise systems are therefore permanently undergoing change and are moved from one stable state to the next by each modification of system parts.

In many cases, enterprise systems are considered to be a supporting tool for existing processes, providing integration and connectivity between different areas or departments of an organization. Enterprise systems used to be custom-made developments for a single organization. Flexibility was achieved by changing program code. This type of system was designed to support an existing process landscape. In the last decades pre-packaged solutions became the most important mode of delivery for enterprise systems. This has led to reduced flexibility in the adaptation to existing processes. At the same time new technologies were integrated in enterprise systems, causing tremendous change in functionality. Therefore, every new software release is an opportunity for process innovation in an organization and a challenge to take maximum advantage of this opportunity.

2 Different Roles of Enterprise Systems in Process Innovation

The following section describes the main roles that an enterprise system can have in a process innovation scenario. These roles relate to the heterogeneous application landscape that makes up such a system. Changes in applications and integration of new technologies lead to opportunities for process innovation. An innovation scenario—besides other components—consists of a trigger (operant resource) and an enabler (operand resource) for innovation (Nambisan, 2013). This basic idea of different roles that IT can take in innovation processes is transferred and extended to the field of enterprise systems in process innovation in the following discussion. Due to the specific characteristics of enterprise systems, three roles are identified.

2.1 Enabler

Enterprise systems are the main component of an organization's IT landscape. Due to the fact that they are highly customized off-the-shelf products or custom-made solutions, a lot of an organization's process knowledge is stored in and represented by these systems.

Process innovation activities always have to relate to an existing enterprise system in an organization in order to create tangible results. The diffusion of process innovation results is achieved by implementing the modified processes in an enterprise system. This is considered to be the role of an enterprise system as an enabler for process innovation. The trigger for process innovation is an event that is not connected to the enterprise system, such as legal changes, business process reengineering projects, mergers, etc.

2.2 Trigger

An external trigger for innovation is usually assumed when discussing the role of an enterprise system as innovation enabler. Process innovation is initiated by activities external to the enterprise system and implemented by changing it. This scenario relates to changes in the enterprise system (e.g. new software releases and adding mobile computing components) triggering the process innovation. Additional capabilities of the system allow a new way of doing business. Process innovation is triggered within the enterprise system in this scenario. The new opportunities offered by the enterprise system lead to a redesign of processes and creates an increased value contribution. An enterprise system represents a strategic resource creating sustainable competitive advantage due to a unique orchestration and usage pattern of applications in this scenario.

2.3 Enforcer

While triggering an innovation is characterized by an increase in possibilities that a system is offering, the role of an enforcer describes the situation when modifications to an enterprise system force a process innovation due to changed system capabilities. An enterprise system consists of applications in different lifecycle phases. Especially the replacement and disintegration of legacy systems forces process change: a new system is brought into use and must be integrated in an organization's process landscape. The significant difference to triggering an innovation lies in the *change* of system capabilities—compared to a capabilities *increase* in the case of triggering. Similar to the trigger role, the source of innovation lies in the enterprise system. In many cases organizations use this role to justify a business process redesign because of the implementation of a new enterprise system component. They back up a process innovation initiative by the changed capabilities of a new system component to achieve increased acceptance of changing routines by the end user. The role of an enforcer is one of the reasons why enterprise system implementation projects are considered to be highly complex, causing tremendous change to an organization.

2.4 Implications

CIOs have to consider all three roles that an enterprise system can play in process innovation when discussing changes to the system. The enterprise system is an innovation platform that triggers innovation and enables the diffusion of process innovation in an organization at the same time. Considering only one of these roles is an oversimplification that is likely to cause the misunderstanding and failure of innovation initiatives. This shows the importance of a thorough understanding of the possibilities of new technologies, as the embedment in enterprise systems (e.g. mobile computing, in-memory computing, cloud computing) is a possible source of process innovation.

To achieve successful process innovation in a digital world, the interrelation between existing enterprise systems, new technologies, and process innovation triggers must be understood and the complexity must be considered. A definition of the enterprise systems' role in an organization process innovation initiative can help to identify the system's importance as a strategic capability supporting a sustainable competitive advantage. Enterprise systems do not only provide a platform for process implementation in an organization—even more, they are *the* process management platform of an organization. One of the latest developments to enable process support is the implementation of a dedicated process management layer, which enables process modeling based on semi-formal process modeling languages, including the invocation of software services by an activity. This new design paradigm enables a detailed adaptation of the software and implementation of process innovation while using the standard methods provided.

However, enterprise systems are only able to provide value contributions when optimized business processes are deployed. Best-practice process templates provided by enterprise system vendors are tempting—especially for SMEs. Adopting standard processes can jeopardize competitive advantages based on company-specific process excellence. The necessity for process standardization evoked by an implementation project represents an important business process improvement activity for many organizations at the same time.

3 Application Example: Implications of Cloud Computing

The following section illustrates the complexity and ambiguous opportunities an organization is confronted with when considering the implementation of a new technology. It exemplarily highlights the potentials of cloud computing paradigm adoption based on company size as classification criterion.

Cloud computing has been a buzzword in the area of enterprise computing for some years now. However, the expectations towards the implementation of a cloud computing model for an organization's enterprise system are ambiguous. In many cases cloud computing is understood as a pure *cost-cutting* measure which enables an easier operation of enterprise systems. Due to economies of scale, a cloud computing provider can deliver higher performance at lower cost compared to on-premise (in-house) operation models. Cloud computing is therefore understood as *new generation outsourcing* within many organizations (Salleh, Teoh, & Chan, 2012). Another field of application is the implementation of an enterprise systems extension, like customer relationship management software or the establishment of a common integration platform along a supply chain. In these areas cloud computing is understood as a *rapid deployment solution* providing flexible scalability in run-time phase, while also providing standardized access for different organizations at the same time.

Cloud computing is, moreover, used for *integration of new technology* while using standardized platforms. Cloud computing enables, inter alia, integration of in-memory computing and mobile device access to enterprise systems. Integration can be achieved much easier *in the cloud* by using the existing infrastructure of a cloud solution provider than by implementation in conventional on-premise solutions.

The examples given above show the different expectations towards cloud computing deployment. While it is a clear cost-cutting measure when it is considered an outsourcing activity, it can be a trigger for business process innovation, driven by the new opportunities offered by technology in other cases. It is therefore of paramount importance to take a closer look at the details of the cloud computing model and especially its service models.

Although there is no common definition of cloud computing and its components, the NIST definition of cloud computing (Mell & Grance, 2011) has achieved wide acceptance in literature and praxis. Following the argumentation above, when considering the opportunities and consequences of cloud computing for an enterprise, the service and deployment models as given in Fig. 1 should receive more attention. In many cases the umbrella term cloud computing is used and no further distinction is made between either different service models or deployment models. This causes ambiguous expectations towards the cloud computing paradigm which lead to fuzzy assumptions about cloud computing's potential value contribution in an organization. This, in turn, can lead to frustration and disappointed expectations in an organization.

In this example a special focus should be placed on the usage of cloud computing in the sector of highly integrated enterprise systems. As stated, these systems differ from other IT solutions as they (1) support the core business processes of an organization, (2) show a high degree of horizontal and vertical integration on different system layers, and (3) are adapted to specific needs of an organization by different means (from configuration to customization by individual code to service orchestration in a process layer). The challenges of process innovation in

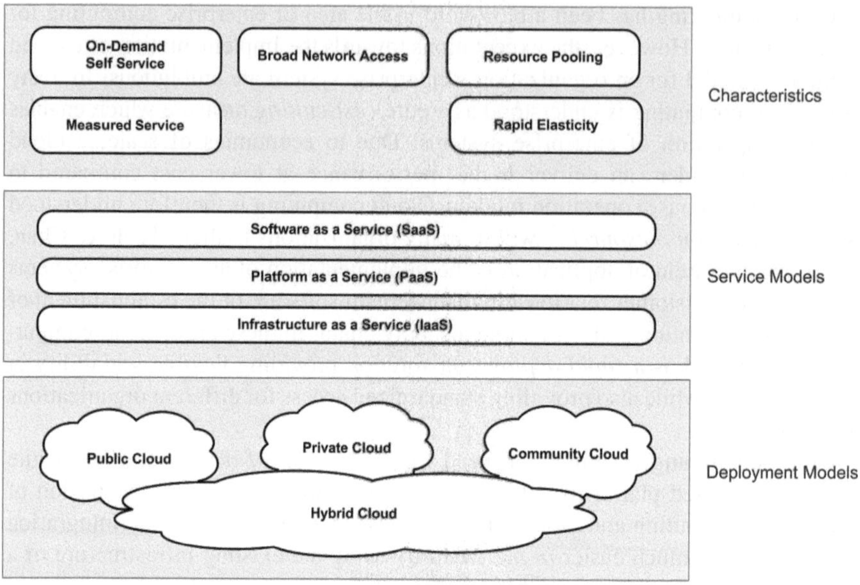

Fig. 1 NIST model of cloud computing (Mell & Grance, 2011)

relation to cloud computing are illustrated by focusing on different service models, which can be divided in SaaS on the one hand, and, on the other hand, PaaS/IaaS.

A seemingly homogeneous paradigm can have different implications for organizations and the way they are using enterprise systems for business operations. Cloud Computing is considered to be a new delivery model enabling a focus on core competences while outsourcing the IT-related activities to professional cloud sourcing providers. Software vendors and consulting companies subsume many different applications and solution packages under this umbrella term. The intention of signaling the capabilities of their solutions is understandable; however, this causes a lot of confusion in the market (Lenart, 2011). It is tempting to use the cloud metaphor in order to emphasize the ease with which such a solution can be used and maintained. However, it implies a set of characteristics, service models, and delivery models, which have the potential to change IT operations and implementation tremendously. An organization must therefore analyze in a detailed manner what functionalities a solution offers and what value contributions can be expected from it.

To exemplarily illustrate the range of opportunities service models do offer, the implications of different service model/delivery model combinations for large enterprises (LE) and small and medium sized enterprises (SME) have been outlined based on experiences from several implementation projects.

The indications illustrated in Fig. 2 are a first evaluation of opportunities for companies of different sizes. The table shows how diversified the implications of cloud computing for an organization are. Coming back to our claim that the usage

		SaaS	PaaS/IaaS
Public	LE	Harmonizing IT Landscape Increasing User Convenience Standardizing Processes	Reducing Cost Increasing Flexibility / Scalability Provisioning of new Company Services Testing new Applications
	SME	Reengineering Processes Accessing new Technologies	Developing new Applications Evaluating Software Increasing Performance Accessing Business Analytics
Private	LE	Deploying own developments Provisioning rarely used software	Standardizing IT Services Industrializing IT Service Delivery Standardizing Device Communication
	SME	*Unusual combination due to high ramp-up costs*	Increasing IT Service Level Virtualizing IT Landscape

Fig. 2 Opportunities of different service model/delivery model combinations with relation to company size

of unclear terminology could lead to unsatisfactory outcomes of an organization's process innovation initiative, the example of cloud computing shows the potential of severe mismatches of expectations and outcomes. A lack of knowledge and understanding of new paradigms like cloud computing and their applicability to enterprise systems might cause obstacles to process innovation in an organization.

Enterprise systems have shown a low frequency of change in the past. Companies try to keep the system in operation as long as possible since the initial investment for a system is high and an implementation project is considered to be a risky endeavor. Nevertheless, the analysis above shows that this picture is changing and enterprise systems play a vital role for innovation in a digital world. We see that a continuous modification process, which enables innovation support in manifold roles, as described above, nowadays characterizes enterprise systems. Their role must be completely understood and carefully considered in order to maximize the value contribution throughout the lifecycle.

Continuing the evaluation of service model/delivery model combinations leads to a mapping of the different roles of an enterprise system in the clusters shown in Fig. 2. Although more than one role can be allocated to a cluster, the differences are clearly visible. In some areas enterprise systems take a more passive role of an enabler for process innovation. In some other areas the modified enterprise system is triggering or enforcing innovation due to modifications in functionality and modes of accessing the system. A brief description of the role allocation is outlined in Fig. 3.

The example showed the potential of enterprise systems for process innovation in connection with technological changes. The enterprise system's importance as a process management platform must be considered to achieve an optimal value contribution from technology adoption initiatives.

		SaaS	PaaS/IaaS
Public	LE	**Enforcer / Trigger** Using standardized software usually reduces the degree of flexibility. Existing procedures must be changed. New functionality is available at the same time.	**Enabler / Trigger** Existing functionalities are transferred to the cloud. The enterprise system is not changed by this. The ubiquitous availability triggers process innovation and is enabled by the enterprise system.
	SME	**Enforcer / Trigger** Using standardized software while having only limited budgets for adaptation usually leads to decreased functionality and a necessity for process standardization. Existing procedures must be changed and standard processes inherent to the solution adopted.	**Enforcer / Enabler** Due to budget restrictions and complexity of the solution, dependency on third-party support is increasing. The flexibility of the solution is therefore reduced and change enforced. New modes of access can be realized at the same time.
Private	LE	**Trigger / Enabler** Standardization of software delivery while keeping the whole solution in-house implicates high ramp-up costs, but allows maximum flexibility for changing processes due to new software functionality.	**Enabler/Trigger** Existing functionalities are transferred to the new service platform. The enterprise system is not changed by this. The ubiquitous availability triggers process innovation and is enabled by the enterprise system. In-house service delivery further increases flexiblity for process innovation.
	SME	*Unusual combination due to high ramp-up costs*	**Enforcer / Enabler / Trigger** Due to budget restrictions and complexity of the solution, dependency on third-party support is increasing. The flexibility of the solution is therefore reduced and change enforced. New modes of access can be realized at the same time and enabled by the solution. The service model might trigger process innovation as well.

Fig. 3 Potential roles of enterprise systems in process innovation while adopting the cloud computing paradigm

4 Openness of Enterprise Systems

In the last years we have seen that a clear differentiation of an enterprise system's lifecycle in the build-time and run-time phase (or even more detailed in different phases of the implementation project (Shanks et al., 2003)) does not serve the purpose of analyzing an enterprise system's role in process innovation. Many such implementation projects are not concerned with an initial greenfield-implementation, but deal with the extension of existing solutions, rollouts to new subsidiaries, merging systems of different branches, or integrating new technologies like in-memory computing or the cloud computing paradigm.

What Weick (1977) calls a chronically unfrozen system in management theory can be transferred to the area of enterprise systems as a new modus operandi. The concept of organizational change (containing the phases unfreeze—change—refreeze) points to the fact that companies can be efficient when working in a stable environment. Enterprise systems are considered to be at the core of enterprise operations and therefore follow the dynamics of organizational change. The tendency to become a chronically unfrozen system (Weick, 1977) is valid for enterprise systems, too. Fast changing environments, like value webs as a form of inter-organizational cooperation, increase the frequency of change for both an organization and its systems, and make permanent openness to change necessary.

A main challenge when trying to bring together enterprise systems and innovation initiatives is therefore to establish such openness for change and a platform for innovation enablement in an organization. A chronically unfrozen system comes with a lack of structure, making employees feel uncomfortable—as their routines can be subject to change anytime. Innovation initiatives have to consider and take precautions against this to keep the enterprise on a high level of productivity permanently.

At the same time, the effects of this trend towards increased openness (as given in open organizations, open innovations, open systems) on enterprise systems must be analyzed. Nowadays, many of these systems are still very stable, monolithic solutions that support the preservation of an existing process landscape, rather than serve as an innovation platform. Enterprise systems must be transformed to chronically unfrozen systems to serve a company's needs. This transformation process is supported by achievements such as new technologies (e.g. in-memory computing enabling real-time-process monitoring and process orchestration during run-time), new modes of service delivery like cloud computing (including SaaS, PaaS, IaaS), and presentation layer extensions (e.g. mobile computing allowing intensified interaction with the system in daily operations).

To transform an enterprise system into a process innovation platform, organizations must have a comprehensive understanding of new technologies and concepts in this area, allowing them to identify possibilities from such advances for their process portfolio and potential innovation.

Interconnectivity can be used as an example. Where interconnectivity between organizations could be established on a long lasting and stable basis in earlier days, the need for a flexible and run-time-based connection of systems is increasingly emerging over time (Nandhakumar, Rossi, & Talvinen, 2005). The requirements for enterprise systems have therefore been changing in the last years—the aim is not to increase efficiency but to redefine the solution space for a problem, finding new levels of effectiveness. The value contribution is not achieved only by doing the same things quicker or more efficiently; enterprise systems are expected to be an important source of innovation as they inherit most of an organization's process knowledge. Combining this with latest achievements in technology makes them an important cornerstone of an organization's process innovation initiative.

System vendors relate to this changing role from a process support tool to a source of process innovation by using innovative thinking in their product development and improvement (e.g. SAP's latest design thinking and business process transformation initiatives)

5 Summary

Enterprise systems research has become a mature area in the field of information systems in the last years. The numerous publications focusing on implementation and critical success factors support this picture. Only in a few cases are the enterprise systems related to current topics like process innovation and challenges of a digital world in general. This chapter should illustrate that enterprise systems must not be neglected when talking about innovation in organizations. Furthermore, the potential touch points and different roles of these systems in an innovation process have been shown.

A necessary and important precondition is a thorough understanding of changes in the area of enterprise systems. Only when the possibilities offered are understood, can the applicability for an organization be recognized and reflected in innovation, which leads to new levels of organizational performance.

References

Davenport, T. H. (1998). Putting the enterprise into the enterprise system. *Harvard Business Review, 76*(4), 121–131.

Lenart, A. (2011). ERP in the cloud – Benefits and challenges. In S. Wrycza (Ed.), *Research in systems analysis and design: Models and methods* (Lecture notes in business information processing, Vol. 93, pp. 39–50). Berlin: Springer.

Markus, L. M. (2004). Technochange management: Using IT to drive organizational change. *Journal of Information Technology, 19*(1), 4–20.

Mell, P., & Grance, T. (2011). *The NIST definition of cloud computing (800–145)*. Gaithersburg: National Institute of Standards and Technology.

Nambisan, S. (2013). Information technology and product/service innovation: A brief assessment and some suggestions for future research. *Journal of the Association for Information Systems, 14*(4), 215–226.

Nandhakumar, J., Rossi, M., & Talvinen, J. (2005). The dynamics of contextual forces of ERP implementation. *Journal of Strategic Information Systems, 14*(2), 221–242.

Salleh, S. M., Teoh, S. Y., & Chan, C. (2012). Cloud enterprise systems: A review of literature and its adoption. *PACIS 2012 Proceedings*. Paper 76.

Shanks, G., Seddon, P., & Willcocks, L. (Eds.). (2003). *Second wave enterprise resource planning systems*. Cambridge: Cambridge University Press.

Turedi, S., & Zhu, H. (2012). Business value of IT: Revisiting productivity paradox through three theoretical lenses and empirical evidence. *AMCIS 2012 Proceedings*. Paper 18.

Wang, P. (2009). Popular concepts beyond organizations: Exploring new dimensions of information technology innovations. *Journal of the Association for Information Systems, 10*(1), 1–30.

Weick, K. E. (1977). Organization design: Organizations as self-designing systems. *Organizational Dynamics, 6*(2), 31–46.

Process Innovation with Disruptive Technology in Auto Insurance: Lessons Learned from a Smartphone-Based Insurance Telematics Initiative

Jens Ohlsson, Peter Händel, Shengnan Han, and Richard Welch

Abstract

Insurance telematics or usage-based insurance (UBI) is a potential game-changer for the insurance industry, especially for innovating auto-insurance. In order to achieve and sustain UBI for auto insurance, insurers are called upon to innovate the marketing and sales processes of the UBI product, as well as related processes such as risk assessment and price calculation. In this chapter, we demonstrate the insurer's process innovation with smartphone-based insurance telematics, using the example of the "*If SafeDrive*" campaign which was commercially conducted by the insurer If P & C in Sweden. The results show that although disruptive technology can trigger process innovation, such innovation cannot succeed and be sustained without fundamental changes in a company's structure, business model and business strategy. We further propose a capability layer model for understanding the insurer's process innovation behaviour. This chapter provokes the critical thinking with regard to the exploration and exploitation of disruptive technology into process innovation. Further, the chapter contributes new knowledge to the research of process innovation with disruptive digital technologies.

J. Ohlsson (✉) • S. Han
Department of Computer and Systems Sciences, Stockholm University, Borgarfjordsgatan 12, 16407 Kista, Sweden
e-mail: jeoh@dsv.su.se; shengnan@dsv.su.se

P. Händel
Department of Signal Processing, KTH Royal Institute of Technology, Osquldas väg 10, 10044 Stockholm, Sweden
e-mail: ph@kth.se

R. Welch
Concord Group Insurance, Bouton Str. 4, 03301 Concord, NH, USA
e-mail: richardewelchjr@me.com

J. vom Brocke, T. Schmiedel (eds.), *BPM – Driving Innovation in a Digital World*, Management for Professionals, DOI 10.1007/978-3-319-14430-6_7

1 Introduction

The smart cellular phone, or smartphone, has become a ubiquitous personal device influencing a large portion of the contemporary individual's daily life. The capabilities of smartphones exhibit a dramatic increase compared to traditional feature phones due to (1) the user-friendly human-machine interface design; (2) the high processing power utilizing multi-core processor architecture and increased memory capabilities, and (3) the sensing capabilities.

Contemporary smartphones are equipped with a large set of sensors which sense the surrounding environment, including means for positioning via e.g., the GPS (that is, the Global Positioning System) or other satellite navigation systems; inertial sensors measuring accelerations and rotations e.g., used for the detection of the orientation of the smartphone for automatic rotation of the displayed information; proximity sensors, light sensors, magnetic compasses, to mention a few. Sensor fusion technologies include the combination of data streams from several different sensors into sought for information, for example the combination of positioning from the GPS with the high resolution information provided by the accelerometers and gyroscopes, which enhance the calculated position, direction and movement of the bearer of the smartphone. By combining measurements from sensors with complementary properties, information with enhanced properties can typically be extracted. Sensor-equipped measurement platforms with processing capabilities existed prior to the introduction of the smartphone, but the smartphone made it a ubiquitous device available in large volumes and distributed to a large portion of the population—a fact that opens up opportunities for developing a range of disruptive technologies.

The sensing capabilities of the smartphone create exciting new application areas (Lane et al., 2010). Connecting millions or even billions of smartphones into large scale sensing systems enable time or location-based services in environment monitoring, intelligent transportation systems, applications in health and support for the ageing populations, to mention only a few. Sheng, Tang, Xiao, and Xue (2013) list two paradigms for sensing via large-scale smartphone-based measurement systems, namely, (1) participatory sensing and (2) opportunistic sensing, where the former is based on an active participation on the part of the smartphone owner and the latter has automated sensing without the interaction of the end-user.

The evolution of smartphone technologies together with its social and technical capabilities creates a solid foundation for innovating business processes in various industries. An innovation is defined as "new to the state of the art," which basically means without known precedent (Abrahamson, 1996; Kimberly & Evanisko, 1981). An innovation can be either disruptive or sustaining. Christensen (1997) defines disruptive innovation (or disruptive technology) as a process of an innovation—usually a product or service—creating a new market and value network, and eventually disrupting an existing market, as well displacing an earlier technology. Disruptive technologies have the great potential to transform life, business and the global economy. Process innovation is adopting a process view in managing business in combination with applying innovation into key processes. By doing so, organizations can achieve major reductions in process cost or time, or major improvements in service level or other business objectives (Davenport, 1993). Innovation of a product or service most often also implies innovation of processes or vice versa (Davenport, 1993; Tidd & Bessant, 2009).

In this chapter, we present a case study in participatory sensing, namely insurance telematics, in which a smartphone-based Usage Based Insurance (UBI) product for a personalised car insurance is realized. It is believed that the findings are of a general interest as an example of a disruptive technology, sometimes designated as Sensing as a Service (Sheng et al., 2013). We argue that the technology has the potential to completely transform the auto insurer's sales and marketing processes of the new UBI products, especially those related processes associated with customer acquisition, risk analysis and price calculation.

2 The Disruptive Technology: Insurance Telematics

Auto insurance is in most cases required by law to cover bodily injuries, property damage liability, for personal injury protection, and the like. Traditionally, the insurance premium is based on measures like driver's age, occupation or place of residence, car model and configuration, and expected mileage over the policy period. Thanks to the development within sensor technology and infrastructure for wireless communication, new premium programs have appeared, not only based on the aforementioned static properties, but also on dynamic measures relying on in-car mounted sensors. Examples include premium based on your driving style (how you drive), your location (where you drive) and time of the day of the trip (when you drive). A common name for these kinds of insurance programs is Usage Based Insurance (UBI), or Insurance Telematics programs. Insurance telematics refers to the technology of sending, receiving, and storing information from and to road vehicles for insurances purposes (Bruneteau, 2012).

The market of UBI is expected to take off in some regions, leading to a penetration of up to a 40 % share of total policies in 2020. Currently, the market penetration is low, with the Progressive Casualty Insurance Company in the US as the market leader with around 1.4 million customers in their program (Insurance Telematics, 2012). The program produced strong intellectual properties for understanding user driving behaviours (Desyllas & Sako, 2013). Forecasts for the United Kingdom are that 60 % of the insured vehicles in 2020 will run under an insurance telematics program (Insurance Telematics, 2013). The corresponding figure for the US is 30 %, which equals to approximately 60 million insured vehicles. The sensors monitoring the location, time and dynamics of the trip can either (1) be installed in the vehicle using a fixed installation—often called a black box, (2) rely on the information that can be extracted about the vehicle via the On-Board Diagnostic (OBD) outlet; or (3) using an independent device, like a smartphone (Fig. 1, pictures from left to right).

An insurer can access actual driving behaviour data through an insurance telematics program. As a result, the insurance premium can be individually adjusted

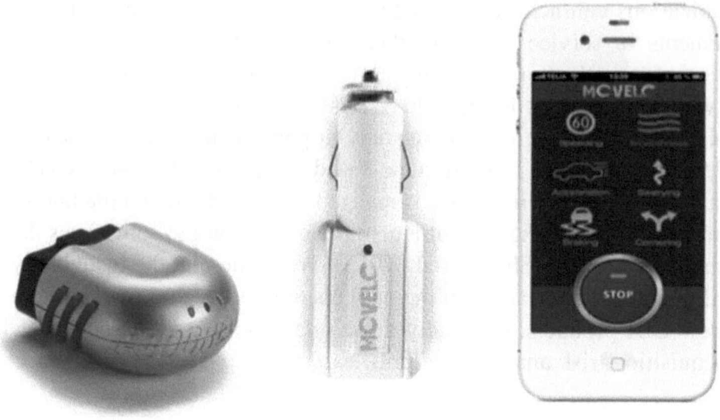

Fig. 1 Progressive insurance snapshot measurement probe for the on-board diagnostics (*left*); sensing device for the cigarette lighter outlet by Movelo (*middle*); and smartphone with insurance telematics software from Movelo (*right*)

based on driving behaviour, and the likelihood of a claim related to that particular driver can be predicted. Insurers have relied on factors such as the age of the driver and place of residence to calculate premiums for a long time. Insurance telematics has helped insurers to use other variables to improve their risk assessment and price calculations.

By using telematics technology, the insurers can improve the pricing accuracy and sophistication, as well as attract favourable risks. As a result, the claims costs will be reduced, which in turn will enable lower premiums for certain customer segments. The technology will help the insurers to increase their overall profits (Progressive, 2012).

There are numerous benefits related to a UBI program for the insured car drivers. UBI leads to premium discounts for the low risk drivers. They can also receive value-added services, such as teen-driver monitoring, emergency services, navigation and infotainment, stolen vehicle recovery, vehicle diagnostics and congestion forecast, allowing for driving in time slots when it is less crowded and/or with reduced risk. In case of an accident, drivers can also use their profile of driving behaviour to prove safe driving behaviour to insurers.

The possibility of obtaining a scalable technology for insurance telematics has increased the insurance companies' interest in smartphone-based programs, also thanks to the smartphones' high penetration, the development talent within the telecom industry, and the ease of deployment by using the regular means for distribution of mobile applications like AppStore or Google Play.

2.1 The Smartphone-Based Insurance Telematics Application

At the Department of Signal Processing, KTH Royal Institute of Technology, vehicle based measurement platforms have been developed and utilized, and have also formed the basis for research for many years. With the progress of the cellular phone from a low-functionality feature phone to versatile software-configurable sensing platform, a new smartphone-based measurement probe is developed and subsequently deployed for commercial purpose (Händel, Ohlsson, Ohlsson, Skog, & Nygren, 2014). The clear advantages using the smartphone in this context include its high availability, competitive price-performance metric, and recognition by the users.

The measurement probe may be a fixed installation in the vehicle, semi-fixed installation using the power and data outlets, or a smartphone, as illustrated in Fig. 1. The probe monitors and transmits risk-related information to the insurers such as the speeding, cornering, braking and accelerating habits, time and date, and road conditions. The information collected by the measurement probe can be used by the insurers to improve their risk assessment, and thus, through use of this data a particular driver's behaviour can be assessed.

2.2 The Vendor Movelo's Motivation to Commercialize the Application

In late 2009, the idea of using the UBI in an innovative business model was initiated. A legal entity was founded and formed outside of academia (Movelo AB, MOving VEhicle LOgger) that had the role of facilitating the business model innovation based on the new technology. A vision, or a BHAG, "Big Hairy Audacious Goal" was set (Collins, 2005):

"*Movelo should be the catalyst for velocity and change of driving behaviour. Swedes are in total spending 350,000 h per week in traffic jams and Americans waste 38 h a year in traffic, costing $87 billion. This creates unnecessary accidents, emissions and expenses. This is what Movelo should change*". (*http://www.movelo.se/wordpress/om-oss/*)

Then a business idea and corresponding strategy to reach the vision was set:

"*With extensive knowledge originated from research in IT and innovation, Movelo creates solutions which generate a positive change in behaviour resulting in increased safety, reduced emissions and saved money. Usage based insurance (UBI) is the starting point. Movelo's strategy is to create commercial partnerships with companies in the automotive eco-system and innovate their business model so (1) money is earned by both parties, and (2) high-valued traffic information is collected taking Movelo closer to its vision and enabling our world class R&D.*" (*http://www.movelo.se/wordpress/om-oss/*)

The trends in sensor and smartphone development in combination with the research activities at the universities were a catalyst for the moving vehicle logger campaign that was set up by Movelo AB and If P & C in early 2013. If P & C was considered to be the most suitable partner for the Movelo campaign. If P & C is a market leader in the Nordic countries with approximately 3.6 million customers in Sweden. As UBI is a new insurance product, enabled by the novel insurance telematics technology, such as a smart-phone solution, the insurers need innovated marketing and sales processes to facilitate and get a maximum effect out of the new product. The old insurance product is marketed and sold by the traditional marketing and sales processes. The insurance company may achieve three aggregated benefits: (1) innovating their marketing and sales process by getting a new customer channel and improved customer relations through the new possibility of communicating to their customers via the smartphone; (2) innovating the related processes, e.g., the risk assessment process and price-calculation process, which results in lowering risks and obtaining more information on driving behaviour and dynamic statistics. By collecting information on driving behaviour, customer segmentation will be improved, for example, by identifying "the dedicated" customers; and (3) the insurance company also gains new possibilities to innovate their business model by cooperating with new key partners, such as companies with customers who are car reliant, for example gas retailers.

3 The Case of the *If SafeDrive* Campaign

In May 2011 a commercial contract was signed between If P & C and Movelo AB. An insurance telematics initiative, *If SafeDrive,* was tested commercially.

The insurance telematics initiative set up the following goals:

- Create a unique solution and mobile application that attracts car-drivers, especially new customers, based on the core-technology;
- Increase sales volumes;
- Improve knowledge regarding car drivers/customer risk-behaviour;
- Improve risk-assessment activities;
- Strengthen the insurer's brand;
- Enable forecasts of traffic flow and congestion and identify the dangerous spots in traffic.

In addition, in the long term, the initiative may

- Contribute benefits to society (traffic safety, sustainable and ecological driving behaviour).

The insurer If P & C applied the new insurance telematics. Moreover, enabled by the insurance telematics solution, the firm innovated their sales and marketing process, introducing the new UBI product to consumers. The initiative started as a small-scale pilot. Because of the insurance telematics solution new capabilities for risk assessment was enabled, such as driving-behaviour. The aim was to capture driving behaviour as early as possible in the marketing and sales process, to capture

Fig. 2 Examples of the smartphone interface and feedback to car-drivers, from *top* to *down/left* to *right*: registration; driving feedback on map; driving feedback history per drive; driving feedback after one drive with score and medals; real time driving feedback; discount and quote after fulfilled qualification

driving behaviour before a consumer/car driver became a customer to the insurance company. This resulted in a higher integration between the risk assessment and marketing and sales processes.

The process innovation and redesign work was done by means of an iterative approach. Movelo prototyped the smartphone solution and evaluated the use-cases. The vendor tested it with different invited user groups and continuously refined the usecases of the solution. All these activities were part of an effort to innovate and redesign the business processes at If P & C. Approximately 1 year was spent in these iterations, i.e. designing, testing and implementing different versions of the solution (Fig. 2) with different test groups. Test groups were both internal test groups, e.g., If P & C employees and project members, and external test groups, e.g., existing customers as well as potential customers.

At the end of March 2013, the first commercial release was done, with the *If SafeDrive* application (Fig. 2) officially released on the AppStore. The purpose of the commercial release was to implement the smartphone application in real driving scenarios with larger group customers/car drivers. The aim was to evaluate if the smartphone-based UBI fulfilled the initiative objectives, e.g., creating sales-volumes and acquiring new customers.

3.1 The Process Innovation: Customer Acquisition Process

The application of the smartphone-based UBI telematics transformed the insurer If's sales and marketing process in the campaign. The related process where the radical innovation was explored was the customer acquisition process. The processes such as risk-assessment process and price calculation were also influenced by the innovation of the UBI and thus innovated simultaneously.

3.1.1 The As-Is Customer Acquisition Process

The As-Is customer acquisition process can be explained as follows (Fig. 3). The starting point, or starting event, is that the end-user (car-driver) has an insurance need. The insurance need can be triggered for different reasons, e.g. the end user has bought a new car or that the end user is at the end of his/her policy period and is actively searching for a better insurance product. The end user can call the insurer, get an outbound call from the insurer, request a quotation via the insurer web-site, or visit an insurance broker to get quotes from several insurers. In Sweden the

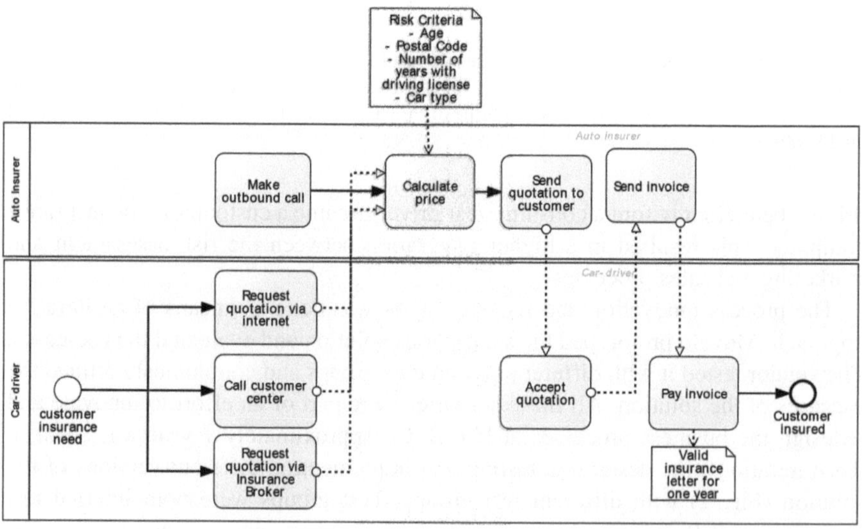

Fig. 3 The As-Is customer acquisition process

broker scenarios are still infrequent, but in other markets such as the UK the broker channel is dominant. The next activity in the customer-acquisition process is the price calculation. This activity is done with system support and the price calculation is done based on risk-criteria data i.e. age, number of years with a driver's license and type of car that the end user wants to insure. The next activity is to send the quote to the end user; if the end-user accepts the conditions in the quotation, then an invoice is sent. When the invoice is paid, the end-user becomes a customer and is, thus, insured. In the As-Is process of selling car insurance, the insurer has few interaction points with the end user and each interaction point has related costs, e.g. call-centre costs, human cost, or web-channel costs.

3.1.2 The To-Be Customer Acquisition Process

Already in the start events, the To-Be process (Fig. 4) differs from the As-Is by engaging end users (Car Drivers) in a novel way. Instead of a reactive approach as in the As-Is, the To-Be process was designed and implemented with the aims of taking maximum advantage of the new customer channel (the Smartphone) and its communication capabilities. This was done to enable the end users (car drivers) to invite other end users whom they considered to be safe and ecological drivers, thus triggering friend invitations, which is the word of mouth effect. Therefore, more end users joined the campaign and met the challenges of qualifying for the UBI car-insurance product. In this case the start event of the sales process was: customer is invited to a safe driving challenge. The design focused on the process interface

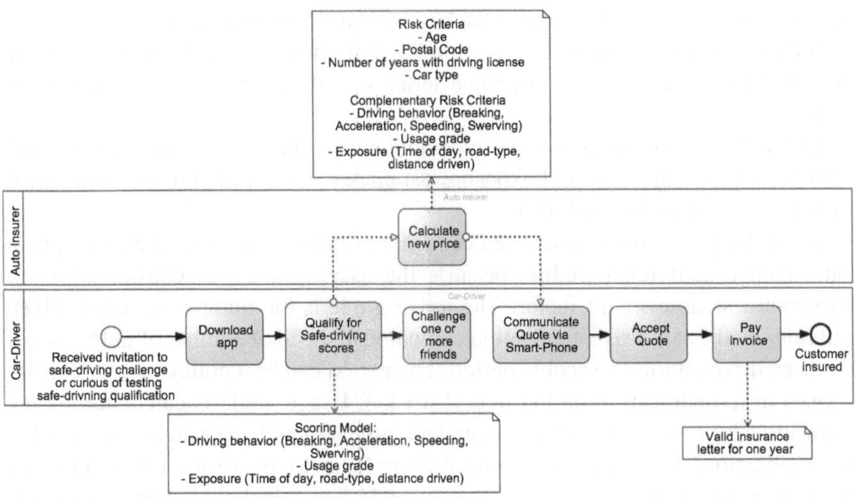

Fig. 4 The To-Be customer acquisition process

between marketing and sales with the target of making the car drivers curious enough about the *If SafeDrive* application to want to download it, test it, and then start a qualification for safe-driving scores, and then qualifying for the new UBI insurance telematics product.

The next phase in the To-Be process was the qualification activity: in the actual case the business rules called for a qualification period of 2 weeks and 200 km of driving. In this activity of the To-Be process the end user received feedback from his/her smartphone on driving behaviour after each drive (see Fig. 2). The feedback consisted of scores 0–100 based on braking, acceleration and speeding behaviour, where 100 points was the best possible score. Feedback was also given in the form of *digital medals*, incentives regarding eco-driving and safe-driving behaviour (Fig. 2). Risk-calculation information such as the road-type and time of day of the driving was also sent to the insurer. These parameters are vital for risk assessment and price calculation. But, for usability reasons, these parameters were not presented to the end user in the feedback and scoring. Another feature of the solution that was not shown to end users was the Movelo real time feedback interface, which provided driving feedback in real time in a dash board view. The reason for this was safety and cost. If real-time feedback is to be presented to end users, the smartphone should be mounted on the dash board, thus, a cradle to put the smartphone in should be fixed in the car, which results in extra costs for end users. Thus, the feedback during the driving was passive, only showing that the solution was running, as indicated by a spinning wheel (Fig. 2).

After the qualification activity the car driver got an aggregated score and an indication of the discount level he or she had qualified for (Fig. 2). The solution sent the aggregated safe-driving score to the insurer's price-calculation and quoting tool and then the system sent the quote back to the car driver in real time.

If the car driver accepted the quote, similar activities as in the As-Is process were executed by insurer and an insurance letter was then sent out to the customer (Fig. 4).

The risk assessment and price calculation are also influenced by the UBI. Therefore, new behaviour and exposure parameters are adopted in the assessment and calculations as outlined next.

In the designed To-Be process a decision was made to measure the usage grade with manual start functionality, because the usage grade was considered as an important risk-assessment factor. The usage grade is the number of miles driven and running the safe-drive application compared to the total number of miles the car has been driven during a specific period. The period can be a policy period (usually 1 year) or a qualification period (e.g. 2 weeks). Usage grade is calculated by the application by comparing the odometer data (mileage) with the mileage recorded in the application. The usage grade and driving behaviours are the complementary parameters for the risk-assessment process and price calculation. The usage grade of the *If SafeDrive* application was measured by a sub-process in the qualification activity. The end user took a picture of his/her odometer when starting the qualification, and made a new picture when finishing the qualification. Then the usage grade was calculated by comparing the actual driving distance of the car during the qualification period, with the distances that the user had the *If SafeDrive* application running while driving. In the smartphone solution one can set up an auto-start function, thus the end users can have the application start by itself when driving.

Driving behaviour parameters were measured by advanced signal-processing algorithms, filtering GPS data combined with sensor fusion from the accelerometer and gyroscope in the smartphone, and combined with map-data in the smartphone (Händel et al., 2014).

The complementary parameters for the risk-assessment process and price calculation regarding exposure were time of day, road type and distance driven. These parameters were given high weight in the price calculation. These exposure parameters have a high effect on risk assessment. For example, a driver who drives in rush hours on a road type with a high frequency of collisions and injuries is assumed to be exposed to a higher risk than a driver who drives at a time when there are few other cars on the road, when the light conditions are good and he or she is driving on a road type with a low frequency of collisions and injuries.

3.1.3 The To-Be Process Advantages

The To-Be process has distinct advantages in comparison with the As-Is process (Table 1). Given the prevalent digital technologies in modern society, more and more end users will adopt the new insurance product based on their driving behaviours, i.e. insurance telematics. The advantages can be summarised as: (1) the To-Be process would save costs with regard to contact end users and communicate with drivers; the insurer has more touch points with consumers in the process; (2) the To-be process provides more accurate and personalized risk assessment for individual drivers; and (3) the price calculation for each customer is based on the dynamic measurements instead of static statistics.

3.2 The Results of the Insurance Telematics Initiative

The *If SafeDrive* campaign was run full scale for 2 weeks between March and April 2013. In total, some 1,000 registered users were involved in the test. The pilot generated in total big data containing 4,500 driving hours and 250,000 km road vehicle traffic data (Händel et al., 2014). The campaign was one of the first campaigns, world-wide, utilizing the processing power of smartphones. The data quality was assured by rigorous soft computing methods. However, the results did not fulfil all the initiative goals. The insurer If P & C decided to put the trial on hold. The insurer delayed the roll-out of the new insurance product to mainstream customers.

Table 1 The advantages of the To-Be customer acquisition process

Process/ sub-process	As-Is (static)	To-Be (dynamic)	To-Be process advantages
Customer acquisition	Consumer makes insurance request through – Internet – Call centre – Broker Or Insurer makes an outbound call to recruit new customer	Consumer makes insurance request through – Smartphone App New customers recruitments are made by word-of-mouth, e.g. inviting friends, social communities, etc.	It reduces the cost dramatically, given it utilizes the prevalent and free marketing channels, i.e. mobile and social. The workload of call centre and broker can be largely reduced. It has increased number of touch-points with the customer since the interactions occur every time the users drive.
Risk assessment	Age, postal code, number of years of driving, gender, car type, previous insurance records/claims	Driving behaviour (breaking, acceleration, speeding) Usage grade (actual driving distances compared with measured driving distance) Exposure measurements (time of day, road type, distance driven)	The rich driving data help predict driving risks, and the loss costs for highest risk driving behaviour. The new process improves the assessment quality. More accurate and personalized risk assessment can be generated.
Price calculation	Based on the static demographic data and historical statistics	Based on the dynamic changes of driving behaviour (UBI)	Customers get an accurate and personalized price. Insurer can identify the safe drivers, which results in less insurance claims/cost.

Although the roll-out attracted some 1,000 signed users in the first 48 h when the campaign was launched, and large majority of the users recommended the smartphone application to friends, it failed to recruit the desired amount of new customers. Most of the users were already customers of If P & C. However, the *If SafeDrive* application created much attention among end users. During the first 48 h after the application was released on AppStore, the *If SafeDrive* application was ranked at number 8 of the downloaded applications within its category in Sweden. The attention helped trigger more consumer awareness of this new insurance product, and achieved the tipping point over a relatively long period (Malcolm, 2000).

The core technology of the smartphone-driven insurance telematics has yielded the advantage of improving risk assessments activities by collecting and analysing customers' driving behaviour. The insurer did improve the knowledge of predicting driving risks. Nonetheless, the media criticized the insurer for being unethical and violating privacy issues in implementing the telematics to analyse end user driving behaviours. For instance, they criticized that "the insurance industry's hunger to chart customers in real-time may prove larger than Facebook and Google" (ComputerSweden, 2013). This criticism also impacted the firm's decision to halt the campaign. We were not able to evaluate the system capacity for providing forecasts of traffic flow, and the long-term contributions to society. Moreover, an insurers' brand cannot be strengthened in only 2 weeks.

4 Lessons Learned: Discussion

In the case of the *If SafeDrive* campaign, the smartphone-based insurance telematics was tested and the information regarding the end users' driving behaviour was gathered. Once the end users qualified as safe drivers, they were offered a new insurance product based on their driving behaviours, and in combination with their demographic backgrounds and previous insurance claims. The insurer If P & C did, accordingly, initiate process innovation, i.e., customer acquisition, risk assessment and price calculation with the aim of supporting the new insurance product, even if on a small scale.

Two lessons stand out from this case: (1) the disruptive technology can trigger process innovation in order to embrace the full benefits of the technology; however, (2) the process innovation cannot succeed without the alignment with organization changes, business model redesign and business strategy transformation. Within the stable insurance industry structure and business environment in Scandinavia, the insurance company has no imperative and immediate motivation to transform the business strategy and redesign the business models for auto insurance. Therefore, the process innovation with disruptive technology such as insurance telematics can't be achieved and sustained at this moment.

The lessons learned have significant theoretical implications. In order to fully understand the implications, we further propose the capability layer model (CLM) with the aim of elaborating the fundamentals of managing process innovation with disruptive technologies, as well as creating a theoretical base for critical thinking concerning process management and innovation in the digital age.

The capability layer model (CLM) (Fig. 5) is inspired by the six elements of business processes management (Rosemann & vom Brocke, 2010) and management model designed by Ohlsson (1999). The CLM consists of seven layers, from the core inner layer, encompassing technology (innovation/disruptive technology design), information (data generated by the disruptive technology), business process design for the core technology implementation, product/services

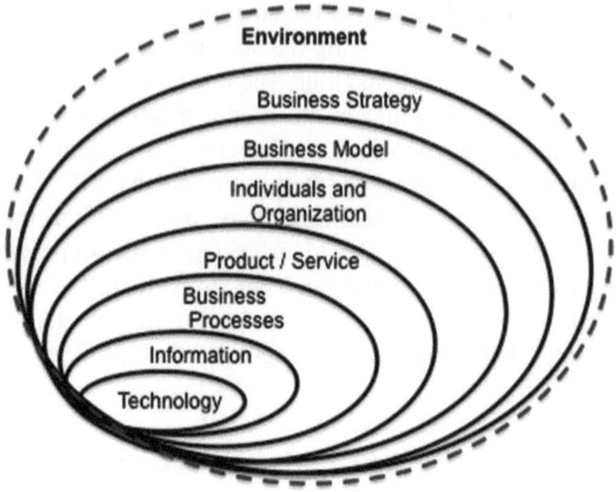

Fig. 5 Capability layer model (CLM)

implementation, individual/organization readiness for innovation implementation, towards business models and the outer layer of business strategy. Business environment is conceptualized as the macro economic and market environment that a company operated within. The management of an innovation goes through two phases: exploration phase and exploitation phase (Tidd & Bessant, 2009). Where exploration can be defined as the investigation and learning phase and exploitation as the full commercial utilization of the innovation.

We define the iterations between the layers of Technology, Information, Business process and Product/Service innovation, and implementation defined by the CLM as the exploration phase of applying disruptive technology in process innovation. In the exploration phase, process innovation by disruptive technologies requires a high number of interactions between the process design phase and implementation phase. Thus, documentation and detailed process modelling at the process activity level is not crucial during these interactions. The traditional approach to a process management cycle emphasizes the documentation phase between the design and implementation (Hammer, 2010). Therefore, people may get stuck in the technical details of process models and lose the focus on value creation by the innovation at the corporate level. The lessons learned from the UBI initiative at If P & C strongly indicate that in the process innovation endeavours, the documentation phase (with detailed process models on the activity level) is not as vital as in the traditional approach. The greatest amount of attention is given to the "*design and implementation*" iterations, which results in a full exploration of the disruptive technology that generates strong stimuli to innovate the processes. In the exploration phase of process innovation, the business process layer simply could not be innovated without the stimuli imperatives and high iterations and experimentation with the inner layers of information and technology.

The campaign did not succeed as expected. We argue that the pressure/resistance from the layers, i.e. business strategy, business model and organization, which are conceptualized in the CLM contributes to the failure. We define the release of the innovated process with the disruptive technology to the main stream market as the exploitation phase of process innovation. In the exploitation phase, the interactions between the process innovations with the outer layers determine the survival and sustainability of the new process. However, in the case of *If SafeDrive*, the resistance from the layers, i.e., organization structure, business model and strategy is stressed in this phase. Therefore, the interactions with exploitation are frozen. We discovered that in the organization layer, the innovation space of the insurer was collapsed in this initiative. Since one or more of the stakeholders who were responsible or accountable for capabilities required for the innovation lacked the necessary motivation, competence or empowerment/mandate, due to a stable business environment and low risk tolerance, it became clear that the layers of organization structure, business model and strategy were not ready for an exploitation of the innovated process. In other words, the process innovation does not encounter all elements that may ensure its successful up-take and exploitation (Rosemann & vom Brocke, 2010). For example, the innovated To Be process lacks an alignment with the firm's strategy. No supportive process innovation culture was established in this case (Schmiedel, vom Brocke, and Recker (2013); see also chapter by Van Looy (2015)). Moreover, people in the firm were satisfied by the performance of the As-Is process, thus, they did not appreciate and accept the disruptive technology and the new process. In short, process innovation cannot succeed in an organization without having all of the necessary elements/layers in place.

5 Conclusions

This chapter describes the unique case of the *If SafeDrive* campaign, where the insurer applied smartphone-based insurance telematics to innovating business processes, i.e. customer acquisition, risk assessment and price calculation. The technology, based on many years scientific research, has created a novel way of offering auto insurance products to customers by analysing their driving behaviours. Therefore, the technology ignited the business processes innovation in this case. However, the insurer made "on-hold" decisions in the campaign. The innovated processes cannot go for exploitation. We argue that the iterations and interactions from the technology layer to the process layer do not generate powerful stimuli to overcome the hindering impacts and stressed resistance from the organization layer to the strategy layer. Thus, the innovated process cannot be sustained in the current environment. Christensen (1997) pinpoints that a market leader with a low risk tolerance, who is acting in a stable business environment with a functional business model, usually avoids the adoption of innovation for fear of provoking the business environment. A possible solution to this dilemma could be to unbundle the business by separating an insurance telematics initiative to another division and brand (Osterwalder & Pigneur, 2010).

Due to the unique context and core subject of this case study, the generalization of the results may be limited. However, implementing the capability layer model (CLM) for understanding process innovation with disruptive technologies may provoke critical thinking on this topic and generate general interests. For instance, before we apply established methods in process analysis and redesign, it is vital to investigate the processes in scope at the macro-level in order to obtain knowledge of potential process innovation from technology layer to business strategy layer. Thus, we can better cope with the resistance of industry structures or radically change the competitive environment.

References

Abrahamson, E. (1996). Management fashion. *Academy of Management Review, 21*(1), 254–285.

Bruneteau, F. (2012). *Why insurance telematics matters—Overview of a future -EUR 50 billion market*. Paper presented at the Telematics Munich, Munich, Germany.

Collins, J. C. (2005). *Built to last: Successful habits of visionary companies*. London: Random House.

Christensen, C. (1997). *The innovator's dilemma: When new technologies cause great firms to fail*. Boston, MA: Harvard Business Review Press.

ComputerSweden. (2013). Safedrive-appen – första steget mot avgrunden. Podcast. Retrieved March 27, 2014, from www.computersweden.idg.se/2.2683/1.499441/podcast--safedrive-appen--forsta-steget-mot-avgrunden

Davenport, T. H. (1993). *Process innovation: Reengineering work through information technology*. Boston, MA: Harvard Business Press.

Desyllas, P., & Sako, M. (2013). Profiting from business model innovation: Evidence from pay-as-you-drive auto insurance. *Research Policy, 42*(1), 101–116.

Hammer, M. (2010). What is business process management? In M. vom Brocke & M. Rosemann (Eds.), *Handbook on business process management* (Vol. 1, pp. 3–16). Berlin: Springer.

Händel, P., Ohlsson, J., Ohlsson, M., Skog, I., & Nygren, E. (2014). Smartphone-based measurement systems for road vehicle traffic monitoring and usage-based insurance. *IEEE Systems Journal, 8*(4), 1238–1248. doi:10.1109/JSYST.2013.2292721.

Insurance Telematics. (2012). *Global study—Free abstract*. Brussels: Ptolemus Consulting Group. Retrieved March 31, 2014, from www.ptolemus.com

Insurance Telematics. (2013). *Usage based insurance global study—Free abstract*. Brussels: Ptolemus Consulting Group. Retrieved March 26, 2014, from www.ptolemus.com

Kimberly, J. R., & Evanisko, M. J. (1981). Organizational innovation: The influence of individual, organizational, and contextual factors on hospital adoption of technological and administrative innovations. *Academy of Management Journal, 24*(4), 689–713.

Lane, N., Miluzzo, E., Lu, H., Peebles, D., Choudhury, T., & Campbell, A. (2010). A survey of mobile phone sensing. *IEEE Communications Magazine, 48*, 140–150.

Malcolm, G. (2000). *The tipping point: How little things can make a big difference*. New York: Little Brown.

Ohlsson, J. (1999). *Medvetande av IT-management – En utveckling av synen på affärssytemet R/3* (in Swedish). Master's series No. 99-33-DSV-SU.

Osterwalder, A., & Pigneur, Y. (2010). *Business model generation: A handbook for visionaries, game changers, and challengers*. Hoboken, NJ: Wiley.

Progressive. (2012). *Linking driving behavior to automobile accidents and insurance rates an analysis of five billion miles driven*. Available at: www.progressive.com/Content/pdf/.../snap shot_report_final_070812.pdf. Last Accessed 8 January, 2015.

Rosemann, M., & vom Brocke, J. (2010). The six core elements of business process management. In J. vom Brocke & M. Rosemann (Eds.), *Handbook on business process management 1* (pp. 107–122). Berlin: Springer.

Schmiedel, T., vom Brocke, J., & Recker, J. (2013). Which cultural values matter to business process management? Results from a global Delphi study. *Business Process Management Journal, 19*(2), 292–317.

Sheng, X., Tang, J., Xiao, X., & Xue, G. (2013). Sensing as a service: Challenges, solutions and future directions. *Sensors Journal, IEEE, 13*(10), 3733–3741.

Tidd, J., & Bessant, J. (2009). *Managing innovation: Integrating technological, market and organizational change*. 4th edition. John Wiley & Sons Ltd. England.

Van Looy, A. (2015). On the importance of non-technical process capabilities to support digital innovations. In J. Brocke & T. Schmiedel (Eds.), *Business process management: Driving innovation in a digital world*. Switzerland: Springer.

Part III

Driving Innovation Through Advanced Process Analytics

Extracting Event Data from Databases to Unleash Process Mining

Wil M.P. van der Aalst

Abstract

Increasingly organizations are using process mining to understand the way that operational processes are executed. Process mining can be used to systematically drive innovation in a digitalized world. Next to the automated discovery of the real underlying process, there are process-mining techniques to analyze bottlenecks, to uncover hidden inefficiencies, to check compliance, to explain deviations, to predict performance, and to guide users towards "better" processes. Dozens (if not hundreds) of process-mining techniques are available and their value has been proven in many case studies. However, process mining stands or falls with the availability of event logs. Existing techniques assume that events are clearly defined and refer to precisely one case (i.e. process instance) and one activity (i.e., step in the process). Although there are systems that directly generate such event logs (e.g., BPM/WFM systems), most information systems do not record events explicitly. Cases and activities only exist implicitly. However, when creating or using process models "raw data" need to be linked to cases and activities. This paper uses a novel perspective to conceptualize a *database view on event data*. Starting from a class model and corresponding object models it is shown that events correspond to the creation, deletion, or modification of objects and relations. The key idea is that *events leave footprints by changing the underlying database*. Based on this an approach is described that *scopes*, *binds*, and *classifies* data to create "flat" event logs that can be analyzed using traditional process-mining techniques.

W.M.P. van der Aalst (✉)
Architecture of Information Systems, Eindhoven University of Technology, P.O. Box 513, 5600 MB Eindhoven, The Netherlands

International Laboratory of Process-Aware Information Systems, National Research University Higher School of Economics (HSE), 33 Kirpichnaya Street, Moscow, Russia
e-mail: w.m.p.v.d.aalst@tue.nl

J. vom Brocke, T. Schmiedel (eds.), *BPM – Driving Innovation in a Digital World*, Management for Professionals, DOI 10.1007/978-3-319-14430-6_8

1 Introduction

The spectacular growth of event data is rapidly changing the Business Process Management (BPM) discipline (Aalst, 2013a; Aalst & Stahl, 2011; Brocke & Rosemann, 2010; Dumas, Rosa, Mendling, & Reijers, 2013; Hofstede, Aalst, Adams, & Russell, 2010; Reichert & Weber, 2012; Weske, 2007). It makes no sense to focus on modeling, model-based analysis and model-based implementation *without* using the valuable information hidden in information systems (Aalst, 2011). Organizations are competing on analytics and only organizations that intelligently use the vast amounts of data available will survive (Aalst, 2014).

Today's main innovations are intelligently exploiting the sudden availability of event data. Out of the blue, "Big Data" has become a topic in board-level discussions. The abundance of data will change many jobs across all industries. Just like computer science emerged as a new discipline from mathematics when computers became abundantly available, we now see the birth of *data science* as a new discipline driven by the torrents of data available in our increasingly digitalized world.[1] The demand for *data scientists* is rapidly increasing. However, the focus on data analysis should not obscure process-orientation. In the end, good processes are more important than information systems and data analysis. The old phrase "It's the process stupid" is still valid. Hence, we advocate the need for *process scientists* that will drive process innovations while exploiting the *Internet of Events* (IoE). The IoE is composed of:

- The *Internet of Content* (IoC): all information created by humans to increase knowledge on particular subjects. The IoC includes traditional web pages, articles, encyclopedia like Wikipedia, YouTube, e-books, newsfeeds, etc.
- The *Internet of People* (IoP): all data related to social interaction. The IoP includes e-mail, facebook, twitter, forums, LinkedIn, etc.
- The *Internet of Things* (IoT): all physical objects connected to the network. The IoT includes all things that have a unique id and a presence in an internet-like structure. Things may have an internet connection or be tagged using Radio-Frequency Identification (RFID), Near Field Communication (NFC), etc.
- The *Internet of Locations* (IoL): refers to all data that have a spatial dimension. With the uptake of mobile devices (e.g., smartphones) more and more events have geospatial attributes.

Note that the IoC, the IoP, the IoT, and the IoL partially overlap. For example, a place name on a webpage or the location from which a tweet was sent. See also Foursquare as a mixture of the IoP and the IoL.

It is not sufficient to just collect event data. The challenge is to exploit it for process improvements. Process mining is a new discipline aiming to address this challenge. *Process-mining techniques form the toolbox of tomorrow's process*

[1] We use the term "digitalize" to emphasize the transformational character of digitized data.

scientist. Process mining connects process models and data analytics. It can be used:

- to automatically discover processes without any modeling (not just the control-flow, but also other perspectives such as the data-flow, work distribution, etc.),
- to find bottlenecks and understand the factors causing these bottlenecks,
- to detect and understand deviations, to measure their severity and to assess the overall level of compliance,
- to predict costs, risks, and delays,
- to recommend actions to avoid inefficiencies, and
- to support redesign (e.g., in combination with simulation).

Today, there are many mature process-mining techniques that can be directly used in everyday practice (Aalst, 2011). The uptake of process mining is not only illustrated by the growing number of papers and plug-ins of the open source tool *ProM*, there are also a growing number of commercial analysis tools providing process mining capabilities, cf. *Disco* (Fluxicon), *Perceptive Process Mining* (Perceptive Software, before Futura Reflect and BPMone by Pallas Athena), *ARIS Process Performance Manager* (Software AG), *Celonis Process Mining* (Celonis GmbH), *ProcessAnalyzer* (QPR), *Interstage Process Discovery* (Fujitsu), *Discovery Analyst* (StereoLOGIC), and *XMAnalyzer* (XMPro).

Despite the abundance of powerful process-mining techniques and success stories in a variety of application domains,[2] a limiting factor is the preparation of event data. The Internet of Events (IoE) mentioned earlier provides a wealth of data. However, these data are a not in a form that can be analyzed easily, and need to be extracted, refined, filtered, and converted to event logs first.

The starting point for process mining is an *event log*. Each event in such a log refers to an *activity* (i.e., a well-defined step in some process) and is related to a particular *case* (i.e., a *process instance*). The events belonging to a case are *ordered* and can be seen as one "run" of the process. Event logs may store additional information about events. In fact, whenever possible, process-mining techniques use extra information such as the *resource* (i.e., person or device) executing or initiating the activity, the *timestamp* of the event, or *data elements* recorded with the event (e.g., the size of an order).

If a BPM system or some other process-aware information system is used, then it is trivial to get event logs, i.e., typically the audit trail provided by the system can directly be used as input for process mining. However, in most organizations one encounters information systems built on top of database technology. The IoE depends on a variety of databases (classical relational DBMSs or new "noSQL" technologies). Therefore, we provide a *database view on event data* and assume that events leave footprints by changing the underlying database. Fortunately, database

[2] For example, http://www.win.tue.nl/ieeetfpm/doku.php?id=shared:process_mining_case_studies lists over 20 successful case studies in industry.

technology often provides so called "redo logs" that can be used to reconstruct the history of database updates. This is what we would like to exploit systematically.

Although the underlying databases are loaded with data, there are no *explicit* references to events, cases, and activities. Instead, there are tables containing records and these tables are connected through key relationships. Hence, the challenge is to convert tables and records into event logs. Obviously, this cannot be done in an automated manner.

To understand why process-mining techniques need "flat event logs" (i.e., event logs with ordered events that explicitly refer to cases and activities) as input, consider any process model in one of the mainstream process modeling notations (e.g., BPMN models, BPEL specifications, UML activity diagrams, and workflow nets). All of these notations present a diagram describing the life-cycle of an instance of the process (i.e., case) in terms of activities. Hence, all mainstream notations require the choice of a single process instance (i.e., case) notion. Notable exceptions are proclets (Aalst, Barthelmess, Ellis, & Wainer, 2001) and artifacts (Cohn & Hull, 2009), but these are rarely used and difficult to understand by end-users. Therefore, we need to relate raw event data to process instances using a single well-defined view on the process. This explains the requirements imposed on event logs.

In this paper, we focus on the problem of extracting "flat event logs" from databases. First, we introduce process mining in a somewhat more detailed form (Sect. 2). Section 3 presents *twelve guidelines for logging*. They point to typical problems related to event logs and can be used to improve the recording of relevant events. Although it is vital to improve the quality of logging, this paper aims to exploit the events hidden in existing databases. We use database-centric view on processes: the state of a process is reflected by the database content. Hence, events are merely changes of the database. In the remainder we assume that data is stored in a database management system and that we can see all updates of the underlying database. This assumption is realistic (see e.g. the redo logs of Oracle). However, how to systematically approach the problem of converting database updates into event logs? Section 4 introduces *class* and *object models* as a basis to reason about the problem. In Sect. 5 we show that class models can be extended with a so-called *event model*. The event model is used to capture changes of the underlying database. Section 6 describes a three-step approach (*Scope*, *Bind*, and *Classify*) to create a collection of flat event logs. The results serve as input for conventional process-mining techniques. Section 7 discusses related work and Sect. 8 concludes this paper.

2 Process Mining

Process mining aims to *discover, monitor and improve real processes by extracting knowledge from event logs* readily available in today's information systems (Aalst, 2011).

Normally, "flat" *event logs* serve as the starting point for process mining. These logs are created with a particular process and a set of questions in mind. An event log can be viewed as a multiset of *traces*. Each trace describes the life-cycle of a particular *case* (i.e., a *process instance*) in terms of the *activities* executed. Often event logs store additional information about events. For example, many process-mining techniques use extra information such as the *resource* (i.e., person or device) executing or initiating the activity, the *timestamp* of the event, or *data elements* recorded with the event (e.g., the size of an order). Table 1 shows a small fragment of a larger event log. Each row corresponds to an event. The events refer to two cases (654423 and 655526) and have additional properties, e.g., the registration for case 654423 was done by John at two past 11 on April 30th 2014 and the cost was 300 euro. An event may also contain transactional information, i.e., it may refer to an "assign", "start", "complete", "suspend", "resume", "abort", etc. action. For example, to measure the duration of an activity it is important to have a start event and a complete event. We refer to the *XES standard* (IEEE Task Force on Process Mining, 2013b) for more information on the data possibly available in event logs.

Flat event logs such as the one shown in Table 1 can be used to conduct four types of process mining (Aalst, 2011).

- The first type of process mining is *discovery*. A discovery technique takes an event log and produces a model without using any a priori information. Process discovery is the most prominent process-mining technique. For many organizations it is surprising to see that existing techniques are indeed able to discover real processes merely based on example behaviors stored in event logs.
- The second type of process mining is *conformance*. Here, an existing process model is compared with an event log of the same process. Conformance checking can be used to check if reality, as recorded in the log, conforms to the model and vice versa.
- The third type of process mining is *enhancement*. Here, the idea is to extend or improve an existing process model by directly using information about the actual process recorded in some event log. Whereas conformance checking measures the alignment between model and reality, this third type of process mining aims at changing or extending the a priori model. For instance, by using timestamps in the event log one can extend the model to show bottlenecks, service levels, and throughput times.
- The fourth type of process mining is *operational support*. The key difference with the former three types is that analysis is not done off-line, but used to influence the running process and its cases in some way. Based on process models, either discovered through process mining or (partly) made by hand, one can check, predict, or recommend activities for running cases in an online setting. For example, based on the discovered model one can predict that a particular case will be late and propose counter-measures.

Table 1 A fragment of an event log: each line corresponds to an event

Case id	Timestamp	Activity	Resource	Cost
654423	30-04-2014:11.02	Register request	John	300
654423	30-04-2014:11.06	Check completeness of documents	Ann	400
655526	30-04-2014:16.10	Register request	John	200
655526	30-04-2014:16.14	Make appointment	Ann	450
654423	30-04-2014:11.12	Ask for second opinion	Pete	100
654423	30-04-2014:11.18	Prepare decision	Pete	400
654423	30-04-2014:11.19	Pay fine	Pete	400
655526	30-04-2014:16.26	Check completeness of documents	Sue	150
655526	30-04-2014:16.36	Reject claim	Sue	100
...	...	...	...	...

The *ProM* framework provides an open source process-mining infrastructure. Over the last decade hundreds of plug-ins have been developed covering the whole process-mining spectrum. *ProM* is intended for process-mining experts. Non-experts may have difficulties using the tool due to its extensive functionality. Commercial process-mining tools such as *Disco*, *Perceptive Process Mining*, *ARIS Process Performance Manager*, *Celonis Process Mining*, *QPR ProcessAnalyzer*, *Fujitsu Interstage Process Discovery*, *StereoLOGIC Discovery Analyst*, and *XMAnalyzer* are typically easier to use because of their restricted functionality. These tools have been developed for practitioners, but provide only a fraction of the functionality offered by *ProM*. Figure 1 shows four screenshots of process-mining tools analyzing the same event log.

In this paper, we neither elaborate on the different process-mining techniques nor do we discuss specific process-mining tools. Instead, we focus on the event data used for process mining.

3 Guidelines for Logging

The focus of this paper is on the input side of process mining: *event data*. Often we need to work with the event logs that happen to be available, and there is no way to influence what events are recorded and how they are recorded. There can be various problems related to the structure and quality of data (Aalst, 2011; Jagadeesh Chandra Bose, Mans, & Aalst, 2013). For example, timestamps may be missing or too coarse (only dates). Therefore, this paper focuses on the "input side of process mining". Before we present our database-centric approach, we introduce *twelve guidelines for logging*. These guidelines make no assumptions on the underlying technology used to record event data.

In this section, we use a rather loose definition of event data: events simply refer to "things that happen" and that they are described by *references* and *attributes*. *References* have a *reference name* and an *identifier* that refers to some object (person, case, ticket, machine, room, etc.) in the universe of discourse. *Attributes*

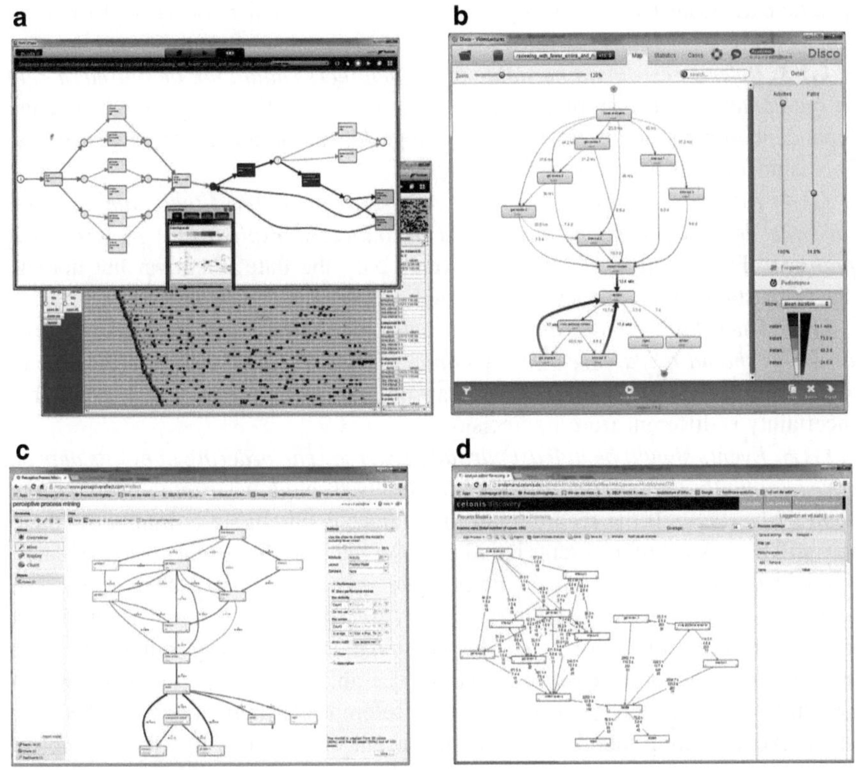

Fig. 1 Four screenshots of different tools analyzing the same event log. (**a**) ProM; (**b**) Disco (Fluxicon); (**c**) perceptive process mining (Perceptive Software); (**d**) Celonis process mining (Celonis GmbH) (Color figure online)

have a *name* and a *value*, e.g., *age* = *48* or *time* = *"28-6-2014 03:14:0"*. Based on these concepts we define our 12 guidelines. To create an event log from such "raw events" (1) we need to select the events relevant for the process at hand, (2) events need to be correlated to form process instances, (3) events need to be ordered using timestamp information, and (4) event attributes need to be selected or computed based on the raw data (resource, cost, etc.). Such an event log can be used as input for a wealth of process-mining techniques.

The guidelines for logging (**GL1–GL12**) aim to create a good starting point for process mining.

GL1: *Reference and variable names should have clear semantics, i.e., they should have the same meaning for all people involved in creating and analyzing event data.* Different stakeholders should interpret event data in the same way.

GL2: *There should be a structured and managed collection of reference and variable names.* Ideally, names are grouped hierarchically (like a taxonomy or ontology). A new reference and variable name can only be added after there is consensus on its value and meaning. Also consider adding domain or organization specific extensions (see for example the extension mechanism of XES (IEEE Task Force on Process Mining, 2013b)).

GL3: *References should be stable (e.g., identifiers should not be reused or rely on the context).* For example, references should not be time, region, or language dependent. Some systems create different logs depending on the language settings. This is unnecessarily complicating analysis.

GL4: *Attribute values should be as precise as possible. If the value does not have the desired precision, this should be indicated explicitly (e.g., through a qualifier).* For example, if for some events only the date is known but not the exact timestamp, then this should be stated explicitly.

GL5: *Uncertainty with respect to the occurrence of the event or its references or attributes should be captured through appropriate qualifiers.* For example, due to communication errors, some values may be less reliable than usual. Note that uncertainty is different from imprecision.

GL6: *Events should be at least partially ordered. The ordering of events may be stored explicitly (e.g., using a list) or implicitly through a variable denoting the event's timestamp.* If the recording of timestamps is unreliable or imprecise, there may still be ways to order events based on observed causalities (e.g., usage of data).

GL7: *If possible, also store transactional information about the event (start, complete, abort, schedule, assign, suspend, resume, withdraw, etc.).* Having start and complete events allows for the computation of activity durations. It is recommended to store activity references to be able to relate events belonging to the same activity instance. Without activity references it may not always be clear which events belong together, which start event corresponds to which complete event.

GL8: *Perform regularly automated consistency and correctness checks to ensure the syntactical correctness of the event log.* Check for missing references or attributes, and reference/attribute names not agreed upon. Event quality assurance is a continuous process (to avoid degradation of log quality over time).

GL9: *Ensure comparability of event logs over time and different groups of cases or process variants.* The logging itself should not change over time (without being reported). For comparative process mining, it is vital that the same logging principles are used. If for some groups of cases, some events are not recorded even though they occur, then this may suggest differences that do not actually exist.

GL10: *Do not aggregate events in the event log used as input for the analysis process.* Aggregation should be done during analysis and not before (since it cannot be undone). Event data should be as "raw" as possible.

GL11: *Do not remove events and ensure provenance. Reproducibility is key for process mining.* For example, do not remove a student from the database after he dropped out since this may lead to misleading analysis results. Mark objects as not relevant (a so-called "soft delete") rather than deleting them: concerts are not deleted—they are canceled, employees are not deleted—they are fired, etc.

GL12: *Ensure privacy without losing meaningful correlations.* Sensitive or private data should be removed as early as possible (i.e., before analysis). However, if possible, one should avoid removing correlations. For example, it is often not useful to know the name of a student, but it may be important to still be able to use his high school marks and know what other courses he failed. Hashing can be a powerful tool in the trade-off between privacy and analysis.

The above guidelines are very general and aim to improve the logging itself. The main purpose of the guidelines is to point to problems related to the input of process mining. They can be used to better instrument software.

After these general guidelines, we now change our viewpoint. We aim to exploit the hidden event data already present in databases. The content of the database can be seen as the current state of one or more processes. Updates of the database are therefore considered as the primary events. This database-centric view on event logs is orthogonal to the above guidelines.

4 Class and Object Models

Most information systems do not record events explicitly. Only process-aware information systems (e.g., BPM/WFM systems) record event data in the format shown in Table 1. To create an event log, we often need to gather data from different data sources where events exist only implicitly. In fact, for most process-mining projects event data need to be extracted from conventional databases. This is often done in an ad-hoc manner. Tools such as *XESame* (Verbeek, Buijs, van Dongen, & Aalst, 2010) and *ProMimport* (Günther & Aalst, 2006) provide some support, but still the event logs need to be constructed by querying the database and converting database records (row in tables) into events.

Moreover, the "regular tables" in a database only provide the *current state* of the information system. It may be impossible to see when a record was created or updated. Moreover, deleted records are generally invisible.[3] *Taking the viewpoint that the database reflects the current state of one or more processes, we define all changes of the database to be events.* Below we conceptualize this viewpoint. Building upon standard class and object models, we define the notion of an *event model*. The event model relates coherent set of changes to the underlying database to events used for process mining.

Section 5 defines the notion of an event model. To formalize event models, we first introduce and define class and object models.

A *class model* defines a set of classes that may be connected through relationships. UML class models (OMG, 2009), Entity-Relationship (ER) models (Chen, 1976), Object-Role Modeling (ORM) models, etc. provide concrete notations for the basic class model used in this paper.

[3] Increasingly systems mark deleted objects as not relevant (a so-called soft delete) rather than deleting them. In this way all intermediate states of the database can be reconstructed. Moreover, marking objects as deleted instead of completely removing them from the database is often more natural, e.g., concerts are not deleted—they are canceled, employees are not deleted—they are fired, etc.

Definition 1 (Unconstrained Class Model) Assume V to be some universe of values (strings, numbers, etc.). An unconstrained *class model* is a tuple $UCM = (C, A, R, val, key, attr, rel)$ such that

- C is a set of class names,
- A is a set of attribute names,
- R is a set of relationship names ($C \cap R = \emptyset$),
- $val \in A \rightarrow \mathcal{P}(V)$ is a function mapping each attribute onto a set of values.[4] $V_a = val(a)$ is a shorthand and denotes the set of possible values of attribute $a \in A$,
- $key \in C \rightarrow \mathcal{P}(A)$ is a function describing the set of key attributes of each class,
- $attr \in C \rightarrow \mathcal{P}(A)$ is a function describing the set of additional attributes of each class ($key(c) \cap attr(c) = \emptyset$ for any class $c \in C$),
- $rel \in R \rightarrow (C \times C)$ is a function describing the two classes involved in a relation. Let $rel(r) = (c_1, c_2)$ for relationship $r \in R : rel_1(r) = c_1$ and $rel_2(r) = c_2$ are shorthand forms to obtain the two individual classes involved in the relationship.

Figure 2 shows a class model with classes $C = \{c_1, c_2, \ldots, c_8\}$ and relationships $R = \{r_1, r_2, \ldots, r_8\}$. Classes and relationships also have longer names, e.g., c_1 is the class "concert hall". We will use the shorter names for a more compact discussion. In this example, each class has a singleton key, i.e., a single column serves as primary key. The keys are highlighted in Fig. 2 (darker color). For example, $key(c_1) = \{hall\_id\}$ and $attr(c_1) = \{name\_of\_hall, address\}$ are the two additional (non-key) attributes of class c_1. $rel(r_4) = (c_5, c_2)$, i.e., relation r_4 relates tickets (c_5) to concerts (c_2). Figure 2 also shows cardinality constraints. These are not part of the unconstrained class model. Later we will define *constrained* class models (Definition 4). However, before doing so, we need to introduce some more notations.

Definition 2 (Notations) Let $CM = (C, A, R, val, key, attr, rel)$ be an (unconstrained) class model.

- $M^{CM} = \{map \in A \not\rightarrow V \mid \forall_{a \in dom(map)}\ map(a) \in V_a\}$ is the set of mappings,[5]
- $K^{CM} = \{(c, map_k) \in C \times M^{CM} \mid dom(map_k) = key(c)\}$ is the set of possible key values per class,
- $A^{CM} = \{(c, map_a) \in C \times M^{CM} \mid dom(map_a) = attr(c)\}$ is the set of possible additional attribute values per class,

[4] $\mathcal{P}(X)$ is the powerset of X, i.e., $Y \in \mathcal{P}(X)$ if $Y \subseteq X$.

[5] $f \in X \not\rightarrow Y$ is a partial function, i.e., the domain of f may be any subset of X: $dom(f) \subseteq X$.

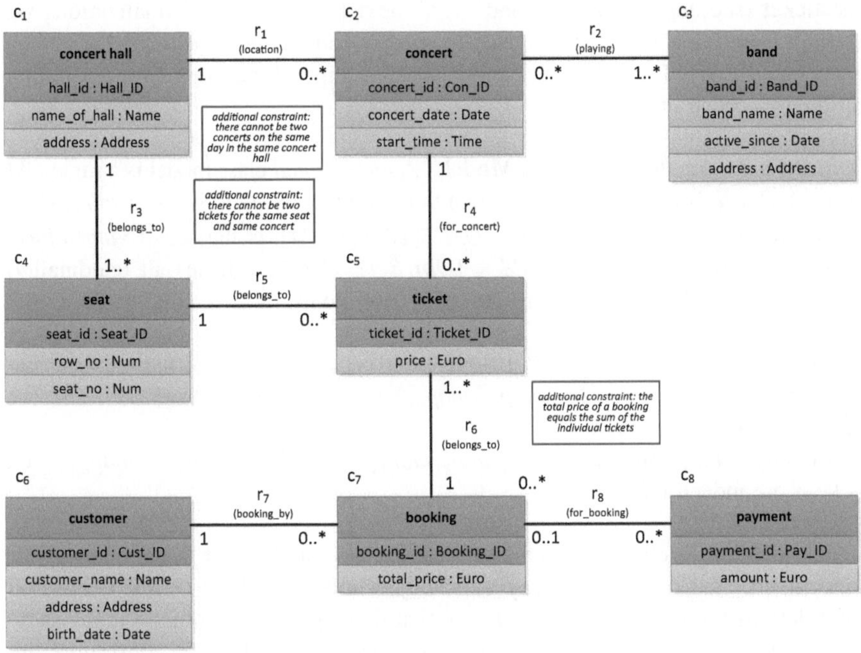

Fig. 2 Example of a constrained class model (Color figure online)

- $O^{CM} = \{(c, map_k, map_a) \in C \times M^{CM} \times M^{CM} \mid (c, map_k) \in K^{CM} \wedge (c, map_a) \in A^{CM}\}$ is the set of objects,
- $R^{CM} = \{(r, map_1, map_2) \in R \times M^{CM} \times M^{CM} \mid \exists_{c_1, c_2 \in C}\ rel(r) = (c_1, c_2) \wedge \{(c_1, map_1), (c_2, map_2)\} \subseteq K^{CM}\}$ is the set of potential relations.

A class model implicitly defines a collection of possible *object models*. Each class $c \in C$ may have multiple objects and each relationship $r \in R$ may hold multiple concrete object-to-object relations.

Definition 3 (Object Model) Let $CM = (C, A, R, val, key, attr, rel)$ be an (unconstrained) class model. An *object model* of CM is a tuple $OM = (Obj, Rel)$ where $Obj \subseteq O^{CM}$ is a set of objects and $Rel \subseteq R^{CM}$ is a set of relations. $\mathcal{U}^{OM}(CM) = \{(Obj, Rel) \mid Obj \subseteq O^{CM} \wedge Rel \subseteq R^{CM}\}$ is the set of all object models of CM.

The cardinality constraints in Fig. 2 impose restrictions on object models. For example, a ticket corresponds to precisely one concert and each concert corresponds to any number of tickets (see annotations "1" and "0..*" next to r_4). Each ticket corresponds to precisely one booking and each booking refers to at least one ticket (see annotations "1" and "1..*" next to r_6). In our formalizations we abstract from the actual notation used to specify constraints. Instead, we assume a given set *VOM* of valid object models satisfying all requirements (including cardinality constraints).

Definition 4 (Constrained Class Model) A *constrained* class model is a tuple $CM = (C, A, R, val, key, attr, rel, VOM)$ such that $UCM = (C, A, R, val, key, attr, rel)$ is an unconstrained class model and $VOM \subseteq \mathcal{U}^{OM}(UCM)$ is the set of *valid object models.* A valid object model $OM = (Obj, Rel) \in VOM$ satisfies all (cardinality) constraints including the following general requirements:

- for any $(r, map_{k1}, map_{k2}) \in Rel$ there exist c_1, c_2, map_{a1}, and map_{a2} such that $rel(r) = (c_1, c_2)$ and $\{(c_1, map_{k1}, map_{a1}), (c_2, map_{k2}, map_{a2})\} \subseteq Obj$, i.e., the referenced objects exist,
- for any $\{(c, map_k, map_{a1}), (c, map_k, map_{a2})\} \subseteq Obj: \; map_{a1} = map_{a2}$, i.e., keys are indeed unique.

All notations defined for unconstrained class models are also defined for constrained class models. For any valid object model $OM \in VOM$ it is ensured that relations refer to existing objects and that there are not two objects in the same class that have the same key values. Moreover, all cardinality constraints are satisfied if $OM \in VOM$.

Definition 4 abstracts from the concrete realization of object and class models in a database. However, it is easy to map any class model onto a set of related tables in a conventional relational database system. To do this foreign keys need to be added to the tables or additional tables need to be added to store the relationships. For example, one may add three extra columns to the table for c_5 ("ticket"): *concert_id* (for the foreign key relating the ticket to a concert), *seat_id* (for the foreign key relating the ticket to a seat), and *booking_id* (for the foreign key relating the ticket to a booking). These columns realize respectively r_4, r_5, and r_6. In the case of a many-to-many relationship an additional table needs to be added to encode the relations. In the remainder we abstract from the actual table structure, but it is obvious that the conceptualization agrees with standard database technology.

5 Events and Their Effect on the Object Model

Examples of widely used *DataBase Management Systems* (DBMSs) are *Oracle RDBMS* (Oracle), *SQL server* (Microsoft), *DB2* (IBM), *Sybase* (SAP), and *PostgreSQL* (PostgreSQL Global Development Group). All of these systems can store and manage the data structure described in Definition 4. Moreover, all of these systems have facilities to *record changes* to the database. For example, in the Oracle RDBMS environment, *redo logs* comprise files in a proprietary format which log a history of all changes made to the database. *Oracle LogMiner*, a utility provided by Oracle, provides methods of querying logged changes made to an Oracle database. Every *Microsoft SQL Server* database has a *transaction log* that records all database modifications. *Sybase IQ* also provides a transaction log. Such redo/transaction logs can be used to recover from a system failure. The redo/transaction logs will grow significantly if there are frequent changes to the database. In such cases, the redo/transaction logs need to be truncated regularly.

This paper does not focus on a particular DBMS. However, we assume that through redo/transaction logs we can monitor changes to the database. In particular, we assume that we can see when a record is inserted, updated, or deleted. Conceptually, we assume that we can see the *creation* of objects and relations (denoted by $\oplus$), the *deletion* of objects and relations (denoted by $\ominus$), and *updates* of objects (denoted by $\oslash$). Based on this we define the set of *atomic* and *composite event types*.

Definition 5 (Event Types) Let $CM = (C, A, R, val, key, attr, rel, VOM)$ be a constrained class model. $ET_{atomic} = ET_{add,obj} \cup ET_{add,rel} \cup ET_{del,obj} \cup ET_{del,rel} \cup ET_{upd,obj}$ is the set of *atomic event types* composed of the following pairwise disjoint sets:

- $ET_{add,obj} = \{(\oplus, c) | c \in C\}$ are the event types for adding objects,
- $ET_{add,rel} = \{(\oplus, r) | r \in R\}$ are the event types for adding relations,
- $ET_{del,obj} = \{(\ominus, c) | c \in C\}$ are the event types for deleting objects,
- $ET_{del,rel} = \{(\ominus, r) | r \in R\}$ are the event types for deleting relations, and
- $ET_{upd,obj} = \{(\oslash, c) | c \in C\}$ are the event types for updating objects.

$ET_{composite}(CM) = \mathcal{P}(ET_{atomic}) \setminus \{\emptyset\}$ is the set of all possible *composite event types* of *CM*.

The atomic event type $(\oplus, c_5)$ denotes the creation of a ticket and $(\oplus, r_8)$ denotes the linking of a payment to a booking. When updating the address of a customer, the atomic event type $(\oslash, c_6)$ is expected to occur. When preparing for a new concert of an existing band in an existing concert hall, we may observe the composite event type $\{(\oplus, c_2), (\oplus, r_1), (\oplus, r_2)\}$, i.e., creating a new object for the concert and relating it to the existing concert hall and band.

The notion of atomic/composite event types naturally extends to concrete atomic/composite events. For an object creation event $(\oplus, c)$ we need to specify (map_k, map_a), i.e., the new key and additional attribute values. For deleting a relation $(\ominus, r)$ we need to specify (map_1, map_2), i.e., the key values of each of the two objects involved in the relation.

Definition 6 (Events) Let $CM = (C, A, R, val, key, attr, rel, VOM)$ be a constrained class model. $E_{atomic} = E_{add,obj} \cup E_{add,rel} \cup E_{del,obj} \cup E_{del,rel} \cup E_{upd,obj}$ is the set of atomic events composed of the following pairwise disjoint sets:

- $E_{add,obj} = \{(\oplus, c, (map_k, map_a)) | (c, map_k, map_a) \in O^{CM}\}$,
- $E_{add,rel} = \{(\oplus, r, (map_1, map_2)) | (r, map_1, map_2) \in R^{CM}\}$,
- $E_{del,obj} = \{(\ominus, c, map_k) | (c, map_k) \in K^{CM}\}$,
- $E_{del,rel} = \{(\ominus, r, (map_1, map_2)) | (r, map_1, map_2) \in R^{CM}\}$, and
- $E_{upd,obj} = \{(\oslash, c, (map_k, map_a)) | (c, map_k, map_a) \in O^{CM}\}$.

$E_{composite}(CM) = \mathcal{P}(E_{atomic}) \setminus \{\emptyset\}$ is the set of all possible *composite events* of *CM*. $fprt \in E_{atomic} \rightarrow ET_{atomic}$ is a function computing the footprint of an atomic event: $fprt((x, y, z)) = (x, y)$ maps an atomic event $(x, y, z) \in E_{atomic}$ onto its corresponding type $(x, y) \in ET_{atomic}$. The footprint function is generalized to composite events, i.e., $fprt \in E_{composite} \rightarrow ET_{composite}$ such that $fprt(CE) = \{(x, y) | (x, y, z) \in CE\}$ for composite event *CE*.

E_{atomic} is the set of atomic events. $E_{composite}(CM)$ is the set of non-empty composite events. *fprt* transforms atomic/composite events into the corresponding types. For example, $fprt((\oplus, r, (map_1, map_2))) = (\oplus, r)$.

An *event model* annotates a constrained class model with event types that refer to composite events. Figure 3 shows an event model that has seven events. Event en_3 models the deletion of a customer. The corresponding composite event type is $\{(\ominus, c_6)\}$. Event en_4 models the adding of a concert. The corresponding composite event type is $\{(\oplus, c_2), (\oplus, r_1), (\oplus, r_2)\}$.

Definition 7 (Event Model) Let $CM = (C, A, R, val, key, attr, rel, VOM)$ be a constrained class model. An *event model* is a tuple $EM = (EN, type, VE)$ where

- EN is a set of event names,
- $type \in EN \rightarrow ET_{composite}(CM)$ is a function mapping each event name onto its composite event type,
- $VE \subseteq EN \times E_{composite}(CM)$ is the set of *valid events* such that for any $(en, CE) \in VE$: $fprt(CE) = type(en)$. Moreover, for any $en \in EN$ there exists a CE such that $(en, CE) \in VE$.

Events should be of the right type and for each event name there is at least one valid event. Note that events may have varying cardinalities, e.g., one event may create five objects of the same class.

In Definition 7, we require $fprt(CE) = type(en)$. Alternatively, one could weaken this requirements to $\emptyset \neq fprt(CE) \subseteq type(en)$. This would allow for the omission of certain events, e.g., in case the object already exists it does not need to be created. Consider for example a new event en_8 with $type(en_8) = \{(\oplus, c_6), (\oplus, c_7), (\oplus, r_7)\}$ that creates a booking and the corresponding

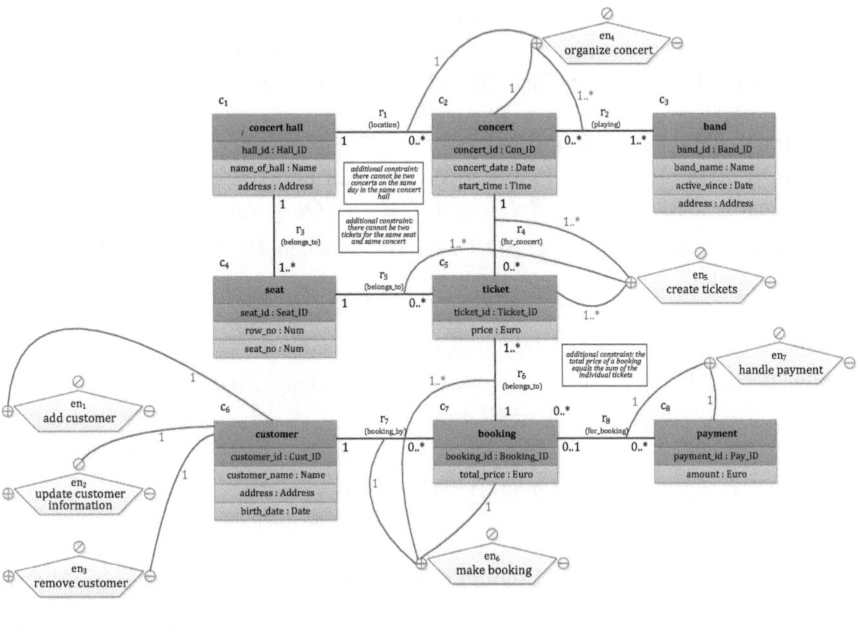

Fig. 3 Example of an event model (Color figure online)

customer. If the customer is already in the database, the composite event cannot contain the creation of the customer object c_6. Instead of defining two variants of the same events (with or without creating a c_6 object), it may be convenient to define one event that allows for both variations. Case studies should show which requirement is more natural (strong versus weak event typing).

Here, we assume an event model to be given. The event model may be created by the analyst or extracted from the redo/transaction log of the DBMS. We also assume that event occurrences (defined next) can be related to events in the event model. Future work aims at providing support for the semi-automatic creation of event models and further investigating the relation with the redo/transaction logs in concrete systems like Oracle.

An *event occurrence* is specified by an event name *en*, a composite event *CE*, and a timestamp *ts*. A *change log* is a sequence of such event occurrences.

Definition 8 (Event Occurrence, Change Log) Let $CM = (C, A, R, val, key, attr, rel, VOM)$ be a constrained class model and $EM = (EN, type, VE)$ an event model. Assume some universe of timestamps TS. $e = ((en, CE), ts) \in VE \times TS$ is an *event occurrence*. $EO(CM, EM) = VE \times TS$ is the set of all possible event occurrences. A *change log* $L = \langle e_1, e_2, \ldots, e_n \rangle$ is a sequence of event occurrences such that time is non-decreasing, i.e., $L = \langle e_1, e_2, \ldots, e_n \rangle \in (EO(CM, EM))^*$ and $ts_i \leq ts_j$ for any $e_i = ((en_i, CE_i), ts_i)$ and $e_j = ((en_j, CE_j), ts_j)$ with $1 \leq i < j \leq n$.

Next we define the effect of an event occurrence, i.e., the resulting object model. If an event is not permissible, e.g., inserting an object for which an object with the same key already exists, the object model does not change.

Definition 9 (Effect of an Event) Let $CM = (C, A, R, val, key, attr, rel, VOM)$ be a constrained class model and $EM = (EN, type, VE)$ an event model. For any two object models $OM_1 = (Obj_1, Rel_1)$ and $OM_2 = (Obj_2, Rel_2)$ of CM and event occurrence $e = ((en, CE), ts) \in EO(CM, EM)$, we denote $OM_1 \xrightarrow{e} OM_2$ if and only if

- $Obj_2 = \{(c, map_k, map_a) \in Obj_1 | (\ominus, c, map_k) \notin CE \ \wedge \ \forall_{map'}, (\oslash, c, (map_k, map')) \notin CE\} \cup \{(c, map_k, map_a) \in O^{CM} | (\oplus, c, (map_k, map_a)) \in CE \ \vee \ (\oslash, c, (map_k, map_a)) \in CE\}$,
- $Rel_2 = \{(r, map_1, map_2) \in Rel_1 | (\ominus, r, (map_1, map_2)) \notin CE\} \cup \{(r, map_1, map_2) \in R^{CM} | (\oplus, r, (map_1, map_2)) \in CE\}$, and
- $\{OM_1, OM_2\} \subseteq VOM$.

Event e is *permissible* in object model OM, notation $OM_1 \xrightarrow{e}$, if and only if there exists an OM' such that $OM \xrightarrow{e} OM'$. If this is not the case, we denote $OM \stackrel{e}{\not\rightarrow}$, i.e., e is not permissible in OM. If an event is not permissible, it will fail and the object model will remain unchanged. Relation $\stackrel{e}{\Rightarrow}$ denotes the effect of event e. It is the smallest relation such that (a) $OM \stackrel{e}{\Rightarrow} OM'$ if $OM \xrightarrow{e} OM'$ and (b) $OM \stackrel{e}{\Rightarrow} OM$ if $OM \stackrel{e}{\not\rightarrow}$.

The event occurrence $e = ((en, CE), ts)$ as a whole is successful or not. If $OM \stackrel{e}{\not\rightarrow}$, then nothing changes. The current definition of $OM_1 \xrightarrow{e}$ is rather forgiving, e.g., it allows for the deletion of an object that does not exist. It only ensures that the result is a valid object model, but relations $\xrightarrow{e}$ and $\stackrel{e}{\Rightarrow}$ can be made stricter if desired. Note that the atomic events in CE occur concurrently if e is successful, i.e., the events do not depend on each other.

Relation $\stackrel{e}{\Rightarrow}$ is deterministic, i.e., $OM_1 \stackrel{e}{\Rightarrow} OM_2$ and $OM_1 \stackrel{e}{\Rightarrow} OM_3$ implies $OM_2 = OM_3$.

Definition 10 (Effect of a Change Log) Let $CM = (C, A, R, val, key, attr, rel, VOM)$ be a constrained class model, $EM = (EN, type, VE)$ an event model, and $OM_0 \in VOM$ the initial valid object model. Let $L = \langle e_1, e_2, \ldots, e_n \rangle \in (EO(CM, EM))^*$ be a change log. There exist object models $OM_1, OM_2, \ldots, OM_n \in VOM$ such that

$$OM_0 \stackrel{e_1}{\Rightarrow} OM_1 \stackrel{e_2}{\Rightarrow} OM_2 \ldots \stackrel{e_n}{\Rightarrow} OM_n$$

Hence, change log L results in object model OM_n when starting in OM_0. This is denoted by $OM_0 \stackrel{L}{\Rightarrow} OM_n$.

The formalizations above provide operational semantics for an abstract database system that processes a sequence of events. However, the goal is not to model a database system. Instead, we aim to relate database updates to event logs that can be used for process mining. Subsequently, we assume that we can witness a change log $L = \langle e_1, e_2, \ldots, e_n \rangle$. It is easy to see atomic events. Moreover, various heuristics can be used to group events into composite events (e.g., based on time, session id, and/or user id). Definition 3 shows that this assumption allows us to reconstruct the state of the database system after each event, i.e., the object model OM_i resulting from e_i can be computed.

6 Approach: Scope, Bind, and Classify

Process-mining techniques require as input a "flat" event log and not a change log as described in Definition 10. Table 1 shows the kind of input data that process-mining techniques expect. Such a conventional flat event log is a collection of events where each event has the following properties:

- **Case id**: each event should refer to a case (i.e., process instance). If an event is relevant for multiple cases, it should be replicated when creating event logs.
- **Activity**: each event should be related to an activity. Events refer to activity instances, i.e., occurrences of activities in the corresponding process model.
- **Timestamp**: events within a case should be ordered. Moreover, timestamps are not just needed for the temporal order: they are also vital for measuring performance.
- Next to these mandatory attributes there may be all kinds of *optional* event attributes. For example:
  - **Resource**: the person, machine or software component executing the event.
  - **Type**: the transaction type of the event (start, complete, suspend, resume, etc.).
  - **Costs**: the costs associated with the event.
  - **Customer**: information about the person or organization for whom or which the event is executed.
  - Etc.

Dedicated process-mining formats like XES or MXML allow for the storage of such event data. To be able to use existing process-mining techniques we need to be able to extract flat event logs and not a change log as defined in the previous section.

Let $CM = (C, A, R, val, key, attr, rel, VOM)$ be a constrained class model, $EM = (EN, type, VE)$ an event model, and $OM_0 \in VOM$ the initial valid object model. In the remainder we focus on the problem of converting a change log $L = \langle e_1, e_2, \ldots, e_n \rangle \in (EO(CM, EM))^*$ into a *collection of conventional events logs* that serve as input for existing process-mining techniques. Given an event occurrence $e_i = ((en_i, CE_i), ts_i)$, one may convert it into a conventional event by taking ts_i as timestamp and en_i as activity. However, an event occurrence needs to be related to zero or more cases and the change log may contain information about multiple processes. Hence, several decisions need to be made in the conversion process. We propose a three-step approach: (1) *scope* the event data, (2) *bind* the events to process instances (i.e., cases), and (3) *classify* the process instances.

6.1 Scope: Determine the Relevant Events

The first step in converting a change log into a collection of conventional events logs is to *scope* the event data. Which of the event occurrences in $L = \langle e_1, e_2, \ldots, e_n \rangle$ are relevant for the questions one aims to answer? One way to scope the event data is to consider a subset of event names $EN_s \subseteq EN$. Recall that EN are all event names in an event model. In Fig. 3, $EN = \{en_1, en_2, \ldots, en_7\}$. Events may also be selected based on a time window (e.g., "all events executed after May 21st" or "all events belonging to cases that were complete in 2013") or the classes involved (e.g., "all events related to Metallica concerts").

6.2 Bind: Relate Events to Process Instances

Process models always describe lifecycles of instances. For example, when looking at any BPMN, EPC, or UML activity model there is the implicit notion of a process instance (i.e., case). The process model is instantiated once for each case, e.g., for an order handling process the activities always operate on a specific purchase order. The notion of process instances is made explicit in process-aware information systems, e.g., Business Process Management (BPM) and Workflow Management (WfM) systems. However, in most other systems the instance notion is implicit. Moreover, the instance notion selected may depend on the questions one would like to answer. Consider for example Fig. 3. Possible instance notions are concert, ticket, booking, customer, band, concert hall, seat, and payment. One could construct a process describing the lifecycle of tickets. Such a lifecycle is different from the lifecycle of a concert or booking. One could even consider discovering the lifecycle of chairs in a concert hall by taking seat IDs as process instances.

Technically, we need to define a set of process instances PI (cases) and relate events to these instances: $bind \subseteq VE_s \times PI$ with $VE_s = \{(en, CE) \in VE \mid en \in EN_s\}$ the subset of the valid events selected (without timestamps). Let $pi \in PI$ be a process instance and $e_i = ((en_i, CE_i), ts_i)$ an event occurrence: event e_i belongs to case pi if $((en_i, CE_i), pi) \in bind$. Note that $bind$ is a relation and not a function. This way the same event occurrence may yield events in different process instances. For example, the cancelation of a concert may influence many bookings.

Relation $bind$ allows us to associate events to cases. This, combined with the timestamps and activity names, enables the construction of event logs.

6.3 Classify: Relate Process Instances to Processes

After scoping and binding, we have a set of events related to process instances. Since we can reconstruct the object model before and after each event occurrence, we can add all kinds of optional element attributes. Hence, we can create a conventional event log with a rich set of attributes. However, as process-mining techniques mature it becomes interesting to compare different groups of process instances (Aalst, 2013b). Instead of creating one event log, it is often insightful to create multiple event logs. For example, to compare the booking process for two concerts we create two event logs and compare the process-mining results.

To allow for *comparative process mining*, process instances are classified using a relation $class \subseteq PI \times CL$ with CL the set of classes. Consider for example the study process of students taking a particular course. Rather than creating one process model for all students, one could create (1) a process model for students that passed and a process model for students that failed, (2) a process model for male students and a process model for female students, or (3) a process model for Dutch students and a process model for international students. Note that $class \subseteq PI \times CL$ does not require a strict partitioning of the process instances, e.g., a case may belong to multiple classes.

In (Aalst, 2013b), the notion of *process cubes* was proposed to allow for comparative process mining. In a process cube events are organized using different dimensions. Each cell in the process cube corresponds to a set of events that can be used to discover a process model, to check conformance, or to discover bottlenecks. Process cubes are inspired by the well-known OLAP (Online Analytical Processing) data cubes and associated operations such as slice, dice, roll-up, and drill-down (Chaudhuri & Dayal, 1997). However, there are also significant differences because of the process-related nature of event data. For example, process discovery based on events is incomparable to computing the average or sum over a set of numerical values. Moreover, dimensions related to process instances (e.g. male versus female students), subprocesses (e.g. group assignments versus individual assignments), organizational entities (e.g. students versus lecturers), and time (e.g. years or semesters) are semantically different and it is challenging to slice, dice, roll-up, and drill-down process-mining results efficiently.

As mentioned before, we deliberately remain at the conceptual level and do not focus on a particular DBMS. However, the "scope, bind, and classify" approach allows for the transformation of database updates into events populating process cubes that can be used for a variety of process-mining analyses.

7 Related Work

The reader is referred to (Aalst, 2011) for an introduction to process mining. Alternatively, one can consult the Process Mining Manifesto (IEEE Task Force on Process Mining, 2011) for best practices and the main challenges in process mining. Next to the automated discovery of the underlying process based on raw event data, there are process-mining techniques to analyze bottlenecks, to uncover hidden inefficiencies, to check compliance, to explain deviations, to predict performance, and to guide users towards "better" processes. Dozens (if not hundreds) of process-mining techniques are available and their value has been proven in many case studies. For example, dozens of process discovery (Aalst, 2011; Aalst et al., 2010; Aalst, Weijters, & Maruster, 2004; Agrawal, Gunopulos, & Leymann, 1998; Gaaloul, Gaaloul, Bhiri, Haller, & Hauswirth, 2009; Bergenthum, Desel, Lorenz, & Mauser, 2007; Carmona & Cortadella, 2010; Carmona, Cortadella, & Kishinevsky, 2008; Cook & Wolf, 1998; Goedertier, Martens, Vanthienen, & Baesens, 2009; Medeiros, Weijters, & Aalst, 2007; Sole & Carmona, 2010; Weijters & Aalst, 2003; Werf, Dongen, Hurkens, & Serebrenik, 2010) and conformance checking (Aalst, Adriansyah, & Dongen, 2012; Adriansyah, Dongen, & Aalst, 2011a, 2011b; Adriansyah, Sidorova, & Dongen, 2011c; Calders, Guenther, Pechenizkiy, & Rozinat, 2009; Cook & Wolf, 1999; Goedertier et al., 2009; Munoz-Gama & Carmona, 2010; Munoz-Gama & Carmona, 2011; Rozinat & Aalst, 2008; Weerdt, De Backer, Vanthienen, & Baesens, 2011) approaches have been proposed in literature. However, this paper is not about new process-mining techniques but about getting the event data needed for all of these techniques. We are not aware of any work systematically transforming database updates into event logs. Probably, there are process-mining case-studies using redo/transaction logs from database management systems like Oracle RDBMS, Microsoft SQL server, IBM DB2, or Sybase IQ. However, systematic tool support seems to be missing.

The binding step in our approach is related to topic of event correlation which has been investigated in the (web) services (Aalst, 2013c). In Aalst, Mooij, Stahl, and Wolf (2009) and Barros, Decker, Dumas, and Weber (2007) various interaction and correlation patterns are described. In Pauw et al. (2005) a technique is presented for correlating messages with the goal to visualize the execution of web services. Also Montahari-Nezhad, Saint-Paul, Casati, & Benatallah (2011) developed techniques for event correlation and process discovery from web service interaction logs.

Most closely related seem to be the work on artifact-centric process mining (ACSI, 2013; Fahland, Leoni, Dongen, & Aalst, 2011a; 2011b), process model repositories (Rosa et al., 2011), event log extraction (Verbeek et al., 2010; Günther & Aalst, 2006), and process cubes (Aalst, 2013b). However, none of these approaches define an event model on top of a class model.

8 Conclusion

To drive innovation in an increasingly digitalized world, the "process scientist" needs to have powerful tools. Recent advances in process mining provide such tools, but cannot be applied easily to selections of the Internet of Events (IoE) where data is heterogeneous and distributed. Process mining seeks the "confrontation" between real event data and process models (automatically discovered or hand-made). The 15 case studies listed on the web page of the IEEE Task Force on

Process Mining (IEEE Task Force on Process Mining, 2013a) illustrate the applicability of process mining. Process mining can be used to check conformance, detect bottlenecks, and suggest process improvements. However, the most time-consuming part of process mining is not the actual analysis. Most time is spent on locating, selecting, converting, and filtering the event data. The *twelve guidelines for logging* presented in this paper show that the input-side of process mining deserves much more attention. Logging can be improved by better instrumenting systems. However, we can also try to better use what is already there and widely uses: database systems. This paper focused on supporting *the systematic extraction of event data from database systems.*

Regular tables in a database provide a view of the actual state of the information system. For process mining, however, it is interesting to know when a record was created, updated, or deleted. *Taking the viewpoint that the database reflects the current state of one or more processes, we define all changes of the database to be events.* In this paper, we conceptualized this viewpoint. Building upon class and object models, we defined the notion of an event model. The event model relates changes to the underlying database to events used for process mining. Based on such an event model, we defined the "scope, bind, and classify" approach that creates a collection of event logs that can be used for comparative process mining.

In this paper we only conceptualized the different ideas. A logical next step is to develop tool support for specific database management systems. Moreover, we would like to relate this to our work on process cubes (Aalst, 2013b) for comparative process mining.

Acknowledgements This work was supported by the Basic Research Program of the National Research University Higher School of Economics (HSE) in Moscow.

References

Aalst, W. van der (2011). *Process mining: Discovery, conformance and enhancement of business processes*. Berlin: Springer.

Aalst, W. van der (2013a). Business process management: A comprehensive survey. *ISRN Software Engineering*, 1–37. doi:10.1155/2013/507984

Aalst, W. van der (2013b). Process cubes: Slicing, dicing, rolling up and drilling down event data for process mining. In M. Song, M. Wynn, & J. Liu (Eds.), *Asia Pacific Conference on Business Process Management (AP-BPM 2013)* (Lecture Notes in Business Information Processing, Vol. 159, pp. 1–22). Berlin: Springer.

Aalst, W. van der (2013c). Service mining: Using process mining to discover, check, and improve service behavior. *IEEE Transactions on Services Computing, 6*(4), 525–535.

Aalst, W. van der (2014). Data scientist: The engineer of the future. In K. Mertins, F. Benaben, R. Poler, & J. Bourrieres (Eds.), *Proceedings of the I-ESA Conference* (Enterprise Interoperability, Vol. 6, pp. 13–28). Berlin: Springer.

Aalst, W. van der, Adriansyah, A., & Dongen, B. van (2012). Replaying history on process models for conformance checking and performance analysis. *WIREs Data Mining and Knowledge Discovery, 2*(2), 182–192.

Aalst, W. van der, Barthelmess, P., Ellis, C., & Wainer, J. (2001). Proclets: A framework for lightweight interacting workflow processes. *International Journal of Cooperative Information Systems, 10*(4), 443–482.

Aalst, W. van der, Mooij, A., Stahl, C., & Wolf, K. (2009). Service interaction: Patterns, formalization, and analysis. In M. Bernardo, L. Padovani, & G. Zavattaro (Eds.), *Formal methods for web services* (Lecture Notes in Computer Science, Vol. 5569, pp. 42–88). Berlin: Springer.

Aalst, W. van der, Rubin, V., Verbeek, H., Dongen, B. van, Kindler, E., & Günther, C. (2010). Process mining: A two-step approach to balance between underfitting and overfitting. *Software and Systems Modeling, 9*(1), 87–111.

Aalst, W. van der, & Stahl, C. (2011). *Modeling business processes: A petri net oriented approach*. Cambridge, MA: MIT Press.

Aalst, W. van der, Weijters, A., & Maruster, L. (2004). Workflow mining: Discovering process models from event logs. *IEEE Transactions on Knowledge and Data Engineering, 16*(9), 1128–1142.

ACSI. (2013). *Artifact-centric service interoperation (ACSI) project home page*. Retrieved from www.acsi-project.eu

Adriansyah, A., Dongen, B. van, & Aalst, W. van der (2011a). Conformance checking using cost-based fitness analysis. In C. Chi & P. Johnson (Eds.), *IEEE International Enterprise Computing Conference (EDOC 2011)* (pp. 55–64). IEEE Computer Society Washington, DC, USA.

Adriansyah, A., Dongen, B., & Aalst, W. van der (2011b). Towards robust conformance checking. In M. Muehlen & J. Su (Eds.), *BPM 2010 Workshops, Proceedings of the Sixth Workshop on Business Process Intelligence (BPI2010)* (Lecture Notes in Business Information Processing, Vol. 66, pp. 122–133). Berlin: Springer.

Adriansyah, A., Sidorova, N., & Dongen, B. van (2011c). Cost-based fitness in conformance checking. In *International Conference on Application of Concurrency to System Design (ACSD 2011)* (pp. 57–66). IEEE Computer Society Washington, DC, USA.

Agrawal, R., Gunopulos, D., & Leymann, F. (1998). Mining process models from workflow logs. In *Sixth International Conference on Extending Database Technology* (Lecture Notes in Computer Science, Vol. 1377, pp. 469–483). Berlin: Springer.

Ana Karla Alves de Medeiros, Weijters, A., & Aalst, W. van der (2007). Genetic process mining: An experimental evaluation. *Data Mining and Knowledge Discovery, 14*(2), 245–304.

Barros, A., Decker, G., Dumas, M., & Weber, F. (2007). Correlation patterns in service-oriented architectures. In M. Dwyer & A. Lopes (Eds.), *Proceedings of the 10th International Conference on Fundamental Approaches to Software Engineering (FASE 2007)* (Lecture Notes in Computer Science, Vol. 4422, pp. 245–259). Berlin: Springer.

Bergenthum, R., Desel, J., Lorenz, R., & Mauser, S. (2007). Process mining based on regions of languages. In G. Alonso, P. Dadam, & M. Rosemann (Eds.), *International Conference on Business Process Management (BPM 2007)* (Lecture Notes in Computer Science, Vol. 4714, pp. 375–383). Berlin: Springer.

Brocke, J., & Rosemann, M. (Eds.). (2010). *Handbook on business process management, international handbooks on information systems*. Berlin: Springer.

Calders, T., Guenther, C., Pechenizkiy, M., & Rozinat, A. (2009). Using minimum description length for process mining. In *ACM Symposium on Applied Computing (SAC 2009)* (pp. 1451–1455). New York, NY: ACM Press.

Carmona, J., & Cortadella, J. (2010). Process mining meets abstract interpretation. In J. Balcazar (Ed.), *ECML/PKDD 210* (Lecture Notes in Artificial Intelligence, Vol. 6321, pp. 184–199). Berlin: Springer.

Carmona, J., Cortadella, J., & Kishinevsky, M. (2008). A region-based algorithm for discovering petri nets from event logs. In *Business Process Management (BPM2008)* (pp. 358–373). Berlin: Springer.

Chaudhuri, S., & Dayal, U. (1997). An overview of data warehousing and OLAP technology. *ACM Sigmod Record, 26*(1), 65–74.

Chen, P. (1976). The entity-relationship model: Towards a unified view of data. *ACM Transactions on Database Systems, 1*, 9–36.

Cohn, D., & Hull, R. (2009). Business artifacts: A data-centric approach to modeling business operations and processes. *IEEE Data Engineering Bulletin, 32*(3), 3–9.

Cook, J., & Wolf, A. (1998). Discovering models of software processes from event-based data. *ACM Transactions on Software Engineering and Methodology, 7*(3), 215–249.

Cook, J., & Wolf, A. (1999). Software process validation: Quantitatively measuring the correspondence of a process to a model. *ACM Transactions on Software Engineering and Methodology, 8*(2), 147–176.

Dumas, M., Marcello La Rosa, M., Mendling, J., & Reijers, H. (2013). *Fundamentals of business process management*. Berlin: Springer.

Fahland, D., Massimiliano de Leoni, Dongen, B. van, & Aalst, W. van der (2011a). Behavioral conformance of artifact-centric process models. In A. Abramowicz (Ed.), *Business Information Systems (BIS 2011)* (Lecture Notes in Business Information Processing, Vol. 87, pp. 37–49). Berlin: Springer.

Fahland, D., Massimiliano de Leoni, Dongen, B. van, & Aalst, W. van der (2011b). Many-to-many: Some observations on interactions in artifact choreographies. In D. Eichhorn, A. Koschmider, & H. Zhang (Eds.), *Proceedings of the 3rd Central-European Workshop on Services and their Composition (ZEUS 2011), CEUR-WS.org, CEUR Workshop Proceedings* (pp. 9–15).

Gaaloul, W., Gaaloul, K., Bhiri, S., Haller, A., & Hauswirth, M. (2009). Log-based transactional workflow mining. *Distributed and Parallel Databases, 25*(3), 193–240.

Goedertier, S., Martens, D., Vanthienen, J., & Baesens, B. (2009). Robust process discovery with artificial negative events. *Journal of Machine Learning Research, 10*, 1305–1340.

Günther, C., & Aalst, W. van der (2006). A generic import framework for process event logs. In J. Eder & S. Dustdar (Eds.), *Business Process Management Workshops, Workshop on Business Process Intelligence (BPI 2006)* (Lecture Notes in Computer Science, Vol. 4103, pp. 81–92). Berlin: Springer.

Hofstede, A. ter, Aalst, W. van der, Adams, M., & Russell, N. (2010). *Modern business process automation: YAWL and its support environment*. Berlin: Springer.

IEEE Task Force on Process Mining. (2011). Process mining manifesto. In *BPM Workshops* (Lecture Notes in Business Information Processing, Vol. 99). Berlin: Springer.

IEEE Task Force on Process Mining. (2013a). *Process mining case studies*. Retrieved from http://www.win.tue.nl/ieeetfpm/doku.php?id=shared:process_mining_case_studies

IEEE Task Force on Process Mining. (2013b). *XES standard definition*. Retrieved from www.xes-standard.org

Jagadeesh Chandra Bose, R.P., Mans, R., & Aalst, W. van der (2013). Wanna improve process mining results? It's high time we consider data quality issues seriously. In B. Hammer, Z. Zhou, L. Wang, & N. Chawla (Eds.), *IEEE Symposium on Computational Intelligence and Data Mining (CIDM 2013)* (pp. 127–134). Singapore: IEEE.

Montahari-Nezhad, H., Saint-Paul, R., Casati, F., & Benatallah, B. (2011). Event correlation for process discovery from web service interaction logs. *VLBD Journal, 20*(3), 417–444.

Munoz-Gama, J., & Carmona, J. (2010). A fresh look at precision in process conformance. In R. Hull, J. Mendling, & S. Tai (Eds.), *Business Process Management (BPM 2010)* (Lecture Notes in Computer Science, Vol. 6336, pp. 211–226). Berlin: Springer.

Munoz-Gama, J., & Carmona, J. (2011). Enhancing precision in process conformance: Stability, confidence and severity. In N. Chawla, I. King, & A. Sperduti (Eds.), *IEEE Symposium on Computational Intelligence and Data Mining (CIDM 2011)* (pp. 184–191). Paris: IEEE.

OMG. (2009). *Unified modeling language, infrastructure and superstructure (Version 2.2, OMG final adopted specification)*. http://www.omg.org/spec/UML/2.2/

Pauw, W., Lei, M., Pring, E., Villard, L., Arnold, M., & Morar, J. (2005). Web services navigator: Visualizing the execution of web services. *IBM Systems Journal, 44*(4), 821–845.

Reichert, M., & Weber, B. (2012). *Enabling flexibility in process-aware information systems: Challenges, methods, technologies*. Berlin: Springer.
Rosa, M. La, Reijers, H., Aalst, W. van der, Dijkman, R., Mendling, J., Dumas, M., et al. (2011). APROMORE: An advanced process model repository. *Expert Systems with Applications, 38* (6), 7029–7040.
Rozinat, A., & Aalst, W. van der (2008). Conformance checking of processes based on monitoring real behavior. *Information Systems, 33*(1), 64–95.
Sole, M., & Carmona, J. (2010). Process mining from a basis of regions. In J. Lilius & W. Penczek (Eds.), *Applications and Theory of Petri Nets 2010* (Lecture Notes in Computer Science, Vol. 6128, pp. 226–245). Berlin: Springer.
Verbeek, H., Buijs, J., Dongen, B. van, & Aalst, W. van der (2010). XES, XESame, and ProM 6. In P. Soffer & E. Proper (Eds.), *Information systems evolution* (Lecture Notes in Business Information Processing, Vol. 72, pp. 60–75). Berlin: Springer.
Weerdt, J., De Backer, M., Vanthienen, J., & Baesens, B. (2011). A robust f-measure for evaluating discovered process models. In N. Chawla, I. King, & A. Sperduti (Eds.), *IEEE Symposium on Computational Intelligence and Data Mining (CIDM 2011)* (pp. 148–155). Paris: IEEE.
Weijters, A., & Aalst, W. van der (2003). Rediscovering workflow models from event-based data using little thumb. *Integrated Computer-Aided Engineering, 10*(2), 151–162.
Werf, J., Dongen, B. van, Hurkens, C., & Serebrenik, A. (2010). Process discovery using integer linear programming. *Fundamenta Informaticae, 94*, 387–412.
Weske, M. (2007). *Business process management: Concepts, languages, architectures*. Berlin: Springer.

Evidence-Based Business Process Management: Using Digital Opportunities to Drive Organizational Innovation

Jan Recker

Abstract

Process improvement and innovation are risky endeavors, like swimming in unknown waters. In this chapter, I will discuss how process innovation through BPM can benefit from Research-as-a-Service, that is, from the application of research concepts in the processes of BPM projects. A further subject will be how innovations can be converted from confidence-based to evidence-based models due to affordances of digital infrastructures such as large-scale enterprise software or social media. I will introduce the relevant concepts, provide illustrations for digital capabilities that allow for innovation, and share a number of key takeaway lessons for how organizations can innovate on the basis of digital opportunities and principles of evidence-based BPM: the foundation of all process decisions in facts rather than fiction.

1 Introduction

One of the key trends that we currently witness not only in academic circles but also in industry—all throughout Australia at least—is that "Innovation" is becoming an important driver for business projects, for change agendas—and in turn, for Business Process Management initiatives.

The first thing that people typically associate with innovation is the development of new products and new technologies. We might go even further and classify innovations in terms of how 'novel', 'appropriate' or 'valuable' these might be. But increasingly, innovation is also seen as applicable to the development of new service offerings, new business models, new processes or new management

J. Recker (✉)
Information Systems School, Queensland University of Technology, 2 George Street, Brisbane, QLD 4000, Australia
e-mail: j.recker@qut.edu.au

J. vom Brocke, T. Schmiedel (eds.), *BPM – Driving Innovation in a Digital World*, Management for Professionals, DOI 10.1007/978-3-319-14430-6_9

practices. Today, there is a greater recognition that novel ideas can transform just about any part of the value chain, and just about every asset and element in an organizational system—and that products and services represent just the tip of the innovation iceberg. Think about it. Steve Job's key innovation was not the i-device itself, it was the business model that centered around this piece of technology, and the novel processes with which people could interact, use, develop, apply or make money on the basis of this technology. So, innovation is much more than a novel product or piece of technology. Thus, the physical IPhone was the obvious attractor, but it was the App store that created an innovative and novel business model that provided a separate ongoing value proposition and added income stream.

What we learn from this example is that innovation is not only deceptively complex but also often a composition of overlapping innovations of different sorts (e.g., new products combined with new process platforms create entire new business models). Focusing on any one type of innovation in itself thus limits our explanatory power as well as our ability to replicate or benefit from innovations.

The increased attention to viewing innovation as a multi-faceted phenomenon that goes well beyond product development brings it also into the focus of process management—where the key organizational asset of focus has always been the 'way an organization manages and executes its work procedures.

The connection between process innovation and process management is by no means new. Colleagues would argue that process innovation was one of the waves that preceded the current enterprise-wide focus on holistically managed business processes. For one thing, Thomas Davenport (1993) published a book on process innovation already in 1993. Today, we understand that process innovation is only one of the many ways in which processes can be improved. Other examples include re-engineering, re-designing or even re-thinking processes (Curtis, 2005).

So, while all would argue and claim that there is indeed an intimate connection between process management and innovation as a key agenda item for organizations, the question remains precisely how this connection manifests itself and—more importantly—specifically how process management can aid organizational innovation.

In this chapter, I will outline some of the challenges of organizational innovation, and then link them back to principles of Research-as-a-Service and Evidence-based Management. Research-as-a-Service describes the idea of applying principles of scientific research, such as independent observation, hypothesis testing and novel conceptual perspectives, to all decision-making processes in management. This, in turn, allows that process management decisions can be made on the basis of facts (evidence) rather than beliefs and perceptions (confidence). I have labeled this type of integration *Evidence-based Process Innovation*, and I will try to illustrate how organizations can innovate on the basis of digital opportunities, evidence-based decisions and principles of BPM.

2 The Innovation Challenge

Innovation is one of the driving forces for redistributing wealth in free markets. While innovation is not necessarily linked to information technology, it is well-established that successful technology innovation can lead to new businesses, can change existing businesses through the introduction of new business models (Chesbrough, 2010), products or services or can change internal procedures and culture to yield higher degrees of efficiency. Clearly, innovative information technology solutions drive organizational change (Markus & Robey, 1988). In fact, new products and services can be sufficiently successful to create entirely new markets (Berry, Shankar, Parish, Cadwallader, & Dotzel, 2006). Conversely, a lack of successful transformation following technology innovation can lead to bankruptcy of established businesses (Lucas & Goh, 2009), more and fiercer competition for established businesses by later market entrants that copy existing models, products or solutions, or, in the best case, a stagnant business.

Approaches to innovation are great in number and exist in isolation as well as in combination. Well-known efforts to create organizational innovation include projects conducted in facilities that are decisively not co-located with corporate headquarters or other corporate offices (Anthony, 2012), conducted through open innovation with customers or other stakeholders (Chesbrough, 2003), or through a focus on mergers and acquisitions to source innovative new products, services or business models. On the other hand, there are numerous examples of case studies of failed innovation (Lucas & Goh, 2009) and attempts to examine the tensions between technology innovations and the institutionalized practices prior to that innovation (Tushman & Anderson, 1986).

There are different types of innovation (Nagji & Tuff, 2012), but key decision makers still struggle to identify, let alone direct the different pathways to successful innovation. Moreover, yielding predictable results from innovation processes is hard. Notably, unsuccessful innovation has its place too. Organizations need to learn to fail, learn how to fail fast and learn from their failures in order to embrace an innovation culture and strategy, all of which are capabilities largely absent in contemporary organizations (Edmondson, 2011) and very hard to attain (Baumard & Starbuck, 2005).

Solutions to a lack of innovation need to address various aspects of primarily cultural and strategic nature at an organization's executive and board level (Leavy, 2005), characterizing innovation as an essential multi-level problem involving essential linkages between different individual and organizational levels. Once an organization has established a strategic framework and defined desirable values and beliefs, it needs to develop processes, skills and capabilities to ensure proper execution of innovation projects (Dreiling & Recker, 2013).

3 Evidence-Based Management

Innovations are essentially complex decision-making problems made under uncertain conditions. This is because innovations require decisions about unstructured and complex problems, the trajectory and solutions of which lie in the future. Risk of failure is high and questions abound: What is a good innovation idea? Which idea should be implemented? Which will be successful? Which innovation option is truly innovative, which will be a waste of money?

Usually, research is performed to tackle and solve such complex problems. Indeed, if problems were not complex, there would be no need for research altogether.

It is on the basis of this connection that an argument can be made that innovation requires research-as-a-service to make innovation work in an organization. But the reality is, of course, that researchers are rarely involved in organizational innovations, and that organizational innovation tends to be seen more as a (co-) *design* exercise rather than a *research* project.

Maybe this is because innovation is a business issue and business and management professionals have always and rightfully emphasized real-world relevance over academic rigor (Clinebell & Clinebell, 2008).

There are other professional communities that value research more, and actively create practices following the research-as-a-service model. Medicine is an example. Evidence-based medicine is promoted as a paradigm in which practice uses timely and relevant research for making clinical decisions (Rosenberg & Donald, 1995). The same principle has also been lauded as evidence-based management (Pfeffer & Sutton, 2006), which is gaining practice in organizational management. One of the most prominent cases-in-point is Michael Lewis's story "Moneyball", which tells the story of the introduction of the sabermetric model to baseball, and is an approach to empirically analyze baseball in-game statistics to support team management decisions such as player sourcing and on-field composition (Lewis, 2003). The adoption of the sabermetric model allowed the Boston Red Sox to win the 2004 championship—after having been unsuccessful since 1918.

Thus, in conclusion, evidence-based management, just like scientific research, is fact based. This means that in decision-making, solid facts are valued over conventional wisdom, status, confidence and common practice. Table 1 summarizes principles of conventional and evidence-based decision-making.

Important to evidence-based management is the realization that the quality of evidence or facts may vary. Two important quality criteria that are typically used to gauge the quality of facts are called validity and reliability (Recker, 2012):

- **Validity** is about whether our evidence comprises accurate measurements of whatever it is that we intended to measure. Anyone that ever stepped on two different weighing scales and received two different results will know that either one or both of the measurements were invalid.
- **Reliability** is about whether our evidence gathering was consistent and replicable. Can it be repeated with the same results, independent of whom we asked?

Table 1 Differences in decision-making

Conventional decision-making	Evidence-based decision making
Relying on status (confidence) rather than facts (evidence)	Seeking an understanding of true cause-effect relations
Using flawed decision models	Realizing the availability of potential evidence
	Opposing tradition, intuition, folklore and rules of thumb

> For example, asking 20 individuals about the performance of a particular mission-critical process is likely to yield 20 different estimates—indicating a lack of consistency in our evidence that we can use to make important decisions about an important process.[1]

Validity and reliability of evidence will vary depending on how the facts have been gathered; viz., what the underlying *research design* looks like. Some research designs provide a stronger level of evidence than others, based on their inherent characteristics. Therefore, evidence-based management requires a basic understanding of the main research designs underlying potential and available evidence. This hierarchy is often shown graphically as a pyramid (see Fig. 1).

The pyramid is an appropriate shape for this graphic, as it represents the quality of evidence and their corresponding research designs by level, and it also conveys how much evidence is actually being gathered through such a design, i.e., what is the quantity of evidence at the different levels. For example, Fig. 1 suggests that most decisions rely on expert opinions (and are therefore susceptible to bias from assumptions), while only few decisions are made based on randomized controlled studies (such as those performed in medicine to test new drugs and medications). For example, many innovation workshops involve experts about the field, the product, the method, and so forth, whose opinions are typically highly valued. Academics, of course, are also within this category. Similarly, many workshop facilitators and leaders use case studies (such as narratives, or even YouTube videos) to convey messages such as "we should be doing this too". Cases—or videos and stories of cases—can provide only limited evidence, simply because they cannot guarantee whether whatever works in one case or context will actually work in another. This problem is called lack of external validity—we don't know whether what we have learned transcends the boundaries of the particular case.

Of course, not all management decisions require evidence-producing research on the basis of controlled experiments and the like. As a case in point, the article about the effectiveness of parachutes (Smith & Pell, 2003) can be recommended. Still,

[1] Of course, interviewing per se is not necessarily unreliable or inappropriate. In fact, interviewing can be a very usefulness method to scientifically explore different situations—for example how appropriate BPM practitioners—in that organization—judge an organizational culture (Schmiedel, vom Brocke, & Recker, 2013). Interviewing can thus become a very useful method for fact finding—but not necessarily for fact checking or hypothesis testing.

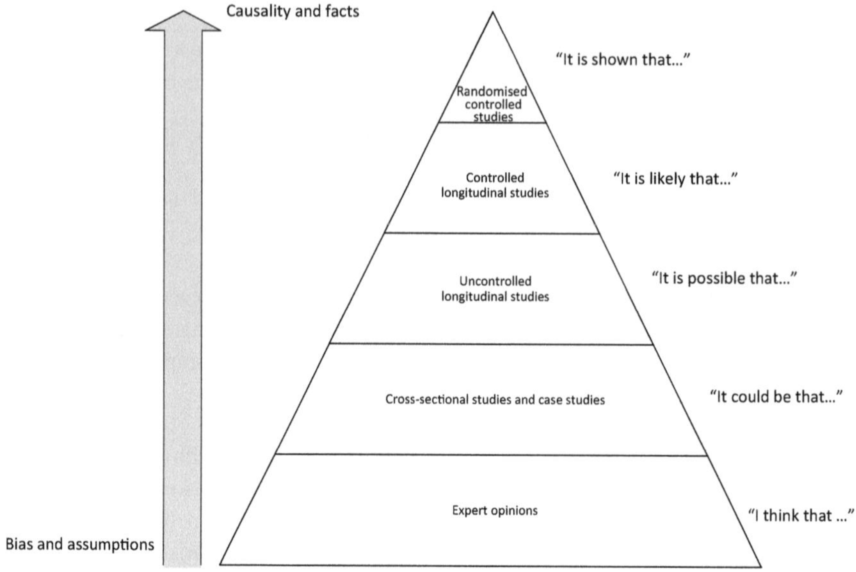

Fig. 1 Levels of evidence

innovation decisions are—as noted above, complex problems under uncertainty and typically concern high risks of failure, potential lack of return on investment or even disruption or failure of entire business models (Lucas & Goh, 2009). Clearly, evidence and fact-based decisions have their place in such endeavors.

4 Research-as-a-Service

To develop evidence-based management capabilities in an organization, that is, to assist organizations in valuing and practicing fact-based decision-making, research can play an essential role as an **innovation support service**.

Moving to reliable, valid and ultimately credible decisions about innovations through evidence-based decision-making requires an ability to work with data and to use scientific analysis principles. For example, innovators need to have an understanding of *appropriate*, *available* and *quality* data that can be used as evidence. They also require a capability to *collect*, *analyze* and *interpret* such data to prepare for decisions. Table 2 summarizes relevant requirements.

These scientific capabilities can obviously be provided by universities and research institutions. And indeed, there is strong evidence to suggest that partnerships between corporate organizations and research institutions can improve innovativeness and performance (Perkmann & Salter, 2012). However, scientific analysis skills are also increasingly sought as an internal capability (Davenport & Patil, 2012).

Table 2 Requirements for evidence-based innovation decisions

Capability	Requirements
Data awareness	Identifying appropriate data
	Finding available data
	Understanding the quality of data
Science appreciation	Understanding validity and reliability of methods and evidence
	Analyzing statistical significance and sample size
	Managing replication and bias
Information management	Determining appropriate analyses
	Identifying appropriate result visualizations
	Considering limitations and assumptions
	Communicating effectively and accurately

Beyond the sheer ability to gather, analyze and interpret data using rigorous scientific methods, research can provide additional innovation support services:

- **Novel conceptual perspectives:** Research can offer new perspectives on an existing problem by proposing and exploring different conceptualizations of an issue or paths to a solution. The example of positive deviance (Spreitzer & Sonenshein, 2004) below is a case in point.
- **Rigorous scientific principles:** The evaluation of innovation ideas and decisions alongside the organizational innovation process (Dreiling & Recker, 2013) can benefit from established principles of science, which have governed the quality evaluation of research studies for centuries, and which, once followed, provide trust in the evidence that forms the basis for innovation decisions.
- **Quality empirical evidence:** Evidence that is converted from data gathered and analyzed scientifically can provide a solid and trustworthy platform for decision-making about innovations, their potential, pitfalls and consequences.
- **Increased research bandwidth:** Research institutes provide extra bandwidth to conduct research, to design potential solutions and prototypes and to explore opportunities for which organizations often do not have the resource or time. In turn, project teams are reinforced by experts who expand the overall bandwidth of resources and provide the knowledge needed for innovation.
- **Unbiased observation:** One key governing paradigm of science is the notion of unbiased observation, that is, the desire to remain as objective as possible by following principles of replicability, independence, precision and falsification (Recker, 2012). This, in turn, also means that researchers often are not biased by organizational cultures, inter-personal relationships or power structures. Moreover, researches often lack the tradition of field expertise stemming from years of practice—which also means they simply do not know conventional wisdom, heuristics and assumptions that may bias decisions about "what" or "how" to innovate.

5 Digital Opportunities for Innovation and Evidence-Based Management

Digital infrastructures play a major role in enabling the use of evidence-based management decisions in process innovation. This is because they allow analysts and managers alike to readily and effectively access and gather objective data that can be used as facts in innovation decisions.

I use the term digital infrastructure in a deliberately loose manner, as an umbrella term to capture all sorts of Information Technology platforms—those that exist to facilitate and enact organizational processes (think or SAP or Oracle solutions), those that transcend organizational and private domains and are used by individuals to connect, share and collaborate (think of social networking or social media) as well as those that exist specifically to create and assist process management and innovation efforts (such as BPM engines, modeling tools or those that allow for open innovation, idea exchange or collaborative design). While some of these technologies, such as enterprise system software, have been around for decades, recent years have also seen a rapid uptake of modern digital infrastructures that transcend the business-private life boundary, such as social networking platforms, or complement historical transaction data with real-time data and analytics, such as in-memory technology.

These digital infrastructures provide ample opportunities for evidence-based management in process innovation. Some of their affordances include:

- **Footprinting:** all actions, decisions and processes carried out on digital infrastructures leave a trace. In turn, all behaviors performed on these technologies can be studied, ex post or even in real-time, in turn creating a wealth of facts of what people have really done and what a process really looks like in reality. This knowledge, which can be mined (van der Aalst, 2011), allows for insights into the existing organizational processes that are in need of innovation; or indeed about the innovation processes themselves.
- **Crowdsourcing:** Most digital infrastructures provide platforms that connect a multitude of users who are geographically and temporally dispersed. This means that every problem that is normally confined to a particular place and time—in the digital world—can be offered to others outside the team, office location or even the organization itself for them to weigh in, explore the problem and offer suggestions. This affordance is creating unheard capacity for open innovation (Chesbrough, 2003), for innovation collaboration (Malsbender, Recker, Kohlborn, Beverungen, & Tanwer, 2013) or for crowdsolving solutions to complex problems (Doan, Ramakrishnan, & Halevy, 2011).
- **Analytics:** Modern digital infrastructures often provide not only facts about behaviors on these platforms or access to other resources and users, but typically also advantages in analytics and computing power; that is, while more data can be generated, more can also be analyzed and used. A classical example is that of Google Analytics that offers free analysis of web browsing behavior, ready at the fingertips of any decision-maker. A more recent trend is in-memory technology,

which provides affordances to process and analyze large volumes of data in real-time (vom Brocke, Debortoli, Müller, & Reuter, 2014).

- **Scaling:** Finally, digital infrastructures provide a frequently overlooked element relevant to fact-finding and evidence-based decision-making: the opportunity to scale up the sheer quantity of available observations, facts et al. Traditionally, fact finding in support of decision-making—in the context of BPM methodologies such as Six Sigma and others—has always been hampered by sheer pragmatic concerns about the feasibility, resourcing and costing of data collection efforts. Data that is generated on digital platforms is typically located at the other end of the scale: Data points are generated well beyond the sample size required to reach conclusive findings about the data. Whereas in the past we relied on observing or interviewing 5–10 process participants, or following a select number of cases through the process, now digital platforms provide footprints of *all* actions ever taken by *all* participants; and store case information about *all* process instances ever generated.

In this brief enumeration of digital infrastructure affordances for evidence-based process innovation, chances are high that the list of potential uses and benefits is much longer than the characteristics I mentioned above. Still, these four attributes should already give a good indication of how the availability and emergence of these technologies allow process innovation and BPM in general to become more evidence-based than ever before. In turn, the opportunity also serves as a warning sign: It is no longer acceptable not to peruse available data and evidence in making process-related decisions. Where in the past it was appropriate (and sometimes unavoidable) to make decisions based on limited information, intuition and confidence, the boundaries of evidence are now well beyond the research of a process decision-maker, demanding evidence in support of all process recommendations, be it during the execution of business process or indeed in the efforts to create new, innovative business processes.

6 Evidence-Based Process Innovation: Two Examples

In the following, I will briefly describe two stories of evidence-based process innovations, which are based on collaborative work we have conducted over recent years with organizations in the retail sector in Australia.

6.1 Positive Deviance

Traditionally, process improvement focuses on processes whose performance is considered inadequate—below acceptable or normal standards of performance. Typically, a root cause for process failure is sought (such as a bottleneck) and a remedy implemented.

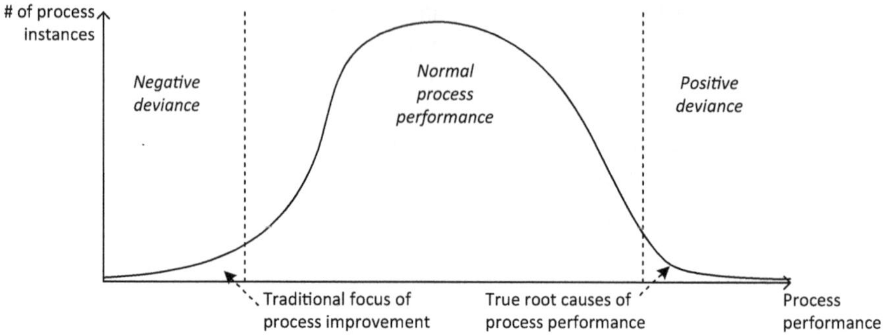

Fig. 2 Positive deviance

Positive deviance reverses this paradigm, and shifts process innovation thinking from "fixing errors" to "rewarding and learning from the best". It describes a practice that stands out from a pool of comparable practices as it shows better performance under the same environmental conditions (Spreitzer & Sonenshein, 2004). Applied to process contexts, a positive deviant is an implementation of a process that is better than the others whilst all environmental conditions are similar. Understanding how and why this process is better is thus an opportunity to increase the performance of all other processes towards the level of the positive deviant process—instead of fixing a negative deviant and bringing it closer to the performance level of a normal process (see Fig. 2).

Identifying and learning from positive deviance requires evidence—evidence about *where* the true positive deviants exist, *how* they come to be positive deviants, and *why* they are positively deviant. True positive deviants are those that are significantly better than all others. Statistically speaking, this means that positive deviants are significantly different from all others, i.e., we are searching for the 1 % of top performance that is different from the performance of all others, given similar conditions and circumstances.

Figure 3 gives an example of identifying positive deviants in bakery sales processes in a retail organization. Imagine a supermarket with an in-built bakery. Most large supermarket chains such as Tesco, Walmart, Metro, Aldi and others have these, and thus thousands of bakery departments are spread about the country or continent. So who is a positive deviant?

A positive deviant bakery is a bakery that sells more than other bakeries when we account for differences in environmental conditions—such as number of customers frequenting the supermarket every day (a bakery in Paris will always sell more bread rolls than a bakery in Vaduz, simply because more people live and eat in Paris). In Fig. 3, the bandwidth of average sales performance by the number of customers is indicated by the two lines traversing the diagram at a 45° angle. This is the normal bandwidth of performance, and 99 % of all bakeries within our sample (about ~1,000 stores, in our case) fall within this band; with some showing a better performance than others, but all behaving as expected. The positive deviants are

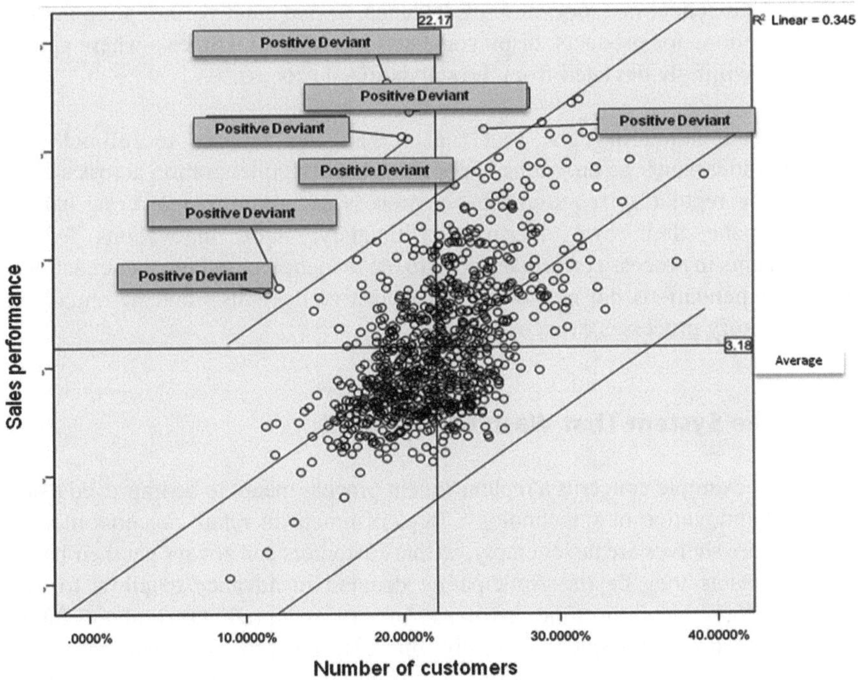

Fig. 3 Finding positive deviants: an example in retail

now those bakeries that fall outside that 99 % band—and as we can see, only 7 out of ~1,000 bakeries are true positive deviants that sell significantly more given their number of customers.

Having identified the positive deviants, the challenge lies in ascertaining how and why these processes are performing significantly better. Again, this is a research challenge where data such as store size, quality of baking, number of competitors in the market, customer demographics, in-store processes, staff attitude and motivation need to be considered. Having examined these factors by studying technology data (such as point-of-sales, HR and payroll systems, census data about customer demographics) as well as empirical data from studying the stores and process participants themselves, conclusions can be made about the occurrence of positive deviance. In a nutshell, in our example the findings were as follows:

- "It's not necessarily the process", meaning that positive deviants as well as all other bakeries followed the same process model.
- Instead, positive deviance stemmed from individual motivation and the willingness to "do something extra", such as the clever use of mark-down prices.
- The process culture mattered in that positive deviants increasingly collaborated and communicated with other departments and exchanged ideas with other bakeries.

- Process personnel is a root cause of deviance, in that creative staff were finding new solutions for products, display and service, and sometimes—where appropriate—willingly deviated from the standardized process.

The identification of these root causes then can be used to roll-out new innovation ideas such as providing support for bakery collaboration across stores, and relaxing regulatory requirements for process execution, empowering bakery staff to make their own decisions. Ultimately, these innovations led to improvements in process performance due to the evidence-based recommendations. The recommendations did not improve the positive deviants—but the remaining 99 % of bakery processes everywhere else.

6.2 The System That Wasn't to Be Used

The second example concerns a replenishment process meant to be improved using a piece of innovative new technology. Replenishment in retail concerns making sure that store shelves are never empty, so that customers can always get their hands on the products they desire. Anticipating demand in advance to allow for the delivery of products on time involves forecasting—predictions about future demands based on past sales. Typically, this essential process is carried out by experienced store managers, who use data from an information system, together with their detailed knowledge of local customers, local events and all other factors that will influence sales. This process is a key responsibility for store managers and can consume up to 70 % of their working hours every week—in turn it is very expensive in process labor costs, over and above all other costs related to transport, over-stocking or indeed lost sales due to under-stocking.

Of course, forecasting means looking into the future and as such is prone to errors due to misjudgment, fragmented and limited information, or simply human error.

One key technological innovation in replenishment processes has been the emergence of a specific kind of information system, namely, automated inventory replenishment systems, which provide order forecasts for regions or even single store outlets (e.g., Cooper, Baron, Levy, Swisher, & Gogos, 1999). If optimized, these systems can enact the replenishment process without intervention from store managers, thereby potentially saving significant amounts of store labor costs across all stores—for a large retailer, these costs amount to several tens of millions of dollars.

The key question here, however, is whether the systems provide adequate forecasts if store personnel do not insert their specialized local knowledge into the process. In simple terms, is the automated process better or more cost-effective with or without human intervention?

Considering the scale of operations of about 1,000 stores in the network, each stocking around 150,000 stock items, out of which on average 30,000 individual stock items are being considered for replenishment every day, one notices that

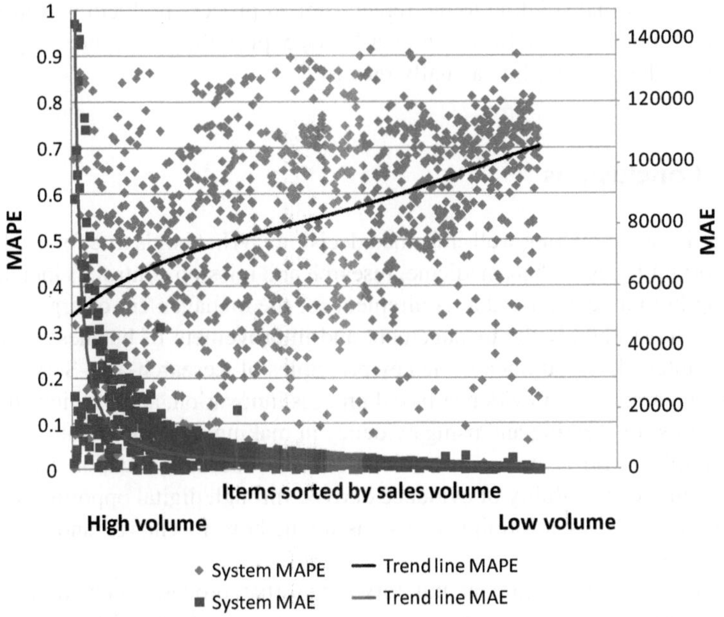

Fig. 4 Data analytics in the replenishment process

making an informed decision about the potential process improvement is a significant data analysis challenge.

Insert Research-as-a-Service. Combining evidence from past sales data, forecasting algorithms as well as observations and evidence from how store managers operate, review and change the replenishment orders allows for creating data-based facts about how the replenishment process can best be organized.

As usual, the answer is not one or the other: Neither a human nor a fully automated process alone is the most appropriate solution to this process. Instead, when examining key performance metrics such as the forecasting errors produced (how far off the forecast was, in retrospect, from actual sales)[2] it becomes evident that automated systems can create very accurate forecasts with low errors for low-volume goods, but not for high-volume goods (see Fig. 4). This means that store managers in the stores tend to have a good sense about high-sales items (such as beverages like Coca-Cola, breads and other every-day goods) perform whilst low-volume items that sell irregularly (but not necessarily make less profit) are hard to predict for humans and are better left to automated systems to forecast.

This example was meant to demonstrate that evidence can not only be used to prove whether one particular innovation is successful or not, but it can also be used to qualify or constrain an innovative solution candidate to workable conditions—in

[2] In replenishment, the forecasting error is typically measured as mean absolute error (MAE) and the mean absolute percentage error (MAPE) (Hyndman & Koehler, 2006).

this case the optimal solution to the replenishment process problem was indeed "a little bit of both"—with Research-as-a-Service providing evidence required to understand what "a little bit" actually means.

7 Conclusions

Evidence is key to making well-informed decisions. What holds true for established and important fields such as medicine, research and mission control, is increasingly becoming both a demand and a requirement for the management of organizational resources, most notably the management and improvement of business processes. In this chapter I have outlined some key principles of Research-as-a-Service as the underlying paradigm for evidence-based process innovation, and I reviewed digital opportunities for creating and using evidence in making decisions about processes. Two examples were given as illustrations of how process innovation projects can benefit from the availability of evidence derived through digital opportunities. This available evidence is informing decisions about how to change and redesign a business process.

In conclusion, the argument put forward is that process innovations require decisions about unstructured and complex problems. Risk of failure in these decisions is high, but avoidable.

Evidence-based decision-making increases process innovation reliability, credibility and, ultimately, the chance of success, and should thus be a requirement in all process innovation projects. Through advances in digital infrastructure, organizations usually have access to—but not necessarily awareness of—internal and external evidence that they can use. In order to capitalize on these digital opportunities, data scientists are becoming an essential resource in developing a capability to identify, understand, analyze and interpret evidence in support of innovation decisions about business processes.

References

Anthony, S. D. (2012). The new corporate garage. *Harvard Business Review, 90*(9), 45–53.

Baumard, P., & Starbuck, W. H. (2005). Learning from failures: Why it may not happen. *Long Range Planning, 38*(3), 281–298.

Berry, L. L., Shankar, V., Parish, J. T., Cadwallader, S., & Dotzel, T. (2006). Creating new markets through service innovation. *MIT Sloan Management Review, 47*(2), 56–63.

Chesbrough, H. W. (2003). The era of open innovation. *MIT Sloan Management Review, 44*(3), 35–41.

Chesbrough, H. W. (2010). Business model innovation: Opportunities and barriers. *Long Range Planning, 43*(2–3), 354–363.

Clinebell, S. K., & Clinebell, J. M. (2008). The tension in business education between academic rigor and real-world relevance: The role of executive professors. *Academy of Management Learning & Education, 7*(1), 99–107.

Cooper, L. G., Baron, P., Levy, W., Swisher, M., & Gogos, P. (1999). PromoCast™: A new forecasting method for promotion planning. *Marketing Science, 18*(3), 301–316.
Curtis, B. (2005). Three levels of process improvement. *BPTrends, 3*(4), 1–5.
Davenport, T. H. (1993). *Process innovation: Reengineering work through information technology*. Boston, MA: Harvard Business School Press.
Davenport, T. H., & Patil, D. J. (2012). Data scientist: The sexiest job of the 21st century. *Harvard Business Review, 90*(10), 70–76.
Doan, A., Ramakrishnan, R., & Halevy, A. Y. (2011). Crowdsourcing systems on the world-wide web. *Communications of the ACM, 54*(4), 86–96.
Dreiling, A., & Recker, J. (2013). *Towards a theoretical framework for organizational innovation*. Paper presented at the 17th Pacific Asia Conference on Information Systems, Jeju Island, Korea.
Edmondson, A. C. (2011). Strategies for learning from failure. *Harvard Business Review, 89*(4), 48–55.
Hyndman, R. J., & Koehler, A. B. (2006). Another look at measures of forecast accuracy. *International Journal of Forecasting, 22*(4), 679–688.
Leavy, B. (2005). A leader's guide to creating an innovation culture. *Strategy & Leadership, 33*(4), 38–45.
Lewis, M. M. (2003). *Moneyball: The art of winning an unfair game*. New York, NY: W. W. Norton.
Lucas, H. C., Jr., & Goh, J. M. (2009). Disruptive technology: How Kodak missed the digital photography revolution. *Journal of Strategic Information Systems, 18*(1), 46–55.
Malsbender, A., Recker, J., Kohlborn, T., Beverungen, D., & Tanwer, S. (2013). *Much ado about nothing? Tracing the progress of innovations borne on enterprise social network sites*. Paper presented at the 34th International Conference on Information Systems, Milan, Italy.
Markus, M. L., & Robey, D. (1988). Information technology and organizational change: Causal structure in theory and research. *Management Science, 34*(5), 583–598.
Nagji, B., & Tuff, G. (2012). Managing your innovation portfolio. *Harvard Business Review, 90* (5), 66–74.
Perkmann, M., & Salter, A. (2012). How to create productive partnerships with universities. *MIT Sloan Management Review, 53*(4), 79–88.
Pfeffer, J., & Sutton, R. I. (2006). Evidence-based management. *Harvard Business Review, 84*(1), 72–77.
Recker, J. (2012). *Scientific research in information systems: A beginner's guide*. Berlin: Springer.
Rosenberg, W., & Donald, A. (1995). Evidence based medicine: An approach to clinical problem-solving. *British Medical Journal, 310*(6987), 1122–1126.
Schmiedel, T., vom Brocke, J., & Recker, J. (2013). Which cultural values matter to business process management? Results from a global Delphi study. *Business Process Management Journal, 19*(52), 292–317.
Smith, G. C. S., & Pell, J. P. (2003). Parachute use to prevent death and major trauma related to gravitational challenge: Systematic review of randomised controlled trials. *British Medical Journal, 327*, 1459–1461.
Spreitzer, G. M., & Sonenshein, S. (2004). Toward the construct definition of positive deviance. *American Behavioral Scientist, 47*(6), 828–847.
Tushman, M. L., & Anderson, P. (1986). Technological discontinuities and organizational environments. *Administrative Science Quarterly, 31*(3), 439–465.
van der Aalst, W. M. P. (2011). *Process mining: Discovery, conformance and enhancement of business processes*. Heidelberg: Springer.
vom Brocke, J., Debortoli, S., Müller, O., & Reuter, N. (2014). How in-memory technology can create business value: Insights from the Hilti case. *Communications of the Association for Information Systems, 34*(7), 151–168.

Enabling Process Innovation via Deviance Mining and Predictive Monitoring

Marlon Dumas and Fabrizio Maria Maggi

Abstract

A long-standing challenge in the field of business process management is how to deal with processes that exhibit high levels of variability, such as customer lead management, product design or healthcare processes. One thing that is understood about these processes is that they require process designs and support environments that leave considerable freedom so that process workers can readily deviate from pre-established paths. At the same time, consistent management of these processes requires workers and process owners to understand the implications of their actions and decisions on the performance of the process. We present two emerging techniques—deviance mining and predictive monitoring—that leverage information hidden in business process execution logs in order to provide guidance to stakeholders so that they can steer the process towards consistent and compliant outcomes and higher process performance. Deviance mining deals with the analysis of process execution logs offline in order to identify typical deviant executions and to characterize deviance that leads to better or to worse performance. Predictive monitoring meanwhile aims at predicting—at runtime—the impact of actions and decisions of process participants on the probable outcomes of ongoing process executions. Together, these two techniques enable evidence-based management of business processes, where process workers and analysts continuously receive guidance to achieve more consistent and compliant process outcomes and a higher performance.

M. Dumas (✉) • F.M. Maggi
Institute of Computer Science, University of Tartu, J. Liivi 2, Tartu 50409, Estonia
e-mail: marlon.dumas@ut.ee; f.m.maggi@ut.ee

J. vom Brocke, T. Schmiedel (eds.), *BPM – Driving Innovation in a Digital World*,
Management for Professionals, DOI 10.1007/978-3-319-14430-6_10

1 Introduction

Traditional approaches to business process management are geared towards regular and predictable processes, where there is in essence one primary and well-understood way of performing a process, with relatively few and well-scoped variations. It is widely accepted that these approaches do not fit the requirements of more flexible processes, such as customer lead management processes, product design processes, patient treatment and related healthcare processes. Moreover, when said traditional approaches are pushed down to the level of fine-grained automation, bottom-up process innovation is stiffed, as process workers are in essence expected to follow a scripted process that tells them what to do, what data to gather and when and how to make decisions.

A number of approaches for flexible process management have emerged in recent years. One family of such approaches encompassing adaptive case management (Swenson, 2010) is based on *flexibility by underspecification* (Schonenberg, Mans, Russell, Mulyar, & van der Aalst, 2008). The idea is to underspecify the process at design-time so that process workers have the freedom to perform tasks in various ways, at almost any point in time, to leave tasks incomplete, and to collect different subsets of data at different points in the process, with as few restrictions as possible. However, while these approaches provide flexibility to process workers and allow managers to scope this flexibility, they do not per se support managers and workers in deciding what to do and when.

In this paper, we outline two emerging techniques that complement flexible process management approaches by identifying patterns of activities associated with positive or negative deviance (deviance mining) and by continuously estimating the probability that ongoing process executions may lead to undesirable outcomes (predictive monitoring). Together, these techniques turn a business process support system into a recommender system that not only enables process innovation, but also channels it towards more consistent and compliant outcomes and higher performance.

In the following section, we outline the architecture of a monitoring system integrating deviance mining and predictive monitoring. We then present each of these techniques in turn and close the paper with a discussion on future challenges on the way to the adoption of these techniques in practice.

2 Business Process Monitoring Architecture

Figure 1 sketches a high-level architecture of a business process system that supports deviance mining and predictive monitoring. The figure highlights that both techniques take as input a log of completed business process execution traces and a set of business constraints. In this context, a business constraint is any condition that can be evaluated to be true or false over every completed case of the process. A business constraint may be a service level constraint such as "every simple insurance claim should be resolved at most 2 weeks after all required

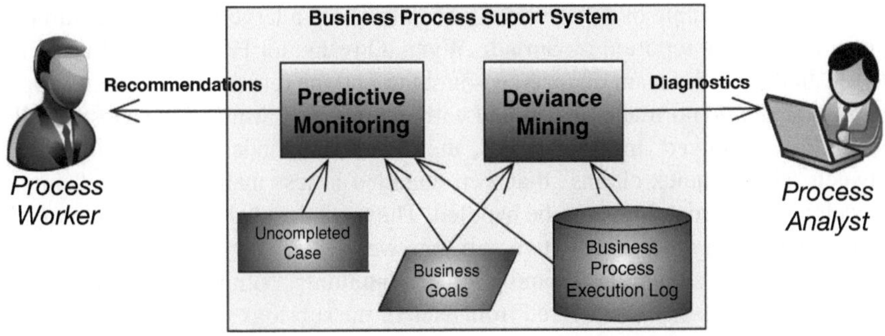

Fig. 1 Business process support with deviance mining and predictive monitoring

documents have been submitted" or it may be a compliance rule such as "every invoice above a given amount should be approved before being paid".

Given an execution log and a set of business constraints, deviance mining allows a process analyst to obtain a diagnostic that explains why certain cases deviate from the intended behavior, meaning that they outperform or underperform the given service level objectives, or fail to fulfill the compliance rules. The diagnostic can take different forms as discussed later, but in any case its purpose is to enable the analyst to identify process improvement opportunities.

Predictive monitoring on the other hand produces recommendations for process workers during the execution of a case. These recommendations refer to a specific (uncompleted) case of the process and tell the user what is the impact of a given action on the probability that the case at hand will fail to fulfill the relevant performance objectives or compliance rules. In particular, predictive monitoring can be used to raise alerts when certain actions are likely to lead to violations of business constraints. In this way, rather than prescribing what to do, the business process support system acts as a compliance monitoring and recommender system, raising flags whenever certain actions heighten the probability of undesirable deviations.

3 Deviance Mining

Business process deviance mining is a family of process mining techniques aimed at analyzing business process execution logs in order to explain the reasons why a business process deviates from its normal or expected execution. Such deviations may be of a negative or of a positive nature—cf. theory of positive deviance (Spreitzer & Sonenshein, 2004). Positive deviance corresponds to executions that lead to high process performance, such as achieving positive outcomes with low execution times, low resource usage or low costs. Negative deviance refers to the executions of the process with low process performance or with negative outcomes or compliance violations.

A concrete example of negative deviance mining in a large Australian insurance company has been reported by Suriadi, Wynn, Ouyang, ter Hofstede, and van Dijk (2013). In this case, a team of analysts sought to find the reasons why certain simple claims that should normally be handled within a few days were taking substantially longer to be resolved. In other words, they needed to understand the difference between "simple quick claims" that were handled in less than x days and "simple slow claims" that took longer to be handled. The team decided to use *delta-analysis* in this context. In other words, two sub-logs were extracted: one containing only traces of "simple slow claims" and another containing "simple quick claims". A process model was then discovered from each of the sub-logs separately—using the Disco process discovery tool[1]—and the resulting models were manually compared. It was found that certain paths and cycles were considerably more frequent for slow claims than for quick claims. The authors also found that two activity metrics were helpful in discriminating slow versus quick claims, namely "average number of occurrences of a given activity X (per case)" and "percentage of cases where a given activity X appears at least once". These two metrics basically indicate how often an activity is executed once, multiple times, or skipped. By calculating these metrics for each activity, the team found it was possible to track down the sources of delays to specific activities in the process, which then allowed them to extract specific process improvement recommendations.

A similar idea was applied by Sun, Du, Chen, Khoo, and Yang (2013) in the context of software defect handling processes in a large commercial bank in China. The authors took a log of over 2,600 defect reports of 4 large software development projects and examined the differences between reports that had led to a correct resolution (normal cases) versus those that had led to complaints by users (anomalous cases). The team defined a number of features to distinguish between normal and anomalous complaints, including "number of occurrences of a given activity X in a case" (for each possible activity X) and "number of occurrences of activity B after an activity A". Since there are many such combinations (A,B) and to avoid having too large a number of features, the authors employed a discriminative itemset mining technique to identify the most relevant of such pairs (A,B). Based on the resulting features, the authors constructed a decision tree that classifies cases into normal and anomalous. Finally, from the decision tree they extracted a set of seven rules that explained the majority of the anomalous cases, thus leading to potential improvement ideas.

Another case study showing the potential of deviance mining, this time in the healthcare domain, is reported by Lakshmanan, Rozsnyai, and Wang (2013). Here, the team applied deviance mining techniques to understand the differences between cases leading to positive clinical outcomes versus those leading to negative outcomes in the process of congestive heart failure treatments at a large US-based healthcare provider. In this case, the team employed a combination of delta-analysis (as in the Australian insurer case study mentioned above) with

[1] http://www.fluxicon.com/

sequence mining techniques. Specifically, the authors used sequence mining to detect typical sequences of activities (e.g. activity B occurring some time after activity A) that were common for positive outcomes but not common for negative ones or vice-versa. The observations made using sequence mining were complemented with additional observations obtained by comparing a process model discovered from cases with positive outcomes with the model obtained for cases with negative outcomes. In this way, the authors extracted a number of pathways and patterns that discriminate between positive and negative cases.

In yet another case study, Bose and van der Aalst (2013) apply a technique for extracting patterns of activities that discriminate between event traces associated to malfunctions (versus normal traces) in components of remotely monitored X-ray machines. The techniques they employ fall under a wider family of techniques known as *discriminative sequence mining techniques* (Lo, Cheng, & Lucia, 2011), which in a nutshell allow one to extract sequential patterns that discriminate between multiple types of sequences (e.g. sequences with positive outcomes versus sequences with negative outcomes).

Finally, Swinnen, Depaire, Jans, and Vanhoof (2012) present a case study in a large European financial institution where analysts sought to understand the reasons for deviations from normative pathways in a procurement process. A dataset of close to 30,000 cases of a procurement process were extracted from the institution's SAP system. Using a process discovery tool, it was found that about 29 % of cases corresponded to deviations from expected (mandated) pathways. Association rule mining was then applied to extract rules to characterize deviant cases. It was found that a total of ten rules could explain almost all deviant cases. Analysis of these rules by business experts revealed characteristic situations where control points in the procurement process were being bypassed, leading to potential weaknesses in the process. The case study highlights that even highly standardized business processes, such as a procurement process, are characterized by frequent deviations. Analysis of such deviations can help to identify and to rectify potential weaknesses. In other words, deviance mining is not only relevant in ad hoc processes, but equally well in standardized scenarios.

The above case studies show that delta-analysis in combination with association rule and sequence mining—particularly discriminative sequence mining—provide a basis for discovering patterns of activities that distinguish negative deviance from normal cases. Setiawan and Sadiq (2013) show that similar techniques can be applied to distinguish positive deviance (i.e. high-performing cases) from normal cases. Specifically, Setiawan and Sadiq propose a method to identify activities or workers that are associated with positive deviance in a business process. The method assumes that the analyst is interested in understanding positive deviance with respect to a given set of process performance measures. The first step of the method is to identify cases that are associated with higher performance according to the given performance measures. Given that there are typically multiple, and sometimes contradicting, process performance measures, the method uses the notion of Pareto frontier to identify cases that strike the best tradeoffs between these multiple measures. In a second step, the method analyzes the performance of process workers to determine which process workers perform better for different types of activities. Finally, in the third step the method analyzes the impact of the performance of different activities on the overall performance of the process. The outcome is a characterization of the best cases of the process with respect to process workers and activity performance observed for these cases, which can be used to identify best practices.

A similar method for positive deviance analysis is outlined by Tregear (2013). Tregear's so-called $^{+}$D method shares common points with that of Setiawan and Sadiq. As in the latter method, the $^{+}$D method starts by determining how success is measured, which entails selecting and defining performance measures. In a second step, data is collected with respect to the chosen performance measures. This is followed (third and fourth steps) by identifying samples of exceptional performance from the data and analyzing the data in an exploratory manner in order to identify what factors might underpin the identified exceptional performance (positive deviance). In a fifth step, statistical tests are used to identify correlations and causal links between the identified factors and positive deviance. This last step leads to the formulation of hypotheses to explain positive deviance. In a sixth step, controlled tests are undertaken in order to validate the hypotheses. Finally, the validated hypotheses are used as a basis to formulate new practices that are implemented and communicated across all relevant process stakeholders.

4 Predictive Monitoring

The execution of business processes is generally subject to internal policies, norms, best practices, regulations, and laws. For example, a doctor may only perform a certain type of surgery a pre-operational screening is carried out beforehand. Meanwhile, in a sales process, an order can be archived only after the customer has confirmed receipt of all ordered items.

For this reason, compliance monitoring is an everyday imperative in many organizations. Accordingly, a range of research proposals have addressed the problem of monitoring business processes with respect to business constraints (Birukou et al., 2010; Ly, Rinderle-Ma, Knuplesch, & Dadam, 2011; Maggi, Montali, Westergaard, & van der Aalst, 2011; Maggi, Montali, & van der Aalst, 2012; Weidlich et al., 2011). Given a process model and a set of *business constraints*, these techniques provide a basis to monitor ongoing executions of a process (a.k.a. *cases*) in order to assess whether they comply with the constraints in question. However, these monitoring approaches are *reactive*, in that they allow users to identify a violation only *after it has occurred* rather than supporting them in *preventing* such violations in the first place.

Predictive Monitoring (Maggi, Di Francescomarino, Dumas, & Ghidini, 2013) is an emerging paradigm based on the continuous generation of predictions and recommendations on what activities to perform and what input data values to provide, so that the likelihood of violation of business constraints is minimized.

In this paradigm, a user specifies a *business goal* in the form of business rules.[2] Based on an analysis of execution traces, the idea of predictive monitoring is to continuously provide the user with estimations of the likelihood of achieving each business goal for a given case. Such predictions generally depend both on: (1) the sequence of activities executed in a given case; and (2) the values of data attributes after each activity execution in a case.

As an example, consider a doctor who needs to choose the most appropriate therapy for a patient. Historical data referring to patients with similar characteristics can be used to predict what therapy will be the most effective one and to advise the doctor accordingly. Meanwhile, in the context of a business process for managing loan applications, the applicant can be advised on the combinations of the loan amount and the length of loan that are the most likely to lead to acceptance of the application, given contextual information about the application and the personal data of the applicant (e.g., age, salary, etc.).

In a previous work (Maggi et al., 2013), we have put forward a specific framework for predictive monitoring aimed at generating predictions at runtime based on user-defined business goals. This technique estimates, for each enabled activity in an ongoing case, and for every data input that can be given to this activity, the probability that the execution of the activity with the corresponding data input will lead to the fulfillment of the business goal. To this aim, we apply a combination of simple string matching techniques with decision tree learning.

An approach for the prediction of abnormal terminations of business processes has been presented by Kang, Kim, and Kang (2012). Here, a fault detection algorithm (local outlier factor) is used to estimate the probability of a fault occurring. Alarms are provided for an early notification of probable abnormal terminations, in order to prevent risks rather than to simply react to them. Castellanos, Salazar, Casati, Dayal, and Shan (2005) present a business operations management platform equipped with time series forecasting functionalities. This platform allows for predictions of metric values on running process instances as well as for predictions of aggregated metric values of future instances (e.g., the number of orders that will be placed next Monday).

Other predictive monitoring techniques have been proposed that are targeted at generating predictions and recommendations focused on temporal aspects. For example, van der Aalst, Schonenberg, and Song (2011) propose predictive monitoring techniques for estimating case completion times and deadline violations based on annotated transition systems encoding temporal information extracted from event logs. Meanwhile, Folino, Guarascio, and Pontieri (2012) propose a predictive clustering approach in which context-related execution scenarios are discovered and modeled through state-aware performance predictors. Finally, Rogge-Solti and Weske (2013) introduce a method for predicting the remaining execution time of a process based on stochastic Petri nets.

---

[2] In line with the forward-looking nature of predictive monitoring, we use the term *business goal* rather than *business constraint* to refer to the monitored properties.

Other approaches focus on generating predictions to reduce risks. Conforti, de Leoni, Rosa, and van der Aalst (2013) for example present a technique to support process participants in making risk-informed decisions by traversing decision trees generated from the logs of past process executions. In a similar vein, Pika, Aalst, Fidge, Hofstede, and Wynn (2013) propose an approach for predicting time-related process risks by identifying indicators observable in event logs that highlight the possibility of deadline transgression.

Finally, initial case studies of predictive process monitoring in the field of transportation and logistics are presented by Metzger, Franklin, and Engel (2012) and Feldman, Fournier, Franklin, and Metzger (2013). These case studies show in particular how predictive process monitoring can be used to explain and predict "late show" events in a transportation process. Here, a "late show" refers to a delay between expected and actual time of delivering the goods to a carrier (e.g. airline). In this case study, standard statistical techniques are used to find correlations between "late show" events and external variables such as weather conditions or road traffic. The uncovered correlations are then used to define complex event processing rules that detect situations where "late show" events are likely to occur. A challenge for predictive process monitoring in this setting is that transportation processes are generally not "case-based" because goods from different customers are often aggregated and dis-aggregated at different points in the process. In other words, multiple "cases" of a transportation process will typically merge and split at runtime and thus delays affecting one delivery might end up affecting others.

5 Discussion and Outlook

Process innovation requires business process support systems that depart from traditional normative approaches to business process execution. Rather than imposing a specific and preconceived course of action, business process support systems are increasingly required to provide process workers with sufficient autonomy to enable continuous adaptation and innovation.

In this setting, we position deviance mining and predictive monitoring as two keystones in modern business process support systems. Predictive monitoring and deviance mining are related since they both try to identify deviations with respect to expected behavior. However, while deviance mining tries to do this off-line (by analyzing process logs), predictive monitoring provides feedback on-the-fly to prevent violations. Together, these techniques turn a business process support system into a recommender system that provides guidance to process analysts and process workers, helping them to recognize actions and decisions that typically drive a process towards desired outcomes and higher performance.

While deviance mining and predictive monitoring techniques are still in their infancy, they are already applicable in real-life scenarios as evidenced by the several case studies discussed in this paper. Going forward, we foresee more sophisticated and automated techniques for deviance mining emerging. For example, techniques for extraction of predictive sequence patterns (Xing, Pei, Dong, &

Yu, 2008) could find useful applications in the context of both deviance mining and predictive monitoring. Another family of techniques that could find applications in this space is that of discriminatively trained hidden Markov models (Collins, 2002). These techniques produce models that could be applied to extract probabilities of an ongoing case falling into either a "deviant" or "normal" category.

In parallel to technical developments, we foresee more sophisticated case studies being carried out, where deviance mining and predictive monitoring are applied not only in the context of specific improvement initiatives, but on an ongoing basis as part of continuous process improvement programs. To achieve this goal, analysts will benefit from more methodological guidance and more user-friendly tool support that allows them to readily apply these techniques on potentially large and complex business process execution logs.

Acknowledgments This work is supported by ERDF via the Estonian Centre of Excellence in Computer Science.

References

Birukou, A., D'Andrea, V., Leymann, F., Serafinski, J., Silveira, P., Strauch, S., et al. (2010). An integrated solution for runtime compliance governance in SOA. In *Proceedings of international conference on service-oriented computing (ICSOC)* (Vol. 6470). Berlin: Springer.

Bose, R. P. J. C., & van der Aalst, W. M. P. (2013). Discovering signature patterns from event logs. In *Proceedings of the IEEE symposium on computational intelligence and data mining (CIDM)* (pp. 111–118). IEEE.

Castellanos, M., Salazar, N., Casati, F., Dayal, U., & Shan, M.-C. (2005). Predictive business operations management. In *Proceedings of the workshop on databases in networked information systems (DNIS)* (pp. 1–14). Springer.

Collins, M. (2002). Discriminative training methods for hidden Markov models: Theory and experiments with perceptron algorithms. In *Proceedings of the ACL conference on empirical methods in natural language processing* (pp. 1–8). Philadelphia, PA: Association for Computational Linguistics.

Conforti, R., de Leoni, M., Rosa, M. L., & van der Aalst, W. M. P. (2013). Supporting risk-informed decisions during business process execution. In *Proceedings of international conference on advanced information systems engineering (CAiSE)* (pp. 116–132). Berlin: Springer.

Feldman, Z., Fournier, F., Franklin, R., & Metzger, A. (2013). Proactive event processing in action: A case study on the proactive management of transport processes. In *Proceedings of ACM international conference on distributed event-based systems (DEBS)* (pp. 97–106). ACM.

Folino, F., Guarascio, M., & Pontieri, L. (2012). Discovering context-aware models for predicting business process performances. In *Proceedings of on the move to meaningful internet systems (OTM)* (pp. 287–304). Berlin: Springer.

Kang, B., Kim, D., & Kang, S.-H. (2012, April). Real-time business process monitoring method for prediction of abnormal termination using KNNI-based LOF prediction. *Expert Systems and Applications, 39*(5), 6061–6068.

Lakshmanan, G. T., Rozsnyai, S., & Wang, F. (2013). Investigating clinical care pathways correlated with outcomes. In *Proceedings of the international conference on business process management* (pp. 323–338). Berlin: Springer.

Lo, D., Cheng, H., & Lucia. (2011). Mining closed discriminative dyadic sequential patterns. In *Proceedings of the international conference on extending database technology (EDBT)* (pp. 21–32). Springer.
Ly, L. T., Rinderle-Ma, S., Knuplesch, D., & Dadam, P. (2011). Monitoring business process compliance using compliance rule graphs. In *Proceedings of on the move to meaningful Internet systems (OTM)* (pp. 82–99). Berlin: Springer.
Maggi, F., Di Francescomarino, C., Dumas, M., & Ghidini, C. (2013). Predictive monitoring of business processes. In *Proceedings of the international conference on advanced information systems engineering (CAiSE)*. Springer.
Maggi, F., Montali, M., Westergaard, M., & van der Aalst, W. (2011). Monitoring business constraints with linear temporal logic: An approach based on colored automata. In *Proceedings of the international conference on business process management (BPM)* (pp. 132–147). Heidelberg: Springer.
Maggi, F. M., Montali, M., & van der Aalst, W. M. P. (2012). An operational decision support framework for monitoring business constraints. In *Proceedings of the international conference on fundamental approaches to software engineering (FASE)* (pp. 146–162). Berlin: Springer.
Metzger, A., Franklin, R., & Engel, Y. (2012). Predictive monitoring of heterogeneous service-oriented business networks: The transport and logistics case. In *Proceedings of the SRII global conference* (pp. 313–322).
Pika, A., Aalst, W., Fidge, C., Hofstede, A., & Wynn, M. (2013). Predicting deadline transgressions using event logs. In *Proceedings of the BPM'2012 workshops* (pp. 211–216). Berlin: Springer.
Rogge-Solti, A., & Weske, M. (2013). Prediction of remaining service execution time using stochastic petri nets with arbitrary firing delays. In *Proceedings of international conference on service-oriented computing (ICSOC)* (pp. 389–403). Berlin: Springer.
Schonenberg, H., Mans, R., Russell, N., Mulyar, N., & van der Aalst, W. M. P. (2008). Process flexibility: A survey of contemporary approaches. In *Proceedings of the CIAO! and EOMAS 2009 workshops* (pp. 16–30). Berlin: Springer.
Setiawan, M. A., & Sadiq, S. W. (2013). A methodology for improving business process performance through positive deviance. *International Journal of Information System Modeling and Design, 4*(2), 1–22.
Spreitzer, G. M., & Sonenshein, S. (2004). Toward the construct definition of positive deviance. *American Behavioral Scientist, 47*(6), 828–847.
Sun, C., Du, J., Chen, N., Khoo, S.-C., & Yang, Y. (2013). Mining explicit rules for software process evaluation. In *Proceedings of the international conference on software and system process (ICSSP)* (pp. 118–125). ACM.
Suriadi, S., Wynn, M. T., Ouyang, C., ter Hofstede, A. H. M., & van Dijk, N. J. (2013). Understanding process behaviours in a large insurance company in Australia: A case study. In *Proceedings of the international conference on advanced information systems engineering (CAiSE)* (pp. 449–464). Springer.
Swenson, K. D. (2010). *Mastering the unpredictable: How adaptive case management will revolutionize the way that knowledge workers get things done*. Tampa, FL: Meghan-Kiffer.
Swinnen, J., Depaire, B., Jans, M. J., & Vanhoof, K. (2012). A process deviation analysis – A case study. In *Proceedings of the BPM'2011 workshops* (pp. 87–98). Springer.
Tregear, R. (2013, January). Insignificant and exceptional. *BPTrends*.
van der Aalst, W. M. P., Schonenberg, M. H., & Song, M. (2011). Time prediction based on process mining. *Information Systems, 36*(2), 450–475.
Weidlich, M., Ziekow, H., Mendling, J., Günter, O., Weske, M., & Desai, N. (2011). Event-based monitoring of process execution violations. In *Proceedings of the international conference on advanced information systems engineering (CAiSE)* (pp. 182–198). Springer.
Xing, Z., Pei, J., Dong, G., & Yu, P. S. (2008). Mining sequence classifiers for early prediction. In *Proceedings of the SIAM international conference on data mining (SDM)* (pp. 644–655). SIAM.

Identification of Business Process Models in a Digital World

Peter Loos, Peter Fettke, Jürgen Walter, Tom Thaler, and Peyman Ardalani

Abstract

Traditionally, business processes are designed using a top down approach. While in top down approaches real process experiences can only be considered in an indirect way, process experiences can be the core input for process model designs using a more innovative bottom up approach with inductive methods, e.g. process mining technologies. The paper introduces a comprehensive seven phases method for inductive reference modelling. Some of the relevant particular techniques in this context are presented. Finally, the vision of the IWi Process Model Corpus is presented. This corpus can serve as a basis for developing and evaluating methods and techniques in the area of inductive reference modelling and currently covers 2,290 single models.

1 Introduction

The usage of reference models offers many advantages for the development of individual enterprise models in practice as well as in science (Fettke & Loos, 2004; Frank, 2008, p. 42). However, it is undisputed that the realisation of these advantages requires the availability of reference models. Thus, methods for a systematic development of high potential reference models are highly relevant.

Based on the established distinction between rationalism and empiricism as two basic paths to knowledge, the distinction within reference modelling differentiates between a deductive and an inductive strategy for developing a reference model (Becker & Schütte, 1997, pp. 428–430; Thomas, 2006, p. 102f):

P. Loos (✉) • P. Fettke • J. Walter • T. Thaler • P. Ardalani
German Research Center for Artificial Intelligence (DFKI), Saarland University, Stuhlsatzenhausweg 3, 66123 Saarbrücken, Germany
e-mail: loos@iwi.uni-sb.de; peter.fettke@iwi.dfki.de; juergen.walter@iwi.dfki.de; tom.thaler@dfki.de; peyman.ardalani@iwi.dfki.de

J. vom Brocke, T. Schmiedel (eds.), *BPM – Driving Innovation in a Digital World*, Management for Professionals, DOI 10.1007/978-3-319-14430-6_11

- *Deductive strategy:* Common principles and theories are the basics for the development of a reference model. The reference model will be refined and concretised during the development phase.
- *Inductive strategy:* On the basis of individual enterprise models, a reference model is developed through the identification of commonalities between the individual models and through the abstraction of particularities. An increasing abstraction from specificities of individual enterprise models is one characteristic of this development process.

Even though both strategies are known in the field, a deeper analysis of the current state-of-the-art reveals a significant gap. Most methods follow the deductive strategy, while the inductive strategy is supported only by a few. However, the inductive strategy also has much potential for reference modelling:

1. Numerous reference models have been constructed inductively, particularly in practice [cf. attribute "construction method" in the reference model catalogue at http://rmk.iwi.uni-sb.de; analogously in (Thomas 2006, p. 103)]. Note that it cannot be concluded from this finding that inductive methods for the reference model development are well known. Rather the opposite seems to be true as, in these works, the exact development steps are not very detailed or not explicitly described. Thus, in particular, the important question of a possible generalization of the actually selected development steps remains unclear.
2. Both development strategies can be combined without problems. Thus, it is possible to use a deductively developed reference model together with individual reference models as a basis for a further inductive development of reference models.
3. Enterprise modelling has gained more importance in organizational practice. Thus, more individual enterprise models, target models and reference models which can be used for inductive reference modelling are available. Some of the models are available as so called "open models" (Koch, Strecker, & Frank, 2006).

To summarise, although there is a considerable lack of methodological knowledge about the inductive development of reference models, the potential of inductive methods is extremely attractive. Especially if one distinguishes between the standard case of reference modelling and non-standard cases, the inductive strategy seems highly beneficial. The standard case delivers a reference model which serves as a basis for creating individual models, e.g. in terms of adapting and enhancing with respect to an individual use case. In contrast to this, the non-standard cases cover different variations: (1) variation of the modelling demand, e.g. best practice, common practice or model reusability; (2) variation of the object, e.g. companies with several locations/offices, parent/subsidiary companies of a horizontally organized enterprise, organization units with comparable function in different sectors; (3) variation of the modelling level, e.g. software reference model or (4) variation of the modelling purpose, e.g. model merging, developing multiperspective reference models, analysis of big model collections. Against this background, the present work aims at a contribution to closing the identified gap in research. Thus, our research objective is to develop a method for inductive reference modelling.

The research approach of this work stands in the tradition of German design science oriented research in the modelling of enterprise information systems (Frank, 2006): On the basis of theoretically as well as practically relevant problems in the (inductive) development of reference models, where no satisfying solutions exist, the authors study and present particular techniques supporting an inductive model development. Following an inductive strategy implies the need for methods and techniques, e.g. identifying correspondences or structural analogies between different process models. Different approaches for merging, abstracting and aggregating particular process models are necessary as well. These streams of research, the development of corresponding methods and the implementation of particular techniques, are therefore highly important in the context of our applied research approach and in the paper at hand. The applicability and usefulness of these methods and techniques are shown by means of an application scenario: Developing reference models for some Dutch government processes based on existing models from 10 municipalities in an inductive manner.

After this introduction, the next section gives an overview of related work on inductive reference modelling. Thereafter, a specific seven phases method for inductive reference modelling is presented. Section 3 describes some central subject areas with corresponding particular techniques supporting this inductive approach, while Sect. 4 introduces a software tool—the RefMod-Miner—realizing these and more techniques. In Sect. 5, the mentioned application scenario is presented. Finally, Sect. 6 closes the article with a conclusion and an outlook on future work. This work is an extended version of Fettke (2014), in particular, different techniques, software tools and application scenarios are described in greater detail in Sects. 3–5.

2 Related Work

Several authors describe a procedure model for reference modelling development (Ahlemann & Gastl, 2007; Becker, Delfmann, Knackstedt, & Kuropka, 2002; Delfmann, 2006; Fettke & Loos, 2004; Schlagheck, 2000; Schütte, 1998; Schwegmann, 1999; Thomas, 2006; vom Brocke, 2003). A first analysis of these methods shows that the inductive strategy does not play a prominent role with regard to most methods. Typically, starting from a general definition of the problem, a reference model is derived by a stepwise refinement and concretisation. In contrast, activities such as the creation of individual enterprise models or the abstraction of enterprise-specific features that would be expected for the inductive strategy are not listed at the top level of the life cycle models.

The analysis of these methods shows that the inductive strategy of reference modelling plays no prominent role. Indeed, none of the outlined methods mentioned before explicitly argues against the inductive strategy. On the contrary, some even noted that existing individual enterprise models and other knowledge sources should be identified and taken into account as part of the reference model development (cf. Becker et al., 2002, p. 49; Schwegmann, 1999, p. 167; Thomas, 2006, pp. 278–280). Nevertheless, besides the programmatic call to consider existing individual enterprise models, only few actual suggestions exist for the systematic derivation of reference models from these models.

Also, the question remains open as to what can be done if appropriate individual enterprise models are neither available nor identifiable prior to the reference model development. Must the development of individual enterprise models for reference modelling be waived in this case? Or is it possible that reference model development benefits from the developments of individual enterprise models while, in a second step, a reference model is derived in an inductive manner? Besides the mentioned methods, various authors (Gottschalk, van der Aalst, & Jansen-Vullers, 2008) and (Li, Reichert, & Wombacher, 2010) present first ideas for an inductive strategy. However, these works do not provide general inductive methods for the development of reference models. Instead, reference modelling is mainly seen as an algorithmic problem. More or less, it is assumed that a reference model can be derived from a set of given process models. Questions, for example with regard to the collection of individual models or the terminological harmonization of labels of the process model, remain largely unaddressed. In addition, these works focus mainly on the process control view and do not consider the modelling of business information systems in general.

Furthermore, some approaches utilize an inductive strategy (Aier, Fichter, & Fischer, 2011; Daun & Matheis, 2005; Karow, Pfeiffer, & Räckers, 2008). However, these approaches focus on the development of a particular reference model. The authors do not claim to present a general method for the inductive development of reference models.

In addition to the works specific to the development of reference models, various approaches are known that have a certain similarity to the inductive development of reference models, e.g. approaches for model comparison (Dijkman, Dumas, van Dongen, Käärik, & Mendling, 2011) or for the integration of enterprise models (Rahm & Bernstein, 2001a, 2001b). These approaches provide very interesting concepts for the analysis of enterprise models but they have not been applied in reference modelling so far.

In conclusion, it can be stated that the deductive strategy significantly dominates the previous methods for reference model development. The inductive strategy and its fundamental ideas are basically known. Nevertheless, there is a lack of general methods for the inductive construction of reference models.

3 Towards a Seven Phase Method for Inductive Reference Modelling

For the inductive development of reference models no concrete requirements are known. Instead, the different requirements for such a method are justified by arguments:

- *Inductive development:* The method is intended to support a modeller so that a reference model can be derived systematically from individual enterprise models. One cannot speak of an inductive development in a meaningful way if this requirement is not met.
- *Identification of commonalities:* If the individual enterprise models contain similarities, these have to be represented in the reference model. In this way, the reference model represents the typical structures of an application domain.
- *Abstraction:* Reference models do not claim to represent all company-specific features. Therefore, the derived reference model should be more abstract than the individual enterprise models.
- *Generativity:* In contrast to the first requirement, it should be possible to derive the individual enterprise models from the inductively generated reference model. This ensures that the reference model is not too far away from the individual enterprise models that it represents.
- *Properties of natural languages:* A common part of enterprise models are natural languages, in which known phenomena such as homonymy, synonymy and linguistic fuzziness are typical. A method must take these aspects into account.

In the following, the seven phases of the proposed method for the inductive development of reference models (Walter, Fettke, & Loos, 2012a) will be presented in greater detail.

Phase 1: Initiation of Reference Model Development

The *goal* of the first step is to identify the requirements that a derived reference model should fulfil. To determine the requirements, the following alternatives are available:

- *Interviews:* Interviews with domain experts or potential model users can give guidance concerning the requirements that the reference model should fulfil.
- *Literature review:* A literature review of relevant literature provides an insight into the aspects to be taken into account by a derived reference model.
- *Analysis of existing reference models:* An analysis of existing reference models provides an overview of the requirements that are already fulfilled by other reference models. It is useful to consider the models of other domains besides directly similar models.

The derived requirements have to be prioritized in order to evaluate the relevancies of the different requirements.

The *result* is a prioritized list of requirements for the reference model.

Phase 2: Acquisition of Individual Process Models

The goal of this step is to collect individual enterprise models that are used for the inductive development of reference models. This should be done in four sub-steps:

- *Class definition:* The class of enterprises for which the reference model should be developed has to be determined. For example, a class can be created by an explicit list of companies or by a specification of characteristic features that a business must meet in this industry branch or domain.
- *Enterprise selection:* In general, individual enterprise models are collected not for all, but only for selected companies of the previously defined class. The selection of suitable companies should take into account at least three aspects: (a) representativeness of the selected companies (b) accessibility to a company or individual enterprise models (c) effort to collect individual enterprise models. In a concrete decision, conflicts between these aspects will occur. For example, the costs will rise if additional enterprise models have to be collected. But this can be essential for reasons of representativeness.
- *Unified modelling conventions:* Modelling conventions concern: (a) the chosen modelling language, e.g. event-driven process chains (EPC) or Business Process Modelling Notation (BPMN); (b) layout conventions, e.g. sequential processes have to be aligned top to bottom; (c) naming conventions, e.g. a single process step has to be described by "subject + predicate"; (d) terminological conventions, e.g. "A customer is a business partner buying goods regularly". The definition of unified modelling conventions noticeably reduces the effort of later analysis. However, it is rather unlikely that such conventions can be enforced, especially in inter-company contexts. Thus, step 3 contains further measures.
- *Collecting individual enterprise models:* Enterprise models of the selected enterprises have to be ascertained. The known methods for enterprise modelling can be used. The inductive development of the reference model can be carried out at a lower cost, especially when individual enterprise models have already been created in the past and can be reused. It is important to document the source ("provenience") of the collected enterprise models because important conclusions can often be drawn from this information (e.g., What was the purpose of the original model? Which changes took place? Are there some legal restrictions which have to be obeyed?).

The *result* is a definition of classes of enterprises as well as individual enterprise models.

Phase 3: Pre-processing of Individual Process Models

The *goals* of the third step are an adjustment and a harmonisation as well as a pre-processing of the individual enterprise models in order to derive an initial reference model. For this purpose, several sub-steps are required:

- *Checking the unified modelling conventions:* If the modelling conventions could be enforced in the collection of individual enterprise models in the second step, it is necessary to check the extent to which they have already been applied. [Appropriate techniques are given in Delfmann (2010)]. Otherwise, the individual enterprise models have to be transformed in this step according to the unified modelling conventions.
- *Generating modelsynsets:* As a next step, modelsynsets have to be built in order to prepare an appropriate grouping of the models in phase 4. The definition of modelsynsets is based on the concept of a linguistic synset, which designates a set of interchangeable words in certain contexts (Miller, 1998, p. 23): A modelsynset is a set consisting of a single word or a group of words that can be interchanged in an enterprise model without changing the intended purpose of the model. An example of a modelsynset is "creditor, supplier (a business partner who has obligations for goods and services)". A synset and a modelsynset are conceptually similar, but they do not have to be the same: General dictionaries for the English colloquial language, such as WordNet, are usually not appropriate because individual business terms are often not available at the necessary level of detail. But such terms are important within individual enterprise models. In addition, individual enterprise models often contain business-specific characteristics which are not covered by general dictionaries. Nonetheless, digital dictionaries can be used as a first step for an automatic generation of modelsynsets, which must be checked afterwards.

The *results* are homogeneous individual enterprise models and modelsynsets.

Phase 4: Exploitation of the Reference Model

The *goal* of this step is the generation of a reference model out of homogeneous individual enterprise models. The following sub-steps have to be processed:

- *Clustering:* In a *clustering* step the different individual models are grouped in a way such that models within one group are similar and models belonging to different groups are different. Here, typical techniques of cluster analysis or multivariate statistics can be used. The modelsynset created in phase 3 can support the grouping. Known similarity measures for enterprise models can also be applied (Dijkman et al., 2011). However, it has to be mentioned that known similarity measures are focussing on the similarity of enterprise models as a whole and do not take into account the similarity of single model fragments. The identification of similarities between individual sub-models provides great potential for the derivation of reference models. Individual enterprise models as a whole exhibit significant differences, although some parts are very similar and, thus, could be summarized in a reference model.

- *Deriving a reference model:* For each cluster, a *reference model* has to be derived. The main idea is based on identifying similar model fragments within a cluster, which are then transformed into a reference model. In this step, individual enterprise models are interpreted as graphs. Within the various graphs, isomorphic sub-graphs have to be identified. These sub-graphs should be as large as possible. The relative frequencies of a sub-graph can be used in order to check which fragments can be used as a reference model. An abstraction parameter α and a configuration parameter β are introduced to describe the extent to which characteristics of individual enterprise models are reflected by the reference model. If α is equal to 0 %, all sub-graphs are used and if α is equal to 100 %, only sub-graphs occurring in all individual enterprise models become part of the reference model. The configuration parameter β determines the value at which a sub-graph becomes a mandatory part of the reference model.

The *result* of this step is a raw reference model.

Phase 5: Post-processing of the Reference Model

The *goal* of the fifth step is the post-processing of the previously derived raw reference model. Here, three different approaches are possible:

- *Concatenation of model fragments:* Interesting relationships can occur between parts of the raw reference model, which should be reflected in the final reference model. For example, some sequences can occur in several different individual enterprise models, so these dependencies should be included in the reference model.
- *Integration of deductively developed reference model fragments:* If fragments of a reference model cannot be derived with the inductive strategy, these fragments can be derived deductively and integrated into the final reference model.
- *Manual extensions:* As a last option, manual extensions can be made in order to correct the reference model, because it is obvious that not all steps can be completely automated.

The *Result* is the reference model.

Phase 6: Evaluation of the Reference Model

The *goal* of this step is to evaluate the developed reference model. In principle, the evaluation can be made from different perspectives where the scope and the content of the perspectives can hardly be defined a priori. Instead, these have to be negotiated in a discourse between the model developers, the users and the evaluators. Within such a discourse, it should be checked to what extent the criteria are justified, how they are weighted and to what extent they are fulfilled. Typical perspectives are:

- *Evaluation with respect to requirements:* It is necessary to check in how far the reference model fulfils the requirements defined in the first step.
- *Evaluation with respect to individual enterprise models:* It is necessary to examine how individual enterprise models can be derived from the reference model. As a benchmark, the initial individual reference models or other models can be used.
- *Evaluation based on an existing framework:* Literature provides several criteria for the assessment of reference models, e.g. the framework by Frank (Frank, 2007), the guidelines for enterprise modelling (Becker, Rosemann, & Schütte, 1995) or ontological quality criteria (Fettke, 2006).

The *result* is an evaluated reference model.

Phase 7: Maintenance and Enhancement
The *goal* of the seventh step is to maintain and improve the reference model after the initial construction. This includes corrections of the reference model as well as necessary additions. It is possible that further individual enterprise models are developed and should be integrated into the reference model during enhancement. It is worth considering whether the previously created reference model should be developed from scratch (redrafted) or whether a check is sufficient and how far aspects of the new individual enterprise models are covered by the reference model, so that only slight changes have to be made (modification draft). Important considerations here are stability of the reference model, the planned development costs and the complexity of necessary changes.

The *result* is an enhanced reference model.

4 Particular Techniques for Inductive Reference Modelling

4.1 Process Matching

Matching describes the process that takes two schemata as input, referred to as the source and the target, and produces a number of matches between the elements of these two schemata based on a particular correspondence (Rahm & Bernstein, 2001a, 2001b). Thereby, the term schema has a broad interpretation and can comprise database schemata (e.g. Evermann, 2009) as well as arbitrary other model schemata.

Process matching can be divided into two different fields—matching process models (1) and matching nodes of process models (2) (Thaler, Hake, Fettke, & Loos, 2014). Matching process models describe the mapping of process models on other models based on criteria like similarity, equality or analogy. A prominent application scenario is the handling of company mergers, where it is necessary to synchronize different processes, e.g. in the context of administration.

In contrast to this, matching nodes of process models, which is mostly associated with the term of process matching, describes the mapping of single nodes, a set of

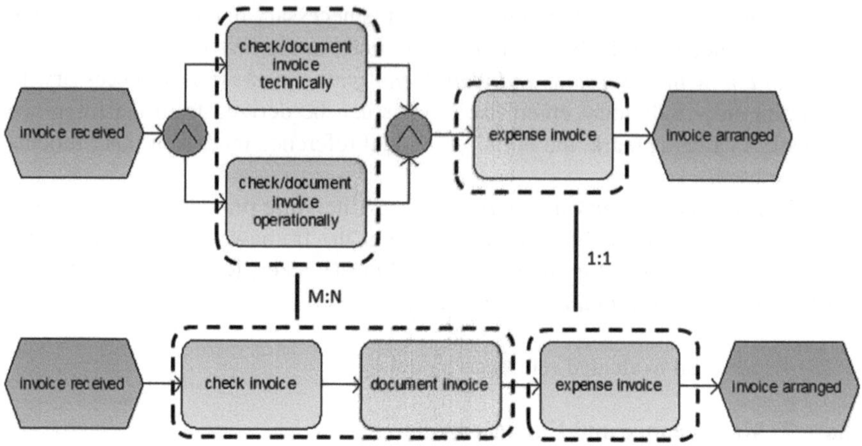

Fig. 1 Node matching example (Thaler et al., 2014)

nodes or node blocks of one model to the corresponding elements of another model. Important application scenarios are the harmonization of business process models and the inductive derivation of reference models from different individual models. In order to determine the matches between process models (1), node matching techniques as described in Becker and Laue (2012), Weidlich, Dijkman, & Mendling (2010) are used in most cases. While Becker and Laue (2012) present 19 different similarity measures for business process models with their underlying—mostly 1:1—node matching techniques (Weidlich et al., 2010) develops a similarity measure for process models based on M:N node matches. The cardinality describes the cardinal number of node sets which are being matched to each other. A sample of a node matching with both 1:1 and M:N matches is visualized in Fig. 1.

Generally, it is not only possible to match nodes (activities, events and connectors in terms of EPCs), but also edges. However, most of the existing techniques and algorithms only take activities into account. There are several different approaches for the automatic detection of correspondences. A common technique is the consideration of (normalized) edit distances like the Levenshtein distance (Dijkman et al., 2011). Many approaches (Cayoglu et al., 2013) also use wordnets with tools like WordNet or GermaNet to take semantic information concerning synonyms, homonyms or antonyms into consideration. Thereby, node labels are split into single terms or n-grams, stop words like "is", "are", "at" etc. are removed and the remaining terms or n-grams are matched to the terms or n-grams of other labels.

As mentioned above, there are several possibilities identifying correspondences between nodes, thus, the particular technique RefMod-Mine/NSCM will be introduced to give an example. First of all, the technique uses a semantic error detection to validate the correctness of node types. The form and the order of nouns and verbs of a label are analyzed, so that the algorithm is able to determine whether a node should be an activity or an event (in case of EPCs).

Generally, one can also distinguish between considering exactly two models, which are matched to each other (binary matching) and a set of models (n-ary matching). The n-ary matching realizes a transitive matching over multiple models, which is generally not the case in the context of binary matches. The RefMod-Mine/NSCM algorithm conducts an n-ary cluster matching, thus, the nodes of all models which should be matched are being compared pairwise, using a semantic similarity measure. The agglomerative (Jain, Murty, & Flynn, 1999) cluster algorithms start with clusters of size 1 (activities) and consolidates two activities to a cluster if their similarity value exceeds a specific threshold.

The used similarity measure consists of three phases: (1) splitting node labels L into single words w_{i_L}, so that $split(L) = \{w_{1_L}, \ldots, w_{n_L}\}$, whereby stop words and waste characters like additional spaces are removed and (2) computing the Porter Stem $stem(w_{i_L})$ (Porter, 1997) and comparing the stem sets of the labels. The similarity is defined as the division of the number of matching stems sets by the sum of all words (cf. Eq. 1).

$$sim(L_1, L_2) = \frac{\left|\left\{stem\left(w_{1_{L_1}}\right), \ldots, stem\left(w_{n_{L_1}}\right)\right\} \cap \left\{stem\left(w_{1_{L_2}}\right), \ldots, stem\left(w_{n_{L_2}}\right)\right\}\right|}{|split(L_1) + split(L_2)|}$$

Equation 1 RefMod-Mine/NSCM node similarity measure

If the similarity value exceeds a specific threshold, the labels are checked for antonyms using a lexical database (3), which decides on the similarity being 0 or $sim(L_1, L_2)$.

In the end, the RefMod-Miner/NSCM technique extracts binary matchings from the calculated node clusters. For each model pair, all clusters are analyzed for the occurrence of nodes in both models. The containing node set of the first model is then matched to the node set of the second model. Finally, the algorithm returns binary simple or complex matches for the nodes of each model pair.

4.2 Structural Analogies

One of the main problems in reference modelling is the identification of correspondences (cf. 4.1). But if there is neither a suitable definition of correspondences between elements nor the means to identify correspondences between elements in another way, it is almost impossible to calculate a useful matching. This is especially the case if the considered schemata belong to different domains utilising completely different vocabulary.

One way to overcome such vocabulary problems is to focus on structural aspects only. Typically, the induced underlying graph structure of most modelling languages is used for the identification of schema matches. One of the most common approaches is the calculation of graph edit distances (GED) (Dijkman et al., 2011; Li, Reichert, & Wombacher, 2008). The derived measure relies on the number of change operations (insertion, modification or deletion of nodes) that are needed to transform one schema into a second one. Commonly, the lower the number of change operations, the greater the similarity.

Another approach in the context of process matching is the refined process structure tree (RPST) (Vanhatalo, Völzer, & Koehler, 2009), in the course of which the underlying graph of a process is decomposed into a hierarchy of fragments. Each fragment is a small subgraph which has exactly one single entry node and exactly one single exit node (SESE). Multiple entry and exit nodes can be handled by adding single dummy starting or end nodes. The fragments of an RPST can be separated into several fragment types, as for example trivial, bond or rigid fragments. Based on this kind of graph decomposition, the analogy is determined through the comparison of the resulting RPSTs.

In contrast to the RPST, the approach in Walter, Fettke, & Loos (2012b) utilises all subgraphs of the underlying graph to determine the degree of structural analogy between two process models, especially EPCs. The main advantage is that this approach is not restricted to SESE fragments. Moreover, this technique is also independent from any previous knowledge about correspondences of elements. For example, in Fig. 2 two EPCs are presented that are *structurally analogous* although they describe different processes. Obviously, only three elements have equal labels ("start", "finish order", "order finished"). In order to match (cf. 4.1) further elements, it is necessary to use advanced mapping algorithms that are able to identify antonyms like "invoice settled" and "payment received". Otherwise, such elements cannot be mapped.

The degree of structural analogy d_s of two given EPCs A and B is calculated as followed Walter et al. (2012a, 2012b):

$$d_s(A,B) = \frac{|S(A) \otimes S(B)|}{|S(A)| + |S(B)| - |S(A) \otimes S(B)|}$$

Equation 2 Degree of structural analogy

In a survey, the method was applied to the Y-CIM reference models (Scheer, 1998) and the Retail-H reference model (Becker & Schütte, 2004). The results show that the reference models contain structurally analogous parts: about 75 % of the structures consisting of 4 nodes are structurally analogous, 54 % with 5 nodes, 36 % with 6 nodes, 23 % with 7 nodes and 14 % with 8 nodes.

In comparison to the linear time computation of an RPST (Vanhatalo et al., 2009), the calculation of subgraph isomorphism is said to be NP complete (Garey & Johnson, 1979). Nonetheless, due to the nature of EPCs, several structural characteristics, e.g. different node types, can be used to speed up the calculation of subgraph isomorphism. Thus, this approach can be used to calculate further process matches which are then utilised for the inductive development of a reference model (Rehse, Fettke, & Loos, 2013).

4.3 Reference Model Development

The terms *reference modelling* and *reference model* have not been consistently defined in literature and a lively discussion about this topic is still underway. In

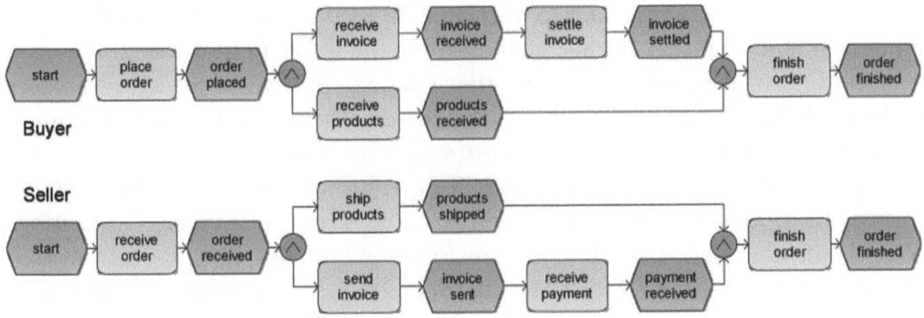

Fig. 2 Structural analogue process chains

general, business process reference models can be understood as business process models which ought to fulfil certain criteria and offer certain features. However, these criteria are still under discussion. Referring to Fettke and Loos (2007), the following features are considered important:

- *Reusability*: Business process reference models represent blueprints for the development of process-oriented IS which can be reused in different IS development projects.
- *Exemplary practices*: Business process reference models can provide common, good or even best practices, describing how business processes are actually designed in practice or how they could or should be designed and executed in order to reach certain goals. In this context, a *descriptive* as well as a *prescriptive* or even *normative* connotation of business process reference models becomes apparent, depending on their interpretation.
- *Universal applicability*: Business process reference models not only represent business processes of one particular organization, but also aim at providing universally applicable business process representations which are valuable for different organizations in a certain domain.

Reference models can provide benefits for both theory and practice. Besides the provision of general descriptions of enterprises, which is especially interesting from a theoretical point of view, practice profits, e.g. from reductions in modelling costs, modelling time and modelling risk, as reference models can represent proven solutions (Becker & Meise, 2011). Furthermore, increases in model quality based on the reuse and adaptation of already validated process models can be expected.

In the following section, the minimal cost of change approach (MCC) (Ardalani, Houy, Fettke, & Loos, 2013) as a solution for inductive reference model development is presented in greater detail. This approach supports the development of reference models with the minimal cost of change in the sense of a minimized graph edit distance to match a set of given underlying process models.

The *MCC algorithm* comprises three main steps: In the first step, a set of *candidateRelations* is calculated out of the existing nodes and edges in given process models. In the second step, this set is filtered through a threshold. In step three the reference model is generated based on the filtered set of step 2.

According to the first step, all existing relations (edges) in the given process models will be extracted into the set of *candidateRelations*. For each relation a *savedValue* ($Nodes \rightarrow [-cost(del), cost(ins)]$) is calculated to prioritize the relations for the later reference model. This value is based on a cost function ($cost : O \times Nodes \rightarrow \mathbb{N}$), which indicates the costs for change operations ($O = \{ins, mov, del\}$) needed to transform one model into another model. Obviously, relations with greater *savedValues* have higher priority to appear in the final reference model. Then, in the filtering step, a *threshold* ($t \in [-const(del), const(ins)]$) is used to filter the *candidateRelations*. Relations that have a *savedValue* greater than the *threshold* will be added to the reference model. By setting the threshold to higher values, only relations with higher *savedValue* are inserted into the final model. Consequently, this results in smaller reference models. And in the final step, the reference model is created from the filtered set considering several refinement rules.

By changing the parameters of the MCC approach, such as the cost function or the threshold, different reference models can be created. To assess the created reference models, a further approach is necessary. In this contribution, a *totalSavedValue* is defined as the sum of *savedValues* of the existing relations in a created reference model. Then, the reference model with the highest *totalSavedValue* within the set of reference models is retrieved as the final reference model. Obviously, in order to achieve higher *totalSavedValues*, the relations with a positive *savedValue* should be inserted into the reference model and therefore the threshold should be equal to zero. In analogy to the parameter α defined in phase 3 of the method, the threshold can be mapped onto a normalised range between 0 and 100 %. As it has been mentioned, if α is equal to 0 %, all elements will be inserted and if α is equal to 100 %, only the relations occurring in all individual models become part of the reference model.

Although the MCC approach especially focuses on providing an *abstracted* reference model, which contains the most relevant relations of the underlying process models, the algorithm is also able to present a completely integrated model containing all nodes of the underlying process models if a low *threshold* is defined. To shed more light on the input and output of this approach, an example is shown in Fig. 3. Three sample EPCs in a model variant collection represent the input data. The approach—with different thresholds set—generates common practice reference models as shown below.

It should be emphasized that the generated models using this approach are not always the favourite reference models. But, with adjustments of the parameters, a reference model meeting the expectations can be created. Therefore, each generated model can be considered as a reference model for certain purposes, while others may not meet the requirements for a reference model.

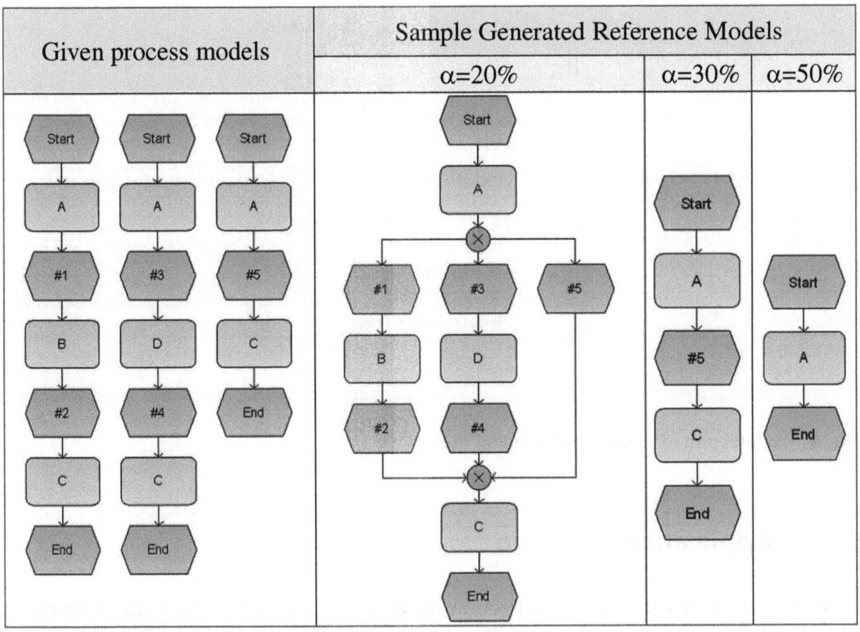

Fig. 3 Given process models and generated reference models with different thresholds

5 RefMod-Miner

In order to support the inductive reference modelling approach, a corresponding software tool was developed. The goal of the tool development was not to support a fully automated development of a reference model. Rather, the tool supports a developer in creating a reference model in an inductive manner.

In order to achieve platform independence, JAVA was used as the programming language. The architecture of the tool consists of three layers that are shown in Fig. 4. At the lowest layer, functionalities for loading, storing, conversion and transformation as well as versioning of model data are available. Generally, two file formats are supported: the ARIS Markup Language (AML) and EPC Markup Language (EPML). The second layer contains concepts and algorithms which support the analysis of individual enterprise models and the derivation of a reference model. The top layer contains several functions for model visualization and editing as well as the possibility of browsing repositories and functions to explain the derivation process.

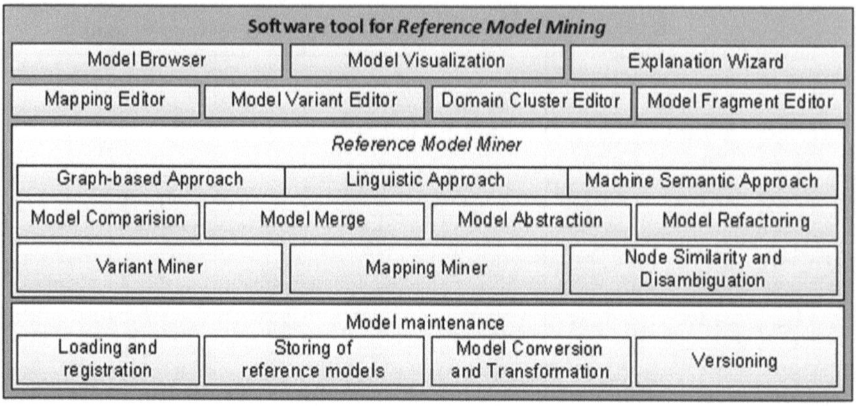

Fig. 4 Architecture of the reference model miner

6 Application Scenario

In order to demonstrate some particular techniques, a holistic application scenario is conducted. Within this scenario, 80 process models from the Dutch government (Vogelaar, Verbeek, Luka, & van der Aalst, 2012), which cover 8 different processes with 10 variants each, are used. The objective is to derive a reference model for these 8 processes based on the variants from different municipalities.

In a first step, clustering techniques are used to identify and reconstruct the given model groups. Since the model repository consists of 80 single models with 8 different processes and 10 variants each, it is necessary to identify the relevant models for generating the reference models. Therefore, a process model similarity measure is used, which quantifies the similarity between two process models based on the percentage of common nodes and edges (Minor, Tartakovski, & Bergmann, 2007) on a scale between 0 and 1.

The results show that it is possible to automatically derive a reference model from a given set of enterprise models. Furthermore, typical similarities and differences of the enterprise models are explicated. Hence, the application scenario gives substantive support for the inductive development of reference modelling to become much more efficient and effective.

7 Conclusion and Future Work

Reference modelling offers several advantages for the practice of enterprise modelling (see also chapters by Becker (2015) and Malinova and Mendling (2015)). These benefits, however, can only be derived if high performing reference models are available. As predominant methods are almost exclusively using deductive approaches, this work presents the possibilities and challenges of an inductive approach, contributing to a more innovative approach to process management (see also chapter by Schmiedel and vom Brocke (2015)). Although the presented method does not allow a purely algorithmic approach, it is still able to significantly support the modeller in the reference model development, e.g. in terms of process standardization or developing common or best practices. This potential support is particularly attractive since neither a deductive nor an inductive strategy has preeminent advantages. Consequently, in the practice of reference modelling, it is suitable to link both strategies.

As deductive methods for reference model development are already well known, the paper at hand focuses on the inductive approach and presents a specific seven phases method for the inductive development of reference models. The authors introduced several important subject areas and described particular techniques which are relevant in the given context. These techniques are also applied to a concrete application scenario in order to give an impression of what is already possible today. However, there is a need for intensive further research since the strengths of the techniques in many fields is far away from being adequate. In fact, the presented RefMod-Mine/NSCM approach for process matching won the Process Model Matching Contest 2013 (Cayoglu et al., 2013), although the evaluation in terms of precision, recall and f-measure was only of moderate value. Thus, a further development of corresponding techniques is still necessary and of high importance.

It is the vision of the authors to develop a comprehensive model corpus containing models in a standardized, digital and processable format. Thus, the following long-term research objectives: (1) Creating a consistent understanding of business application systems in different domains, (2) reusing the contained models in other contexts, (3) creating a homogeneous data basis for different application and analysis scenarios. Moreover, the authors aim at publishing the model corpus in terms of open models, much as in the open source idea in the context of software development. However, this very much depends on the license holder of the model corpus' content.

The initial starting point for this ongoing work is the reference model catalogue provided by Fettke & Loos (2002) (rmk.iwi.uni-sb.de/). It contains 98 reference model entries with lexical data and meta-data, such as the number of contained single models. However, this catalogue contains neither digitally processable models (in terms of the used modelling language and a consistent exchange format) nor entries of individual models from different domains. Each model collection or each model within the developed model corpus could be assigned to exactly one of the following three categories based on their origin or type: (1) r*eference model, (2) individual model, and (3) model from controlled modelling scenarios.*

In order to support this further research, the authors developed a process model corpus which could serve as a standardized basis for the evaluation of methods and techniques. Indeed, the corpus currently covers 2,290 single models. Nevertheless, it is limited in terms of scope and diversity. Against this background the corpus should be enhanced by additional models and collections, and provided to other scientists.

Further needs for future work are mentioned in the following:

- Development of further high performing concepts for inductive reference modelling,
- a wide application of new methods to gain more experience in terms of performance,
- an application of the inductive method to develop new reference models and
- the development and application of techniques and algorithms for the corpus development.

Acknowledgement This research has been co-funded by the German Research Foundation DFG, Project "RefMod-Miner", (LO 752/5-1).

References

Ahlemann, F., & Gastl, H. (2007). Process model for an empirically grounded reference model construction. In P. Fettke & P. Loos (Eds.), *Reference modeling for business systems analysis* (pp. 77–97). Hershey, PA: Idea.

Aier, S., Fichter, M., & Fischer, C. (2011). Referenzprozesse empirisch bestimmen – Von Vielfalt zu Standards. *Wirtschaftinformatik und Management, 3*(3), 14–22.

Ardalani, P., Houy, C., Fettke, P., & Loos, P. (2013). Towards a minimal cost of change approach for inductive reference model development. In *Proceedings of the ECIS 2013 completed research*, Utrecht, The Netherlands.

Becker, J. (2015). Designing process modeling tools to facilitate semantic standardization: Increasing the speed of innovation in a digital world. In J. vom Brocke & T. Schmiedel (Eds.), *Business process management: Driving innovation in a digital world*. Berlin: Springer.

Becker, J., Delfmann, P., Knackstedt, R., & Kuropka, D. (2002). Konfigurative Referenzmodellierung. In J. Becker & R. Knackstedt (Eds.), *Wissensmanagement mit Referenzmodellen. Konzepte für die Anwendungssystem- und Organisationsgestaltung* (pp. 25–144). Berlin: Springer.

Becker, M., & Laue, R. (2012). A comparative survey of business process similarity measures. *Computers in Industry, 63*(2), 148–167.

Becker, J., & Meise, V. (2011). Strategy and organizational frame. In J. Becker, M. Kugeler, & M. Rosemann (Eds.), *Process management. A guide for the design of business processes* (pp. 91–132). Berlin: Springer.

Becker, J., Rosemann, M., & Schütte, R. (1995). Grundsätze ordnungsmäßiger Modellierung. *Wirtschaftsinformatik, 37*(5), 435–445.

Becker, J., & Schütte, R. (1997). Referenz-Informationsmodelle für den Handel: Begriff, Nutzen und Empfehlungen für die Gestaltung und unternehmensspezifische Adaption von Referenzmodellen. In H. Krallmann (Ed.), *Wirtschaftsinformatik '97 – Internationale Geschäftstätigkeit auf der Basis flexibler Organisationsstrukturen und leistungsfähiger Informationssysteme* (pp. 427–448). Heidelberg: Physica.

Becker, J., & Schütte, R. (2004). *Handelsinformationssysteme. Domänenorientierte Einführung in die Wirtschaftsinformatik* (2nd ed.). Frankfurt am Main: Redline Wirtschaft.

Cayoglu, U., Dijkman, R., Dumas, M., Fettke, P., Garcia-Banuelos, L., Hake, et al. (2013). *The process model matching contest 2013*. In: BPM 2013 Workshops, LNBIP 171, pp. 442–463, Beijing.

Christine, D., & Matheis, T. (2005). Constructing a reference process model for E-government. In R. Mosca, et al. (ed.) *Proceedings of the 7th International Conference on "The Modern*

Information Technology in the Innovation Processes of the Industrial Enterprises (MITIP)" (pp. 10–14). o.A.
Delfmann, P. (2006). *Adaptive Referenzmodellierung. Methodische Konzepte zur Konstruktion und Anwendung wiederverwendungsorientierter Informationsmodelle* (Vol. 25). Berlin: Logos Verlag.
Delfmann, P. (2010). *Verteilte Informationsmodellierung – Methodische und technische Konzepte zur Disambiguierung und Analyse arbeitsteilig entwickelter Informationsmodelle*. Münster.
Dijkman, R., Dumas, M., van Dongen, B., Käärik, R., & Mendling, J. (2011). Similarity of business process models: Metrics and evaluation. *Information Systems, 36*(2), 498–516. doi:10.1016/j.is.2010.09.006.
Evermann, J. (2009). Theories of meaning in schema matching: An exploratory study. *Information Systems, 34*(1), 28–44. doi:10.1016/j.is.2008.04.001.
Fettke, P. (2006). *Referenzmodellevaluation. Konzeption der strukuralistischen Referenzmodellierung und Entfaltung ontologischer Gütekriterien* (Vol. 5). Berlin: Logos Verlag.
Fettke, P. (2014). Eine Methode zur induktiven Entwicklung von Referenzmodellen. In D. Kundisch, L. Suhl, & L. Beckmann (Eds.), *Tagungsband Multikonferenz Wirtschaftsinformatik 2014 (MKWI 2014)* (pp. 1034–1047). Paderborn: Universität Paderborn.
Fettke, P., & Loos, P. (2002). Der Referenzmodellkatalog als Instrument des Wissensmanagements – Methodik und Anwendung. In J. Becker & R. Knackstedt (Eds.), *Wissensmanagement mit Referenzmodellen. Konzepte für die Anwendungssystem- und Organisationsgestaltung* (pp. 3–24). Berlin: Springer.
Fettke, P., & Loos, P. (2004). Referenzmodellierungsforschung. *Wirtschaftsinformatik, 46*(5), 331–340.
Fettke, P., & Loos, P. (Eds.). (2007). *Reference modeling for business systems analysis* (1st ed.). Hershey, PA: Idea.
Frank, U. (2006). *Towards a pluralistic conception of research methods in information systems research*. Essen: Institut für Informatik und Wirtschaftsinformatik (ICB) der Universität Duisburg-Essen.
Frank, U. (2007). Evaluation of reference models. In P. Fettke & P. Loos (Eds.), *Reference modeling for business systems analysis* (pp. 118–140). Hershey: Idea Group.
Frank, U. (2008). Reflexionen zur sprachlichen Konstruktion von Informationssystemen. In E. Heinemann (Ed.), *Anwendungsinformatik. Die Zukunft des Enterprise Engineering. Festschrift für Erich Ortner zum 60. Geburtstag* (pp. 37–49). Baden-Baden: Nomos.
Garey, M. R., & Johnson, D. S. (1979). *Computer and intractability: A guide to the theory of NP-completeness*. San Francisco, CA: Freeman.
Gottschalk, F., van der Aalst, W. M. P., & Jansen-Vullers, M. H. (2008, November 9–14). Mining reference process models and their configurations. In R. Meersman, Z. Tari, & P. Herrero (Eds.), *On the move to meaningful Internet systems: OTM 2008 workshops, OTM confederated international workshops and posters, ADI, AWeSoMe, COMBEK, EI2N, IWSSA, MONET, OnToContent + QSI, ORM, PerSys, RDDS, SEMELS, and SWWS 2008, Monterrey, Mexico* (pp. 263–272). Berlin: Springer.
Jain, A. K., Murty, M. N., & Flynn, P. J. (1999). Data clustering: A review. *ACM Computing Surveys (CSUR), 31*, 264–323.
Karow, M., Pfeiffer, D., & Räckers, M. (2008). Empirical-based construction of reference models in public administrations. In M. Bichler, T. Hess, H. Krcmar, U. Lechner, F. Matthes, A. Picot, B. Speitkamp, & P. Wolf (Eds.), *Multikonferenz Wirtschaftsinformatik*. Berlin: GITO-Verlag.
Koch, S., Strecker, S., & Frank, U. (2006). Conceptual modelling as a new entry in the bazaar: The open model approach. In E. Damiani, B. Fitzgerald, W. Scacchi, M. Scotto, & G. Succi (Eds.), *Open source systems, IFIP 203* (pp. 9–20). Berlin: Springer.
Li, C., Reichert, M., & Wombacher, A. (2008). On measuring process model similarity based on high-level change operations. In Q. Li, S. Spaccapietra, E. Yu, & A. Olivé (Eds.), *Conceptual modeling – ER 2008* (Vol. 5231, pp. 248–264). Berlin: Springer.
Li, C., Reichert, M., & Wombacher, A. (2010). The MinAdept clustering approach for discovering reference process models out of process variants. *International Journal of Cooperative Information Systems, 19*(3), 159–203.

Malinova, M., & Mendling, J. (2015). Leveraging innovation based on effective process map design: Insights from the case of a European insurance company. In J. vom Brocke & T. Schmiedel (Eds.), *Business process management: Driving innovation in a digital world*. Berlin: Springer.

Miller, G. A. (1998). Nouns in WordNet. In C. Fellbaum (Ed.), *WordNet: An electronic lexical database* (pp. 23–46). Cambridge: The MIT.

Minor, M., Tartakovski, A., & Bergmann, R. (2007). Representation and structure-based similarity assessment for agile workflows. In R. O. Weber & M. M. Richter (Eds.), *Case-based reasoning research and development, 7th international conference on case-based reasoning, ICCBR 2007* (LNCS, Vol. 4626, pp. 224–238). Berlin: Springer.

Porter, M. F. (1997). *An algorithm for suffix stripping*. *Readings in information retrieval* (pp. 313–316). San Francisco, CA: Morgan Kaufmann.

Rahm, E., & Bernstein, P. A. (2001a). A survey of approaches to automatic schema matching. *The Very Large Database Journal, 10*, 334–350.

Rahm, E., & Bernstein, P. A. (2001b). A survey of approaches to automatic schema matching. *International Journal on Very Large Data Base, 10*(4), 334–350.

Rehse, J.-R., Fettke, P., & Loos, P. (2013). Eine Untersuchung der Potentiale automatisierter Abstraktionsansätze für Geschäftsprozessmodelle im Hinblick auf die induktive Entwicklung von Referenzprozessmodellen. In *Proceedings of the 11th international conference on Wirtschaftsinformatik (WI-2013)*, Leipzig, Germany.

Scheer, A.-W. (1998). *Wirtschaftsinformatik – Referenzmodelle für industrielle Geschäftsprozesse [Studienausgabe]* (2nd ed.). Berlin: Springer.

Schlagheck, B. (2000). *Objektorientierte Referenzmodelle für das Prozess- und Projektcontrolling – Grundlagen – Konstruktion – Anwendungsmöglichkeiten*. Wiesbaden: DUV.

Schmiedel, T., & vom Brocke, J. (2015). Business process management: Potentials and challenges of driving innovation. In J. vom Brocke & T. Schmiedel (Eds.), *Business process management: Driving innovation in a digital world*. Berlin: Springer.

Schütte, R. (1998). *Grundsätze ordnungsmäßiger Referenzmodellierung – Konstruktion konfigurations- und anpassungsorientierter Modelle*. Wiesbaden: Gabler.

Schwegmann, A. (1999). *Objektorientierte Referenzmodellierung – Theoretische Grundlagen und praktische Anwendung*. Wiesbaden: DUV.

Thaler, T., Hake, P., Fettke, P., & Loos, P. (2014). Evaluating the evaluation of process matching techniques. In L. Suhl & D. Kundisch (Hrsg.), *Tagungsband der Multikonferenz Wirtschaftsinformatik (MKWI-14)*. Paderborn: Universität Paderborn.

Thomas, O. (2006). *Management von Referenzmodellen. Entwurf und Realisierung eines Informationssystems zur Entwicklung und Anwendung von Referenzmodellen*. Berlin: Logos.

Vanhatalo, J., Völzer, H., & Koehler, J. (2009). The refined process structure tree. *Data and Knowledge Engineering, 68*(9), 793–818. doi:10.1016/j.datak.2009.02.015.

Vogelaar, J. J. C. L., Verbeek, H. M. W., Luka, B., & van der Aalst, W. M. P. (2012). Comparing business processes to determine the feasibility of configurable models: A case study. In F. Daniel, K. Barkaoui, & S. Dustdar (Eds.), *Business process management workshops* (LNBIP, Vol. 100, pp. 50–61). Berlin: Springer.

vom Brocke, J. (2003). *Referenzmodellierung – Gestaltung und Verteilung von Konstruktionsprozessen*. Berlin: Logos.

Walter, J., Fettke, P., & Loos, P. (2012a). *How to identify and design successful business process models: An inductive method*. Paper presented at the Promoting Business Process Management Excellence in Russia – Proceedings and Report of the PropelleR 2012 Workshop. Innovation Forum PropelleR (PropelleR-2012). Moscow, Russian Federation (02.2013).

Walter, J., Fettke, P., & Loos, P. (2012b). *Zur Identifikation von Strukturanalogien in Prozessmodellen*. In Leena Suhl; Dennis Kundisch (Hrsg.), *Tagungsband der Multikonferenz Wirtschaftsinformatik (MKWI-14)*. Paderborn: Universität Paderborn.

Weidlich, M., Dijkman, R., & Mendling, J. (2010). The ICoP framework: Identification of correspondences between process models. In B. Pernici (Ed.), *Advanced information systems engineering: 22nd international conference, CAiSE 2010* (LNCS, Vol. 6051, pp. 483–498). Berlin: Springer.

Part IV

Driving Innovation Through New Generation Process Modeling

Designing Process Modeling Tools to Facilitate Semantic Standardization: Increasing the Speed of Innovation in a Digital World

Jörg Becker

Abstract

Business process management (BPM) projects are increasing in size and becoming ever more complex. With companies being subject to increasing degrees of competition and a more dynamic market environment, it is crucial to implement organizational changes rapidly in order to remain innovative and competitive. BPM projects are an important tool to achieve this, yet they are often delayed or fail completely. Frequently they suffer from a high degree of heterogeneity resulting from huge project teams modeling hundreds of processes. Modeling conventions can help harmonize process models, yet they are hard to develop and enforce in large teams. Building modeling tools such that modelers must comply with conventions can alleviate these problems. In this chapter, I present five design principles for such tools and one prototypical implementation, the *icebricks* modeling tool.

1 Motivation

In today's globalized world, business process management (BPM) endeavors undertaken by companies have to cope with increasing degrees of organizational complexity. Multinational corporations work in spatially and temporally distributed teams, large enterprises integrate vertically to manage all parts of the value chain in a unified way, and networks of highly specialized firms collaborate to efficiently provide products and services. Often, large parts of the work have become digital, with complex sociotechnical systems driving the business. Hence, BPM projects are conducted in large, possibly interorganizational environments (Houy, Fettke,

J. Becker (✉)
Department of Information Systems, University of Muenster, Leonardo-Campus 3, 48149 Münster, Germany
e-mail: joerg.becker@ercis.uni-muenster.de

J. vom Brocke, T. Schmiedel (eds.), *BPM – Driving Innovation in a Digital World*, Management for Professionals, DOI 10.1007/978-3-319-14430-6_12

Loos, van der Aalst, & Krogstie, 2011). In addition, increasingly dynamic markets and short innovation cycles require companies not only to change faster in general, but also faster than their competitors. Hence, it is important that BPM projects—vehicles to prepare and implement change—are conducted rapidly despite the complexities with which they have to cope.

Business process modeling languages are important means to document the current state of a company's process landscape and to conceptualize how improvements and innovations could be designed and implemented. Against the backdrop of the organizational setting described above, it is not surprising that BPM project teams are well staffed. When modeling processes in such very large teams, it is hard for a single person to maintain an overview of all the models being created. Lack of standardization may be the result, which is an obstacle for the subsequent implementation of models.

Sources of ambiguities are manifold [see, e.g., Pfeiffer (2008)]. For instance, a modeling language's constructs often allow different modelers to express similar things in different ways, thereby obfuscating structural analogies. The most important source of ambiguity, though, is the use of natural language to describe modeling constructs. Without standardization, different modelers will use different terms to express the same things, will use the same terms for different things, and will describe processes on very different levels of abstraction. As a result, a process landscape documented by a huge team can easily be heterogeneous enough to make major consolidation efforts necessary before productive work, i.e., designing innovations, can start. Combating ambiguities automatically with digital systems, e.g., by using ontologies or techniques from natural language processing, is often not feasible in practical settings.

Instead of fixing these problems after they have been caused, I argue that it is better to avoid making them in the first place. For BPM projects, this means primarily to standardize the vocabulary and the level of abstraction before modeling even the first process. This can be accomplished by setting up a comprehensive glossary upfront, either by using an existing one or defining it oneself, and mandating modelers to comply. It also helps to provide them with standardized modeling layers, limited freedom with regard to layout and control flow design, and, possibly, a reference model of the domain under analysis. To ensure modelers follow the rules, modeling software must be built such that the rules are impossible to violate. Adherence to semantic standardization rules not only ensures that ambiguities inherent to free use of natural language are eradicated, it also guides modelers in choosing an adequate level of abstraction at which processes should be described.

As a consequence of having standardized and comparable process models, BPM project teams can avoid lengthy consolidation phases and start working on actual improvements immediately after having completed modeling, thereby increasing the pace of change and facilitating rapid organizational innovation.

The remainder of this article is structured as follows. Section 2 discusses guidelines of modeling, by which I mean best practices that should be obeyed in process modeling projects. Section 3 illustrates how modeling tools can be designed against the backdrop of modeling guidelines. In particular, five design principles are discussed which all have a positive effect on guideline adherence. In Sect. 4, I demonstrate the *icebricks* approach, which is a prototypical implementation of a modeling tool that obeys the design principles. Finally, Sect. 5 presents the conclusion.

2 Guidelines of Modeling

As mentioned in the previous section, business process modeling is central to any BPM project. The goal of business process modeling is to create transparency regarding a company's business processes. Numerous different methodologies exist to organize a BPM project [cf. Kettinger, Teng, and Guha (1997) or more recent books such as Becker, Kugeler, and Rosemann (2011) or Schmelzer and Sesselmann (2010)]. It is not this article's purpose to delve into the details of these methodologies, and thus, I will adhere to a generic four-step procedure which is compatible with most methodologies. It is illustrated in Fig. 1. Starting with a preparation phase, whose purpose is to set up the project in the organization and to prepare modeling activities, a project typically proceeds with the modeling itself. This may involve, for instance, as-is- and to-be-modeling if the project's purpose is to improve business processes, or it may simply involve as-is-modeling, e.g., if the goal is to select a suitable Enterprise Resource Planning (ERP) tool. Following that, models are used to achieve a goal, e.g., incorporation of innovations. Obviously, the nature of these activities is diverse and depends on the project's purpose. Finally, an evaluation should be conducted to see if the goals have been attained.

All too often, only limited attention is paid to the preparation phase of modeling projects. Consequently, this is what I will emphasize in this article. In fact, preparation is essential in modeling projects as the ability of a project team to use process models heavily depends on the models' quality. While quality assurance might be relatively easy to handle if only one or two persons create the models, in large projects with huge modeling teams one can quickly end up with an incomparable pile of process models that is of no use in subsequent phases.

One answer to such problems is to alleviate them after they have been identified. This reactive approach is the idea behind much of the research published in the BPM field. Consider the example of semantic ambiguities in modeling element descriptions such as functions in an Event-driven Process Chain (EPC). In large distributed modeling projects, modelers will likely not use the same terms for the same things (thereby introducing synonym conflicts) or may even accidentally use the same terms for two different things (thereby introducing homonym conflicts). Most techniques supporting management of large model collections process natural

Fig. 1 Generic modeling methodology

language and must resolve these inconsistencies, which is a major challenge (Dijkman, La Rosa, & Reijers, 2012). Approaches do exist (Weidlich, Dijkman, & Mendling, 2010), yet given the fact that, for instance, Tweets are known to be particularly hard to analyze computationally as they are very short (Kouloumpis, Wilson, & Moore, 2011), and given that modeling element descriptions are even shorter, it is worth thinking about alternatives.

Instead of reacting to problems after model creation, it is also conceivable to work on avoiding the emergence of problems. In fact, this is a constituent part of a model project's preparation phase. In the example above, standardization endeavors could be undertaken before modeling, e.g., by creating a glossary of terms to be used. If all modelers strictly follow this glossary, modeling element descriptions can be harmonized significantly. Other problems can also be addressed prior to modeling by defining appropriate modeling conventions.

In the literature, different guidelines can be found that describe best practices for modeling projects. One of these–the guidelines of modeling (GoM)–(Becker, Probandt, & Vering, 2012; Becker, Rosemann, & von Uthmann, 2000; Schütte & Rotthowe, 1998) have been developed as a set of recommendations for high quality process modeling. The idea was to formulate rules analogously to generally accepted accounting principles. In this paper, I follow the presentation of Becker et al. (2000), which divides the guidelines of modeling into three basic guidelines (correctness, relevance, economic efficiency) which can be considered as mandatory for high quality modeling and three optional guidelines (clarity, comparability, systematic design) which are not strictly necessary but helpful nevertheless.

GoM1, *Guideline of correctness*: In modeling, a modeler should produce both syntactically and semantically correct models. Syntactic correctness can be evaluated easily by checking compliance with a meta model (if such a meta model exists). Semantic correctness refers to the real world aspects described by the process model. The goal is to faithfully represent this part of the real world such that model interpretation does not lead to false conclusions.

GoM2, *Guideline of relevance*: Obviously, the universe of discourse, the modeling language, and the modeled system should be relevant with respect to the goals of the modeling endeavor. If there is any modeling element that could be removed without hampering project success, then this element is not relevant and should not have been modeled in the first place. This is a motivation for creating models of minimal size, constrained by the fact that they must serve a purpose.

GoM3, *Guideline of economic efficiency*: Ultimately, any modeling endeavor is an organizational activity from which some benefit should be derived, but which generates cost at the same time. Hence, adherence to any of the guidelines is only justified if the cost-benefit-ratio is appropriate.

GoM4, *Guideline of clarity*: This guideline encourages a modeler to prepare the model in such a way that it can easily be read and understood by viewers. Besides using appropriate descriptions for modeling element labels, modelers should also design the model in a graphically appealing way. Graphical aspects of modeling have been investigated by Moody (2009). Models should also be clear from a conceptual point of view. For instance, this means that the constructs of a modeling language should have clear meanings. Attempts to analyze this aspect are frequently undertaken based on the Bunge-Wand-Weber (BWW) ontology (Wand & Weber, 1993).

GoM5, *Guideline of comparability*: To ensure comparability among different models, it is vital that all modeling conventions are applied consistently within a project. This includes all guidelines regarding modeling style, layout, naming, etc.

GoM6, *Guideline of systematic design*: If not only the process view but also other views (e.g., data view or organizational view) are modeled, it is important to maintain a systematic relationship between modeling elements from different views to ensure all models are properly integrated. Usually, a solid meta model provides such integration.

Another set of guidelines has been proposed by Mendling, Reijers, and van der Aalst (2010). They are called the seven process modeling guidelines (7PMG) and primarily address control flow design and model size.

7PMG1, *Use as few elements in the model as possible*: as small models are more easily understood than large ones, it is desirable to keep models as small as possible. Moreover, modelers are more likely to make mistakes when creating large models.

7PMG2, *Minimize the routing paths per element*: the control flow should be kept as simple as possible, since modeling complex control flows increases the likelihood of modeling mistakes.

7PMG3, *Use one start and one end event*: to increase understandability and avoid mistakes, it is recommendable to model processes such that their beginnings and endings are found at one place in the models, not at multiple places.

7PMG4, *Model as structured as possible*: In this guideline, the adjective *structured* refers to modeling such that each modeling element branching the control flow comes with a corresponding element merging the control flow at a later place in the model. What results is a block-structured model whose control flow structure is less confusing than that of a model for which the guideline has been disobeyed.

7PMG5, *Avoid OR routing elements*: Not only does adhering to this guideline avoid the famous vicious circle paradox, but it also facilitates model comprehension as OR routing semantics can be very complicated if excessively used.

7PMG6, *Use verb-object activity labels*: A consistent style of labeling activities makes models more readable and avoids strange mistakes (such as not using a verb at all) that might otherwise occur if modelers are in hurry or believe the activity is self-explanatory.

7PMG7, *Decompose the model if it has more than 50 elements*: In line with the first guideline, the recommendation is to keep models as small as possible and to never exceed a size of 50 modeling elements.

Many other sets of guidelines have been put forth in scientific literature [e.g., see Rosemann (2006a, 2006b)] and even more can be found in management literature targeting practitioners. It is commonly believed that carefully designed modeling conventions do increase model quality. Empirical investigations conducted on this topic support this claim [e.g., in UML modeling, see Lange, DuBois, Chaudron, and Demeyer (2006)].

3 Guideline-Driven Tool Design

Whilst modeling conventions can improve model quality, an organization will only enjoy these benefits if the modelers consistently apply the conventions. Unfortunately, people in practice often violate them even if the trouble of defining conventions has been taken. Reasons can be manifold. Additional effort for applying conventions may appear unjustified if modelers are under time pressure. Individual work results may appear to be of inferior quality and hammered into a framework that does not fit to the case at hand. The benefits of standardization though unfold only when looking at the big picture, after each individual modeler has done his part of the job.

Modeling research often focuses on modeling languages, yet it is also important not to forget that digital products—modeling tools—are the means by which languages are provided to the modelers (Recker, 2012). Consequently, the idea is to build modeling tools in such a way that it is impossible to violate modeling conventions. Alternatively, if this cannot be done, build it such that violating conventions comes along with prohibitively much effort. In this section, I propose five design principles for modeling tools that support one or many modeling guidelines, thus contributing to homogenizing process models in large modeling projects. Their correspondence to the guidelines is made explicit in Table 1 at the end of this section.

3.1 Enforce Naming Conventions

As the primary source of heterogeneity is free use of natural language, the first principle is to enforce naming conventions. In literature, it is often recommended to label activities of process models in accordance with the verb-object style (Sharp & McDermott, 2008). For instance, checking an invoice should be represented by an activity labeled *check invoice*. Labels such as *invoice checking* might convey the same information but are discouraged. Also, novice modelers sometimes use labels such as *invoice management*, assuming that the kind of work they refer to is self-explanatory. Such descriptions should always be avoided.

In an empirical study, Reijers, Recker, and Mendling (2010) analyze results from an experiment in which different naming styles were compared in terms of ambiguity and usefulness. Participants clearly favored the verb-object style over other styles of labeling activities. Unfortunately, although modelers appear to like

Table 1 Design principles and how they address best practices in process modeling

Design principle	GoM	7PMG	Description
Naming conventions	GoM4 GoM5	7PMG6	Naming conventions make models easily readable as any activity is described in a standardized way
Glossary	GoM1 GoM4 GoM5	7PMG6	The glossary ensures that only well-defined terms are used and that all members of a project team share a common understanding (which is made explicit in the glossary). This facilitates a semantically faithful representation of the domain
Reference models	GoM1 GoM2 GoM3 GoM4 GoM5		Reference models provide a generic structure to start with and thereby facilitate a common understanding of the domain among all team members. This facilitates a semantically faithful representation of the domain and avoids the modeling of irrelevant aspects. It also saves the effort of creating an appropriate structure
Variants	GoM4	7PMG1 7PMG2 7PMG3 7PMG4 7PMG5	Variants avoid cognitively complex control flow structures and make models more readable. Important choices are captured as different variants. Each variant is a simple, mostly linear process. As it only captures a part of the entire process, it also makes models graphically smaller compared to an integrated model
Automatic layout	GoM4 GoM5		Automatic layout ensures that modelers do not try to encode meaning by arranging modeling elements in a specific way. Otherwise, modelers can try to express aspects that are not reflected in the abstract syntax of the language

verb-object labeling most, they do not use this style consistently when they create models. Hence, Reijers et al. (2010) argue that modelers should be supported by a modeling tool. They propose using algorithms to parse labels written by modelers in order to detect grammatical mistakes and to prompt users to fix them.

3.2 Use a Glossary

As naming conventions only refer to standardizing the grammatical part, the logical next step is to also standardize the meaning of terms. To do so, Reijers et al. (2010) also envision the use of controlled vocabularies for verbs and objects. In such controlled vocabularies, modelers may only use verbs and objects from a predefined list. Hence, what they propose is a glossary.

Different styles of enforcing the use of a glossary are conceivable. The simplest solution would be to not allow users to type in textual descriptions into activities and make them choose verbs and objects from lists. This solution is most transparent to the user and provides him with an overview of existing terms, which is of great help when searching for appropriate words. If lists become too long, it may be necessary to provide some automatic support in finding the correct terms.

Techniques to narrow down the list might involve adding structure, such as organizing the terms in a hierarchy.

More elaborate approaches can be designed when using techniques from computational linguistics. A user could be allowed to type in natural language text, as he would do if there were no controlled vocabulary. An algorithm can then parse his sentence and deconstruct it into its parts. This allows not only a verification of the phrase structure, i.e., whether it is compliant with the desired naming convention such as verb-object style. It is also possible to identify the words and to check whether they comply with any word contained in the glossary. If not, known synonyms of the user's term, e.g., taken from WordNet (Fellbaum, 1998), can be used to find an appropriate glossary term. Such a system can be built, as has been demonstrated by a prototypical software artifact (Delfmann, Herwig, & Lis, 2009).

The most challenging task, though, is not to use the terms but to create the glossary in the first place. Relevant verbs and objects must be identified before modeling. Process modeling projects benefit from carrying out technical term modeling before actually starting with modeling processes (Becker et al., 2011). In a technical term model, the key objects an organization is working with (either material objects such as goods or immaterial objects such as certain information) are laid down. These technical terms correspond to the objects processed in the organization's activities. Hence, technical term models can be used to supply organization-specific terms for the glossary. However, instead of specifying terms for each and every object manually, it can be more economical to use existing dictionaries and modify them accordingly. For instance, Reijers et al. (2010) recommend using the XML Common Business Library (xCBL)[1] or the Health Level 7 (HLC) reference information model[2] to extract terms.

Similar approaches can be used to define verbs. With a list of those objects most important to the organization's business, a list of activities that modelers will likely encounter can be deduced. Again, much effort can be saved by starting with a standardized, domain-specific set of verbs, and only customizing this if necessary. Standardized sets of verbs describing business activities have been put forth in the literature. For instance, Mendling, Recker, and Reijers (2010) extracted from the SAP reference model (Keller & Teufel, 1998) the most frequently used verbs and tried to apply two different verb sets to classify and standardize the notations. The first was a set of eight verbs taken from the MIT process handbook (Malone, 2003), which consists of "create", "modify", "preserve", "destroy", "combine", "separate", "decide", and "manage". Second, they have used a verb classification scheme by Levin (1993), which consists of 49 different classes. Although these classes are not directly verbs themselves, a representative for each could be chosen to come up with a list of verbs to be used in a process modeling project. Applied to the SAP reference model, both classification schemes left many verbs unclassified (Mendling et al., 2010). Nevertheless, they can be suitable starting points for

[1] http://www.xcbl.org/

[2] http://www.hl7.org/implement/standards/rim.cfm

developing better verb sets. Moreover, the fact that these schemes do cover all verbs in the SAP reference model does not imply that they are inappropriate for modeling. Quite the contrary may be true, as a reduced set of verbs may reduce the use of exotic verbs, thereby facilitating standardization and understandability of the models. To illustrate this, consider the example of PICTURE (Becker, Algermissen, Pfeiffer, & Räckers, 2007b), a domain-specific modeling methodology tailored to the pubic administrations domain. It was developed in an EU research project and has been applied in numerous BPM projects, e.g., in the administration of the University of Münster (Becker, Algermissen, Pfeiffer, & Räckers, 2007a) or in a Brazilian municipal public administration (Matzner, Alexandrini, Araujo, & Becker, 2009). It can be shown that ambiguities typically found in natural language labels of process models can be avoided with such a language (Breuker, Pfeiffer, & Becker, 2009).

3.3 Incorporate Reference Models

Providing structured domain descriptions can help when modeling processes. They reduce the effort of forming an understanding of the domain as a whole. Even if the description is inaccurate, partly erroneous, or outdated, a reference model can still be of value, as modifying it may be easier than doing green-field modeling.

A reference model may provide actual process models created in a (semi-) formal language, but it could also have any other form, e.g., a pictorial framework. The only requirement is that it should provide structure and guide modeling activities. Pinggera et al. (2010) show that particularly casual (i.e., inexperienced) modelers benefit from a structured description of the domain. In an experiment, 83 master's students were asked to model a process based on a textual description with varying degree of structure. Those students provided with well-structured descriptions created more accurate processes, presumably due to their improved understanding of the domain.

3.4 Represent Decisions as Variants

Empirical studies identified that models will be much more comprehensible if their modelers adhere to a structured style of modeling (Claes et al., 2012). They can achieve this by focusing, at any time, only on a very small part of the overall model. Although it is the ultimate purpose of a model to grasp the big picture, this appears to be harmful when done during modeling. Theories such as the cognitive load theory (Sweller, 1988) are sometimes used to explain this phenomenon. The complexity involved in trying to design too many parts of the process simultaneously tends to simply overwhelm modelers.

Other empirical studies aim at explaining understandability of process models and related concepts with respect to certain model factors [e.g., see Cardoso (2006), Piattini, Visaggio, Canfora, Ruiz, and García (2005), or Reijers and Mendling

(2011)]. Model factors refer to properties of the process models. Typically, these factors can be thought of as drivers of model complexity. For instance, it has been shown in a study by Reijers and Mendling (2011) that an increased number of control flow arcs per activity leads to decreased understandability of the model. Hence, it is generally desirable to keep the complexity of the control flow as low as possible so that models are easy to work with. Although we also know that modeling expertise can compensate for the negative effects of complexity (Reijers & Mendling, 2011), it is also true that—by the very nature of a BPM project—not each and every stakeholder can be a modeling expert. Non-experts hire experts to create models, yet the non-experts nevertheless need to understand these models. For this reason, the need to reduce model complexity is even more pressing.

To reduce the complexity of a process model, it can be advantageous to explicitly create different variants of the same process. Each variant may look quite similar to the others, yet with subtle differences in parts of the model. The advantage over distinguishing between all the different variants by means of split and merge control flow constructs is that each time someone views a model, he or she first chooses the appropriate variant and then sees only the relevant part of the model. The single variant can be much easier to read than a model comprising all variants. Languages with emphasis on variants avoid complex modeling situations such that overly complex models cannot be created.

A huge challenge with variants is that there is danger of redundancy. If you fully embrace the concept of variants (i.e., if you create models as individual variants instead of creating an integrated model from which variants are derived), different people working at different variants will effectively work on the same parts of the model. To keep things consistent, the concept of occurrence copies comes to the rescue. Variants can be created by copying and modifying other variants, so that commonalities can be tracked by the tool. Nevertheless, regular reviews of all variants are necessary for complex processes. See Dijkman et al. (2012) for more information on strategies to maintain consistency among process model variants.

Variants have been implemented in several modeling tools. Provop, for instance, is one approach providing functionality for managing process model variants and avoiding redundancy (Hallerbach, Bauer, & Reichert, 2010). Another implementation of a similar variants concept is based on Eclipse (Weber, Reichert, Mendling, & Reijers, 2011).

3.5 Automate the Layout

For any kind of model, it is essential to prepare it in a visually appealing way to make it understandable (Moody, 2009). Moreover, visual cues can also be used to convey additional information beyond that which the modeling language is supposed to express. A simple example would be a convention to model processes from left to right, which implies that an activity occurs prior to another if and only if it is on the other activity's left side. In the literature, the term secondary notation has been coined to describe such phenomena (Petre, 2006; Schrepfer, Wolf, Mendling, & Reijers, 2009).

For these reasons, it is desirable to have the tool carry out the layout of process models. Not only can this help to create more clearly arranged models (provided that the algorithm is good), it also prevents different modelers from using different aspects of secondary notation. All information expressed in the process models should follow the same conventions, including secondary notation. These conventions should be codified in the form of a layout algorithm which is the same for each modeler. Otherwise, there is a risk that readers misinterpret certain aspects of some models.

4 The Icebricks Approach

The *icebricks* tool is a process modeling software prototype developed to support BPM consulting projects in the retail industry. The tool's purpose is to capture a broad, conceptual overview of the business processes. Its process models can be used for process-oriented reorganization, software selection, and similar project objectives. Not in its scope is the generation of highly detailed workflow models that are meant to be executed (or at least have execution semantics). Icebricks models are meant to be interpreted by humans only and serve as a basis for discussion.

The icebricks modeling environment is structured in four layers (cf. Fig. 2). On the first layer, modelers design a framework, which should represent an overview of the entire process landscape within a single picture. Its modeling elements represent main processes. Each main process is modeled on the second layer using modeling elements corresponding to detail processes. In turn, detail processes are modeled on the third layer using modeling elements called process bricks. These bricks are the atomic elements. On the fourth layer, they can be described using attributes. This

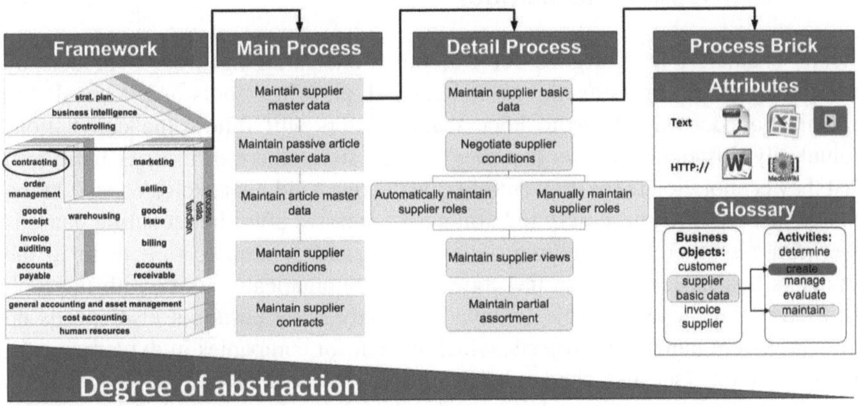

Fig. 2 Exemplary overview of the icebricks tool (Becker et al., 2013)

includes both standardized attributes with predefined domains (working time, IT systems, organizational units, etc.) and any kind of free form attribute, which could be anything that can be stored as a file on a computer (MS Office documents, pictures, videos, BPMN diagrams, etc.).

Modeling on the first layer is done virtually without any restrictions. Elements can be arranged freely and may have any form of visual appearance. As there is only one framework per modeling project, standardization on this layer would be counterproductive. The second and third layers, though, are fairly restrictive in terms of modeling. Each element is described in verb-object-style and a glossary is used to maintain semantic consistency. The control flow is deliberately kept simple. There is only one start and one end element, no cycles in the control flow are allowed, but elements can have multiple predecessors and successors. Complex decisions are represented using the variants concept as explained in the previous section. The model layout is generated automatically following the convention of top to bottom modeling. The fourth layer may contain both structured and unstructured information. Hence, the tool can integrate more detailed process descriptions if necessary. By default, the tool is shipped with the retail-H reference model (Becker & Schütte, 2004) to guide modelers through their projects. It could be replaced if the tool were to be applied in a different industry.

We used the icebricks tool in various case studies in the retail sector. As an example, consider one project in which we applied icebricks for ERP-system selection and process optimization. Modeling preparation involved selecting appropriate attributes that the customer deemed relevant for the project. No other activities, most importantly crafting a full-fledged modeling conventions document, were necessary, since the tool's enforced conventions were impossible to violate by modelers. Not only has much effort been saved this way, the project has also been accelerated a great deal. More details can be found in Becker, Clever, Holler, Püster, & Shitkova (2013).

5 Conclusion and Outlook

In this chapter, I have argued for rigorously standardizing process models by embedding modeling conventions into digital modeling tools. As a result, an organization does not have to hope that modelers will follow the conventions voluntarily. Instead, it knows that they will do so, as the tool itself is built such that they cannot violate the conventions. On the one hand, this avoids consolidation phases that are often necessary to harmonize processes after the modeling phase is over. On the other hand, defining conventions and communicating them to the modelers is also easier, since the conventions automatically come with the tool. This saves time in BPM projects, which not only saves costs but also speeds up innovative reorganization projects, which is vital for companies in dynamic, competitive markets [see also chapter by Schmiedel and vom Brocke (2015)].

With icebricks, a prototype has been developed that demonstrates the feasibility of this concept. Hence, future research can focus on extending icebricks with other features that might facilitate standardization and easy comprehension of process models. As an example, labeling activities to visualize the nature of the verbs used within their labels could be pursued to visualize the nature of the activities in a process. It has been proposed by Mendling et al. (2010) and was also applied in a domain-specific modeling language for public administrations (Becker et al., 2007a). A next step could be to develop visualizations for retail processes.

References

Becker, J., Algermissen, L., Pfeiffer, D., & Räckers, M. (2007a). Bausteinbasierte Modellierung von Prozesslandschaften mit der PICTURE-Methode am Beispiel der Universitätsverwaltung Münster. *Wirtschaftsinformatik, 49*(4), 267–279.

Becker, J., Algermissen, L., Pfeiffer, D., & Räckers, M. (2007b). Local, participative process modelling – The PICTURE-approach. In *1st international workshop on management of business processes in government* (pp. 33–48). Brisbane, Australia.

Becker, J., Clever, N., Holler, J., Püster, J., & Shitkova, M. (2013). Integrating process modeling methodology, language and tool – A design science approach. In *6th IFIP WG 8.1 working conference, PoEM 2013* (pp. 221–235). Riga, Latvia.

Becker, J., Kugeler, M., & Rosemannm, M. (2011). *Process management: A guide for the design of business processes* (2nd ed.). Berlin: Springer.

Becker, J., Probandt, W., & Vering, O. (2012). *Grundsätze ordnungsmäßiger Modellierung: Konzeption und Praxisbeispiel für ein effizientes Prozessmanagement*. Berlin: Springer.

Becker, J., Rosemann, M., & von Uthmann, C. (2000). Guidelines of business process modeling. In W. M. P. van der Aalst, J. Desel, & A. Oberweis (Eds.), *Business process management models, techniques, and empirical studies* (pp. 30–49). Springer: Berlin.

Becker, J., & Schütte, R. (2004). *Handelsinformationssysteme* (2nd ed.). Frankfurt am Main: Redline Wirtschaft.

Breuker, D., Pfeiffer, D., & Becker, J. (2009). Reducing the variations in intra- and interorganizational business process modeling – An empirical evaluation. In *Internationale Tagung Wirtschaftsinformatik*. Vienna, Austria.

Cardoso, J. (2006). Process control-flow complexity metric: An empirical validation. In *2006 I.E. international conference on services computing (SCC'06)* (pp. 167–173). Chicago, IL.

Claes, J., Vanderfeesten, I., Reijers, H., Pinggera, J., Weidlich, M., Zugal, S., et al. (2012). Tying process model quality to the modeling process: The impact of structuring, movement, and speed background on the process of process modeling. In *10th international conference on business process management (BPM 2012)* (pp. 33–48). Tallinn, Estonia.

Delfmann, P., Herwig, S., & Lis, L. (2009). Unified enterprise knowledge representation with conceptual models – Capturing corporate language in naming conventions. In *30th international conference on information systems*. Phoenix, Arizona.

Dijkman, R., La Rosa, M., & Reijers, H. A. (2012). Managing large collections of business process models – Current techniques and challenges. *Computers in Industry, 63*(2), 91–97.

Fellbaum, C. (1998). *WordNet: An electronic lexical database*. Cambridge, MA: MIT Press.

Hallerbach, A., Bauer, T., & Reichert, M. (2010). Capturing variability in business process models: The Provop approach. *Journal of Software Maintenance and Evolution: Research and Practice, 22*(6–7), 519–546.

Houy, C., Fettke, P., Loos, P., van der Aalst, W. M. P., & Krogstie, J. (2011). Business process management in the large. *Business and Information Systems Engineering, 3*(6), 385–388.

Keller, G., & Teufel, T. (1998). *SAP R/3 process–oriented implementation: Iterative process prototyping*. Boston, MA: Addison-Wesley.

Kettinger, W. J., Teng, J. T. C., & Guha, S. (1997). Business process change: A study of methodologies, techniques, and tools. *MIS Quarterly, 21*(1), 55–80.

Kouloumpis, E., Wilson, T., & Moore, J. (2011). Twitter sentiment analysis: The good the bad and the OMG! In *fifth international AAAI conference on weblogs and social media* (pp. 538–541). Barcelona, Spain.

Lange, C. F. J., DuBois, B., Chaudron, M. R. V., & Demeyer, S. (2006). Experimentally investigating the effectiveness and effort of modeling conventions for the UML. In *9th international conference on model driven engineering languages and systems (MoDELS 2006)* (pp. 27–41). Genova, Italy.

Levin, B. (1993). *English verb classes and alternations: A preliminary investigation* (Vol. 37). Chicago, IL: University of Chicago Press.

Malone, T. W. (2003). *Organizing business knowledge: The MIT process handbook.* Cambridge, MA: MIT Press.

Matzner, M., Alexandrini, F., Araujo, T. S., & Becker, J. (2009). Process modeling in Brazilian public administrations: The domain-specific PICTURE approach. In *Americas conference on information systems*. San Francisco, CA.

Mendling, J., Recker, J., & Reijers, H. A. (2010). On the usage of labels and icons in business process modeling. *International Journal of Information System Modeling and Design, 1*(2), 40–58.

Mendling, J., Reijers, H. A., & van der Aalst, W. M. P. (2010). Seven process modeling guidelines (7PMG). *Information and Software Technology, 52*(2), 127–136.

Moody, D. L. (2009). The "physics" of notations: Toward a scientific basis for constructing visual notations in software engineering. *IEEE Transactions on Software Engineering, 35*(6), 756–779.

Petre, M. (2006). Cognitive dimensions "beyond the notation". *Journal of Visual Languages and Computing, 17*(4), 292–301.

Pfeiffer, D. (2008). *Semantic business process analysis – Building block-based construction of automatically analyzable business process models*. Dissertation, University of Münster, Germany.

Piattini, M., Visaggio, C. A., Canfora, G., Ruiz, F., & García, F. (2005). A family of experiments to validate metrics for software process models. *Journal of Systems and Software, 77*(2), 113–129.

Pinggera, J., Zugal, S., Weber, B., Fahland, D., Weidlich, M., Mendling, J., & Reijers, H. (2010). How the structuring of domain knowledge helps casual process modelers. In *29th international conference on conceptual modeling (ER 2010)* (Vol. 6412, pp. 445–451). Vancouver, BC.

Recker, J. (2012). "Modeling with tools is easier, believe me": The effects of tool functionality on modeling grammar usage beliefs. *Information Systems, 37*(3), 213–226.

Reijers, H. A., & Mendling, J. (2011). A study into the factors that influence the understandability of business process models. *IEEE Transactions on Systems, Man, and Cybernetics – Part A, 41* (3), 449–462.

Reijers, H. A., Recker, J., & Mendling, J. (2010). Activity labeling in process modeling: Empirical insights and recommendations. *Information Systems, 35*(4), 467–482.

Rosemann, M. (2006a). Potential pitfalls of process modeling: Part A. *Business Process Management Journal, 12*(2), 249–254.

Rosemann, M. (2006b). Potential pitfalls of process modeling: Part B. *Business Process Management Journal, 12*(3), 377–384.

Schmelzer, H. J., & Sesselmann, W. (2010). *Geschäftsprozessmanagement in der Praxis: Kunden zufrieden stellen – Produktivität steigern - Wert erhöhen* (7th ed.). Munich: Carl Hanser.

Schmiedel, T., & vom Brocke, J. (2015). Business process management: Potentials and challenges of driving innovation. In J. vom Brocke & T. Schmiedel (Eds.), *Business process management: Driving innovation in a digital world.* Berlin: Springer.

Schrepfer, M., Wolf, J., Mendling, J., & Reijers, H. A. (2009). The impact of secondary notation on process model understanding. In *Second IFIP WG 8.1 working conference, PoEM 2009* (pp. 161–175). Stockholm, Sweden.

Schütte, R., & Rotthowe, T. (1998). The guidelines of modelling as an approach to enhance the quality of information models. In *17th international conference on conceptual modeling (ER'98)* (pp. 240–254). Singapore.

Sharp, A., & McDermott, P. (2008). *Workflow modeling: Tools for process improvement and applications development. Data management* (2nd ed.). Norwood, MA: Artech House.

Sweller, J. (1988). Cognitive load during problem solving: Effects on learning. *Cognitive Science, 12*(2), 257–285.

Wand, Y., & Weber, R. (1993). On the ontological expressiveness of information systems analysis and design grammars. *Information Systems Journal, 3*(4), 217–237.

Weber, B., Reichert, M., Mendling, J., & Reijers, H. A. (2011). Refactoring large process model repositories. *Computers in Industry, 62*(5), 467–486.

Weidlich, M., Dijkman, R., & Mendling, J. (2010). The ICoP framework: Identification of correspondences between process models. In *Proceedings of the 22nd international conference on advanced information systems engineering CAiSE* (pp. 483–498).

(Air)port Innovations as Ecosystem Innovations

Mikael Lind and Sandra Haraldson

Abstract

Airports, among other transport hubs, are settings that rely on multi-actor collaborations for the co-production of high-quality services to its beneficiaries. Digital innovations enabling optimal and integrated performance for the actors' value production become essential in such settings. Innovating in such contexts requires an understanding of each actor's contribution to a common object of interest. Business process modelling approaches could provide an understanding of the distributed value production that constitutes such collaborative settings. In ecosystems, involved actors need to share this common object of interest in order to produce value on behalf of the actors as well as on behalf of the ecosystem. This chapter will elaborate on how business process modelling has been used, inter alia, as a driver to facilitate the emergence of digital innovations aimed at contributing to sustainable passenger flow (door-to-door) as the common object of interest. The case of Future Airports will be used to illustrate the emergence of three airport driven (digital) innovations that qualify as ecosystem innovations. These innovations are integrated measurement systems, information sharing platforms for common situation awareness, and passenger dashboards as a mean for the well-informed and well-prepared passengers.

M. Lind (✉)
Viktoria Swedish ICT, Sustainable Transports, Lindholmspiren 3A, 41756 Gothenburg, Sweden

Swedish Centre of Digital Innovation, Chalmers University of Technology/University of Gothenburg, 41296 Gothenburg, Sweden
e-mail: mikael.lind@viktoria.se

S. Haraldson
Viktoria Swedish ICT, Sustainable Transports, Lindholmspiren 3A, 41756 Gothenburg, Sweden
e-mail: sandra.haraldson@viktoria.se

J. vom Brocke, T. Schmiedel (eds.), *BPM – Driving Innovation in a Digital World*, Management for Professionals, DOI 10.1007/978-3-319-14430-6_13

1 Introduction

Traditionally, within the field of business process management, the main focus has been on the business processes of the *single* organization. This means that efforts and focus have been on creating value for the beneficiaries of the organization concerned (Hammer, 1990). In order to respond to contemporary societal challenges such as globalization and the three pillars of sustainability (Elkington, 1998), one needs to expand the scope beyond the single organization (Adner, 2006). The transport sector is one example where the value production is distributed among several actors enabling responses to the different needs of beneficiaries of the transportation process. Examples of such needs are seamless integration and that the performance of the single actor is valued based on contributions provided to the multi-modal needs of the beneficiaries and to the transport system as a whole. Performances of the actors need thus to be integrated.

Such expansion of the scope requires that the involved co-producing actors, including the beneficiaries, share and agree upon the constituents and the performance indicators of a "common object of interest". Ecosystems are to be distinguished through the identification of such common objects of interest. Distributed value production in multi-organizational business processes (Haraldson & Lind, 2011a, 2011b) is an example of such a common object of interest. Since most innovative efforts have historically been oriented towards the single organization's value production, there exists a need for new innovations enabling excellence in multi-organizational performance.

Co-ordinated and integrated efforts within ecosystems require the collaboration of involved actors, which nowadays could be enabled through digitalization. Actors within the telecommunication sector forecast 50 billion connected devices just within a couple of years. An increased connectivity for enhanced collaboration could be met by digital innovations that bring new values and opportunities for existing and new actor participation in the ecosystem [see also chapter by Schmiedel and vom Brocke (2015)].

In this chapter we explore how (air)port innovations, as examples of digital (ecosystem) innovations, deployed and disseminated by transport hubs, enable a digital collaboration between co-producing actors within the ecosystem, all sharing the same common object of interest: sustainable door-to-door processes. Due to its relational capital, transport hubs do have a strong influence on behaviour in ecosystems focusing on transport processes. Transport hubs thus become a suitable empirical object when exploring ecosystem innovations. The purpose of this chapter is thus to explore how digital innovations can be developed further based on a view of business processes as multi-organizational business processes as the common object of interest in ecosystems.

The research approach adopted in this chapter is based on a case study with the purpose to identify innovative digital solutions in the airport system. The airport as the transport hub is chosen as the empirical context. Many of the characteristics of an airport are however applicable to other types of transport hubs, such as e.g. seaports and railway stations. The common object of interest of the ecosystem was the door-to-door passenger flow. The case study was conducted as an action and design research project adopting a multi-organizational perspective on business processes (cf. Haraldson & Lind, 2011a, 2011b) at Stockholm-Arlanda, a larger airport in Sweden, and included several stakeholders involved in realizing the door-to-door process. The empirical data was derived from a series of workshops and interviews with the key stakeholders along the process steps, in conjunction with observations. Among other things, this project resulted in several process models that covered the entire door-to-door process and a design vision that guided several improvement projects for a number of areas addressing the future airport.

An elaboration on the concept of ecosystems and needs for innovations that enable synchronized and integrated co-production of value performed by multiple actors follows this introduction [see also chapter by Møller (2015)]. A section describing value production in multi-organizational processes is covered in the subsequent section. Then, the case will be introduced by examining three airport innovations as ecosystem innovations that enable sustainable door-to-door processes. The chapter is concluded by some reflections on how the elaborated examples of digital innovations have emerged and the role of such innovations at other transport hubs.

2 Multi-Actor Co-production in Ecosystems

2.1 Conceiving Ecosystems and Their Innovation Needs

Ecosystems, such as e.g. health care, airports and transportation hubs, are emerging as an idea. As claimed by Adner (2006), actors operating in an ecosystem take the issue of boundaries to a new level of complexity. These new boundaries result in the development of choices with regard to determining which activities will be undertaken by the firm, which are to be undertaken by partners, and which to be taken to the open market. "Firms face a choice between taking an active or a passive role in guiding ecosystem development. If you lead an ecosystem, you'll have a chance to tailor its development to your own strengths" (Adner, 2006, p. 107). Due to the fact that ports, such as airports and other types of transportation hubs, do manage the relationships to many actors operating in the ecosystem, the hub can become a powerful actor, which is orchestrating the ecosystem.

A common object of interest, such as e.g. patient flow or passenger flow, characterizes an ecosystem. These are typically covered within multi-organizational business processes (cf. e.g. Haraldson & Lind, 2011a, 2011b). This requires a shared understanding of the performance of the object of interest, such as e.g. a consensus around the target values for what constitutes a good passenger flow, etc. However, ecosystems are made up of several organizations, legally all separate entities. As a consequence we lack ecosystem-wide integrated performance systems. "Traditional models of strategy that emphasize internal competencies fail to account for these dynamics because they focus on the evolution of the firm capabilities and business models instead of on the relationship between the firm and its external ecosystem" (Iansiti & Levien, 2004). Performance issues will increase in significance in the sense that we now see how these ecosystems are beginning to grow, such as e.g. airtropolis. There is a huge gap in the practice, but also in the whole body of academic knowledge. Up to now there are no approaches on how to measure, monitor, and evaluate ecosystem-wide performance. Coming to an understanding of how to conceive ecosystem is one essential step towards the development of such approaches.

A single organization will never own the whole process that a common object of interest represents due to the involvement of several organizations as co-producers, since they provide services along the flow. Instead, it is the beneficiaries (such as e.g. the passengers/patients) themselves who are responsible for arranging the process based on the opportunities (and constraints) and possible process variants of a particular flow. However, in this chapter we argue that a shared understanding of the objectives around the "flow", and its variants, can facilitate an increased consensus among the involved stakeholders. Optimal and integrated performance within ecosystems does however need to be facilitated and monitored by a common measurement system reflecting desired states of the different business processes that each party are involved in, in their co-production of value. In today's ecosystems there are too few innovations being brought forward that would facilitate and enable an integrated performance for involved actors going beyond the organization's performance itself and thereby satisfying the "holistic" needs of the beneficiaries.

2.2 Value Creation in Multi-Organizational Business Processes

Originally, a business process was conceived as a holistic concept capturing value-adding activities that transform input to output, which should be of value to the customer. This viewpoint is based on the classical definition of business processes given by Hammer and Champy (1993, p. 35): "a collection of activities that takes one or more input and creates an output that is of value to the customer" (cf. e.g. Davenport, 1993). At the core of this traditional view, defined by Goldkuhl and Lind (2008) as "business process as sequential transformation", is the idea that activities performed for the customer should have value-creation characteristics. In the literature, value creation is often described and structured as value chains or value networks, which are often argued to be contrasting views on value creation.

Within the management literature different ways of framing value creation have been proposed (Peppard & Rylander, 2006). Initiated by Porter (1985) the value chain model was the first step towards portraying the "chained linkage of activities that exist in the physical world within traditional industries, particularly manufacturing". This metaphor has however been questioned by numerous scholars looking at networks (Allee, 2000; Håkansson & Snehota, 2006) and thus, the notion of the value network concept was introduced: "The focal of the value chain is the end product and the chain is designed around the activities required to produce it. The logic being that every company occupies a position in the chain; upstream suppliers provide inputs before passing them downstream to the next link in the chain, the customer. With the value network concept, value is co-created by a combination of players in the network." (Peppard & Rylander, 2006, p. 131). In contrast to a focus on the role of the single company in a value chain, this shift from value chain to value network, placed the focus upon the value-creating system itself in which different actors co-produce value.

Peppard and Rylander (2006, p. 131) identifies a value chain perspective as "the logic being that every company occupies a position in the chain; upstream suppliers provide inputs before passing them downstream to the next link in the chain, the customer". A value network on the other hand consists of specific roles and value interactions oriented towards the achievement of a particular task or outcome. The notion of relationship is the key in value networks. "From a network perspective relationships are viewed as part of a larger whole—a network of interdependent relationships [. . .]. These relationships are 'connected' since what happens in one relationship affects positively and negatively in others." (Peppard & Rylander, 2006, p. 133). The value network perspective is promising, but does however reject a value chain perspective by, as for example, "is it not of interest to focus upon actions performed in business processes?". Allee (2000, p. 439) claims "Value network analysis provides an opportunity to overcome the 'split' in business management practices where human interactions and relationships reside in one world of models and practices and business processes and transactions reside in another". "The active agents of any organization are real people who play particular roles to convert both tangible and intangible assets into negotiable offerings and fulfil different functions" (Allee, p. 429). A value network is therefore to be seen as "any purposeful group of people or organizations creating social and economic good through complex dynamic exchanges of tangible and intangible value" (Allee, 2000, p. 429). Allee (2000, p. 439) further claim that "reorienting toward networks means supporting people in wearing different 'hats' and filling roles in multiple value creating networks".

Building on both these complementary views on creating value, a multi-organizational perspective conceives value creation to be structured as value chains in value networks, meaning that value is created both in actor relationships, in interactions, and in the actions performed. A multi-organizational perspective on value creation in business processes argues that all these value components and their interrelations are required to conceive value creation in multi-organizational settings. Multi-organizational business processes (MOBP) build upon the fact that different organizations, by undertaking different actor roles, co-produce value. MOBP captures both condition-creating processes for establishing a basis for the realization of value propositions aimed towards potential customers as well as realizing business transactions with particular end-customers. As identified in Haraldson and Lind (2011a, 2011b), a multi-organizational perspective on business processes adopts an integrated (synthesized) view on value creation, taking identified strengths from both the Value Chain and the Value Network Perspective (see Fig. 1). In MOBP value is created in the actor relationship (i.e. capabilities to perform future actions), through the interaction among actors (i.e. value creation

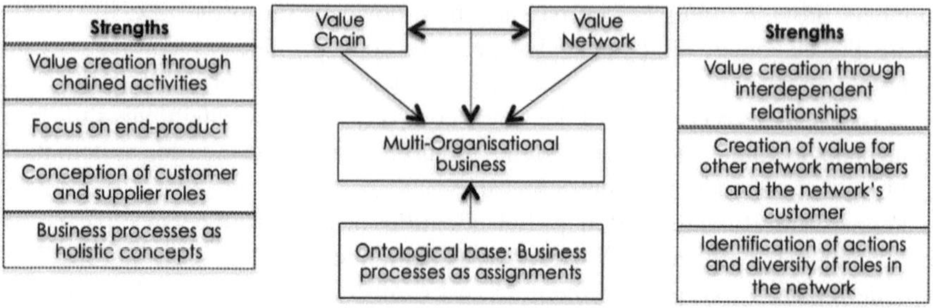

Fig. 1 A multi-organizational analysis on value chains and value networks (cf. Haraldson & Lind, 2011a, 2011b)

through interaction) and through the actions performed by the actors in the value network (i.e. value creating activities).

One of the main purposes of a business process orientation is to conceptualize structures for actions (cf. Lind, 2002). This means that a viewpoint on business processes needs to rely on a pragmatic foundation (cf. Goldkuhl, 2001) emphasising different types of social actions (material and/or communicative) performed by actors acting on behalf of organizations and the business network. To address the weaknesses of the value network perspective, specifically the lack of clarity as to how value is created through inter-dependent relationships, an assignment view on business processes is adopted. This means that business processes are conceived as interactions between different roles in the creation of actor, role, and action relationships (cf. Haraldson, 2008). A multi-organizational perspective on business processes acknowledges business processes as assignments (cf. Haraldson & Lind, 2011a, 2011b) in which establishing, fulfilling, and evaluating expectations are made core issues, thereby constituting structures for actions. Expectations are covered by the assignment in which participating actors come to an agreement on what to realize. The ontological base for a view on business processes as multi-organizational thus relies on business processes as an assignment (cf. Fig. 1).

An assignment view on business processes has its foundation in the language-action tradition in which the viewpoint on business processes could be framed as "business processes as coordination" (cf. Goldkuhl & Lind, 2008). Within this tradition, inspired by the conversation-for-action schema (cf. Winograd & Flores, 1986), commitment as the key construct for capturing the establishment, fulfilment, and conclusion of assignments has formed the far most important coordination mechanism for business processes (cf. e.g. Medina-Mora, Winograd, Flores, & Flores, 1992).

A multi-organizational perspective on business processes (cf. Haraldson & Lind, 2011a, 2011b) using assignment structures as a basis to identify interaction patterns is inspired by the work of Goldkuhl and Röstlinger (2002) and adapted to multi-organizational settings. In action relationships, i.e. expectations and commitments for future actions within assignments are created through the performance of actions based on some role relationships. In multi-organizational business processes (MOBP) value is created through action relationships based on role relationships between several actor roles. Consequently, value-adding activities are seen as parts of the establishment, fulfilment, and conclusion of assignments. Assignment structures form the basis for coordinating the ecosystem in which the (co-)production of value is coordinated and realized. Due to an increased degree of digital connectedness and increased flow of data from assets and actions within the ecosystem, there are great possibilities to ensure that the value production becomes even more coordinated and optimized than they are today. In this way the ecosystem's ability becomes expanded, which would potentially enable a higher degree of competiveness, attracting beneficiaries and, consequently, more service providers. Digital ecosystems innovations therefore need to support the interaction and collaboration between engaged actors through its ability to enable actors to share desired data.

To summarize, a multi-organizational view on business processes is different from the traditional firm-focused conception of business processes. The most obvious difference is that different organizations, by undertaking different actor roles, are involved in realizing different parts of an overall customer assignment, as well as the embedded or condition-creating assignments (integrated) constituting MOBP. Founded on a pragmatic conception of business processes, reflecting both transformative and coordinative dimensions of organizational work, our definition of a multi-organizational business process reads as follows (cf. Haraldson & Lind, 2010): "*A multi-organizational business process consists of a set of actions where multi-organizational network actor roles create value (customer value [components] and business value) aimed for beneficiaries. Beneficiaries of such processes are end-customers utilizing the products being offered through value propositions from a main actor in the business network, as well as other network member utilizing business values in their production of customer value (components). These actions utilize infrastructure and can be of coordinative and/or transformative character. The value, often operationalized and described as products (goods and/or services), produced, delivered, utilized, and consumed is enabled and coordinated through embedded and integrated business assignments. Within multi-organizational business processes, assignments are established, fulfilled, and evaluated, in patterns of interactions constituted by transformative and coordinative actions. Multi-organizational business processes both cover actions performed for potential as well as particular end-customers. Actions performed for potential customers are oriented towards the establishment of conditions for efficient realization of customer assignments as well as embedded/integrated assignments. Successful multi-organizational businesses rely on the ability to coordinate value creation processes, based on assignments as coordination mechanisms, throughout the value chain using network capabilities*".

3 Three (Air)port Innovations

To exemplify how digital innovations could act as a means for an increased capability of an ecosystem, the future airport project (www.futureairports.se) is used as the case. Airports are hubs integrating the performance of numerous different actors, which is why airport innovations could contribute to the ecosystem, of which the airport is a part, in a substantial way. In the following sections the future airport project is introduced, the door-to-door passenger flow as the common object of interest is characterized, and three digital innovations are introduced.

3.1 The Case of Future Airports: Balancing Performance Areas

Future Airports, as a research and innovation initiative, was initiated as a joint effort between Viktoria Swedish ICT (an applied research institute), Swedavia (the owner and operator of 10 airports in Sweden), and the Swedish Transport Administration. In the project, Swedavia acted as a representative and interface towards actors acting on the airport, and the Swedish Transport Administration acted as a representative and interface for ground transportation actors. The Future Airports project was used for engaging co-producing actors to share the same common object of interest as well as involving them in the realization and evaluation of digital innovations. Future Airports was formed based on a pre-study with the purpose to identify relevant areas needing improvement; towards making Stockholm-Arlanda a world-class airport integrated in a larger transportation system. The project was inspired by and positioned in relation to the Australian initiative, Airports of the Future (www.airportsofthefuture.qut.edu.au). The Swedish initiative was unique due to the strong focus on environmental concerns and passenger experiences from a door-to-door perspective.

In order to enable a solid focus on desired actions and enabling innovations, the passenger flow, as door-to-door processes, was modelled using contemporary process modelling techniques. The constituents of such door-to-door processes are covered in the next section. Sub-processes covered in detailed process models are depicted in Fig. 2 below (in blue).

This definition of the door-to-door process formed the basis for bringing the focus on different actions to be performed within Future Airports. It was determined as essential to pinpoint activities that occur prior to the actual transportation, such as a passenger's activities in planning, preparing, and booking a trip. Understanding these preparatory steps would enable the establishment of expectations on diverse organizations/actors involved in satisfying the needs of different stakeholders. The well-prepared and well-informed traveller is to be seen as a key driver for overall passenger satisfaction. By adopting a door-to-door perspective, essential actions can be identified in earlier processes (conditional processes) in order to arrive at a prepared passenger, necessary in later processes. This means that enabling the prepared passenger builds upon knowledge about where and when to provide a basis for supporting different patterns of behaviour. The prepared passenger is however one characteristic

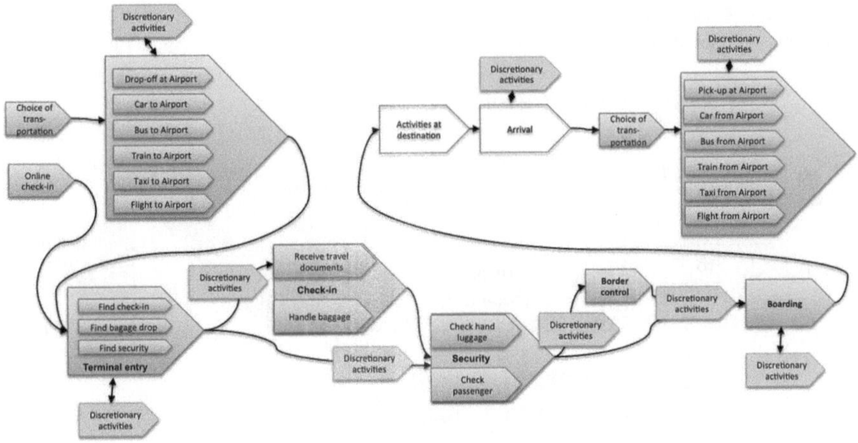

Fig. 2 Processes captured in the door-to-door process

of what can be conceived as traveller satisfaction. Also other characteristics governing such satisfaction are relevant and need to be identified. Besides traveller satisfaction (being at the traveller's service), the Future Airports project identified five additional (inter-linked) key performance areas (KPA) that are essential to acknowledge in the future developments of the door-to-door process. This means that the following key performance areas were brought into focus:

1. traveller satisfaction
2. profitable business (business revenue) and acting for the public good
3. environmentally friendly operations
4. state of the art collaboration management with involved stakeholders
5. operational excellence
6. safe and secure travel

An efficient process realization builds upon the fact that each actor acknowledges the other actors operating in the door-to-door process. Thus, to a large extent Stockholm-Arlanda becomes a governing actor of infrastructure for efficient traveller processes. The influence and governance of actor relationships differ due to characteristics of the relationship (i.e. the constituents of the relationship in relation to the overall value network) and where the actor operates within the door-to-door process. Future Airports thus focused upon the example of Stockholm-Arlanda to enable them to be an efficient infrastructural provider.

As a result of the Future Airports project, a design vision has been formulated as a guide to help keep the focus within the project incorporating the different dimensions mentioned above (see Fig. 3 below).

A design vision is a conceptualization of key concepts and a contextualization for desirable outcomes for the design of the concepts in use. As can be derived from

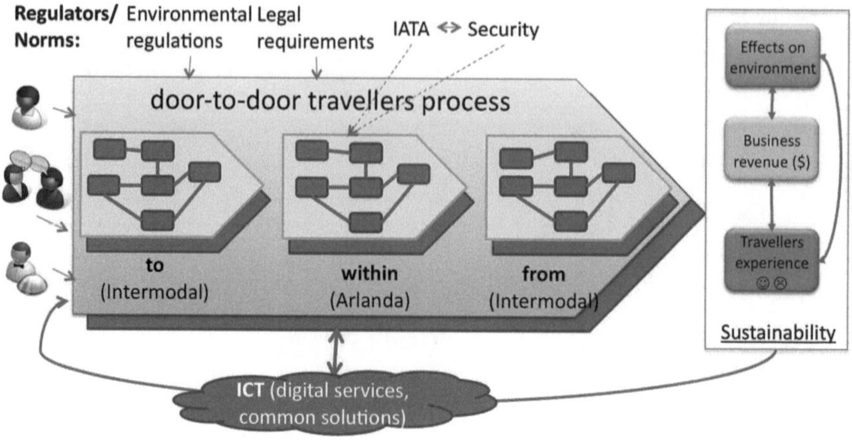

Fig. 3 The design vision of future airports

the figure, the focus is put upon the door-to-door traveller's process with three core processes (to, within, and from the airport) and their outcomes addressing the three pillars of sustainability (cf. Elkington, 1998): environmental impact (as environmental sustainability), the generation of business revenue (as economic sustainability), and traveller experience (as social sustainability). Putting these expected outcomes in relation to the key performance areas identified above KPA #1 (traveller satisfaction), #6 (safe and secure travel), and #4 (collaboration management) relates to social sustainability, #2 (business revenue) and #5 (operational excellence) to economic sustainability, and #3 (environmentally friendly operations) to environmental sustainability. In the design vision the necessity to understand regulations/norms as well as the role of ICT (digital services and common solutions) are put forward.

3.2 Understanding the Door-to-Door Process as the Common Object of Interest

In order to understand the essentials of the door-to-door process (as depicted in Fig. 2), the following section covers a textual description summarizing the detailed process models.

3.3 The Initiation of the Door-to-Door Process: Getting to the Airport

The point of departure in the door-to-door perspective adopted in the project is the booked trip. As is shown by Fig. 2 above, there is a selection of means of transportation for the passenger to utilize. A distinction is made between public transportation (bus, train, taxi) and the utilization of a private car (own car or drop-off). It is also revealed that pre-booking (of taxi) as well as pre-payment (of train, bus or taxi) might be offered, which requires digital infrastructure as well as interaction.

Bus transportation and train transportation reveals a need to combine one means of transportation with other transport solutions (such as walking, taxi, car, ride or subway) to the desired pick-up point (bus stop or train station). In other words, inter-modal transport and information about inter-modal transport chains is essential to get to/from the airport.

Both bus and train transportation tickets can be purchased in advance or on board the bus/train. Taxi is usually booked in advance and can potentially be pre-paid. Taking the own car to the airport requires information about possible parking opportunities. Some parking lots can be pre-booked via the airport website. When the car has been parked the passenger needs to get to the right terminal either by walking or utilizing the transfer bus (on-site transportation). This means that utilizing the own car as the means of transport to the airport requires additional time for arriving at the terminal, which may not be the case when utilizing other means of transportation.

Drop-off at Airport means that the passenger is accompanied by another person. Arriving at the airport, this person might accompany the passenger inside the airport or just drop-off the passenger at a desired drop-off zone.

For all means of transportation it is necessary that the passenger knows or finds out which terminal he/she is expected to depart from.

3.4 At the Core of the Door-to-Door Process: Actions Performed Within Airports

After arriving at the airport the passenger enters the terminal building. The process (terminal entry) depicts the fact that the passenger can have utilized different means of transportation to get to the airport. The passenger's entrance in the terminal building triggers this process. At this stage the passenger verifies that he/she is in the right terminal.

In both the terminal entry stage and the boarding process, discretionary activities are captured as a phenomenon—in terms of optional activities—within the processes. For other processes such activities are rather seen to occur between the different core processes. Since these activities are outside the project scope, they are depicted in the models as grey coloured sub-process (see Fig. 2), without in-depth description.

Dependent on the action taken by the passenger before arrival at the airport (such as online check-in), different flows occur upon the arrival at the airport. In situations where check-in occurs in the terminal entry process, either with personal assistance or by utilizing the check-in kiosk (or the cuss-machine depending on actual airline), it becomes necessary to find the check-in location and, possibly, also a baggage drop (if the passenger wishes to check baggage). If the passenger is already checked in and is travelling without baggage, he/she can proceed directly to security screening. Besides the information provided by the airport and possible discretionary activities performed, such passengers utilize fewer resources (in terms of personnel and/or infrastructural) in some of the compulsory processes.

When heading to check-in, there could be different paths taken depending on the choice of check-in means; personal check-in or the utilization of a check-in kiosk. Travellers may however potentially encounter queues, regardless of choice. In situations where the passenger also needs to check in baggage, the time gained is less in relation to check-in using kiosks. Assistants are available to help passengers checking in via machines, especially when it is crowded.

The baggage is managed in different ways, depending on the choice of medium. If the information kiosk is utilized, the passenger needs to find the baggage drop, which might be automatic, and in case of personal check-in, the luggage is taken care of by the handling agent. In regular check-ins a number of different actions are performed by the handling agent.

In some cases (i.e. the passenger who has checked in online, without luggage to check in) the first meeting between handling agents, operating on behalf of the airline, and passengers occurs late in the process, i.e. in the boarding process. This means that the passenger's travelling documents may still be unverified when he/she approaches the gate. In these cases it is essential for the passenger to be well prepared in order to avoid the risk of not being able to solve the issues in time for departure.

One important role for an airport is to ensure that passengers travelling on airlines are checked by security. The security process captures the detailed actions taken by the passenger (such as preparing luggage as well as himself/herself) for scanning. Some exceptions are also brought forward acknowledging additional actions (such as the rescanning of passengers) taken in order for the passenger to be considered secure. The process can result in that the passenger is denied access (into the secure airport zone). In situations where the passenger carries illegal goods or refuses actions requested by the security personnel, the police become involved in further actions.

After security the passenger is in the secure airport zone. Between security and boarding there are various opportunities for discretionary activities (such as shopping, dining, visiting a lounge, etc.). These opportunities are managed by numerous organizations and contribute to the airport income. Balancing between actions to enable different types of income is a great challenge for airports, which is why it has become important to offer attractive opportunities for passengers to spend valuable time at the airport. If the passenger is travelling internationally, the passenger needs to pass border control. In this process the passenger's passport (and other travelling documents) are checked, to approve/disapprove whether the passenger can leave the country.

At this point the passenger is ready to board the plane. In the boarding process the passenger and the hand luggage is checked with regard to the allowed size and weight. The passenger could use different ways of identifying himself/herself (such as card, digital barcode, finger print, and physical boarding card). The process might result in that the passenger discovers that he/she will not arrive in time for boarding. Three such situations where this is likely to occur has been identified; (1) if there is a need to resolve identification issues, (2) if the passenger needs to go back to check in over-sized luggage, or (3) if the passenger needs to store over-sized luggage. An important part of the boarding process is to ensure that there is a match between the number of passengers on board the plane and the number of checked-in passengers. If there are checked-in passengers who are not on the plane, the handling agents are, according to the law, required to off-load the luggage. This might jeopardize the possibilities for the passengers already on the plane to catch connecting flights.

3.5 The Final Steps of the Door-to-Door Process: Getting from the Airport

The same means of transportation is taken as a basis for the transportation from the airport as the one to the airport. However, the transportation from the airport is initiated by the passenger arriving at the airport with or without a pre-determined choice of transportation. At the time of arrival to the airport, the passenger might already have chosen and arranged his/her transport. This pre-arrangement can be done in three different ways:

- pre-paid/pre-booked public transportation (i.e. train, bus and taxi)
- own car at a parking lot to pick up
- arranged pick-up transportation

When the passenger chooses a means of transportation that can be considered as public transportation (such as bus, train, and/or taxi), the passenger also needs to choose an operator. At Stockholm-Arlanda different (public and private) operators are offered the possibility to provide services to passengers, all with equal conditions. Instructions for the passenger to choose and find the right means of transportation are provided without prioritizing any of the operators. Besides using bus, train, and taxi transportation from the airport, additional means of transportation might be used for onward travel to the final destination. As for the transportation to the airport, this is an expression for inter-modal transportation in the passenger's final stage of his/her door-to-door process.

The passenger's utilization of the own car as a means of transport from the airport requires the passenger to locate his/her car at the parking lot. Payment of the parking lot can be completed at different physical locations (in the terminal building, on the way to the parking area, at the parking area, or when leaving the parking area). A bus services for transferring passengers to the parking area is provided by Stockholm-Arlanda.

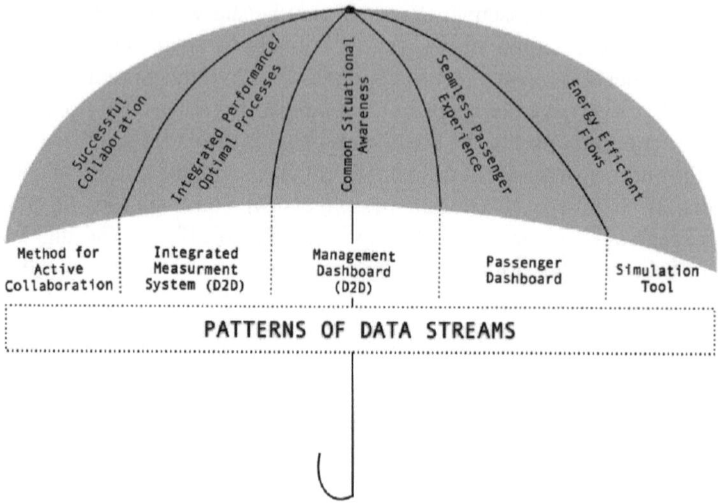

Fig. 4 Key values and innovations addressed in future airports as a basis for future work

3.6 Three Digital Innovations as Ecosystem Innovations

The identification of different innovations that would matter for a more sustainable door-to-door process has been guided by some key values of such a sustainable ecosystem. These key values are a means for the key performance areas identified as drivers for the development of a sustainable door-to-door process. These guiding key values that were identified in the future airport project were: successful collaboration (as means for KPA #4), integrated performance/optimal processes (as means for KPA #2 and #5), common situational awareness (as means for KPA #5 and #6), seamless passenger/traveller experience (as means for KPA #1), and energy efficient flows (as means for KPA #3). Each of the (digital) innovations initiated in the Future Airport project had the goal to contribute to these values (see Fig. 4 below) founded on patterns of data streams as the common information environment.

In this chapter, three of the innovations are given special attention: integrated measurement system, management dashboard (D2D), and passenger dashboards. The choice of focusing on these three innovations is due to space limitations, their strong resemblance with the understanding of current and future business processes, their use of digitalization as a digital innovation, and their maturity (the degree to which they have been implemented). These innovations place the focus on desired refinements of the door-to-door process. The constituents of these three innovations are described below.

3.7 Innovation 1: Integrated Measurement System

As indicated in the beginning of this chapter, there is a lack of approaches to measure, monitor, and evaluate the performance of ecosystems covering co-production of value by multiple actors. A Measurement System integrating the different processes is an essential basis for enabling optimal processes realization based on common situational awareness. For a successful realization, estimates and changes in the state of door-to-door processes are to be continuous monitored and shared among the actors. It is therefore important to identify relevant points to be measured. A measurement system is also an essential foundation for predicting possible future deviations, and thus a basis for identifying actions needed to ensure optimal punctuality. Such a measurement system is also identified as an important foundation for a Management Dashboard (D2D) (see innovation 2 below).

The integrated measurement system D2D, developed in Future Airports, identifies critical control and measurement points based on the idea of optimal (sustainable) traveller flows D2D, which consists of an integrated approach to three main processes: traveller, baggage, and turnaround (see Fig. 5 below). This integrative approach drove the project to refer to the European initiative Airport-CDM (Collaborative Decision Making), BRS (Baggage Reconciliation system) and various process measures in passenger movements door-to-door (including ground transport).

What is meant here is a measurement system that goes beyond organizational boundaries and is, instead, defined by the processes and activities contained in a door-to-door journey. Performance targets founded in different key performance areas govern the optimal traveller flows. As mentioned above, six key performance areas were pinpointed within Future Airports: Traveller Satisfaction, Business Revenue, Environmentally Friendly Operations, Collaboration Management, Operational Excellence, and Safe and Secure Travel.

Besides the control and measuring points, a measuring system D2D includes target values, metrics, outcome analysis, explanatory factors, and actions. This means that the measurement will be using relevant target values and performance metrics, allowing correct measurement data to be obtained and for the results to be interpreted based on relevant contextual factors (explanatory factors), and, further, to provide a basis for correct action to be taken. In this way, the measurement system also works as a decision support system and thereby has an advisory function regarding actions to take in the continuous efforts to optimize the door-to-door processes. The measurement system determines, inter alia, the requirements concerning what data should be replicated in a management dashboard.

3.8 Innovation 2: Information Sharing Platforms for Situational Awareness: Management Dashboard (D2D)

The aim with this innovation is to create a digital tool for the use in, among other things, a future operative centre (OPC) with appurtenant operational roles that

Abbrev.	Definition
AmBag	Amount of baggage pieces
AmBT	Amount of booked trips
AmSecCH	Amount of security checked travellers
AmTrCh	Amount of travellers checked-in
AmTrT	Amount of travellers in terminal
AOBT	Actual off-block time
BagLo	Baggage loaded
BagSo	Baggage sorted
BMCT	Baggage Minimum Connection Time
BoPa	Boarded passengers
DistInf	Disturbance information
IBT	In-block time
MCT	Minimum connection time
QTCh	Queuing time check-in
QTS	Queuing time security
RegFl	Regularity flights
RegTrpt	Regularity transportation mean
ReLo	Ready for loading
SecChBag	Security checked baggage
Tbag	Time to bag
TMCT	Traveller minimum connection time
TIBT	Target in-block time
TOBT	Target off-block time

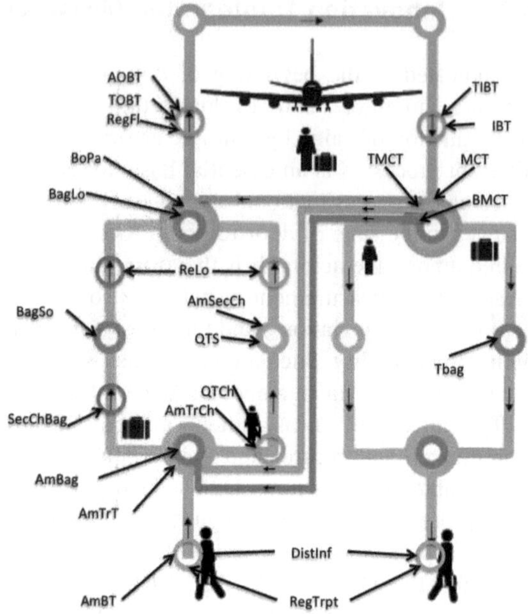

Fig. 5 Integrated approach with connection points to three processes constituting the D2D-process; traveller (covering ground transportation as well as air/airport operations), baggage, and turn-around

would benefit from an increased situational awareness based on the awareness of status on one or more operational processes (D2D). The tool should serve to support—in addition to visualizing the status—the prediction of shortcomings in punctuality (in respect to flight and to passenger and luggage punctuality) founded in the measurement system (see innovation 1). The information-sharing platform for situational awareness, operationalized as a Management Dashboard D2D, is based on four integrated operational processes with their measurement points: the turn-around process, the traveller process, the luggage process, and the ground transportation process.

The joint efforts in developing a Management Dashboard D2D have been an enabler to increase the information exchanges between several actors of the D2D-process. The plan has been to integrate status information on rail and road traffic with information related to airport operations (including arriving and departing flights). The basis for enabling co-producing actors to contribute to seamless travelling processes could thus be created by the common situational awareness provided by a Management Dashboard D2D.

The ambition with a management dashboard is to enable digital images providing status of the D2D process for key stakeholders with relevant data in real time for the purpose of increased punctuality and customer satisfaction. At the

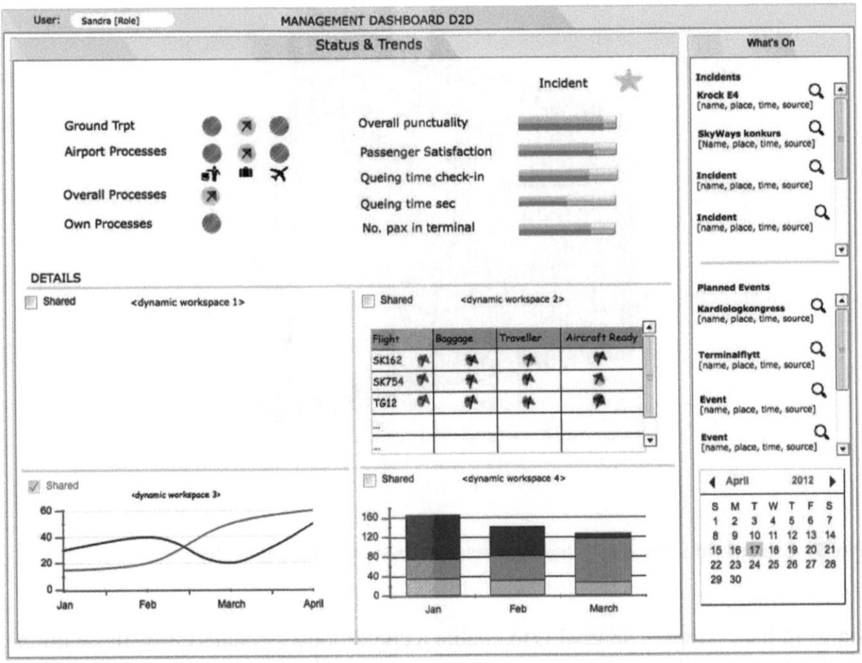

Fig. 6 Example of a view from the management dashboard D2D covering different aspects of the door-to-door process

core of this innovation is a tool for providing digital images (see Fig. 6 above) based on information from different key actors, constituting a common situational awareness for different actors. The development of this tool followed a repetitive process of design, realization, and evaluation. For reaching the full effects of this innovation it was also seen as important to include the development of an Application Protocol Interface (API) enabling external D2D-actors to include information from the management dashboard D2D in their internal governance structures. The successful realization of the management dashboard D2D builds upon a measurement system integrating different "measurement" domains with each other, providing forecasts of process punctuality based on the actual and future status of the processes.

3.9 Innovation 3: Passenger Dashboards

The passenger is seen as an important actor in the ecosystem. The passenger is both a beneficiary who needs to be well informed and well prepared as well as a source of information, as parts for defining the overall situational awareness. It is therefore seen as essential to establish digital relationships with the passenger.

The purpose with Passenger Dashboards is to give each traveller a personalized picture of their whereabouts in the door-to-door process, the steps to take, and the

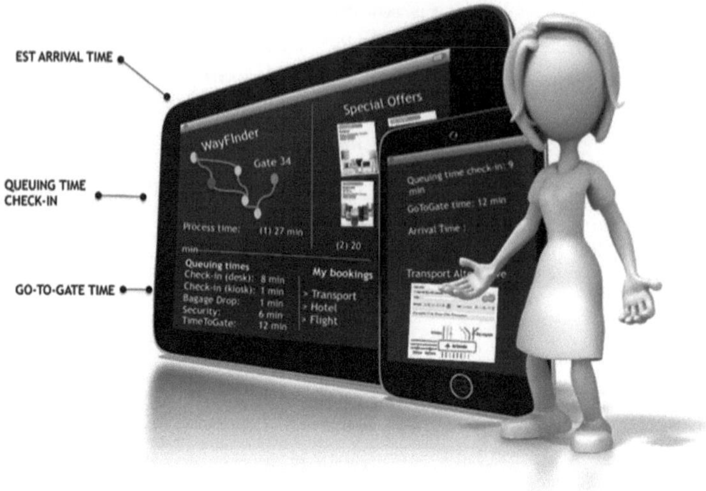

Fig. 7 Example of a passenger dashboard channelized via different media

status of these steps. The goal is to enable a continuously updated traveller with the right information in the right time and through the right channel. Thus, there exists a strong correlation between Management Dashboard (D2D) and Passenger Dashboards. Passenger Dashboards builds on the same foundational information and the aggregated information generated within the scope of the Management Dashboard (D2D). In Fig. 7, below, examples of what such a passenger dashboard looks like.

Recently, service innovation within the digital realm has gone through fundamental changes. Examples such as the Apple Appstore, followed by others, shows that an open innovation model has come to dominate the previous, closed models of service innovation in some markets. Indeed, the notion of the supply chain has been exchanged with that of the ecosystem, which better describes the fluid manner of interaction between developers and users of information services. This development is being replicated in numerous accounts of how citizens and small third party developers design the latest traveller support services using commonly available data. There are a number of novel insights to be made. First, according to open innovation theory, it is acknowledged that not all the smartest people work for you, and it is important to capture the best ideas using other means than those traditionally used. Second, consumers of digital services (e.g. the travellers) are also suppliers of feedback data, encompassing feedback on digital services, new ideas on digital services, the use of physical infrastructures and transport services, their opinion of such services, and their travelling behaviour. Among other things, this facilitates (1) the improvement of digital services, (2) the design of new digital services, (3) the discovery of new ideas on which data should be provided.

4 Concluding Discussion

In this chapter we have covered the emergence of three digital innovations as examples of ecosystem innovation. By expanding beyond the scope of the single organization, mostly focused in contemporary business process management approaches, a multi-organizational perspective on business processes has been used to conceive the characteristics of an ecosystem. Such expansion of the scope has driven the identification of (digital) innovations enabling a higher degree of performance in the ecosystem. The innovations have focused on enabling engaged actors (including the beneficiaries) to coordinate their efforts towards an improved high utilization of available infrastructure. Enabling actors to share information to a higher degree has lead to an increase in the situational awareness enabling travellers and other actors to make well-founded decisions about future steps to take.

The Future Airport project has been driven from the need to contribute to a (more) sustainable ecosystem enabled by digital (airport) innovations. This ecosystem is characterized by sustainable passenger flow as the common object of interest. It has therefore been essential to be informed of the different state of changes that occur throughout the door-to-door process. It has been possible to reveal the state of such changes using detailed business process models, cf. e.g. the details of the measurement system depicted as innovation 1 above, which has been derived from the state of changes depicted in these models.

The key performance areas driving the development of sustainable door-to-door processes are applicable to other ecosystems, including similar systems that have airports as their core connection point, for ecosystems within the transport domain, but also for ecosystems covering other work practices. In the maritime domain there are similar challenges. In the MONALISA project (www.monalisaproject.eu) information sharing environments are being set up to achieve safer, more efficient, and more environmentally friendly transportation by integrating ship-shore (port) actions.

This chapter has had the purpose to illustrate the necessity to expand the scope beyond the single organization in order to reach desirable effects when adopting business process management approaches. Steps towards conceiving the common object of interest as multi-organizational business processes have been taken. Reliance on distributed value production brings forward a need to ensure that (informational) conditions are established for the different actors to perform and act on behalf of themselves and on behalf of the ecosystem as such. The value production performed by the different actors should be valued from an integrated point of view. This requires that common information environments are being set up in which different actors, including the beneficiaries, can share information. This also requires a joint understanding of which information is relevant for sharing. The three innovations brought forward do provide a basis for integrated performance within ecosystems. Innovation 1 depicts which information is relevant for sharing, Innovation 2 is the artefact being used for enabling co-producing actors to increase their situational awareness as a basis for coordinating their actions, and Innovation 3 is the artefact enabling the passenger/traveller to be well-informed and well-

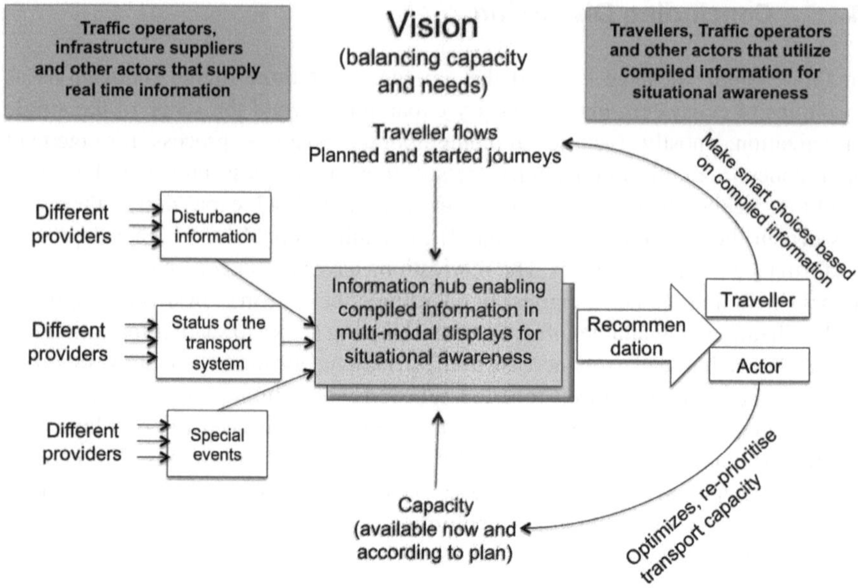

Fig. 8 Balancing capacity and needs in transportation systems based on recommendation to travellers and actors founded on compiled information from multiple sources

prepared, which in turn enables him/her to make relevant decisions about his/her journey (both before and in real-time). The emergence of these innovations has been driven from the need to balance capacity and needs in an optimal way based on information compiled from many different sources (see Fig. 8 below).

To arrive at optimized transportation systems, as examples of an ecosystem characterized by distributed value production, it becomes essential to balance capacity management and mobility management. As someone quoted in the Future Airports project, "When a queue occurs it is too late. A possible queue should be predicted and fended off before it starts forming" means that bottlenecks should be predicted in advance and thus avoided.

The next step in our research is to further develop approaches and methods for (digital) ecosystem innovations founded on business processes as multi-organizational business process.

References

Adner, R. (2006). Match your innovation strategy to your innovation ecosystem. *Harvard Business Review, 84*(4), 98–107.

Allee, V. (2000, July/August). Reconfiguring the value network. *Journal of Business Strategy, 21* (4), 36–39.

Davenport, T. H. (1993). *Process innovation – Reengineering work through information technology*. Boston, MA: Harvard Business School Press.

Elkington, J. (1998). *Cannibals with forks: The triple bottom line of 21st century business*. Gabriola Island: New Society Publishers.

Goldkuhl, G. (2001). Communicative vs. material actions: Instrumentality, sociality and comprehensibility. In *Proceedings of the 6th international workshop on the language action perspective (LAP2001)*. Aachen: RWTH.

Goldkuhl, G., & Lind, M. (2008). Coordination and transformation in business processes: Towards an integrated view. *Business Process Management Journal, 14*(6), 761–777.

Goldkuhl, G., & Röstlinger, A. (2002), Towards an integral understanding of organisations and information systems: Convergence of three theories. In *Proceedings of the 5th international workshop on organisational semiotics*, Delft.

Håkansson, H., & Snehota, I. (2006). No business is an island: The network concept of business strategy. *Scandinavian Journal of Management, 22*(3), 256–270.

Hammer, M. (1990). Reengineering work: Don't automate, obliterate. *Harvard Business Review, 68*(4), 104–112.

Hammer, M., & Champy, J. (1993). *Reengineering the corporation. A manifesto for business revolution*. London: Nicholas Brealey.

Haraldson, S. (2008). *Design principles for action quality in collaboration – A multi-organizational perspective on third party logistics* (in Swedish). Licentiate Thesis, Linköping University, Sweden.

Haraldson, S., & Lind, M. (2010, August 12–15). The emergence of a multi-organizational view on business processes – Experiences from a double-loop action research approach. Lima: AMCIS.

Haraldson, S., & Lind, M. (2011a). Value chains in value networks: A multi-organizational business process definition. In *Australian conference on information systems*, Australia.

Haraldson, S., & Lind, M. (2011b). Dividing multi-organizational businesses into processes: Capturing value creation in assignment structures. In *Australian conference on information systems*, Australia.

Iansiti, M., & Levien, M. (2004). *The keystone advantage – What the new dynamics of business ecosystems mean for strategy, innovation, and sustainability*. Boston, MA: Harvard Business School.

Lind, M. (2002). Dividing businesses into processes – Foundations for modelling essentials. In K. Liu, R. J. Clarke, P. B. Andersen, R. K. Stamper (Eds.), *Organizational semiotics – Evolving a science of information systems* (pp. 211–230). IFIP TC8/WG8.1. Kluwer.

Medina-Mora, R., Winograd, T., Flores, R., & Flores, F. (1992). *The action workflow approach to workflow management technology, CSCW'92*. New York, NY: ACM.

Møller, C. (2015). Business process innovation as an enabler of proactive value chains. In J. vom Brocke & T. Schmiedel (Eds.), *Business process management: Driving innovation in a digital world*. Berlin: Springer.

Peppard, J., & Rylander, A. (2006). From value chain to value network: Insights for mobile operators. *European Management Journal, 24*(2–3), 128–141.

Porter, M. E. (1985). *Competitive advantage – Creating and sustaining superior performance*. New York, NY: Macmillan.

Schmiedel, T., & vom Brocke, J. (2015). Business process management: Potentials and challenges of driving innovation. In J. vom Brocke & T. Schmiedel (Eds.), *Business process management: Driving innovation in a digital world*. Berlin: Springer.

Winograd, T., & Flores, F. (1986). *Understanding computers and cognition: A new foundation for design*. Norwood, NJ: Ablex.

Leveraging Innovation Based on Effective Process Map Design: Insights from the Case of a European Insurance Company

Monika Malinova and Jan Mendling

Abstract

Business process modeling plays an important role in supporting various stages of the BPM lifecycle. While academia and practice have developed a thorough understanding of how to work with fine-granular models, as for instance defined using BPMN, research only recently started to investigate the relationship between good process map design and its impact on process innovation. In this paper, we discuss the current state of process map design in practice. We utilize the case of a European insurance company to illustrate the benefits of a systematic approach to designing process maps to support the framing of business process management in a company and its relationship to process innovation.

1 Introduction

Business process management (BPM) is increasingly used as an approach to continuously improve the operations of a company. Often, the management activities of BPM are illustrated as a lifecycle which refines the general plan-do-check-act cycle. The BPM lifecycle refers to two perspectives on business processes. The first one describes the overall company and its collection of processes as a whole. This perspective is important for defining the boundaries of processes and assessing their strategic importance. Often, this perspective is referred to as multi-process management or as process portfolio management. The second perspective considers a singular process and the different management activities to which it relates.

M. Malinova (✉) • J. Mendling
Institute for Information Business, Wirtschaftsuniversität Wien, Welthandelsplatz 1, 1020 Vienna, Austria
e-mail: monika.malinova@wu.ac.at; jan.mendling@wu.ac.at

J. vom Brocke, T. Schmiedel (eds.), *BPM – Driving Innovation in a Digital World*,
Management for Professionals, DOI 10.1007/978-3-319-14430-6_14

It is generally accepted that business process models are a useful analysis aid for conducting various BPM-related management activities [see also chapters by van der Aalst (2015), Loos, Fettke, Walter, Thaler, and Ardalani (2015), and Lind and Haraldson (2015)]. Research in this area has essentially focused on modeling languages that help to describe a single process. Prominent examples are languages such as Business Process Model and Notation (BPMN), Event-driven Process Chains (EPCs) or Petri Nets. Despite its strategic importance, there has been limited research into the concepts for representing the overall collection of processes as a whole. In practice, so-called process maps are frequently used for capturing multiple processes and their interrelations. Except for their reference to established management concepts like Porter's Value Chain, Scheer's Value-Added Diagram or the Supplier-Input-Process-Output-Customer (SIPOC) scheme from Six Sigma, they hardly build on any theoretical pillars.

In this paper, we discuss how process map design as implemented in practice can be integrated towards a sound conceptual framework. Furthermore, we discuss the benefits of process maps as a tool to support continuous process innovation. On the one hand, we investigate the cognitive foundations behind this argument. On the other hand, we utilize the case of a European insurance company to illustrate the advantages of good process map design.

Against this background, this paper is structured as follows. The next section presents the foundations of process map design with a reference to the BPM lifecycle. Then, we discuss barriers of process innovation and in how far process maps can help to overcome these. Afterwards, we present findings from a case study conducted with an insurance company that reworked their process map. The paper closes with a summary and implications.

2 Foundations of Process Map Design

In this section, we first discuss the essential concepts of BPM. Afterwards, we cover process map design.

2.1 Business Process Management

The essential subject of BPM is that of processes. In this context, a business process is typically defined as a set of activities which are related to one another in a temporal and logical way in order to provide a product or service to a customer (Davenport, 1993; Hammer & Champy, 2009). BPM can then be understood as the entirety of management tasks that are related to business processes. As such, it aims to explicate and organize the coordination needs stemming from division of labor. The BPM-related tasks are often described as a lifecycle model. The first phase of the BPM lifecycle is the process identification, which has the goal of identifying a complete and abstract list of the company's processes (Dumas, La Rosa, Mendling, & Reijers, 2013; Weske, 2007). The main outcome of this phase is the process map,

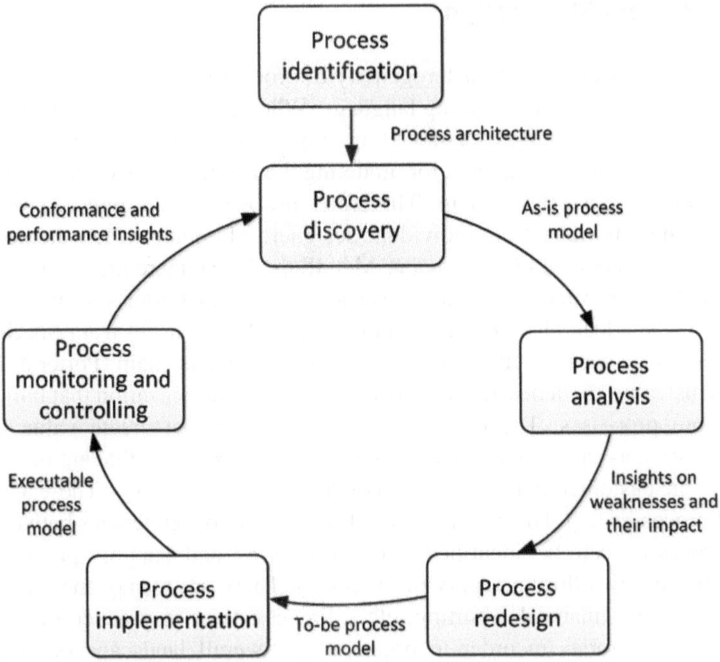

Fig. 1 BPM lifecycle according to Dumas et al. (2013)

which depicts all processes of the organization and the relations between them (Malinova & Mendling, 2013). The process map is considered as the top and most abstract view of the company's process architecture, while the lower levels serve to store the different levels of process granularity (Malinova, Leopold, & Mendling, 2013a). The process map is typically used as a guide for the subsequent steps of the BPM lifecycle, where the processes shown in the map are being discovered, modeled, analyzed for weaknesses, redesigned accordingly, and implemented so that some organizational change could occur due to BPM. Once processes are implemented, monitoring and controlling facilities can be put into practice, such that insights into performance and conformance can trigger another turn of the lifecycle (see Fig. 1).

Process architectures typically define different levels of abstraction along with corresponding modeling notations. In this way, they provide a systematic classification of processes and define a means for understanding a company from a process-oriented perspective (Malinova, Leopold, & Mendling, 2013a). Process maps are often used as a means for representing the top-level view of the company. More fine-granular models from level three onwards then show details of individual processes, for instance, represented as BPMN models.

2.2 Process Map Design

In practice we observe a high heterogeneity of process map designs. This is due to the lack of a standardized modeling language. Whereas there are a number of well-defined modeling languages for modeling singular processes (e.g. BPMN, EPC), there is still no standard available for modeling the abstract view of processes of an organization, i.e., a process map. Therefore, process map design is very much driven by the intuition of the individual designer. Although neither elements nor symbols are standardized (Malinova & Mendling, 2013), there are some recurring concepts that are often included. These are related to Porter's value chain, to Scheer's value-added chain diagram, and to the SIPOC concept from Six Sigma.

Process maps usually reflect Porter's concept of a value chain (Porter & Millar, 1985). This value chain describes a process view of an organization that builds on a set of core processes. The core processes are those that create value for the customer, such as sales, logistics, etc. There are also processes that are not directly related to the customer, but required for conducting core processes. These are called support processes (e.g. HR, finance, etc.). Explicit interdependencies between both these processes can be identified. Core processes and support processes are complemented by a third category of processes. These are management processes (e.g. controlling, financial reporting, etc.). Process maps in practice often define these three categories in order to organize the overall landscape of processes. However, the assignment of processes to each category depends entirely on the context of the corresponding company.

The second source of inspiration for process map design is the value-added chain diagram as defined by Scheer (2000). This diagram describes the essential elements for representing basic relationships between processes that are defined at a high level of abstraction. The first concept is the concept of sequential order. Certain processes can only start when others have been completed. The second concept is a notion of refinement. A single process can be broken down into a set of sub-processes, which, together, define it. Process maps also adopt the chevron symbol from the Scheer proposal.

A third source of inspiration is Six Sigma. Six Sigma uses the SIPOC scheme, which is an abbreviation for supplier-input-process-output-customer (Eckes, 2002). This scheme essentially wants to help with the identification of inputs and outputs of a process and the parties who provide or consume these. In process maps, this concept is often reflected in an end-to-end representation of processes from the supplier to the customer. Also inputs (e.g. customer order) and outputs (e.g. customer satisfaction) are frequently defined.

Figure 2 shows an example of a process map, which was found on the website ariscommunity.com. It shows an abstract process-oriented representation of an insurance company. Similar to the ideas of Porter, core processes and support processes are explicitly categorized, along with management processes. Each of the 14 processes is shown as a chevron symbol and subordinated to their respective category. This is fully in line with the Scheer proposal. The small green and purple symbols at the right-hand side of each process visualize that there are sub-processes

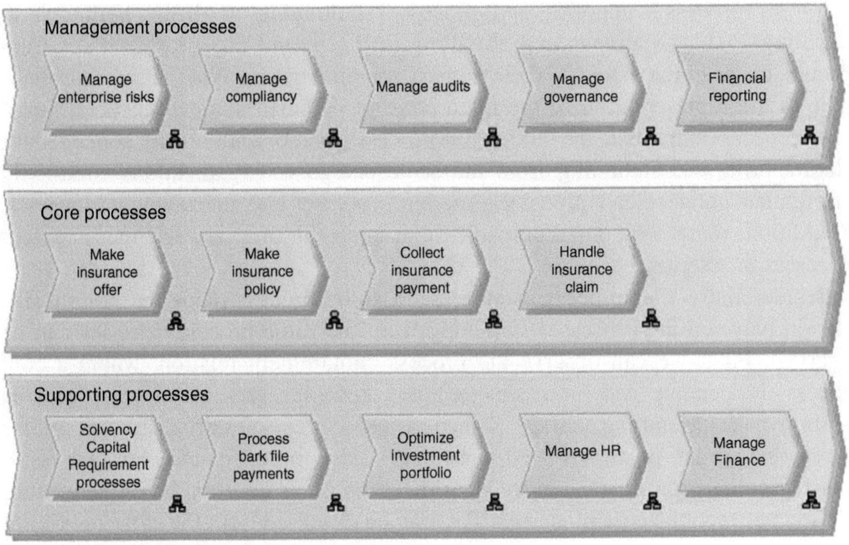

Fig. 2 Process map example found at http://www.ariscommunity.com

defined. Suppliers and customers are not explicitly defined in this example; also, inputs and outputs are not shown.

3 Process Map Design and Its Impact

In this section, we discuss why good process map design is important and what kind of impact it may have on the overall success of a BPM initiative. As process maps provide an abstract overview of how an organization operates as a whole, they are a crucial aid to organizing the whole BPM initiative. The process map design could potentially influence the consequent process innovation. In prior research, we have observed that process maps from practice vary in their level of quality (Malinova & Mendling, 2013). We first discuss primary notation and secondary notation of process maps. Then, we discuss their benefits for process innovation and potential risks.

3.1 Primary Notation

The purpose of a process map is to show in an abstract manner how an organization operates without necessarily going into process details (Malinova & Mendling, 2013). Hence, a process map is well designed when any end-user can clearly understand the information the process map attempts to convey.

Primary notation concerns the formal syntax of process maps, which are the concepts a process map includes without the aid of visual representation, such as the notion of process categories and processes belonging to them (Malinova & Mendling, 2013). Malinova and Mendling (2013) found that process maps from practice differ in the extent of their primary notation usage. What all process maps share is the representation of the main concept of business process. In addition, most process maps use the notion of process categorization and concepts for relating processes stemming from the same category. Organizations commonly differentiate between core processes, support processes and management processes. In addition, there are some companies that keep the analysis and measurement processes in a separate category.

Besides these four process categories, in some process maps the notion of a relation between the processes stemming from the same process category can be observed. First, we can observe the process containment relation, where a core process is decomposed into smaller part-processes, so-called sub-processes (Malinova & Mendling, 2013). When a core process starts, the set of its corresponding sub-processes need to be executed in order for the core process to finish. Another commonly observed primary notation concept is the sequential relation between the core processes. This can be observed from the close proximity of two core processes, when these stand next to each other. For this, many maps use Porter's value chain concept (Malinova & Mendling, 2013; Porter & Millar, 1985). As a result, all core processes are represented in such a way that there is a temporal sequential order between them. In this way, it is easier to see when each core process is executed. Moreover, when process maps that represent the core processes in a value chain manner, they also indicate the input of the value chain and its consequent output. The input is usually a customer request, while the output is customer satisfaction (Malinova & Mendling, 2013).

3.2 Secondary Notation

In addition to the primary notation, process maps also use visual variables, which serve the purpose of increasing the cognitive effectiveness of the information that an organization intends to convey about their operations (La Rosa et al., 2011). These complement the primary notation and are referred to as the secondary notation. We can discuss the secondary notation of process maps in reference to the visual variables identified by Bertin (1983), i.e. horizontal position, vertical position, size, shape, orientation, color, texture, and brightness. These aim to ease the understanding of the information conveyed by the process map. This is done because the resultant process map will not only be used by its creator, but by all employees of the organization, thus, all those that are directly or indirectly involved in the process execution. For example, a process represented only with its name only uses primary notation. When, in addition, this process is represented as a chevron symbol, the symbol is a visual variable which increases the meaning of the process. By adding this symbol the designer intends to convey a message that the process has some sequence of occurrence.

Process maps from practice appear to make use of an extensive set of common visual variables (Malinova & Mendling, 2013). The most often used visual variable is that of symbols (shape) to represent a single process. Because of the lack of standardized language for process map design, process maps tend to use a set of different symbols to represent the different types of processes. For example, core processes are represented either by a rectangle-shaped symbol, which obviously indicates a singular process, or a chevron-shaped symbol, which in addition also infers some sequence of occurrence. On the other hand, the support and management processes are generally represented either by using the rectangle-shaped symbol or by using the pentagon-shaped symbol, pointing to the direction of the core process category. This direction (position and orientation) also infers some meaning, in which the support processes apparently are there to support the core processes, while the management processes manage the execution of the core processes. This way, a relation also between the processes that belong to different categories can be implicitly depicted.

Moreover, the close proximity of two core processes typically implies a sequential order between these processes. In order to make this implicit relation explicit—so that by looking at the two processes we can be sure that they are indeed carried out in a sequential order—an organization in addition uses a directed arrow between these two processes. Another way to capture the same meaning of sequence is to use a chevron symbol. Hence, when two chevron-shaped processes are positioned next to each other, it illustrates a process order.

Beyond the notion of process order, most process maps visually depict the process containment relation. This is typically illustrated with the use of the visual variables size and position. Also, some use a narrower chevron-shaped symbol (size) to indicate inputs and outputs. The position of the input/output visual representation also indicates a particular meaning. For example, an input pointing only to the core process category means that this particular input will trigger the execution of one or a set of core processes. Some process maps additionally emphasize the importance of certain parts by increasing the size or using different colors of the respective concept. Table 1 summarizes all secondary notation aspects observed in 15 process maps from practice (Malinova & Mendling, 2013). These concepts concern the visual variables shape, position and orientation.

3.3 Impact of Process Map Design

The design of a process map has a strong impact on how stakeholders cognitively capture the operations of a company. The availability of a process map can therefore have substantial benefits for management. Nonetheless, there is the risk that a process map can be designed in a misleading way.

Research on innovation and technology transfer has identified a problem of sticky information, which refers to information on technical problem solving being costly to acquire, transfer, and use in a different context (von Hippel, 1994). Furthermore, a local search bias is established through the fact that obtaining

Table 1 Symbol description adopted from Malinova and Mendling (2013)

Symbol	Description	Symbol	Description
s1 ——→	Explicit process order	s7	Process
s2 -----→	Implicit process order		
s3 --------	Implicit process influence	s8	
s4	Explicit process order	s9	
s5	Input/output	s10	
s6	Process contains subprocesses	s11	(Process category)

such information might be too costly. For BPM, these observations imply that the creation of a process map can have substantial benefits for understanding the operations of a company and for making well-informed decisions.

On the downside, information artifacts in general tend to be subject to anchoring and adjustment heuristics (Parsons & Saunders, 2004). This means that humans tend to question an information artifact too little in the context of a particular task. As a consequence, errors might be accepted unquestioned, omissions overlooked, and extraneous matters considered when they should be ignored. For these reasons, it is important for a process map to be correct and complete, and to represent its content in an efficient and effective manner.

4 The Case of a European Insurance Company

In this section, we describe the case of a European Insurance Company. We used an action research approach, in which we joined their efforts of reworking their process map.

4.1 BPM in the European Insurance Company

Organizations are triggered for various reasons to adopt BPM. These reasons typically map to a set of goals that a company desires to reach through modeling their business processes. Accordingly, a company identifies and models all those processes that will contribute to reaching the pre-defined goals. All these processes and the relations between them are shown in the company's process map. The main objective of the European insurance company is to achieve transparency of its work processes, to increase its efficiency and to reduce the associated risk. Consequently, the singular and measurable goals that will lead to the organization accomplishing these three objectives are:

- Make processes easier to understand and secure process-relevant information
- Identify process weaknesses in order to create the basis for increasing efficiency
- Achieve common understanding over all processes
- Enable easier updates of process-relevant information
- Use process models as work manuals for employees
- Reduce process-related risks
- Measure and control process performance

As a first step towards attaining all the listed goals, the company designed its process map in order to achieve an abstract overview over its processes. It used the process map as a guide for selecting the right processes to model, which in turn will assist the company in reaching its initial goals.

4.2 The Original Process Map

The process map of the European insurance company is considered as the top-view of its process architecture. It includes all processes the organization is involved with. An abstract version of its original process map can be seen in Fig. 3. From the figure, we can observe that the company incorporated both, primary and secondary notation into its process map design. On the primary notation side, we observe three categories of processes. Compliant to most process maps we observed in practice, clusters are defined for core, support and management processes. Beyond this, the map also indicates a notion of process containment within the core process

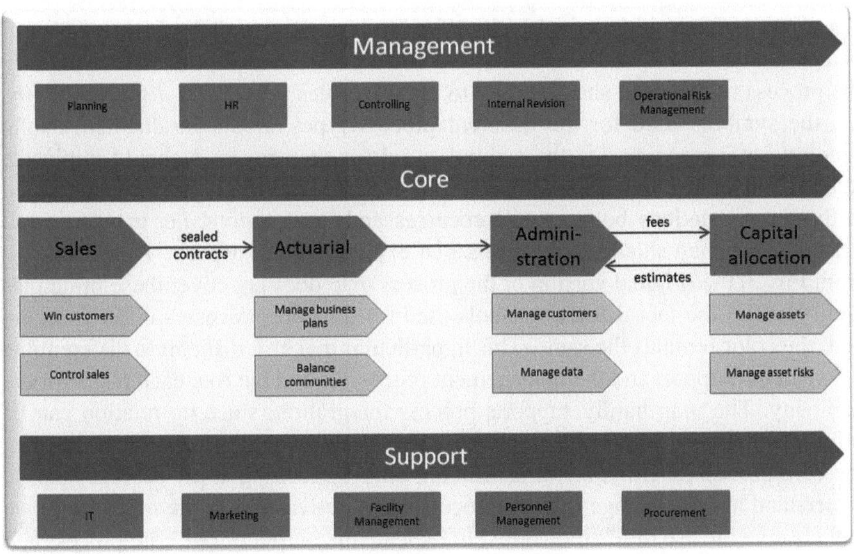

Fig. 3 The original process map of a European insurance company

category. This we infer from the labels used for each sub-process. For example, the processes shown in the core process category *win customers* and *control sales* are clearly a subset of the core process *sales*. In addition, based on the order of the four core processes (sales, actuarial, administration and capital allocation) and the inputs and outputs coming from and to some of the core processes (sealed contracts, fees, estimates) we could infer certain sequence of execution.

This company used few visual variables to complement the primary notation. First of all, we can see three different colors in this map. The color blue is used to highlight the type of each process category, whereas the color green is used to indicate the importance of each type of process. On the other hand, the light brown color differentiates between core processes and their corresponding sub-processes. The management and support processes are using the rectangle-shaped symbol, while the core processes and sub-processes use a pentagon-shaped symbol positioned horizontally. This might indicate that these processes include activities that are done in a particular order. Similarly, the title of each process category also uses the same shaped symbol, but with a different color (blue) and size (longer and narrower). The input/output notions we found to be primary concepts are complemented by an arrow between the core processes. Using this arrow strengthens the relation by explicitly showing that, indeed, there is a sequential order between the core processes. The explicitly labeled inputs and outputs, together with the directed arrow, clearly depict what a core process needs to produce in order to finish, thus starting the execution of the next in line process.

4.3 Discussion of the Original Process Map

For a process map to be cognitively effective it needs to reflect the principles of visual notations by Moody (2009). In order to achieve overall process transparency the process map design should apply to the principles *perceptual discriminability*, i.e. the symbols used for the different process types should be distinguishable; *semantic transparency*, i.e. the symbols used for the processes should imply the intended meaning; *cognitive integration*, i.e. there should be process integration with shown relations between all processes and *dual coding*, i.e. in addition to graphics, the map should include text that explain certain aspects. As we can see from Fig. 3, the original version of the process map does not cover these principles well. Despite the fact that the symbols used for the core processes differ from the rest, the color remains the same. This in particular makes it difficult to differentiate between the support and the management processes, and the role each plays for the company. The map hardly supports process integration, since no relation can be inferred between the process categories. There is a notion of process order between the core processes. However, it is difficult, only by looking at the process map, to understand at which stage the sub-processes are activated. On the other hand, we can observe the use of additional text to indicate the output of one core process and the input of another (e.g. sealed contracts). While this significantly assists in understanding the nature of the respective core processes, this input/output text is not shown between all core processes (e.g. actuarial). As such, it will potentially lead to misinterpretations and misunderstandings among the end-users.

Core processes in such an insurance company are typically cross-functional, which means that several departments are involved in their execution. As such, it is important for the process map to be designed in a way that it facilitates process integration. This is crucial considering that one of the BPM goals of this company is to use the process models as a work manual for employees. This means that, when an employee (new or existing) views the process map, he or she should gain a basic understanding of how the company operates as a whole. If the employee requires some additional in-depth information about a particular process, then the process model details from the lower levels of the corresponding process architecture have to be inspected. Facilitating cross-functional thinking will in return lead to increased employee communication and collaboration. Moreover, a process map is used as a foundation for the subsequent detailed modeling. Excluding the relation between the processes could potentially be an obstacle for the modeling team when trying to capture the details of processes. This is mainly because the relations between the processes shown in the process map should also be reflected in the detailed process modeling.

4.4 The New Process Map

Towards the reworking of the process map, we conducted three workshops with the members of the BPM team of the insurance company. The objective of these workshops was to establish a new process map that reflects the insights of our investigations on process map design.

The result of the reworked project is shown in Fig. 4. First, several matters are modified on the level of the secondary notation. Now, management as well as support processes are visualized with symbols different to the ones of the core processes. Also, the notion of visual containment is more explicitly used. Second, the core business has been subdivided into three segments, which are interrelated. The customer-facing processes partially interact with the recipient-facing processes. The community-related processes reflect the lifecycle of how assets are managed. In addition, the map now makes more explicit use of naming guidelines, although not to the full extent. It was suggested to use names that reflect the operations and to give less consideration to department names.

The most important impact of the reworking was the identification of business segments. The company was mostly struggling with the interfaces between these segments. This was also the main reason for the missing input between the actuarial and administrative core processes from Fig. 3. The original process map provided an inappropriate representation of the interfaces, which were in fact necessary for the relation between the two core processes. In this way, innovation at these cross-roads was blocked by the fact that it was simply not captured in an explicit manner. This lack meant that the company was not at all times aware of the impact the

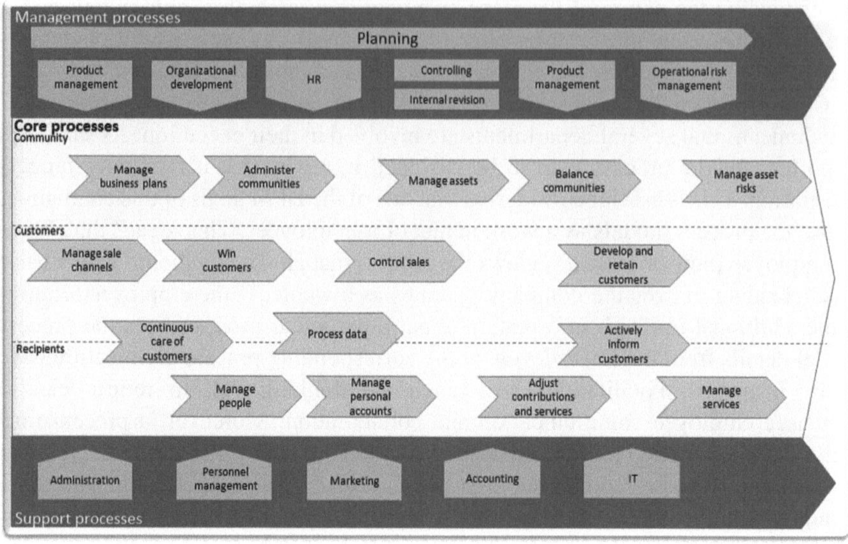

Fig. 4 The new process map of a European insurance company

different business segments could have on their BPM initiative. Having them explicitly depicted in the reworked process map will eventually lead to a correct undertaking of all subsequent steps of their BPM implementation, such as correctly modeling the details of each process depicted in the process map.

5 Lessons Learnt and Conclusions

In this paper, we studied process map design and its impact. We have identified potential weaknesses of process maps in terms of their primary and secondary notation. We used the case of an insurance company to highlight the benefits of good process map design. The lessons learnt include the following three major points. First, make sure that different concepts are also visually discriminable. Second, show explicitly how processes relate to one another. Finally, consider the strategic importance of process map design and assure that they are correct and complete. Because, the process map should be used as a reliable source for modeling the singular processes in detail, thus it should enable process redesign, implementation and innovation.

References

Bertin, J. (1983). *Semiology of graphics: Diagrams, networks, maps*. Madison, WI: University of Wisconsin Press.

Davenport, T. (1993). *Process innovation: Reengineering work through information technology*. Boston, MA: Harvard Business Press.

Dumas, M., La Rosa, M., Mendling, J., & Reijers, H. A. (2013). *Fundamentals of business process management*. Berlin: Springer.

Eckes, G. (2002). *The six sigma revolution: How general electric and others turned process into profit*. New York, NY: Wiley.

Hammer, M., & Champy, J. (2009). *Reengineering the corporation: Manifesto for business revolution*. New York, NY: HarperCollins.

La Rosa, M., ter Hofstede, A. H. M., Wohed, P., Reijers, H. A., Mendling, J., & van der Aalst, W. M. P. (2011). Managing process model complexity via concrete syntax modifications. *IEEE Transactions on Industrial Informatics, 7*(2), 255–265.

Lind, M., & Haraldson, S. (2015). Airport innovations as ecosystem innovations. In J. vom Brocke & T. Schmiedel (Eds.), *Business process management: Driving innovation in a digital world*. Berlin: Springer.

Loos, P., Fettke, P., Walter, J., Thaler, T., & Ardalani, P. (2015). Identification of business process models in a digital world. In J. vom Brocke & T. Schmiedel (Eds.), *Business process management: Driving innovation in a digital world*. Berlin: Springer.

Malinova, M., Leopold, H., & Mendling, J. (2013a). An empirical investigation on the design of process architectures. Paper presented at the Internationale Konferenz Wirtschaftsinformatik, Leipzig.

Malinova, M., & Mendling, J. (2013). *The effect of process map design quality on process management success*. Paper presented at the 21st European Conference on Information Systems, Utrecht, The Netherlands.

Moody, D. L. (2009). The "physics" of notations: toward a scientific basis for constructing visual notations in software engineering. *Software Engineering, IEEE Transactions 35(6)*, 756–779.

Parsons, J., & Saunders, C. (2004). Cognitive heuristics in software engineering: Applying and extending anchoring and adjustment to artifact reuse. *IEEE Transactions on Software Engineering, 30*, 873–888.

Porter, M. E., & Millar, V. E. (1985). How information gives you competitive advantage. *Harvard Business Review, 63*(4), 149–160.

Scheer, A.-W. (2000). *Aris: Business process modeling*. Berlin: Springer.

van der Aalst, W. M. P. (2015). Extracting event data from databases to unleash process mining. In J. Brocke & T. Schmiedel (Eds.), *Business process management: Driving innovation in a digital world*. Berlin: Springer.

von Hippel, E. A. (1994). Sticky information' and the locus of problem solving: Implications for innovation. *Management Science, 40*(4), 429–439.

Weske, M. (2007). *Business process management: Concepts, languages, architectures*. Berlin: Springer.

Part V

Driving Innovation Through Organizational Capabilities

Implementing a Digital Strategy through Business Process Management

César A.L. Oliveira, Ricardo M.F. Lima, and Hajo A. Reijers

Abstract

While digital innovations are transforming people's personal lives like never before, there are facets of corporate management that are still running behind the digital era. For instance, are there new ways through which a manager could ensure that employees are aligned with the company's strategy? This chapter describes a design approach and the implementation architecture for what we call Strategy-Aware Business Process Management (SA-BPM). In SA-BPM, while employees are guided through the execution of the workflow, they are also informed about the company's strategic goals and how these affect the execution of their activities. Such an approach increases the alignment between employees' decisions and the strategic priorities of the company. Moreover, it offers an innovative way to allow the company to implement strategic changes more efficiently. SA-BPM affords organizations an unprecedented capacity to integrate strategic planning and BPM concepts, making them more prepared to deal with changing and uncertain business environments.

C.A.L. Oliveira (✉) • R.M.F. Lima
Center for Informatics, Federal University of Pernambuco, Av. Jornalista Anibal Fernandes, s/n - Cidade Universitária, 50740-560 Recife, PE, Brazil
e-mail: calo@cin.ufpe.br; rmfl@cin.ufpe.br

H.A. Reijers
Department of Mathematics and Computer Science, Eindhoven University of Technology, Den Dolech 2, 5612 AZ Eindhoven, The Netherlands
e-mail: h.a.reijers@tue.nl

J. vom Brocke, T. Schmiedel (eds.), *BPM – Driving Innovation in a Digital World*, Management for Professionals, DOI 10.1007/978-3-319-14430-6_15

1 Introduction

The role of strategic planning in highly unpredictable or turbulent environments has extensively been discussed by management researchers (Brews & Purohit, 2007; Grant, 2003). According to Sanchez (1997), the "traditional strategic management objective of choosing a single best plan of action is likely to be an unrealistic objective in an uncertain environment". Modern organizational management requires the capacity to continually evaluate the company's performance and to rapidly adjust strategies in response to market changes. However, organizations often have difficulties in implementing strategic changes at the speed required by the market environment (Shimizu & Hitt, 2004). One of the reasons for such difficulties is that the relationship between a company's strategic goals and the operations that are necessary in order to achieve the goals is not clearly understood. Without such an understanding, the organization cannot guarantee that its operations are in alignment with its strategic requirements.

The importance of Business Process Management (BPM) (Dumas, Rosa, Mendling, & Reijers, 2013) in modeling and managing the execution of an organization's operations has been recognized by both academics and the industry. However, BPM and strategic planning have been studied by the literature as separate fields, with very limited approaches for connecting the two (Lepmets, McBride, & Ras, 2012). Due to this, ensuring the alignment between strategies and business processes in changing environments becomes a difficult task for organizations. Although we now live in a digital world, most organizations cannot exploit the opportunities given by information technology to solve these issues [see also chapter by Schmiedel and vom Brocke (2015)].

In this chapter, we describe the concept of Strategy-Aware Business Process Management (SA-BPM) as a means to improve strategic alignment and to increase the capacity of the organization to implement strategic changes. In SA-BPM, while employees are guided through the execution of the workflow, they are also informed about the company's strategic goals and how these affect the execution of their activities. An architecture for the implementation of this concept in information systems is presented, as well as a prototype system that we have constructed and an application scenario that illustrates its usefulness.

2 Related Work

The concept of *line of sight* (LOS) (Boswell, Bingham, & Colvin, 2006; Buller & McEvoy, 2012) in management research explains that human resources play a considerable part in the achievement of a firm's strategy. However, to fully benefit from their human potential, organizations need to ensure that their employees understand their own role in the strategy of the organization. LOS has been defined as "an employee's understanding of the organization's goals and what actions are necessary to contribute to those objectives" (Boswell et al., 2006). The challenge in enhancing LOS is how to implement efficient communication channels that transmit strategic objectives and performance targets from top managers to employees (Boswell et al., 2006).

The alignment between business processes and strategic goals has been approached by information systems literature in different ways. A common framework used to connect strategic goals and process goals is the Balanced Scorecards methodology (BSC) (Harmon, 2003; Kaplan & Norton, 1992). This methodology helps managers to design strategies and performance metrics in a way that links operations to results. In systems that employ this approach, business process goals can be mapped to the strategy through BSC performance metrics. Then, the system collects and monitors such metrics during the execution of the process. Due to the popularity of the BSC methodology among executives, many packaged solutions offer standard business process models that are already mapped into BSC metrics (Brignall & Ballantine, 2003).

Kang, Lee, and Kim (2010) propose the use of fact-based ontologies (OMG, 2008) to capture the relationships between a firm's strategic goals, performance metrics, business processes, and resources. Through their ontology, an organization can describe the links between these elements. This information is, then, used to compute matrix visualizations that help people understand the company's alignment requirements for each task.

Despite the fact that these works have approached the link between business processes and strategic goals, it can be noticed that current studies do not approach the fact that the strategy of the organization may affect the way business process models are designed and the way employees execute the processes. According to Lepmets et al. (2012), the literature is lacking studies on how process improvement methodologies can be used to align the goals of a process with the business goals of an organization. These authors argue that any connection between an organization's business goals and process improvement "has relied on coincidental concern" 'rather than on the direct representation of business goals within the improvement methodology context (Lepmets et al., 2012). They empirically tested these arguments through a survey with IT service providers and software development companies. The survey analyzed whether process assessment, the activity of identifying and quantifying which aspects of the process should be improved, was linked with business goals alignment. Their results show no correlation between process assessment and goals alignment in the process improvement projects conducted by their 63 respondents.

Therefore, the approaches used by related work to connect business processes and strategic goals have been superficial and mostly used to help managers to collect metrics about the process. There is a need for a methodology for ensuring the alignment of business processes and the company's strategy both at design and run-time.

3 Strategy-Aware BPM

To define SA-BPM, we firstly introduce some basic concepts that help us understand what a strategy is and how strategy and operations can be connected. Then, we describe an architecture for SA-BPM that employs these concepts. Our architecture is designed both to improve the alignment between process models and strategic requirements and to improve employee understanding of their role in the success of the strategy.

3.1 Basic Concepts

When employees know the expected outcomes of their activities, they are able to improve their job to meet the expectations of the organization (Buller & McEvoy, 2012). Unfortunately, current information systems do not offer support towards making the users aware of their role in the success of the organization's strategy.

Common practices to improve LOS rely on workshops, company-wide presentations, e-mail communication, and goal-based performance assessment (Boswell et al., 2006). These approaches have been in practice for decades. But new technologies delivery opportunities for making strategies go digital, offering much more automation opportunities for making employees aware of their role in the company's strategy.

We define *strategy awareness* as an information system's capacity to influence users to work towards the strategic priorities of the organization. SA-BPM is a management approach in which business processes not only define how employees should conduct their work, but are also used to inform these employees about the relationship between what they do and what is needed for the success of the company's strategy. To explain how this relationship is expressed, we must have a concrete definition of what a strategy is and of how strategy and operations can be connected. Two concepts are introduced with this purpose: the *results-chain* model and *work products*. The first is used to model strategies, the second is used to model the outputs of an employee's tasks. Finally, we use the concept of *strategic recommendations* to inform the employee about the connection between their tasks and what is required by the organization's strategy.

3.1.1 Results-Chain

Our first task in building an SA-BPM architecture is to make strategies go digital, i.e., to build a strategy model that is not only stored in an information system but that can also be interpreted by a computer to extract useful information from it.

To clearly express the elements that make up a strategy and how they relate to each other, we employ the framework of Results-Oriented Management (ROM) (Schouten & Beers, 2009). This is a management approach currently used by several organizations, which describes strategies as hierarchical structures called *results-chains*. This structure reflects cause-effect relationships between what the company does and the goals it wants to achieve. Figure 1 illustrates a graphical

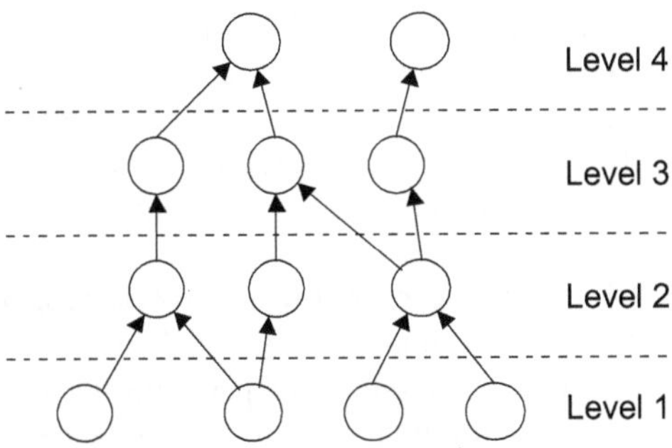

Fig. 1 Example of the graphical representation of a results-chain

representation of a results-chain. It can be defined as a graph whose nodes are the elements that make part of the strategy and whose edges express a relationship (a, b), such that element a contributes to the achievement of element b, which is in the level above a.

Usually, a results-chain is composed of the following *levels*: **inputs** (resources and competences), **actions** (projects and initiatives), **outputs** (the products of the actions), **outcomes** (short/mid-term business results obtained through the outputs), and **impacts** (long-term business results) (OECD, 2008).

Through the results-chain model, an organization can clearly express the steps necessary to meet long-term objectives. By analyzing the structure of the graph, we can also identify the cause-effect relationships between two distant elements of the strategy. For instance, we can identify that two outcomes depend on the same output, or find all actions required to produce a certain output. This capacity is explored in this work to clarify the relationship between the activities executed by a process participant and their relevance to the strategy of the organization.

3.1.2 Work Products

Employees in an organization execute activities to produce some output that is valuable to the company. Through the products of the employees' work, organizations perform their daily operations and implement the actions necessary to meet their strategic objectives. A *work product* is defined as the output of a single operation executed by an employee. For instance, an "order delivered" or an "invoice issued". This operation may correspond to the completion of a business process, of a set of activities within a business process, or even to the completion of more general tasks such as the conclusion of a project.

To connect the concept of work products to the results-chain, we propose a results-chain model in which the lowest level is the level of the work products. These work products are, then, connected to the "actions level", to express the relationship between these and the actions that require their execution to be completed. For example, we can define a strategy that contains the following action: "*improve quality assessment in the production process*", which generates the output "*reduced number of product defects*". Imagine that the production process was changed and an additional *quality assessment* activity was added to this process. Each time the activity is executed, it generates a work product

"*product quality assessed*". In the results-chain, we connect the "*product quality assessed*" work product to the action "*improve quality assessment in the production process*". It means that the quality assessment is required to implement the action.

Therefore, the work product concept is useful to describe the relationship between what an employee does and the strategic goals connected to that activity.

3.1.3 Strategic Recommendations and Recommended Work Products

For any given operation executed by the company, strategic requirements may affect the way the employee performs his job. We call a *strategic recommendation* any information that helps the user take decisions and perform activities in alignment with the strategic priorities of the organization. For instance, think in a company that has the strategic goal to "*reduce travel expenses*". At the time that travel expenses are involved in a business process, a strategic recommendation would be advice to the user telling him whether he should or should not proceed with a path that involves such expenses. If the employee finishes an operation generating an output that is in accordance with its strategic recommendations, then we say that he generated the *recommended work product.*

Decision-making algorithms can be used to compile and present to the user recommendations about how to perform their job in alignment with the organization's priorities. Then, the output of their work can be monitored and compared to the recommended work products in order to measure the fit between an employee's work and strategic requirements.

3.2 Architecture

SA-BPM differs from regular BPM both at design and run-time. At design time, business process models are decomposed into separate modules according to their strategic purpose. The aim of such decomposition is to facilitate the implementation of changes when strategies are changed. At run-time, these modules are joined together into a single workflow and strategic recommendations are compiled to inform the user about the strategic requirements of his work.

To implement the infrastructure for SA-BPM system, we apply concepts drawn from the architectures of context-aware information systems. In general, these systems are composed of three main elements: (1) the user application services; (2) a context acquisition and reasoning module; and (3) an adaptation mechanism. The *context* is the information that comes from the environment and that defines the situation in which the application is being employed. The adaptation mechanism uses such context information to adapt the system's functions and provide services to the user in a way that is optimized to the current context of use.

On the basis of these concepts, we design four main modules that compose an SA-BPM system's architecture: (1) the *strategic context provider*, (2) the *strategic adaptation agent*, (3) the *BPM engine*, and (4) the *strategic adapters*. The BPM engine is the underlying BPM system that executes the business process model and interacts with the user. The other modules communicate with the BPM engine to

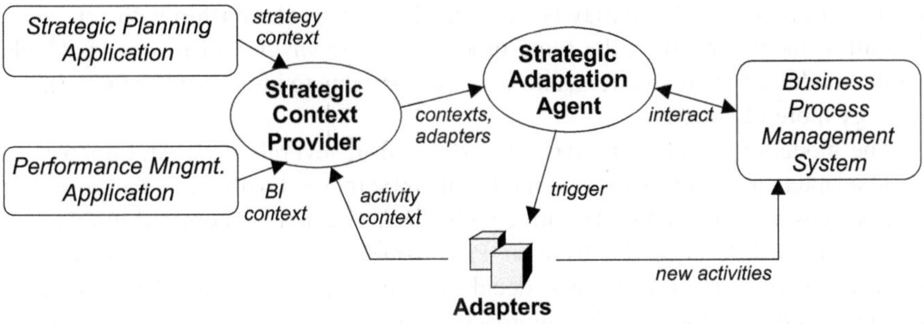

Fig. 2 Information flow between elements that make part of SA-BPM's architecture

implement the strategy-related features. Strategic Planning and Performance Management applications are also integrated into the system to retrieve the information that make up the strategic context. Figure 2 depicts a diagram of the information flow between these modules and applications. They are described in detail at this point.

3.2.1 Strategic Context Provider

The task of the Context Provider is to acquire information from the organization's management support systems and make this information available to the other modules. It is the responsibility of the Context Provider to store a results-chain that represents the company's strategy, to compare the priorities of goals, to trace the relationship between an action and the outcomes and impacts connected to it, and so on. It is also responsible for obtaining data about the performance indicators, their historical data and current values, as well as the performance targets that are defined in the strategy (the desired values of the indicators).

During process enactment, the Context Provider creates a specific area for storing the context of each process instance. This area stores information that is specific to that instance, such as, strategic recommendations that should be presented to the user during the execution of that instance of the process.

3.2.2 Strategic Adapters

The Strategic Adapters (or just *adapters*) are pieces of software that affect the execution of the process to include new activities, alternative paths, and strategic recommendations. For example, during the execution of an Order Fulfillment process, an adapter may insert into the process instance activities that aim at improving customer relationship metrics, while another adapter may warn the employee that the order is delayed and should have processing priority to avoid customer complaints. A third adapter may give the user a recommendation to avoid printing a document when a digital copy is available and a fourth one may insert an automatic activity that applies additional discounts due to a marketing campaign.

Each adapter addresses a specific strategic concern. So, while one adapter may be concerned with customer relationship, another may be concerned with cost reductions, and a third one may be concerned with the relationship with suppliers. But all of them can affect the same process. This *separation of concerns* affords higher modularity to the system, allowing the company to implement changes in the strategy more efficiently.

The modeling of adapters may be performed in several ways. An option is to build adapters as business process models that are merged with the main process to include new activities and alternative paths to it. The adapters created in this way may communicate with the Context Provider through *web services* to acquire information from the context and decide which information should be shown to the user. The advantage of this approach is that the company can build adapters using the same knowledge that is used to design a regular business process.

3.2.3 Strategic Adaptation Agent

The Adaptation Agent is the module responsible for monitoring the execution of the business process instance and making the adapters effective when they are necessary. The Adaptation Agent can interact with the business process engine and change the workflow that is being executed *even without the process modeler being aware of this*. The Adaptation Agent will check the description of all adapters, identify the points in the process in which they should be inserted and trigger their execution at the right moment. The activities and strategic recommendations provided by the adapters are incorporated into the process that is being executed.

To show the strategic recommendations to the user, the Adaptation Agent also affects the user interface of the BPM system to enrich the user's experience. All recommendations stored in the *context* of the process instance are made available to the user, so that he can become aware of them and perform the activities in accordance. The information shown to the user includes also the connections between the work products generated by the activity and all elements of the results-chain that are affected, their corresponding performance indicators and targets, as well as their current value. Thus, the process participant is aware of the overall relationship between the activities and the strategy of the organization and also about specific recommendations about how that process instance should be executed to meet the expectations of the organization.

4 Prototype Implementation

This section describes a prototype SA-BPM system constructed to show the feasibility of the architecture proposed. The system is called *ROSAS—the Results-Oriented Strategy Automation System*. ROSAS is built on top of the *Bonita BPM System*, produced by *BonitaSoft* (www.bonitasoft.com).

In ROSAS, the Context Provider is a web service that stores the results-chain and that uses *business intelligence* mechanisms to extract data from performance indicators. Both regular business processes and adapters are modeled using BPMN notation and deployed to the engine. Adapters differ from regular processes with respect to their initiation. They can only be initiated by the system. The Adaptation Agent is a stand-alone application that monitors the process execution in the Bonita BPM engine, looking for the moment when certain activities are ready to be executed. These are the activities that are registered as the *targets* of adapters. When such an activity becomes ready, the Adaptation Agent interrupts the process, blocking its execution. It then starts the execution of all adapters that are registered to affect the process at that execution point. All variables from the process instance are copied to the adapters so all adapters can have access to the process data. On the basis of this data, the adapters can compute recommendations and store them in the Context Provider. If adapters request the execution of manual activities, these activities are communicated to the user, as usual in any regular business process.

As soon as all adapters have concluded their execution, the Adaptation Agent returns the control flow to the initial process. During this process, the Agent changes the user interface so that the user can become aware of the execution of these adapters and of the strategic recommendations computed by them. The Bonita BPM's interface enriched by ROSAS with strategic recommendations is illustrated in Fig. 3. This picture shows a typical input form shown by Bonita BPM during the execution of a process. Over this form a sliding panel is added by ROSAS where recommendations specifically targeted for the activity being executed are shown.

When the organization changes its strategic goals or changes its approach to meet those goals, the corresponding adapters can be updated or removed from the set. New adapters can be added to take new strategic concerns into account. All these changes are automatically identified by ROSAS so that they are effective in the next execution of the process affected by them. When the users execute the process, the visual feedback given by ROSAS helps them recognize changes in the

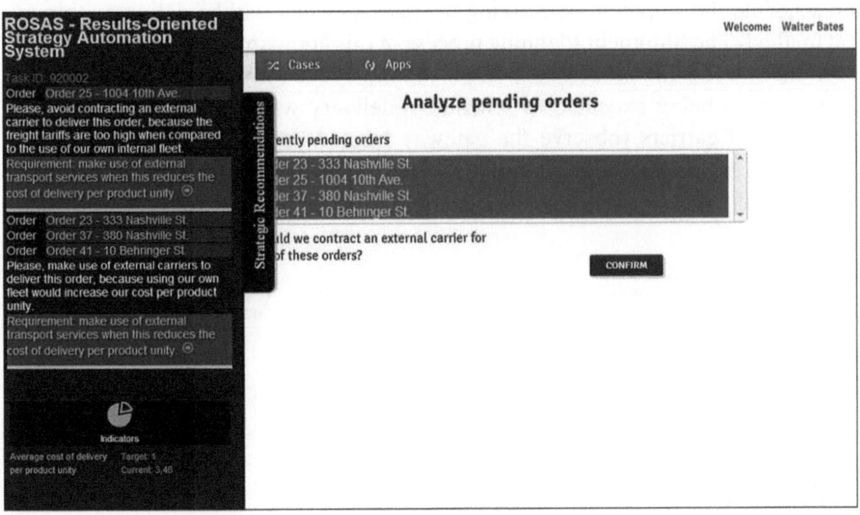

Fig. 3 Bonita BPM interface enriched by ROSAS to display strategic recommendations

priorities of the organization and understand how these changes impact their own job.

5 Application Scenario

To demonstrate the application of SA-BPM concepts and tools, we describe a fictitious scenario of a manufacturing company. This company wants to improve their distribution agility while keeping the delivery costs low. They also want to improve financial stability by increasing their Free Cash Flow (FCF), which is the cash available to the organization after all debits are subtracted.

5.1 Distribution

To improve the distribution agility, this company decided to get rid of all of their large trucks, adopting the principle that smaller trucks can make faster deliveries and can better supply smaller retail stores. Their decision showed to be effective in most cases. However, when the amount of packages to be delivered to a certain area is too large, a larger truck would reduce the delivery costs. The managers observed this situation and also included in their operations an option to contract an external carrier for handling such a situation. Whenever the volume of packages is large, an external carrier can be contracted to perform the delivery.

The decision to how packages will be delivered is taken during the *Shipment Planning* process. Every day, the distribution department must schedule the deliveries and plan the routes for the trucks of the company's fleet. When an external carrier is needed, the distribution department must contract the carrier and schedule the shipment, specifying the packages that will be delivered through that method. The Shipment Planning process of this company is illustrated in Fig. 4.

At the start of this process, the employee must take the decision about whether the process is being executed to schedule a delivery with the company's fleet or with external carriers (observe the gateway labeled "need to contract carrier?"). Depending on the user's decision, the process will finish with the generation of either one of two *work products*:

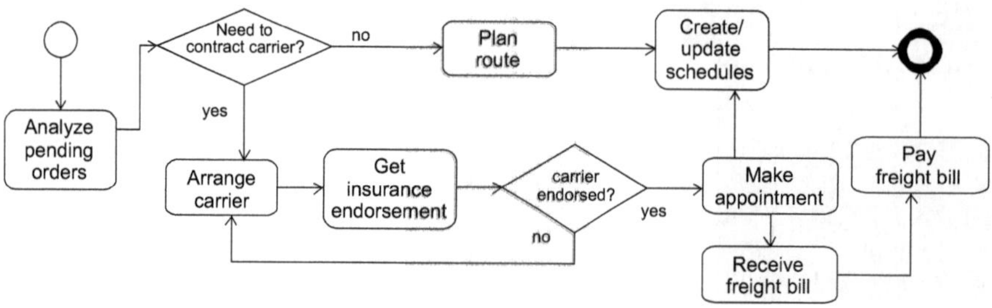

Fig. 4 Shipment planning process of the manufacturing company

- *Truck assigned to shipment schedule;*
- *External carrier contracted to perform shipment.*

At this point, the employee is actually facing a difficult decision. Is it an advantage to the company to contract a carrier? Will this delay the delivery too much? Will the costs be reduced? This decision depends on a set of information, including an estimate of the freight tariffs that would have to be paid to deliver the packages through an external carrier. The decision taken by the employee at this point has a direct impact on the strategic performance of the company. If the user is not aware of the trade-offs involved and the objectives of the organization, he may take the wrong decision and cause a detrimental impact to the capacity of the organization to meet its performance targets.

To ensure the alignment between the Shipment Planning process and the strategic goals of the organization, we implemented an adapter for making recommendations about which shipment method should be chosen, in other words, to determine which is the *recommended work product* of each process instance. This adapter is implemented in ROSAS and is illustrated in Fig. 5.

The adapter firstly identifies the amount of packages that must be delivered through each of a set of pre-determined routes. When it identifies that there are too many packages to the same route, it requests the user to estimate the freight tariffs for external carriers. As soon as the employee has gathered this information and input into the system, a decision algorithm is automatically employed to determine the recommended path to be followed by the user. This information is stored in the system's Context Provider.

After the execution of this adapter, when the employee reaches the decision point in the process flow, the SA-BPM system will display the recommendations computed by the adapter in a textual form, as well as the performance indicators and strategic goals that are affected by his decision at this point. In this example, the performance indicator directly affected by the decision is the "average cost of delivery per product unity". The textual representation of the recommendation computed by the adapter will be one of the following two:

Fig. 5 Distribution department's adapter for reducing cost of delivery per product unity

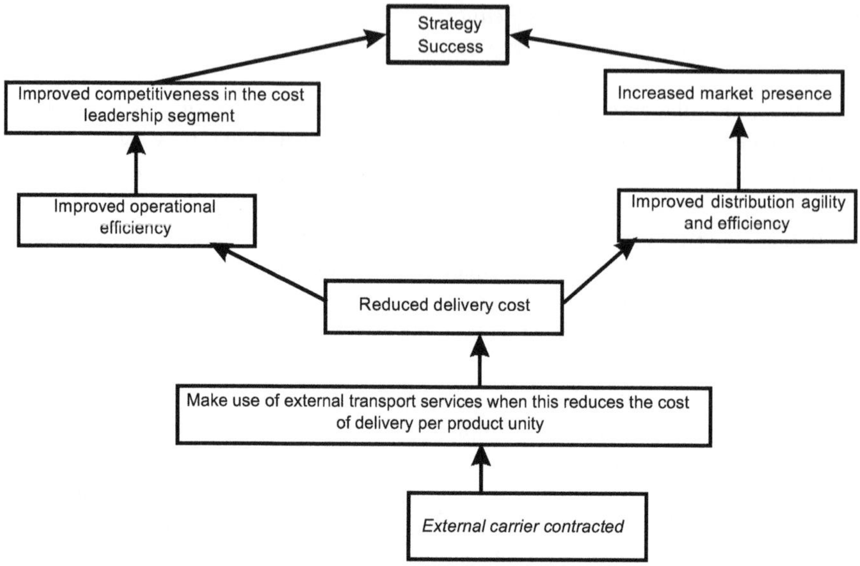

Fig. 6 Results-chain linked to the work product "external carrier contracted"

- **Recommended work product:** *Truck assigned to shipment schedule*
  Text shown to the user: "Please, avoid contracting an external carrier for these packages, because the cost of delivery per product will be lower if our company's truck are used."
- **Recommended work product:** *External carrier contracted to perform shipment*
  Text shown to the user: "Please, contract an external carrier to deliver these orders, because this will reduce the cost of delivery per product unity."

The results-chain that is linked to this activity is illustrated in Fig. 6. The work product contributes to the implementation of the "make use of external transport services" action, which, in turn, contributes to the achievement of output "reduced delivery time and costs". This output is linked to outcomes "improved operational efficiency" and "improved distribution agility and efficiency". The first one is proposed to generate the impact "improved competitiveness in cost leadership", while the second one contributes to "increased market presence". All these strategic goals, thus, are affected by the decision that the user is going to make at this moment. Through the SA-BPM system, the user becomes aware of the relevance of the activity he is executing and of what he should do to contribute to the success of the strategy.

5.2 Finance

Although contracting external carriers has been shown to be useful to improve the performance from the distribution department's viewpoint, the finance department is not that happy with this approach. It happens that carriers must be paid in advance. Thus, the more carriers are contracted, the less FCF is available to the company. Since this department is particularly concerned with increasing FCF, they determine that the use of external carriers should be limited when the company's free cash has been decreased due to other debits. To implement these concerns, we modeled the adapter illustrated in Fig. 7.

Finance's adapter checks current cash of the company. When it is too low, it recommends the instance of the Shipment Planning process to avoid contracting external carriers. The recommended work product here is the "truck assigned to shipment schedule".

After the addition of the Finance's adapter, the employee that is executing the Shipment Planning process will also be informed that his decision affects the FCF of the organization and that, in certain instances, what appears to be a good decision from the cost effectiveness perspective has, indeed, other undesirable impacts to the organization.

Notice that, in this case, the user needs to balance the trade-offs between cost reduction and financial stability, because the recommendations of the adapters may conflict with each other. Should the user prefer one to the other? What is more important for the company?

In SA-BPM, all information necessary to help the user in taking a decision that affects the strategic performance of the company must be made accessible to him. In the situation of a conflict between recommendations, the system must rank the recommendations according to the company's priorities at the time. We propose in our work two main criteria to be taken into consideration when ranking recommendations:

- **Strategic coverage**: which recommendation covers the largest number of goals in the company's strategy?
- **Performance gap**: which recommendation addresses goals that are at a high distance from meeting their targets?

To automatically weight the recommendations according to these criteria, a multi-criteria decision making method can be employed, such as the Analytic Hierarchy Process (AHP) (Saaty, 2008). Through the application of a method like

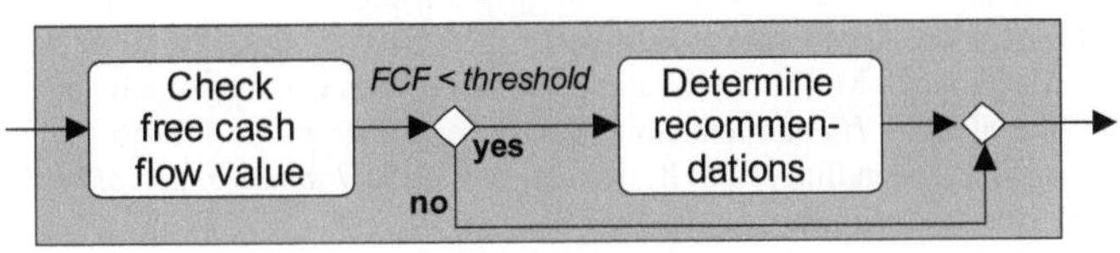

Fig. 7 Finance department's adapter to increase free cash flow

AHP, the recommendations can be shown to the user together with their ranks. So, the user can know that, for instance, the financial stability of the company is in a critical situation and that this much more important than reducing the cost of delivery—which may be less critical at the time.

6 Conclusions

Companies in complex and uncertain environments need means to adapt their strategies and operations quickly in response to unexpected situations. In this chapter, we describe the concept and tool support for Strategy-Aware Business Process Management (SA-BPM). The objective of SA-BPM is to close a gap that separates strategy management and business process management subjects. SA-BPM helps companies to overcome a number of difficulties that surge due to this gap:

- **unclear linkages between business processes and strategic goals**, which makes achieving and maintaining the alignment between processes and strategies more difficult;
- **the difficulty in disseminating strategic change throughout the organization**, which reduces the agility to react to unforeseen changes;
- **the difficulty in monitoring the fitness between an employee's activities and corresponding strategic requirements**, which makes it more difficult to identify and address internal weaknesses.

Through a set of concepts that express the links between strategic goals and operations, SA-BPM offers possibilities to overcome these barriers and allow companies to achieve higher flexibility. The architecture for the implementation of these concepts exploits the benefits already offered by BPM and builds a new layer on top of that. It offers means through which both process designers and participants are engaged in the pursuit of the strategic goals of the organization.

References

Boswell, W. R., Bingham, J. B., & Colvin, A. J. S. (2006). Aligning employees through "line of sight". *Business Horizons, 49*, 499–509.

Brews, P., & Purohit, D. (2007). Strategic planning in unstable environments. *Long Range Planning, 40*(1), 64–83.

Brignall, S., & Ballantine, J. (2003). Strategic enterprise management systems: New directions for research. *Management Accounting Research, 15*, 225–240.

Buller, P. F., & McEvoy, G. M. (2012). Strategy, human resource management and performance: Sharpening line of sight. *Human Resource Management Review, 22*, 43–56.

Dumas, M., Rosa, M. L., Mendling, J., & Reijers, H. A. (2013). *Fundamentals of business process management*. Berlin: Springer.

Grant, R. M. (2003). Strategic planning in a turbulent environment: Evidence from the oil majors. *Strategic Management Journal, 24*(6), 491–517.

Harmon, P. (2003). *Business process change: A manager's guide to improving, redesigning, and automating processes.* San Francisco, CA: Morgan Kaufmann.

Kang, D., Lee, J., & Kim, K. (2010). Alignment of business enterprise architectures using fact-based ontologies. *Expert Systems with Applications, 37*(4), 3274–3283.

Kaplan, R. S., & Norton, D. P. (1992). *The balanced scorecard: Translating strategy into action.* Boston, MA: Harvard Business School Press.

Lepmets, M., McBride, T., & Ras, E. (2012). Goal alignment in process improvement. *The Journal of Systems and Software, 85*, 1440–1452.

OECD. (2008). *Sourcebook on emerging good practice in managing for development results.* Washington, DC: Organisation for Economic Co-operation and Development. (book available at http://www.mfdr.org/sourcebook/)

OMG. (2008). *Semantics of business vocabulary and business rules (SBVR), v1.0.* Needham, MA: Object Management Group. (book available at http://www.omg.org/spec/SBVR/1.2/)

Saaty, T. L. (2008). Decision making with the analytic hierarchy process. *International Journal of Services Sciences, 1*, 83–98.

Sanchez, R. (1997). Preparing for an uncertain future: Managing organizations for strategic flexibility. *International Studies of Management and Organization, 27*(2), 71–94.

Schmiedel, T., & vom Brocke, J. (2015). Business process management: Potentials and challenges of driving innovation. In J. vom Brocke & T. Schmiedel (Eds.), *Business process management: Driving innovation in a digital world.* Berlin: Springer.

Schouten, J., & Beers, W. (2009). *Results-oriented management.* Zaltbommel: Thema. ISBN 9789058714220.

Shimizu, K., & Hitt, M. A. (2004). Strategic flexibility: Organizational preparedness to reverse ineffective strategic decisions. *Academy of Management Executive, 18*(4), 44–59.

Flexible Workflows and Compliance: A Solvable Contradiction?!

Stefan Sackmann and Kai Kittel

Abstract

Managing workflows is increasingly becoming flexible on both the conceptual and technical level. Reacting directly to new context situations and adapting workflows to changing requests both rapidly and flexibly are seen as key characteristic for future agile companies. Providing flexibility in process execution for single workflow instances is also a promising basis for expanding the scope of Business Process Management to other application fields and for integrating so-called dark processes into the system. However, workflows are not only subject to "pure" business needs but also increasingly to compliance requirements. To validate that a workflow is compliant with relevant laws and regulations, in principal, each change of a workflow has also to be checked according to its consequences for compliance. Not surprisingly, validating compliance is currently a well-known challenge for many companies, specifically their IT governance, and is, usually, a time-consuming manual task dealing with the challenge of fast adaptations and changes. Management has to balance the trade-off between flexible but (possibly) non-compliant workflows and compliant but (mostly) inflexible workflows. Addressing this trade-off, we present a novel approach called FlexCom and its prototypical implementation in this contribution. It aims at solving the trade-off by allowing a person in charge to change a workflow, even during execution, according to business needs, and by automatically integrating required control processes for achieving the correspondent compliance requirements. It is demonstrated that with such "sticky" controls at hand, the balance between flexibility of processes and compliance can be managed in a novel and promising way.

S. Sackmann (✉) • K. Kittel
Martin Luther University Halle-Wittenberg, Universitätsring 3, 06108 Halle (Saale), Germany
e-mail: stefan.sackmann@wiwi.uni-halle.de; kai.kittel@gmx.de

J. vom Brocke, T. Schmiedel (eds.), *BPM – Driving Innovation in a Digital World*,
Management for Professionals, DOI 10.1007/978-3-319-14430-6_16

1 Balancing Flexibility and Compliance

Beyond doubt, business process management (BPM) has driven many innovations in companies and is still massively changing traditional organization forms. By standardizing processes and separating execution of activities from its control on a conceptual level, higher process transparency, efficiency, and customer satisfaction are now within reach. Thus, to remain competitive, many companies decided to actively manage their processes and to use information systems (IS) to support these. In particular, enterprise resource planning systems (ERP) or workflow management systems (WfMS) have been implemented and successfully used by many companies.

A very welcome "side effect" of applying ERP or WfMS is that such systems support not only process design by arranging activity sequences, assignment of predefined resources, realizing IS support of functionalities, etc., they also provide a way to technically enforce process execution as planned and to realize so-called compliance-aware process engines (Cabanillas, Resinas, & Ruiz-Cortes, 2011). The capability to enforce execution of workflows exactly in an ex-ante specified way does, in turn, not only maintain the achievement of "pure" or "original" business goals. It also has raised the interest of other management fields, since integration (and automated enforcement) of additional control activities provide powerful mechanisms and tools for realizing effective internal control systems (Sackmann, Hofmann, & Kühnel, 2013) that are an essential part of any risk and compliance management. For example, enforcing separation of duty or monitoring (and logging) actual execution states of each activity doubtlessly support achievement and validation of compliance to relevant laws, rules, and regulations like, e.g., Sarbanes Oxley Act (SOX), laws and regulations issued by the Basel Committee on Banking Supervision, Health Insurance Portability and Accountability Act (HIPAA), German Freedom of Information Act and many others more. So far, efficiently and effectively realizing both original process goals and compliance goals in one single workflow is a challenging issue that quickly turns into a real problem when either processes or compliance requirements (or, worse, both) change very frequently.

For actively managing the balance between flexibility and compliance, a methodical approach called FlexCom is presented in this paper. FlexCom has also been prototypically implemented within the adaptive workflow management system AristaFlow, demonstrating the general functionality of the approach. The remainder of this contribution is organized as follows: initially, some background information on the "trade-off" between flexibility of workflows and validation of compliance by controls together is given in the following section. Afterwards, the developed method FlexCom (third section) followed by a demonstration of its prototypical implementation called KitCom (fourth section) are presented and explained by means of a continuous workflow example. A short discussion and conclusion completes the contribution.

2 Flexibility XOR Compliance?

Achieving flexibility and compliance does, in general, not involve an inherent or insolvable contradiction. In practice, however, aiming for both goals usually means searching for an efficient and effective balance between flexible but (possibly) non-compliant workflows and compliant but (mostly) inflexible workflows. Thus, achieving both goals together frequently seems out of reach. Since achieving compliance (and also risk management) is substantially based on internal control systems, i.e., controls non-detachably integrated into workflows (e.g., approval to pay an invoice given by a supervisor), every change within the workflows should be validated against several management goals and requirements.

In doing so, current compliance approaches quickly reach their limits (Kittel, 2013): so-called hard-wired controls that are integrated on the level of workflow schemes have to be checked and validated, in principal, for each change of the process specification with regard to their effects on process performance as well as on compliance validation. Since validation is the core of compliance (Cannon & Byers, 2006) and it is usually a "manual" task requiring noteworthy time and effort, either flexibility or compliance can be achieved. For example, when important production parts for a time-critical order are ruined by accident late in the night and there is no person to authorize a necessary re-ordering, either the order can be executed by skipping the authorization process to the next morning (flexibility) or the workflow/production has to halt until all required persons are available and give their approval (compliance). Thus, changing a workflow (instance) in real-time and validating that the integrated controls are still achieving relevant compliance requirements appears as an inherent trade-off in many situations. Otherwise, if process designers aim at integrating necessary controls for all thinkable situations in advance, the convenient side effect results immediately in a plethora of conditional branches and control activities leading to a state that some authors already named "process pollution" (Schumm, Leymann, Ma, Scheibler, & Strauch, 2010).

Although more advanced approaches like the so-called repository solutions are usually capable of relieving the situation by defining for each foreseeable situation a single version of a compliant workflow scheme, enriched with adequate controls (see, e.g., Sadiq, Governatori, & Namiri, 2007), they usually bring their own complexity and do not solve the issue on a methodical or general level. Further methods and tools like the so-called (rule-based) monitors or ex post auditing approaches, e.g., process mining, also reveal several disadvantages in the light of the (typically) conflicting goals of business process management and compliance management (for a more detailed discussion see, e.g., Kittel, 2013): while the former is usually capable of enforcing compliance without adequately taking economic risk (e.g., interrupting a process instance) into consideration, the latter is usually capable of providing high flexibility of process execution, but this is inherently combined with a high risk of violating compliance goals (Sackmann, 2011). For realizing the opportunities for both business process and compliance management, it becomes obvious that both have to work together and, in practice, companies have to find a balance between flexibility and compliance and the required controls integrated into their workflows.

As extensively discussed in the literature, a flexible adaptation of ongoing workflows to new demands or changing contexts is challenging (see, e.g., Smith & Fingar, 2003; van der Aalst, Weske, & Grünbauer, 2005). Indeed, it is actually achievable on the level of workflow design or modelling (see, e.g., Weske, 2012) as well as on the technical level (see, e.g., Krafzig, Banke, & Slama, 2005) within so-called adaptive workflow management systems (see, e.g., Reichert, Rinderle, Kreher, & Dadam, 2005; Rinderle, Reichert, & Dadam, 2004). However, this available flexibility has not yet been exploited to its full potential, but the momentum to do so can be expected to become more pressing and serious when progressive methods, tools, and technologies in the fields of, e.g., cyber physical systems, big data analysis, business intelligence approaches, or process mining provide more and more results in real-time. Such developments will change the landscape of BPM further and form a promising basis for innovation, process improvement, and adaptation according to the actual execution context, quasi in real-time (some impressive examples are presented in other chapters of this book). Existing approaches towards solving the apparent trade-off and, in turn, the achievable "balance" can be expected to become increasingly unsatisfactory. Thus, it is not really surprising that the development of new methods and tools for changing workflows at run-time in accordance with actual environmental conditions and without violating compliance requirements is an emerging field of research (see, e.g., Ly, Rinderle-Ma, Knuplesch, & Dadam, 2011; Sadiq et al., 2007).

3 FlexCom: An Approach for Integrating Control Activities into Workflow Instances at Run-Time

The basic idea of our FlexCom approach is, at first, to allow managers of business processes to change the workflows if necessary. However, each change is actively monitored by FlexCom and analyzed according to its meaning for compliance management: if required and feasible, the change is allowed and the (ongoing) workflow is automatically adapted by controls in accordance with the compliant requirements. Thus, FlexCom does not focus on flexibility already provided by advanced WfMS but provides the methodic basis for identifying and adapting effective control activities in real-time for ongoing and changing workflows. FlexCom is based on a separation of controls and processes on the conceptual level (design time, see Fig. 1) and, thus, does not focus on the level of workflow schemes. In fact, this conceptual separation is the basis for our automated integration of control processes directly into single workflow instances during their execution (for more details see also Kittel, 2013; Kittel & Sackmann, 2011, 2012; Kittel, Sackmann, Betke, & Hofmann, 2013a). At least for several types of compliance requirements, this approach facilitates validation of compliance before workflow execution while still maintaining the possibility to adapt workflow instances at run-time.

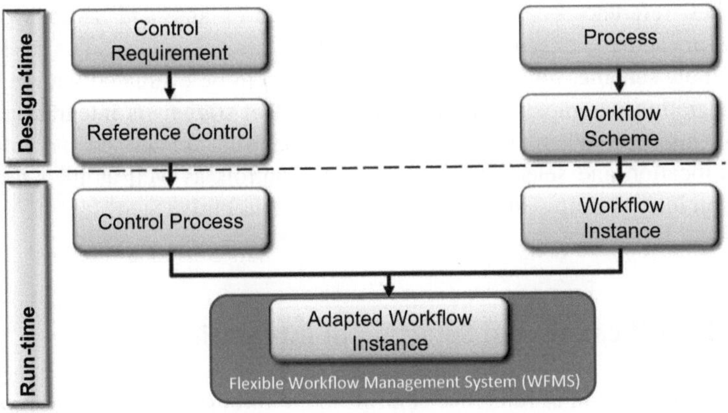

Fig. 1 FlexCom: a general approach for integrating control processes into workflow instances at run-time (Kittel & Sackmann, 2012)

On a general level, the FlexCom approach can be separated into three main areas: firstly, the formal definition of reference controls that show how control activities can be executed to achieve a given compliance requirement; secondly, for each reference control, the identification and selection of integration points at which it is possible or, rather, reasonable to integrate them into workflow instances; and thirdly, the integration of control activities into workflows at run-time.

3.1 Defining Reference Controls

The generic starting point for a methodic integration of control activities into workflows is to define (formal) compliance requirements. For each compliance requirement, at least one or a set of general reference controls has to be defined. Such reference controls can be seen as a template where the activities and objects involved, as well as the general structure of the controls, are already designed (Kittel, Sackmann, & Göser, 2013b). For instance, the "second set of eyes" principle (compliance requirement) can be performed in several ways: it can be realized as a sequential execution of control activities or with two control activities in parallel. Furthermore, it can be performed executing two control activities successively or with other workflow activities in between. This template has to be substantiated at the moment when the reference control is instantiated. Thus, reference controls are similar to the scheme of workflows which can produce several instances if executed (van der Aalst & van Hee, 2004) and can be modeled with the same tools (Betke, Kittel, & Sackmann, 2013).

Furthermore, several parameters that are typical for workflows (and WfMS) can be used for the specification of reference controls and the conditions for their integration (integration parameters), e.g., data elements, values, organizational units, or temporal characteristics. Finally, similar to classical "by design" approaches, reference controls should be validated ex ante and before workflow instances are actually executed. In addition to the classical validation on the level of the workflow scheme, reference controls have also to be evaluated with regard to their integration parameters, i.e., the conditions that trigger its integration into a workflow instance. When all relevant reference controls are defined and validated, the identification and selection of appropriate controls as well as their technical integration into workflow instances are the next consecutive steps.

3.2 Identification and Selection of Integration Points

A dynamic integration of reference controls in the form of actual control processes into workflow instances during their execution has a significant advantage: there is more information available than at design time. This information can be used for flexibly adapting a workflow as well as control activities to the actual process context, for instance to implement (control) activities. Furthermore, integration at run-time allows control activities to be integrated only if they are actually needed in a specific instance and, consequently, can reduce the complexity of business process execution.

In order to realize such integration at run-time, all entities that can be used in a process model could be taken into account as relevant parameters. Based on the parameters identified by Sadiq et al. (2007), control integration parameters are assigned to three categories: structural, validity, and conditional control integration parameters. Within these categories, concrete information like the validity period, activities as precondition, and/or activities as post-condition have to be defined (Kittel et al., 2013b). This additional information is also part of our reference controls and named control parameters (see above). Then, using all these pieces of information it becomes possible to identify points for integrating concrete control activities into workflows. This can be realized by having automated search algorithms check the actual control parameters against the workflow instance information.

Since there might be a large number of different points in a workflow where integration is theoretically possible, a reduction to efficient control points is necessary. This reduction can be achieved by several methods, e.g., by calculating the so-called critical path and selecting an integration point that is not an active part of it. In our prototype KitCom, we decided to integrate the controls as early as possible, following a prudence principle [for a detailed description of the identification and selection algorithm see Kittel (2013)]. While the identification of possible integration points works on a general level, this selection is only a first heuristic. However, a method for finding the economically optimal integration point is not yet available and still part of current research [see, e.g., Sackmann et al. (2013)].

3.3 Integration of Controls into Workflows at Run-Time

Last but not least, the identified and selected reference control(s) have to be technically integrated as control processes into the workflow instance at the identified points. How integration actually takes place depends mainly on the WfMS engine that is used for executing and enforcing the workflow instances. Since workflow engines of specific WfMS are constructed with different capabilities and modus operandi, a general discussion of technical integration seems not to be appropriate. Therefore, in the following, we demonstrate the integration (as well as the definition of reference controls) by means of a prototypical implementation within the adaptive WfMS AristaFlow (see http://www.aristaflow.com).

4 Prototype KitCom: Integrating Controls at Run-Time

A prototype called KitCom, originally presented at the CeBIT 2013 and published by Kittel et al. (2013b), was created to integrate reference controls at run-time into ongoing workflow instances. Following the FlexCom approach, the prototype requires two parts: firstly, reference controls, including the definition of situations in the workflow instance (status of integration parameters) where an integration of a control process becomes necessary, have to be modeled, e.g., by a compliance officer. Secondly, the execution engine of a workflow management system needs to be extended to automatically perform the modeled actions and integrate the modeled reference controls. Therefore, we extend the Aristaflow BPM Platform (for more details see, e.g., Dadam et al. (2009) and http://www.aristaflow.com): on the client side, the Process Template Editor is extended for modeling reference controls. On the server side, the LogManager is extended for intercepting execution events (see Fig. 2, where white/blue fields are the original components of AristaFlow, grey/yellow fields are the extensions characterizing KitCom).

To easily follow the working of KitCom, an exemplary workflow is modeled that describes activities if an invoice is received. In a first step, a process designer has to create and develop the workflow in the Process Template Editor as shown in Fig. 3.

Due to compliance requirements, all orders above 5,000€ which are captured by user "Meyer13" must be checked. Thus, in a second step, a compliance officer has to define a corresponding reference control. In this simplified example, only one control activity is defined: an accounts clerk has to compare the invoice amount

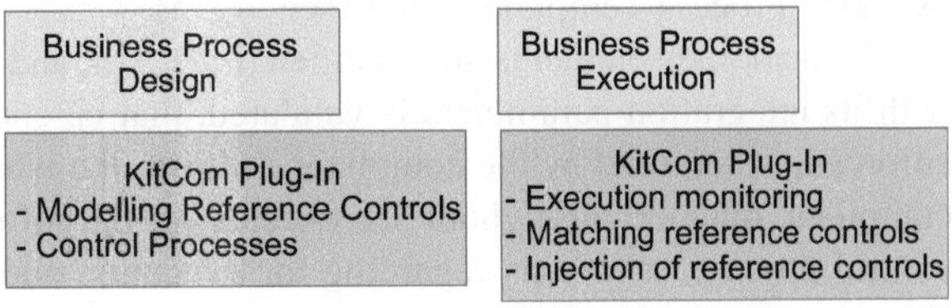

Fig. 2 The two conceptual parts of KitCom

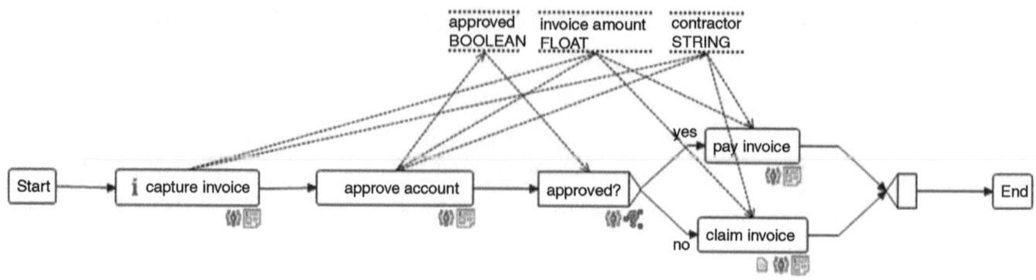

Fig. 3 Exemplary workflow created with the AristaFlow process template editor

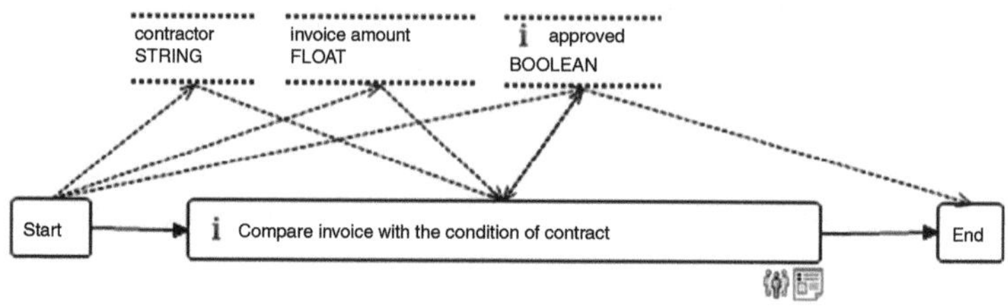

Fig. 4 Exemplary reference control modeled with KitCom

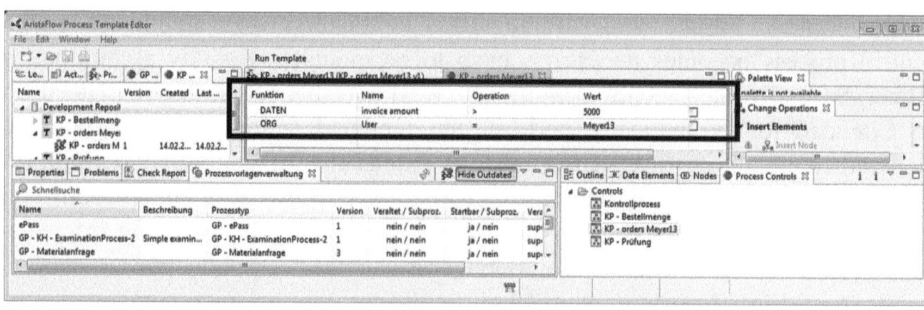

Fig. 5 Control parameter specification in KitCom

with the condition of the contract (see Fig. 4). Since the AristaFlow Process Template Editor is implemented using Eclipse RCP, it can be easily extended with additional plug-ins (Reference Control Editor, Control Process Repository, Control Parameter). Therefore, a separate view in the AristaFlow Process Template Editor was created.

Subsequently, the definitions of the control parameters have to be specified in the extended Process Template Editor (see Fig. 5).

When all three elements are specified (Figs. 3, 4, and 5) and the reference control with its integration parameters is validated, that is, confirming that compliance is enforced, as required by the compliance officer, the workflow can be executed in a compliant manner throughout its execution. To enforce the integration of the control process, all events regarding the execution and adaptations of an ongoing workflow instance are monitored by KitCom. Therefore, all events within the AristaFlow Platform are monitored, i.e., start of a new workflow instance, finishing a workflow step, etc. All these events are centrally logged in the Execution History using the inbuilt Log Manager Service of the platform. The Execution History is updated synchronously and the Log Manager Service is extensible. Therefore, the execution/server side was chosen as an ideal place for integrating the extending elements of KitCom. The information of execution events in the extended Log Manager is used for identifying relevant reference controls. If the requirement of a control is detected, the execution of the workflow instance is suspended. Using the API for ad hoc-deviations (Rinderle, 2004), the control process is integrated into the workflow instance. Figure 6 shows an overview of the architecture of our KitCom prototype (light grey fields are the original components of AristaFlow, dark grey fields are the extensions characterizing KitCom). After the integration of the control process or, rather, the corresponding control activities, the execution of the workflow instance is resumed.

Resuming the simplified exemplary workflow from above, a new instance of a workflow for paying out an invoice is started. The instance is started as a "pure" business process without any control at the beginning (see Fig. 7).

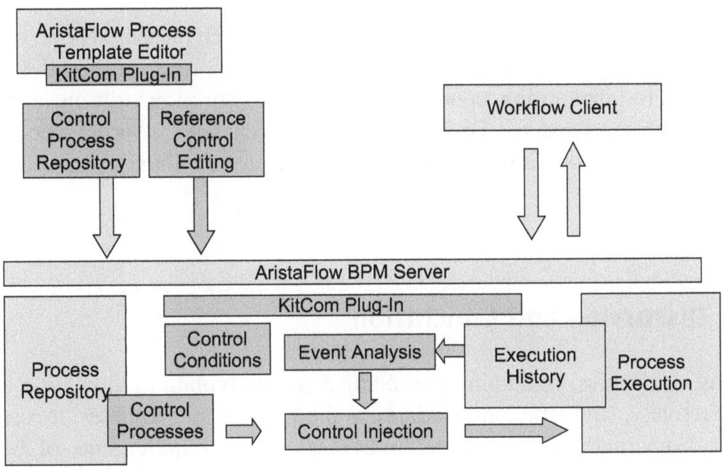

Fig. 6 KitCom architecture extending AristaFlow BPM server

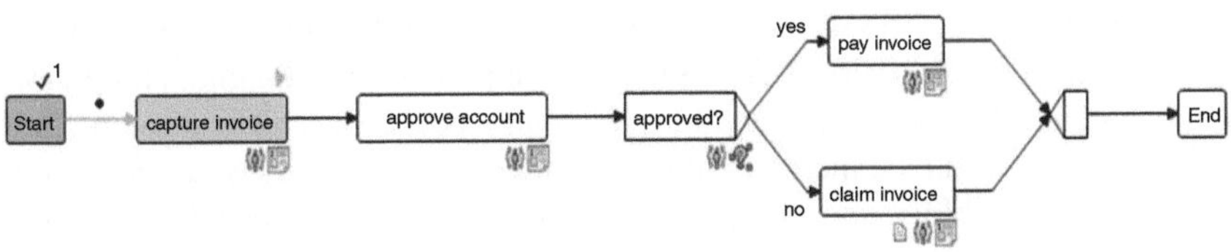

Fig. 7 Usual workflow execution with the software AristaFlow

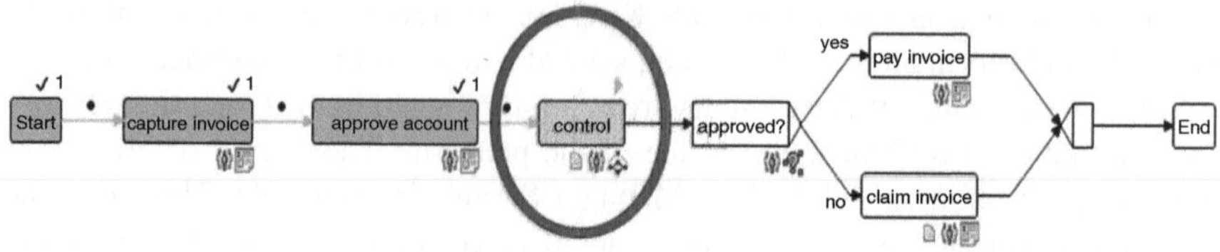

Fig. 8 Automatic integration of the reference control into the workflow instance by KitCom

Secondly, if the user "Meyer13" captures an invoice with an amount over 5,000 €, the reference control will automatically be integrated as a sub-process called "control" shown in Fig. 8, following the definition of reference controls and control parameters (Figs. 4 and 5).

While only one demonstration example is shown in this chapter, a lot of other information can be integrated with KitCom. Known approaches on business process compliance provide several criteria for modeling controls, such as the COMPAS project (Compas, 2008) which identifies generic criteria on the basis of a comprehensive compliance legislation review. Other authors, such as Sadiq et al. (2007), Goedertier and Vanthienen (2006), or Pitthan and Philipp (1997) identify generic criteria, too. As aggregated in Kittel et al. (2013a), all these control parameters can be defined as control parameters in KitCom.

Although the underlying control model of the approach presented is very general and obviously requires a more detailed analysis, the prototype has the general functionality for integrating control activities into workflows during execution, satisfying both the need for flexibility by ad-hoc changes of processes-schemes and the compliance with policy rules through dynamic integration of required reference controls.

5 Discussion and Conclusion

For many companies, remaining competitive means remaining flexible, i.e., rapidly, effectively, and efficiently adapting their business processes to changing demands from markets, customers' individual needs, requirements of business networks, or changing laws. Current technological progress and the ongoing trends to analyze business data quasi in real-time will, in the near future, allow direct reactions to the actual context, e.g., by adapting ongoing business processes "on the fly". Such flexibility, however, is challenging the ability to control workflow execution in an efficient and effective manner. In particular, validating compliance with regard to relevant laws, regulations, or contracts becomes difficult in the light of high flexibility and the methods and tools that are available today are not able to provide both flexibility and compliance at the same time. Research for finding solutions in this area, thus, is expected to drive innovation in BPM further. Compliance management becomes a necessary companion to other current BPM-relevant issues that mainly address the "business view", e.g., process design, intra-organizational business processes, integrating emerging technologies or social media, real-time adaptation to changing workflows to execution context, advanced process analytics results, or management decisions, etc.

Addressing this research gap, we presented a novel approach called FlexCom in this contribution. FlexCom aims at solving this practical trade-off between achieving compliance and remaining flexible within process execution in a systematic and automated manner. To achieve both aims, FlexCom enables companies on the level of single workflow instances to react to process changes from the business side with an automatic process adaptation from the compliance side.

While the functioning of the approach and the prototypical implementation called KitCom were only shown with one simple demonstration example in this contribution, KitCom is a promising application for integrating any kind of control activities into workflows during execution. In principal, the tool is independent of the implementation of a Workflow Client since it is integrated directly into the process engine. The screenshots show the AristaFlow Workflow Client. However, the prototype implementation also works for any custom Workflow Client implementation. Thus, KitCom is seen as a promising next step in automating compliance, that is, an aide to reacting in an automatic manner—if business processes need to remain flexible.

Although there are many open research questions, in particular in the field of how efficiently and effectively reference controls can be modelled and how an economically optimal integration point for control processes can be evaluated, it can already be shown for at least a small set of compliance requirements that it is possible on the level of workflow instances to combine the advantages of ex ante validation and flexible enforcement.

Last but not least, current research suggests that the FlexCom approach is not only valid for compliance but also offers new opportunities for other domains to use WfMS that are dependent on flexibility and on achieving multiple goals, e.g., from the health-sector or the field of disaster response management. Exploiting these opportunities provided by BPM in the long run can be expected to drive innovation further in our digital world.

References

van der Aalst, W. M. P., & van Hee, K. M. (2004). *Workflow management: Models, methods, and systems*. Cambridge, MA: The MIT.

van der Aalst, W. M. P., Weske, M., & Grünbauer, D. (2005). Case handling: A new paradigm for business process support. *Data Knowledge Engineering, 53*, 129–162.

Betke, H., Kittel, K., & Sackmann, S. (2013). Modeling controls for compliance – An analysis of business process modeling languages. In *Proceedings of the 27th IEEE international conference on advanced information networking and applications workshops (WAINA-2013)* (pp. 866–871). Barcelona, Spain.

Cabanillas, C., Resinas, M., & Ruiz-Cortes, A. (2011). Exploring features of a full-coverage integrated solution for business process compliance. In C. Salinesi & O. Pastor (Eds.), *CAiSE 2011 workshops (GRCIS'11)* (LNBIP, Vol. 83, pp. 218–227). Berlin: Springer.

Cannon, J., & Byers, M. (2006). Compliance deconstructed. *ACM Queue, 4*, 30–37.

Compas. (2008). *State-of-the-art in the field of compliance languages*. Tilburg University. Retrieved from http://ec.europa.eu/information_society/apps/projects/logos/5/215175/080/deliverables/D2.1_State-of-the-art-for-compliance-languages.pdf

Dadam, P., Reichert, M., Rinderle-Ma, S., Lanz, A., Pryss, R., Predeschly, M., et al. (2009). From ADEPT to AristaFlow BPM suite: A research vision has become reality. In *Proceedings of the 1st international workshop on empirical research in business process management (ER-BPM'09)* (pp. 529–531).

Goedertier, S., & Vanthienen, J. (2006). Designing compliant business processes with obligations and permissions. *Business Process Management Workshops, 4103*, 5–14.

Kittel, K. (2013). Agilität von Geschäftsprozessen trotz Compliance. In R. Alt & B. Franczyk (Eds.), *Tagungsband der 11. Internationale Tagung Wirtschaftsinformatik* (pp. 967–981).

Kittel, K., & Sackmann, S. (2011). Gaining flexibility and compliance in rescue processes with BPM. In *Proceedings of the ARES conference – Workshop on "Resilience and IT-Risk in Social Infrastructures" (RISI 2011)*. Vienna, Austria.

Kittel, K., & Sackmann, S. (2012). Flexible controls for compliance in catastrophe management processes. In *Proceedings of the Multikonferenz Wirtschaftsinformatik (MKWI'12)* (pp. 1675–1687). Berlin: GITO.

Kittel, K., Sackmann, S., Betke, H., & Hofmann, M. (2013a). Achieving flexible and compliant processes in disaster management. In *Proceedings of the HICSS 2013* (pp. 4687–4696).

Kittel, K., Sackmann, S., & Göser, K. (2013b). Flexibility and compliance in workflow systems – The KitCom prototype. In *Proceedings of the 25th international conference on advanced information systems engineering (CAISE'13)* (pp. 154–160). Valencia, Spain.

Krafzig, D., Banke, K., & Slama, D. (2005). *Enterprise SOA: Service-oriented architecture best practices*. Upper Saddle River, NJ: Prentice Hall.

Ly, L., Rinderle-Ma, S., Knuplesch, D., & Dadam, P. (2011). Monitoring business process compliance using compliance rule graphs. In *On the move to meaningful internet systems: OTM 2011* (pp. 82–99). Berlin: Springer.

Pitthan, D. K. J., & Philipp, D. W. I. M. (1997). Einsatz von Petri-Netzen für die Aufnahme, Dokumentation und Analyse Interner Kontrollsysteme im Rahmen der Jahresabschlußprüfung. In W. Stucky & U. Winand (Eds.), *Petri-Netze zur Modellierung verteilter DV-Systeme* (pp. 87–104). Karlsruhe: University of Karlsruhe.

Reichert, M., Rinderle, S., Kreher, U., & Dadam, P. (2005). Adaptive process management with ADEPT2. In *Proceedings of the 21st ICDE* (pp. 1113–1114).

Rinderle, S. (2004). *Schema evolution in process management systems*. Ph.D. thesis, University Ulm, Germany.

Rinderle, S., Reichert, M., & Dadam, P. (2004). Correctness criteria for dynamic changes in workflow systems – A survey. *Data and Knowledge Engineering, 50*, 9–34.

Sackmann, S. (2011). Economics of controls. In *Proceedings of the international workshop on information systems for social innovation 2011 (ISSI 2011)* (pp. 230–236). Tachikawa, Tokio.

Sackmann, S., Hofmann, M., & Kühnel, S. (2013). Return on controls invest – Ein Ansatz zur wirtschaftlichen Spezifizierung von internen Kontrollsystemen. *HMD – Praxis der Wirtschaftsinformatik, 289*(2), 31–40.

Sadiq, S. W., Governatori, G., & Namiri, K. (2007). Modeling control objectives for business process compliance. In G. Alonso et al. (Eds.), *International conference on business process management* (LNCS, pp. 149–164). Berlin: Springer.

Schumm, D., Leymann, F., Ma, Z., Scheibler, T., & Strauch, S. (2010). Integrating compliance into business processes: Process fragments as reusable compliance controls. In *Proceedings of the Multikonferenz Wirtschaftsinformatik (MKWI'10)*. Göttingen, Germany.

Smith, H., & Fingar, P. (2003). *Business process management: The third wave*. Tampa, FL: Meghan-Kiffer.

Weske, M. (2012). *Business process management – Concepts, languages, architectures*. Berlin: Springer.

On the Importance of Non-technical Process Capabilities to Support Digital Innovations

Amy Van Looy

Abstract

This article elaborates on the interrelationship between business processes and technologies to innovate. As business processes are generally seen as important contributors to digital innovations, the perspective of process capabilities is taken to specify this contributing role. In particular, the author investigates which process capabilities have been identified as critical success factors in the current literature, and to which degree they are non-technical. The author's process capability framework is a two-layered framework that recognizes the essential role of an upper layer with (non-technical, but process-oriented) organizational capabilities, and, complementing this, a lower layer with (mostly technical) process capabilities. It is shown that the non-technical process capabilities generally relate to a process-oriented management, structure and culture. This non-technical perspective on business processes is stimulated by a more holistic view on business processes in the recent literature.

1 Introduction

Organizations may foster business innovations in order to realize a business strategy and increase business performance. When information technology (IT) is used to enable business innovations, one also speaks of digital innovations (SAP, 2013). While it is generally accepted that IT and business processes have a key part to play in innovating an organization, the article's strength lies in its explicit focus on the non-technical aspects of business processes for digital innovations.

In order to estimate the presence of such non-technical aspects in the process literature, Sects. 2 and 3 first look at key domains in which digital innovations and

A. Van Looy (✉)
Ghent University, Tweekerkenstraat 2, 9000 Ghent, Belgium
e-mail: Amy.VanLooy@UGent.be

J. vom Brocke, T. Schmiedel (eds.), *BPM – Driving Innovation in a Digital World*, Management for Professionals, DOI 10.1007/978-3-319-14430-6_17

business processes affect one another. Subsequently, Sect. 4 presents a current process capability framework to verify whether and how the technical and non-technical process aspects (i.e. capabilities like skills and knowledge) can actually be distinguished. In addition, in order to discuss the relationship of business processes to digital innovation more specifically, Sect. 4 will verify which process capabilities are important to digital innovation and in what way.

2 How Digital Innovations Can Support Business Processes

As a first stage in explaining the interrelationship (or bilateral relationship) between digital innovations and business processes, this section illustrates how IT can support the creation of new business processes, as well as (drastic or continuous) improvements of existing business processes. To this end, we first turn to IT development in general, and then focus on social media as new technologies.

2.1 IT Supports Drastic Process Improvements

Business process reengineering (BPR) is the ultimate domain of drastic process improvements to create IT-enabled end-to-end processes. It is defined as:

> the fundamental rethinking and radical redesign of business processes to bring about dramatic improvements in performance (Hammer & Stanton, 1995, p. 3).

The need for BPR was initially explained by advanced technologies in the late 1980s and early 1990s, and also by economic motives, like higher international competition, altered customer expectations, and work redundancies with high costs (Hammer & Champy, 2003). Hence, BPR promotes the use of IT to redesign end-to-end business processes from a clean slate (instead of merely automating existing departmental processes) in order to increase organizational performance. Davenport (1993) prefers the term 'business process innovation', because reengineering implies the design of new processes. Business process innovation also encompasses new work strategies and the implementation of change, with its technological, human and organizational dimensions. In general, IT is not seen as a prerequisite for radical redesign, but rather as an enabler and implementer.

Nevertheless, studies have shown that the majority of BPR projects failed because of misconceptions and a corporate culture resistant to cross-functional collaboration. For instance, many organizations introduced individual departmental IT strategies, resulting in multiple, incompatible IT systems within the same organization (Basu & Palvia, 2000; O'Neill & Sohal, 1999). Or failures occurred when external IT consultants suggested generic best practices without really differentiating between organizations (Chang, 2006).

In the 2000s, Champy (2002) responded to criticism of BPR by explaining how BPR can create value for all stakeholders. Moreover, his X-engineering approach recognizes a new cross-organizational business climate, in which partnering organizations must cross X (or a number of) organizational boundaries.

> X-engineering is the art and science of using technology-enabled processes to connect businesses with other businesses and companies with their customers to achieve dramatic improvements in efficiency and create value for everyone involved (Champy, 2002, p. 3).

For instance, in a business-to-business environment, an organization consists of a web of interacting processes and people (like in a supply chain, a business network or for outsourcing). In this digital age, organizations face new challenges of connectedness and interdependency. IT, especially the Internet, is now seen as the most important enabler to connect the world in a seamless web of transactions. As such, X-engineering responds to the trend of e-business.

2.2 IT Supports Continuous Process Improvements

Radical process improvements co-exist with incremental process improvements. For instance, between two drastic improvement projects business processes must be continuously improved by means of smaller efforts (Chang, 2006; Davenport, 1993; O'Neill & Sohal, 1999).

In the 1990s, Harrington (1991), Harrington and Harrington (1995) reacted to the failed BPR projects by promoting IT-enabled continuous process improvements in line with the mainstream idea of Total Quality Management. Similar to BPR, the focus was on end-to-end business processes, and not on the individual tasks or activities. Other advocates of continuous process improvements are Smith and Fingar (2002), who promote a third wave of business process management (BPM) for the new century (after Taylor's scientific management and BPR). Like X-engineering, Smith and Fingar (2002) see IT as the most important enabler for cross-organizational business processes in e-business. In order to obtain automated and agile processes, the authors propose using:

- open standards (e.g. BPMN, BPQL) to facilitate the integration of applications and communication between integrated organizations, and
- process-aware information systems (e.g. a BPM suite) to allow business people to model, deploy and optimize business processes themselves (i.e. without manual programming by software engineers).

This third BPM wave initiated by Smith and Fingar (2002) is a synthesis of existing techniques for process representation and collaboration (e.g. Enterprise Resource Planning, Service-Oriented Architecture, Enterprise Architecture Integration and workflow management). According to the authors, a BPM system or suite can close a gap between the intentional process design and its implementation, which is created if software architectures and application development methods pose technical constraints to the execution of BPM.

2.3 New Technologies Support Process Change

This third key domain illustrates that IT continues to support business processes, also through new technologies like social media. Nowadays, social media have gained in importance. Not only do millions of people (or customers) have an account with one or more of the social media tools like Twitter, Facebook, LinkedIn, Google+, YouTube, Pinterest, etc., but many organizations have also jumped on the social bandwagon, and try to create value from social media. Since social media make use of Web 2.0 as a technological platform, they can be seen as the next step in the Internet evolution (DachisGroup, 2012; Woodcock, Green, & Starkey, 2011).

Social media use within an organization requires a multi-disciplinary approach, which means that it is not limited to marketing or IT departments. Social Customer Relationship Management (social CRM) is the ultimate key domain to illustrate how social media can affect new and existing business processes. Social CRM is:

> a philosophy and a business strategy, supported by a technology platform, business rules, workflow, processes and social characteristics, designed to engage the customer in a collaborative conversation in order to provide mutually beneficial value in a trusted and transparent business environment (Greenberg, 2009).

As such, social CRM means truly listening to customers, wherever they are, responding, anticipating and making the commitment to improve products and services. It is user-driven in order to turn fans and followers into customers and even advocates of a brand. Consequently, social CRM has a real impact on both existing and new business processes, as illustrated below (Ang, 2011; Altimeter, 2010; Woodcock et al., 2011).

- Regarding existing business processes, feedback or complaints received by means of social media can give insightful input towards adjusting an organization's way of working (i.e. business rules and operations). For instance, Forrester (2011) surveyed 200 US companies and found out that already 88 % monitor customer feedback and conversations on social media platforms and 64 % of respondents collect online feedback and also turn them into process improvements or product improvements. Social media can also stimulate internal collaboration, for instance by internal networks like Yammer, resulting in a better customer service delivery.
- Social media can also facilitate people's involvement from idea generation to the realization of new products and services, and thus new business processes. Particularly, forums, communities, contests and polls can stimulate customer collaboration and can request the submission of new ideas that other community member will discuss and rate. For instance, LEGO (i.e. a brand of toy building bricks) uses their CLICK community (http://www.legoclick.com/) to gather ideas from clients for product innovation, which may lead to new R&D processes and new production processes. Similarly, the computer company Dell has a community for crowdsourcing ideas called IdeaStorm (http://www.ideastorm.

com/). This approach involves several opportunities for an organization, like more innovative insights from the external environment and engaged community members who are more likely to buy the (new) product or service afterwards.

2.4 Learnings

Although the presented key domains are frequently interpreted as separate approaches, they all aim at change and innovation to achieve higher business (process) performance or excellence. The most suitable approach for a specific situation still depends on the business strategy, to which business processes must contribute. As the opportunities for more efficiency and effectiveness change over time, we can see that, in practice, a balance is required between drastic and continuous process improvements.

Another similarity is based on the fact that all previous key domains describe IT (e.g. software and social media) as an enabler for (re-)designing business processes. Particularly the first two key domains still present business processes as being dominated by engineering. Only recently has the process literature been examining the human side of business changes, similar to current quality programs (e.g. Total Quality Management) and quality models (e.g. EFQM). Consequently, two perspectives in the process literature can be distinguished (vom Brocke & Sinnl, 2011).

- In the 1990s, the process literature mostly covered technically-oriented articles on how IT supports business processes, for instance, by means of Enterprise Resource Planning, Service-Oriented Architecture, and workflow management. Currently, this first perspective is still present in many articles that investigate extensions of process modeling languages, simulation techniques, process mining applications, etc.
- As from the 2000s, studies also start taking a holistic view on business processes, and extend BPM towards business process orientation (McCormack & Johnson, 2001). Such studies recognize the relevance of non-technical capabilities to support process innovations and digital innovations.

3 How Business Processes Can Support Digital Innovations

The third section further elaborates on the interrelationship between IT and business processes by illustrating how business processes can support digital innovations. In particular, this section shows that IT should not be developed or used as such, but must contribute to a business strategy of the organization. Consequently, information systems should provide business-specific functionality, which typically requires knowledge of business processes. As in the previous section, the interrelationship is first discussed for IT development. Subsequently, we look at digital capabilities (i.e. the critical success factors for digital innovations) to verify how business processes are included, i.e. whether only technical aspects of business processes are recognized or also non-technical aspects (i.e. as embedded in the overall contribution of this chapter).

3.1 Business Processes Support IT Development

Studies have shown that only a minority of IT projects succeed, that is, are delivered on time, on budget and within scope (i.e. with the required features and functions) (Resch, 2011; Stepanek, 2005; The Standish Group, 2013). Particularly, time, budget and scope constitute the so-called "Triple Constraint" in project management (Schwalbe, 2010). Although requirements analysis and BPM are crucial to IT development (i.e. scope definition), they are also difficult to conduct properly. For instance, according to The Standish Group (2013), a root cause of many IT project failures was process ignorance (i.e. with business functions being poorly or not documented) in 2004, whereas the desire to fulfill all requirements (instead of focusing on high-value requirements) caused many time and budget problems in 2012. Or, due to poor requirements, applications frequently lack business-specific functionality and process-support (Forrester, 2006).

Consequently, clear requirements and business processes are inherently important to IT development, being part of the Triple Constraint of any IT project. As a result, their importance is also recognized in frameworks for IT development (e.g. RUP) and enterprise architecture (e.g. Zachman).

- IBM's Rational Unified Process (RUP) is an iterative and incremental IT development framework with disciplines across project lifecycle phases.
  - RUP distinguishes nine disciplines with six engineering disciplines and three supporting disciplines: (1) business modeling, (2) requirements, (3) analysis/design, (4) implementation, (5) test, (6) deployment, (7) configuration/change management, (8) project management, and (9) environment.
  - Business value is realized in four project lifecycle phases: (1) inception, (2) elaboration, (3) construction and (4) transition.

  By mapping the disciplines to the lifecycle phases, RUP shows that an IT project should start with business process modeling and requirements analysis, primarily during the early inception and elaboration phases, while functional and technical analyses, implementation and testing only start as of the elaboration phase (Kruchten, 2004).
- Zachman's enterprise architecture framework (1987) categorizes different artifacts of organizational data that are required for IT development, e.g. design documents, specifications, and models. The categorization is a two-dimensional matrix with six communication questions in the columns and five stakeholder perspectives in the rows, resulting in 36 categories.

- The six communication questions are: (1) what (data), (2) how (function or process), (3) where (network), (4) who (people), (5) when (time), and (6) why (motivation).
- The five perspectives are arranged from the abstract to the more concrete: (1) contextual (scope/planner), (2) conceptual (business models/owner), (3) logical (system models/designer), (4) physical (technology models/builder), and (5) detailed (out-of-context/subcontractor).

The matrix is a template that must be filled out by different representations of a particular organization. Business process models are typically situated in the category of 'how' and 'conceptual model' from the owner's perspective (McGovern et al., 2004; Zachman, 1987). Nevertheless, business processes can also specify inputs and outputs ('what'), resources ('who'), and timing ('when'). Regarding the rows, low-level process models can also serve the designer's perspective if a BPM suite or system is used. Furthermore, the planner's perspective is covered if high-level process models describe the scope and functionalities of a system. Consequently, depending on the level of detail, business processes can be used in four of the six questions and three of the five perspectives.

3.2 Business Processes Support Digital Innovations

The previous key domains have shown that business processes and IT both matter for business innovations (Forrester, 2005), e.g. to realize IT-enabled processes, to request customer feedback, or to obtain successful IT development projects. As stated in the introduction, business innovations that are enabled by IT are also referred to as digital innovations. Digital innovations may result in a digital enterprise, which can be defined as any organization:

> whose IT plays a dominant role in the corporate strategy, i.e. where IT is used in internal and external operations to create competitive advantage (SAP, 2013, p. 1).

In order to become a digital enterprise, SAP (2013) has designed a digital capability framework with digital transformation enablers and goals.

- The two digital transformation enablers express the readiness of an organization to (1) transform and (2) innovate.
- The four digital transformation goals that a digital enterprise must pursue are (1) customer centricity, (2) effective knowledge worker, (3) operational excellence, and (4) IT excellence.

Consequently, operational or process excellence is recognized as one of the six digital capabilities. This means that business processes can support digital innovations. Although the name suggests otherwise, digital capabilities are not limited to a technical interpretation. Instead, in the SAP framework (2013), they also refer to a non-technical culture with values such as customer centricity, knowledge sharing, management by objectives, coaches instead of managers, teamwork instead of hierarchies, and collaboration between departments, customers and suppliers instead of a vertical organogram with silos, etc. (SAP, 2013).

3.3 Learnings

The first key domain in this section still takes a technical perspective on business processes by focusing on process modeling and deployment, as in the mainstream BPM literature. Nevertheless, in line with the recent BPM literature (vom Brocke & Sinnl, 2011), the second key domain shows that digital capabilities (with business processes, among others) do not necessarily have a technical interpretation. It shows that also the human side of business changes counts. Subsequently, different process capabilities are discussed to illustrate which tend to be non-technical.

4 Managing Digital Innovations by Process Capabilities

Business process excellence can be reached by improving different critical success factors, also known as process capabilities (Van Looy, De Backer, & Poels, 2011). While the previous key domains mainly emphasize technical process capabilities, examples of non-technical or people-related process capabilities are process-oriented values, governance bodies [see also chapter by Kettenbohrer, Kloppenburg, and Beimborn (2015)], roles and responsibilities, and human resources, like training and appraisals. They are considered in contemporary maturity models which focus on gradually improving specific business processes (Ahern, Clouse and Turner, 2004; Harrington, 2006; OMG, 2008), the whole process portfolio in an organization (de Bruin & Rosemann, 2007; McCormack & Johnson, 2001), or both (Hammer, 2007). Many maturity models on business processes exist nowadays that cover the process capabilities to varying extents and/or with different names [see, for instance, the overview in Rosemann and vom Brocke (2014)]. Hence, previous research (Van Looy, 2014; Van Looy, De Backer, & Poels, 2014) has designed and validated an exemplary framework that categorizes the process capabilities of 69 sampled maturity models focusing on specific and/or all business processes in an organization (and which are, as such, independent of a single maturity model). For the purpose of this article, the framework will be used to discuss the contribution of process capabilities to digital innovations. The framework is shown in Fig. 1.

The framework consists of a lower layer and an upper layer, which should be complementary to reach process excellence (Van Looy, 2014; Van Looy et al., 2014).

- The lower layer contains capabilities that should be present per business process: process modelling, deployment, optimization, and its management (by a process

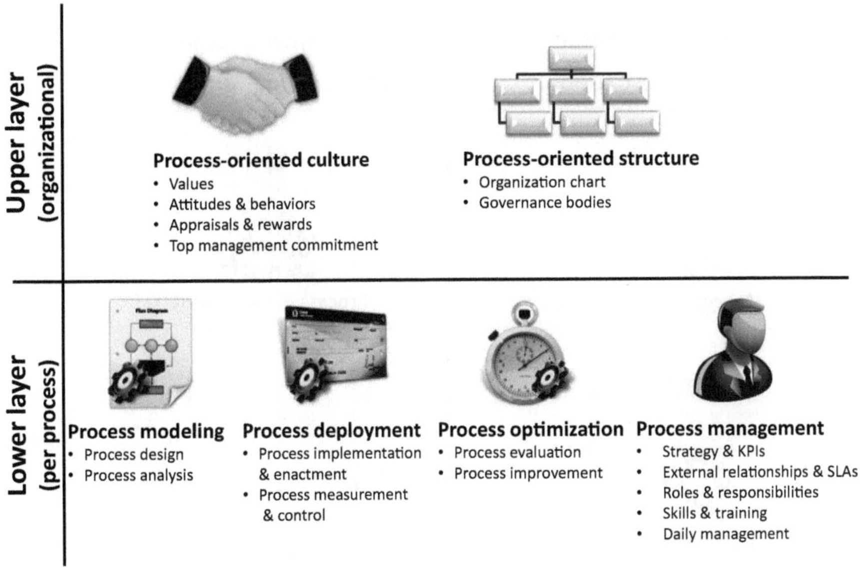

Fig. 1 The process capability framework of Van Looy et al. (2014)

owner and, possibly, an optimization team). These capabilities refer to the traditional process lifecycle (Weske, 2010), in which inter-dependent phases are logically and iteratively related in a cycle. The process management capability surrounds (or supports) the other three process capabilities in the process lifecycle.

- Besides the required efforts per business process, the upper layer adds some organizational capabilities that may influence the whole process portfolio in an organization. It particularly refers to a culture and structure that support (not impede) process excellence (Schmiedel, vom Brocke, & Recker, 2013, 2014), similar to the examples shown for the SAP digital capability framework (SAP, 2013). A process-oriented culture means that business processes are generally seen and promoted as a way of doing business, while a process-oriented structure also institutionalizes this point of view in the organization chart (e.g. by appointing a Chief Process Officer, a program manager who coordinates all process owners, and a Center of Excellence (Rosemann, 2014) which methodologically supports the process capabilities in the lower level).

In order to show the relationship with digital innovations, Fig. 2 proposes a distinction between the mainly technical and non-technical process capabilities.

- The lower layer of the framework (Fig. 1) is mostly technical, because advanced process modeling, deployment and optimization are frequently IT-enabled (i.e. by means of methods and IT, like in a BPM suite). Nevertheless, the process management capability takes a people perspective on business processes, and can be better classified as non-technical.

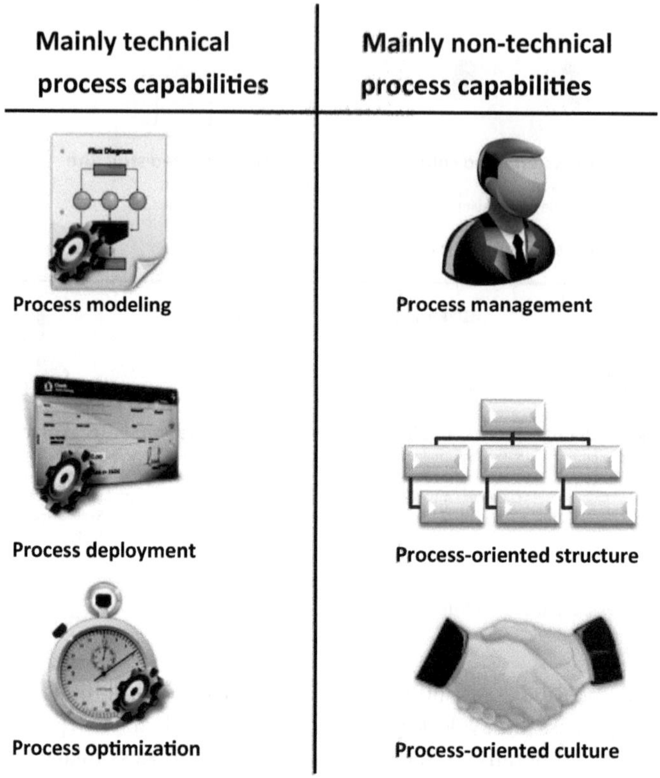

Fig. 2 Technical and non-technical process capabilities, based on Van Looy et al. (2014)

- The human side of business processes is predominant in the upper layer, with culture and structure being typical non-technical capabilities.

We must, however, note that this high-level distinction is only valid to a certain degree, particularly: (1) process management and a process-oriented culture and structure may also have a technical side in its use of methods and IT, whereas (2) process modeling, deployment and optimization may also have a non-technical or human side. In other words: the so-called non-technical capabilities tend to have a technical side too, and vice versa. This finding suggests a minor overlap between what is generally considered as being technical and non-technical. Therefore, the process capabilities of Van Looy et al. (2014) are subsequently discussed to elicit the way in which they are important to digital innovations.

The mainly technical capabilities (i.e. process modeling, deployment and optimization) are best known from the traditional process lifecycle (Weske, 2010). The key domains in the previous sections mostly relied on the methods and IT of these capabilities (e.g. for designing process models in a process language, like BPMN, as well as their subsequent execution and evaluation by means of a process-aware information system), entailing a clear link to digital innovations. Some non-technical examples for these capabilities may include, among others: (1) workshops between business and IT for gathering requirements regarding new processes or eliciting improvement opportunities, (2) linking process output metrics to business performance outcomes during business-activity monitoring (because digital innovations generally aim at increasing business performance by taking advantage of opportunities), as well as (3) the use of a process architecture or hierarchy of layered process models to help orient (new) employees or estimate the impact of risks and changes.

As the other process capabilities are mainly non-technical, they are discussed in more detail. First, the process management capability consists of the following sub areas:

- Strategy and Key Performance Indicators (KPIs)
- External relationships and Service Level Agreements (SLAs)
- Roles and responsibilities
- Skills and training
- Daily management

This process management capability plays an essential role in digital innovations by maintaining communication and collaboration between process participants, customers and other external stakeholders, while aligning the process strategy with a global business strategy. As mentioned in the introduction, each innovation should be seen in the context of realizing a business strategy with corporate goals (instead of just innovating for the sake of innovating). This aim will be hard to realize if the involved actors are either not communicating and collaborating or are doing so inappropriately due to the opposing forces that may emerge. Similarly, the process participants should be well aware of their function and properly trained to perform the required actions. Other non-technical examples for this capability that relate to digital innovations are daily decision-making and the supervision of a process improvement plan by the process owner (or process manager) of the business process that is involved in a particular innovation. In general, if the roles and responsibilities of the process owner, his or her improvement team and the process participants are not clearly defined, it is less likely that the process goals will be achieved, thus impacting the innovation projects and corporate goals as well. On the other hand, methods and IT can be used to assist such non-technical assignments, like e-learning, to acquire the necessary process knowledge and tools for project management (e.g. MS Project) or communication (e.g. Skype). Also the ability to interpret and use the technical process output metrics may facilitate the mentioned strategic alignment, as well as business-IT alignment. Nevertheless, the non-technical impact of this process management capability prevails.

Regarding a process-oriented structure, two sub areas can be distinguished:

- Organization chart
- Governance bodies

Digital innovations may bring about changes in the organization chart by (re-) designing business processes, which may in turn impact the existing roles and responsibilities. For instance, product development can lead to a new business process or supply chain, introducing new collaboration between the departments and an additional process owner. Reconsidering the organization chart can also reveal more efficient and effective lines of authority, resulting in less bureaucracy. Furthermore, the governance bodies that coordinate the whole process portfolio in an organization should decide which digital innovations will be approved, and when. Due to monetary constraints, not all innovative projects can be realized and priorities should be defined in accordance with the global business strategy (e.g. after conducting a SWOT analysis to determine the strengths, weaknesses, opportunities and threats of certain business situations that require innovation). Besides these non-technical values for digital innovations, the activities of a process competence center (called Center of Excellence) can be seen as more technical by methodologically supporting the previous process capabilities. In particular, a Center of Excellence will typically transfer knowledge on how to use the required methods and IT (e.g. management controls and standards) for process modeling, deployment, optimization and management. One example is teaching the process owners and their improvement teams how to design AS-IS and TO-BE process models by using the BPMN process language in order to enhance a standardized way of working or to find process steps that need innovation. Other examples may involve learning how improvement programs like Lean and Six Sigma should be conducted, how actual processes should be mined and compared with their initial process design, and how Prince2 or PMBOK may guide innovative projects. As it mainly concerns knowledge exchange, the non-technical side of a process-oriented structure is predominant.

Finally, a process-oriented culture covers the following sub areas:

- Values
- Attitudes and behaviors
- Appraisals and rewards
- Top management commitment

This process capability is the most straightforward example of non-technical aspects influencing digital innovations. First of all, digital innovations strongly depend on top management commitment and leadership attention to business processes. As argued in the previous key domains, business processes reflect the organizational way of working, and can therefore build a bridge between IT and corporate goals (e.g. by process-aware information systems). However, if top managers rather support vertical departments working as silos instead of horizontal end-to-end value chains, they are likely to miss out on a wider perspective on business opportunities to create innovation through IT. Further, the organization should be responsive (instead of resistant) to change, which may lead to more successful (or accepted) innovations. Such responsiveness can be stimulated by promoting horizontal or process-oriented values like customer orientation, team spirit, cross-departmental collaboration and empowerment. Change and innovations can also be facilitated through process-oriented attitudes and behaviors that transcend the boundaries of a specific process and represent process-oriented values, like promoting success stories and sharing lessons learned across business processes and digital innovations. Another way to stimulate digital innovations might be to include process performance metrics in the appraisals of all employees (instead of only departmental or individual metrics), and (financially or non-financially) rewarding people when the processes in which they work show an increase in performance. As this form of extrinsic motivation needs top management approval, the human resources appraisals and rewards can support a certain way of doing business and the concretization of process-oriented values among business processes. The technical side of a process-oriented culture remains negligible, i.e. limited to tools for tracking human resources activities or knowledge sharing databases.

4.1 Learnings

The process capability framework and the underlying maturity models illustrate that BPM can be approached from a technical perspective and/or a people perspective.

- The technical perspective gives a limited interpretation of BPM by focusing on process modeling, business rules, specifications, automation, Service Oriented Architecture, workflows, suites and tools, optimization techniques, etc.
- The non-technical perspective gives a broader interpretation of BPM by also focusing on process roles and responsibilities, human resources rewards, organizational values, organization chart, governance bodies, etc.

As discussed earlier, the perspectives are covered as different research streams in the BPM literature. By combining them into a framework or maturity model, evidence is given that both perspectives are critical success factors, and thus required to achieve process excellence and digital innovations. However, the importance of the non-technical process capabilities should not be underestimated.

5 Conclusion

This article has shown that business processes and digital innovations are closely linked, and affect one another. The process capabilities to facilitate digital innovations are, however, not limited to a digital or technical interpretation. Likewise, in addition to technical studies, the process literature is beginning to recognize the human side of business processes and innovations. This article has taken the perspective of a process capability framework to explicitly focus on the non-technical process capabilities.

While technical process capabilities are mostly related to the traditional process lifecycle (modelling, deployment, and optimization), the non-technical process capabilities are typically related to process management and a process-oriented structure and culture. In particular, they may involve:

- Process management
  - Strategic alignment of a process strategy to the corporate strategy
  - External relationships with customers, suppliers, and other stakeholders
  - Roles and responsibilities (e.g. a process owner + an optimization team)
  - Skills to perform such roles (+ training, if required)
  - Daily management of the activities conducted by such roles
- Process-oriented structure
  - Organogram visualizing end-to-end processes (e.g. horizontal or matrix)
  - Governance bodies (e.g. a program manager + a Center of Excellence)
- Process-oriented culture
  - Values that stimulate horizontal process thinking
  - Attitudes and behaviors that visualize such values outside the process boundaries
  - Appraisals based on process outcomes, in order to reward the realization of such values
  - Top management support (i.e. seeing business processes as a way of doing business)

Since the dichotomy between technical and non-technical process capabilities fits in with the two research streams in the BPM literature, other BPM researchers can relate their work to the discussed process capability framework (Fig. 1). For instance, based on information found on the website http://www.bpmroundtable.eu/ , the cultural research conducted in Liechtenstein is mainly situated in the upper layer of the framework (with organizational characteristics that impact the whole process portfolio), whereas the technical research on process modeling and mining in the Netherlands (Eindhoven) and Austria (Innsbruck) is mainly situated in the lower layer (with characteristics per business process). Hence, the presented framework can currently be used to organize the BPM discipline as a reference for BPM researchers too. Additionally, BPM practitioners can profit from the framework, as the use of BPM suites (which focus on the lower layer) should be complemented by non-technical capabilities to facilitate process excellence.

Consequently, for BPM to advance as an academic discipline, scholars and organizations are encouraged to continue collaborating to stimulate knowledge about the capabilities in the framework.

References

Ahern, D. M., Clouse, A., & Turner, R. (2004). *CMMI distilled*. Boston, MA: Pearson Education.

Altimeter. (2010). *Social CRM use cases: 5Ms and marketing*. Retrieved from http://www.slideshare.net/jeremiah_owyang/20100407-s-c-r-m-part1-final5-n-o-n-o-t-e-s

Ang, L. (2011). Community relationship management and social media. *Database Marketing and Customer Strategy Management, 18*(1), 31–38.

Basu, S. C., & Palvia, P. C. (2000). Business process reengineering. In A. Kent (Ed.), *Encyclopedia of library and information science* (Vol. 67, pp. 24–34). New York, NY: Marcel Dekker.

Champy, J. (2002). *X-engineering the corporation. Reinventing your business in the digital age*. New York, NY: Warner Business Books.

Chang, J. F. (2006). *Business process management systems. Strategy and implementation*. Boca Raton, FL: Taylor & Francis.

DachisGroup. (2012). *Social business index*. Retrieved from http://www.socialbusinessindex.com/

Davenport, T. H. (1993). *Process innovation. Reengineering work through information technology*. Boston, MA: Harvard Business School.

de Bruin, T., & Rosemann, M. (2007, December 5–7). Using the Delphi technique to identify BPM capability areas. In *Proceedings of the 18th Australasian conference on information systems* (pp. 642–653). Toowoomba, Australia.

Forrester. (2005). *Make IT matter for business innovation*. Retrieved from http://c.ymcdn.com/sites/www.simnet.org/resource/group/62BDE4A1-974A-4105-BE98-BA41ED782AA3/presentations/makingitmatterinbusinessinno.pdf

Forrester. (2006). *The root of the problem: Poor requirements*. Retrieved from http://es.slideshare.net/Timothy212/carey-schwaber-analyst-forrester-research-3916521

Forrester. (2011). *Listening and engaging in the digital marketing age. Companies progress their customer-centric approaches and see positive business outcomes*. Retrieved from http://i.dell.com/sites/doccontent/corporate/secure/en/Documents/listening-and-engaging-in-the-digital-marketing-age.pdf

Greenberg, P. (2009). *Time to put a stake in the ground on social CRM*. Retrieved from http://the56group.typepad.com/pgreenblog/2009/07/time-to-put-a-stake-in-the-ground-on-social-crm.html/

Hammer, M. (2007). The process audit. *Harvard Business Review, 85*(4), 111–123.

Hammer, M., & Champy, J. (2003). *Reengineering the corporation. A manifesto for business revolution* (2nd ed.). New York, NY: HarperCollins.

Hammer, M., & Stanton, S. A. (1995). *The reengineering revolution. A handbook*. New York, NY: HarperCollins.

Harrington, H. J. (2006). *Process management excellence*. Chico, CA: Paton Press.

Harrington, H. J. (1991). *Business process improvement. The breakthrough strategy for total quality, productivity, and competitiveness*. New York, NY: McGraw-Hill.

Harrington, H. J., & Harrington, J. S. (1995). *Total improvement management. The next generation in performance improvement*. New York, NY: McGraw-Hill.

Kettenbohrer, J., Kloppenburg, M., & Beimborn, D. (2015). Driving process innovation: The application of a role-based governance model at Lufthansa Technik. In J. vom Brocke & T. Schmiedel (Eds.), *Business process management: Driving innovation in a digital world*. Berlin: Springer.

Kruchten, P. (2004). *The rational unified process: An introduction* (3rd ed.). Boston, MA: Pearson Education.

McCormack, K., & Johnson, W. C. (2001). *Business process orientation: Gaining the e-business competitive advantage*. St. Lucie, FL: St. Lucie Press.

McGovern, J., Ambler, S. W., Stevens, M. E., Linn, J., Sharan, V., & Jo, E. K. (2004). *A practical guide to enterprise architecture*. Englewood Cliffs, NJ: Prentice Hall.

O'Neill, P., & Sohal, A. S. (1999). Business process reengineering. A review of recent literature. *Technovation, 19*, 571–581.

OMG. (2008). *Business process maturity model (BPMM). Version 1.0*. Retrieved from http://www.omg.org/spec/BPMM/1.0/PDF
Resch, M. (2011). *Strategic management transformation: Delivering maximum ROI & sustainable business value*. Plantation, FL: J. Ross.
Rosemann, M. (2014). The service portfolio of a BPM center of excellence. In J. vom Brocke & M. Rosemann (Eds.), *Handbook on business process management* (Vol. 2, pp. 267–284). Berlin: Springer.
Rosemann, M., & vom Brocke, J. (2014). The six core elements of business process management. In J. vom Brocke & M. Rosemann (Eds.), *Handbook on business process management* (Vol. 1, pp. 107–122). Berlin: Springer.
SAP. (2013). *Business transformation award 2013 application*. Retrieved from http://global.sap.com/campaigns/2013_06_bt_award/assets/BT%20Award%20Application.docx
Schwalbe, K. (2010). *Information technology project management*. Boston, MA: Course Technology, Cengage Learning.
Schmiedel, T., vom Brocke, J., & Recker, J. (2013). Which cultural values matter to business process management? Results from a global Delphi study. *Business Process Management Journal (BPMJ), 19*(2), 292–317.
Schmiedel, T., vom Brocke, J., & Recker, J. (2014). Development and validation of an instrument to measure organizational cultures' support of business process management. *Information and Management, 51*(1), 43–56.
Smith, H., & Fingar, P. (2002). *Business process management: The third wave. The breakthrough that defines competitive advantage for the next fifty years*. Tampa, FL: Meghan-Kiffer.
Stepanek, G. (2005). *Software project secrets: Why software projects fail*. Berkeley, CA: Apress.
The Standish Group. (2013). *CHAOS Manifesto 2013*. Retrieved from http://versionone.com/assets/img/files/ChaosManifesto2013.pdf
Van Looy, A., De Backer, M., & Poels, G. (2011). Defining business process maturity. A journey towards excellence. *Total Quality Management and Business Excellence, 22*(11), 1119–1137.
Van Looy, A., De Backer, M., & Poels, G. (2014). A conceptual framework and classification of capability areas for business process maturity. *Enterprise Information Systems, 8*(2), 188–224.
Van Looy, A. (2014). *Business process maturity. A comparative study on a sample of business process maturity models* (Springerbriefs in business process management). Berlin: Springer.
vom Brocke, J., & Sinnl, T. (2011). Culture in business process management: A literature review. *Business Process Management Journal, 17*(2), 357–377.
Weske, M. (2010). *Business process management. Concepts, languages and architectures*. Berlin: Springer.
Woodcock, N., Green, A., & Starkey, M. (2011). Social CRM as business strategy. *Database Marketing and Customer Strategy Management, 18*(1), 50–64.
Zachman, J. A. (1987). A framework for information systems architecture. *IBM Systems Journal, 26*(3), 276–292.

Driving Process Innovation: The Application of a Role-Based Governance Model at Lufthansa Technik

Janina Kettenbohrer, Mirko Kloppenburg, and Daniel Beimborn

Abstract

Many stakeholders are involved in process operation and, consequently, also in process improvement and innovation. For the coordination of all stakeholders, an effective governance model with clearly defined roles and tasks can support process-oriented decision-making, which drives improvement and innovation. In this chapter, such a Business Process Management governance model is introduced. The role-based model FAR+ (Framework for Assignment of Responsibilities) provides precise assignment of process accountabilities and responsibilities. In the following, we apply FAR+ to an exemplary process at Lufthansa Technik. Based on this application, we derive implications for research and practice.

1 Introduction

Business processes have not just to be managed at initial design or at re-engineering initiative stages but — to a greater extent — on-going operation and continuous improvement have to be ensured throughout (Markus & Jacobson, 2010).

J. Kettenbohrer (✉)
Department of Information Systems and Services, University of Bamberg, An der Weberei 5, 96047 Bamberg, Germany
e-mail: janina.kettenbohrer@uni-bamberg.de

M. Kloppenburg
Lufthansa Technik AG, Weg beim Jäger 193, 22335 Hamburg, Germany
e-mail: mirko.kloppenburg@lht.dlh.de

D. Beimborn
Management Department, Frankfurt School of Finance & Management, Sonnemannstraße 9-11, 60314 Frankfurt am Main, Germany
e-mail: d.beimborn@fs.de

J. vom Brocke, T. Schmiedel (eds.), *BPM – Driving Innovation in a Digital World*, Management for Professionals, DOI 10.1007/978-3-319-14430-6_18

Numerous stakeholders are involved therein and need to be coordinated (e.g., managers, process owners, process participants) (Dumas, La Rosa, Mendling, & Reijers, 2013) whereby designing and implementing an effective governance model is essential (Doebeli, Fisher, Gapp, & Sanzogni, 2011; Markus & Jacobson, 2010; Rosemann & De Bruin, 2005).

Governance comprises authority, accountability, stewardship, leadership, direction, and control for a firm's activities (Doebeli et al., 2011; Markus & Jacobson, 2010; McPhee, 2008). As a consequence, business process performance, business success (Rosemann & De Bruin, 2005), and stakeholder relations (Doebeli et al., 2011) are influenced positively. By adapting and modifying Weill and Ross' (2004) definition of IT governance to BPM, BPM governance can be defined as "the establishment of relevant and transparent accountability, decision making and reward processes to guide desirable process actions. This includes how process related decisions are made at various levels within an organization" (De Bruin, 2009, p. 725).

Defining roles and responsibilities, which are a core part of a governance model, supports process-oriented decision-making and managing cross-functional processes more effectively (Braganza & Lambert, 2000; Doebeli et al., 2011).

Complementing the chapters by Oliveira, Lima, and Reijers (2015) and Sackmann and Kittel (2015), we introduce a BPM governance model which bears large potentials for continuous improvement and innovation in practice [see chapter by Schmiedel and vom Brocke (2015)]. The model provides a role-based framework for precise assignment of process management responsibilities, especially with regard to process operations and strategy. It is designed to fit to any organizational setup, but has been implemented as a pilot at Lufthansa Technik within an international context.

2 Framework for Assignment of Responsibilities

In the following, we introduce the role-based *Framework for Assignment of Responsibilities* (*FAR+*) which enables an organization to assign process management roles with defined accountabilities and responsibilities to designated persons.

FAR+ was conceptually developed in a joint research project by the University of Bamberg and Lufthansa Technik Group in accordance with an action design research approach. The central objective of this research project was to define a process management role framework which helps to handle the growing complexity caused by the international operations of processes at the different locations of Lufthansa Technik Group. In particular, a clear assignment of accountabilities and responsibilities for process operations and improvement to all involved parties and structured decision making procedures was requested (Braganza & Lambert, 2000; Doebeli et al., 2011).

In the context of the action design research approach, existing literature regarding BPM governance models was analyzed and the definition of the FAR+ roles is based on it (e.g., Braganza & Lambert, 2000; Osterloh & Frost, 2006; Spanyi, 2010). Core of the framework is the differentiation between Process Responsibility and Disciplinary Responsibility (Davenport, 1993; Nesheim, 2011). The Disciplinary Responsibility defines *what* an employee is supposed to do. This comprises signing legal contracts and issuing the power of attorney whereby Disciplinary Responsibility also bears the risk of possible organizational fault. Furthermore, business strategy for an organizational unit is defined, goals are derived, and the accountability for their fulfillment is taken on. This includes planning and controlling revenues, earnings, costs, capital, and expenditure related to resources such as personnel, material, infrastructure, etc. Disciplinary Responsibility is granted to the two roles of the Administrative Responsible and the Resource Responsible.

In contrast, Process Responsibility defines *how* an employee is supposed to perform an activity within a business process. As such, Process Responsibility defines a process-related strategy and issues directives for process execution. Furthermore, Process Responsibility takes over ownership of processes, master data, and customized system settings. This includes the definition of process trainings and participation in the appointments of process management roles. Process Responsibility is delegated to four roles: Process Domain Owner, Process Owner, Process Architect, and Process Manager. Figure 1 shows the roles of FAR+ at a glance.

The roles are introduced in a logical order starting with the Administrative Responsible as initial role of the framework, followed by the Resource Responsible with a task-assigning role, and finishing with the roles of the Process

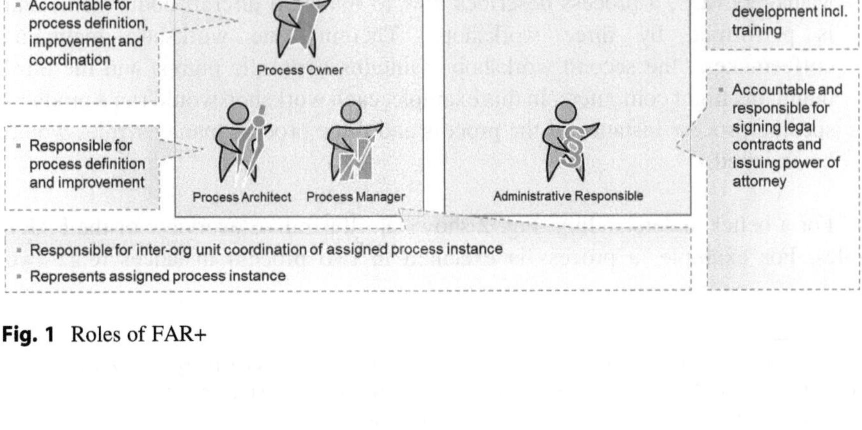

Fig. 1 Roles of FAR+

Responsibility. For a precise specification of these roles, parts of the RACI[1] framework (Loshin, 2008) are applied.

Roles of the Disciplinary Responsibility:

- The *Administrative Responsible* is accountable and responsible for signing legal contracts and issuing the power of attorney to the Resource Responsible and to the various Process Responsibility roles. Thus, the Administrative Responsible also bears the risk of organizational faults occurring.
- The *Resource Responsible* is accountable for the process accomplishment in the respective organizational unit. This includes budget fulfillment as well as the leading of employees (e.g., role assignment to employees, target agreement, personnel development) within the organizational unit.

Roles of the Process Responsibility:

- The *Process Domain Owner* is accountable for the strategic direction of a process domain. A process domain groups several business processes within a defined topic (e.g., accounting processes or production processes). The Process Domain Owner nominates the Process Owners of the processes within his or her domain.
- The *Process Owner* is accountable for the definition, improvement, and overall coordination of a process. A process describes an end-to-end sequence of process activities from one customer to another customer. In this context, 'customer' refers to both internal and external entities.
- The *Process Architect* is responsible for definition and continuous improvement of a process by operationally driving the activities to support the Process Owner (e.g., definition of trainings for process employees, specification of IT tools).
- The *Process Manager* is responsible for cross-unit coordination of a process instance. A process instance could be the product-, location-, or customer-specific execution of a process. For each process instance, a Process Manager has to be nominated. Consequently, a process can have several Process Managers (e.g., a process describes how to maintain aircraft components and is performed by three workshops. Therein, one workshop maintains coffeemakers, the second workshop maintains hydraulic pumps and the third maintains flight computers. In this example, each workshop would run a product-specific process instance of the process and three process manager roles would be assigned.).

For a better understanding, Fig. 2 shows an illustrative overview of the FAR+ roles. For example, a process is executed in two process instances (e.g., two

[1] R = role is responsible for an activity, A = role is accountable for an activity, C = role has to be consulted, I = role has to be informed. Particularly, R (role is responsible for a task) and A (role is accountable for a task) are used. C and I are not used in our classification.

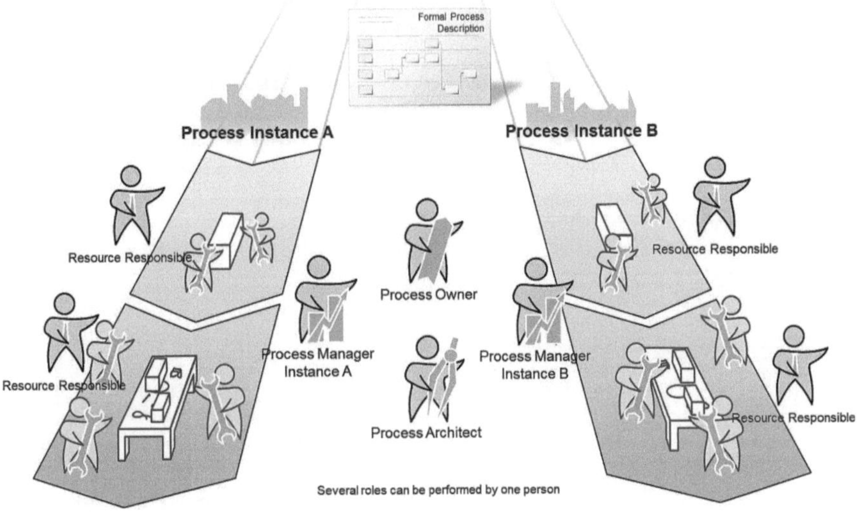

Fig. 2 Illustrative overview of FAR+ roles

locations). In both process instances the process runs through two organizational units. Each organizational unit is headed by a Resource Responsible who leads the employees from a disciplinary perspective. The employees perform the process according to the formal process description issued by the Process Owner, who is operationally supported by the Process Architect and the Process Managers. The latter are responsible for cross-unit process accomplishment and coordinate the overall execution of the process instance.

To enable a fit to any organizational structure, several setups for the assignment of the Process Manager role are possible. In the following, two extremes will be introduced. On the one hand, for each process instance the Process Manager role can be assigned to a single person. This maximizes the contact of the Process Manager to the employees and Resource Responsibles of the process instance, but increases the overall coordination effort due to the number of involved Process Managers. On the other hand, due to the organizational structure, it could be possible to cluster the process instances so that one person can take over the Process Manager role of several process instances. This reduces the coordination effort, but the contact to employees may also decrease. Due to the clustering of process instances, this person can work fulltime as a Process Manager and the professionalism (i.e., methodological know-how and BPM expertise increases) can be raised. Figure 3 shows the different setups.

For a successful realization of the framework's benefits, it is insufficient to merely assign roles. It is essential to establish structured and goal-directed communication and collaboration (Spanyi, 2010; Spender & Kessler, 1995) by defining communication flows which are presented in Fig. 4.

FAR+ uses five core communication flows, which are explained from a bottom-up perspective, starting with the operational communication flows:

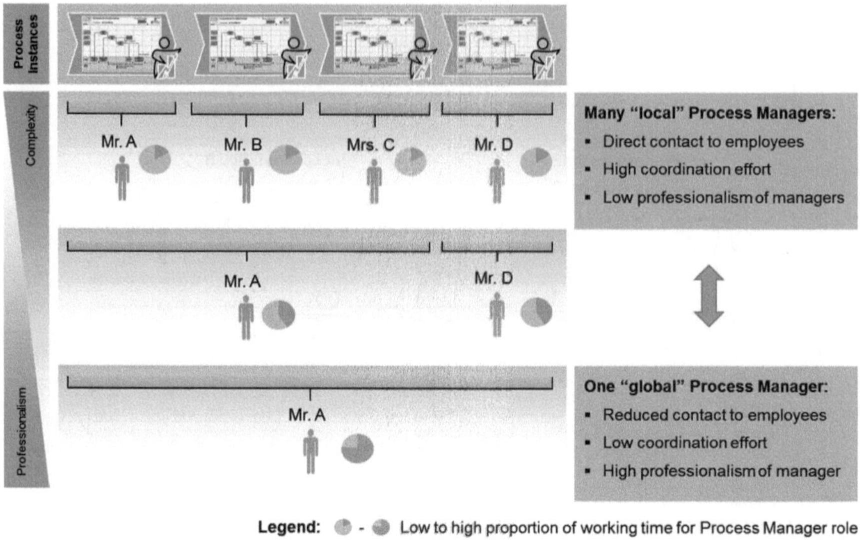

Fig. 3 Different setups for assignment of process manager role

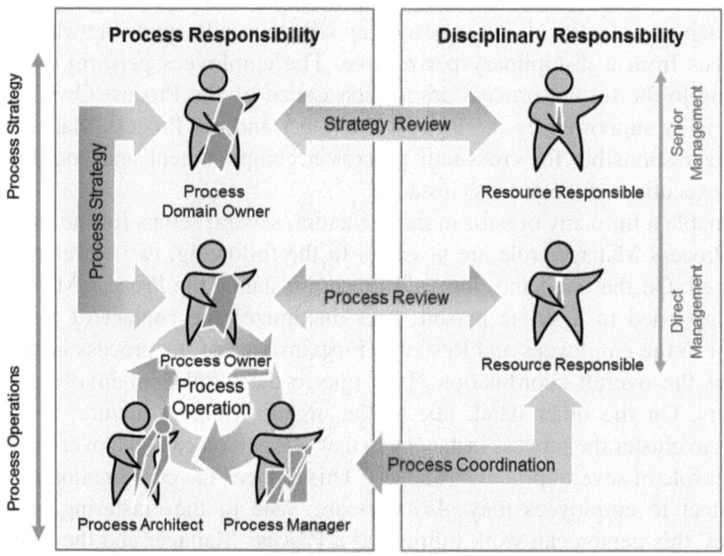

Fig. 4 Communication flows of FAR+

- *Process Coordination*: To ensure the cross-unit execution of a process instance, the Process Manager communicates with the respective Resource Responsibles on a regular basis. Thereby, ideas for improvement are identified and exchanged.

- *Process Operation*: Process Owner, Process Architect, and Process Manager discuss all topics related to the execution of a specific process within Process Operation meetings. In this context, a structured procedure for continuous process improvement is defined. Hereby, the different Process Managers represent their process instances and bring in the ideas for improvement identified within the Process Coordination.
- *Process Strategy*: To align the process results defined at the Process Operation and the further development of a process with the process domain strategy, coordination between Process Owner and Process Domain Owner is necessary.
- *Process Review*: In addition to Process Operation, the coordination between Process Owner and Resource Responsibles of the process participants ensures applicability of the process improvements. These improvements are developed by Process Operation participants to the requirements of the involved organizational units (e.g., coordination of adjusted capacity, increased qualification requirements, or additional tools and equipment).
- *Strategy Review*: Similar to Process Review, coordination between Process Domain Owner and Resource Responsibles on senior management level facilitates the alignment of process domain strategy and corporate strategy.

For the implementation of the communication flows, a cascaded meeting structure is suggested. This structure is designed according to the different phases of a process lifecycle (Dumas et al., 2013) and will be explained in detail, based on the Lufthansa Technik example, within the next section.

3 FAR+ Application

FAR+ was rolled out at Lufthansa Technik (LHT). LHT is the maintenance, repair and overhaul division of the Lufthansa Aviation Group and comprises a total of 54 companies around the globe within the LHT Group.

To show how FAR+ drives innovation in practice, the application of the approach is explained in the following by applying it to the business process "Operations of management system". This specific process describes the creation and publishing of process documentations in a role-based, process-oriented software system. Within this system, processes are described as swim-lane process diagrams (sequencing of activities along workflows and allocation of roles to single activities). To link the processes with the organizational structure, roles are assigned to organizational units. A business process documented within this system is applicable to all subsidiaries that use the system.

Table 1 shows a simplified overview of applying FAR+ to this process.

In this example it is important to point out that the person who adopts the Process Owner role is also Resource Responsible of the Process Architect, but there is no direct disciplinary relationship operating from the Process Owner to the Process Managers. In most cases the Process Manager role is assigned to the quality managers of the different subsidiaries. With regards to the organizational structure

Table 1 Overview of FAR+ application

Person A	• Process owner • Employee within quality management • Head of management system team • Resource responsible of process architect
Person B	• Process domain owner • Head of quality management • Resource responsible and administrative responsible of process owner
Person C	• Process architect • Employee within management system team
Person D to P	• Process manager • Mainly quality managers of the subsidiaries • In some cases, a person represents more than one process instance and takes over the role of process manager for several process instances • In some cases, resource responsibles of employees perform core roles of the process

Table 2 Overview of FAR+ communication flows

Process coordination	• On demand communication between process manager and resource responsible • No structured meeting • No fixed schedule
Process operation	• Quarterly video conference meeting • In advance to the process strategy
Process review	• Quarterly meeting • Subsequent to the process operation
Process strategy	• Quarterly meeting • In advance of the strategy review
Strategy review	• Quarterly meeting

of the LHT Group, it is possible to cluster the process instances and to assign several Process Manager roles to one person. This reduces the number of involved persons and the related coordination effort.

For continuous improvement, it is insufficient to merely assign roles, but structured coordination and communication flows are essential. Table 2 presents the application of the communication flows in our exemplary process.

The specific implementation of these communication flows by a meeting structure according to the process (improvement) lifecycle is described in Fig. 5. Only Process Coordination is not integrated into the lifecycle view due to its unstructured characteristic (i.e., on-demand meetings).

In our example the cycle starts by checking the current process to identify ideas for process improvement as a basis for Process Operation. It was agreed to ask all process participants for their feedback by conducting an online survey. The survey is designed to evaluate all areas of process operations, including communication of process changes, training of process participants, execution of process, and process performance.

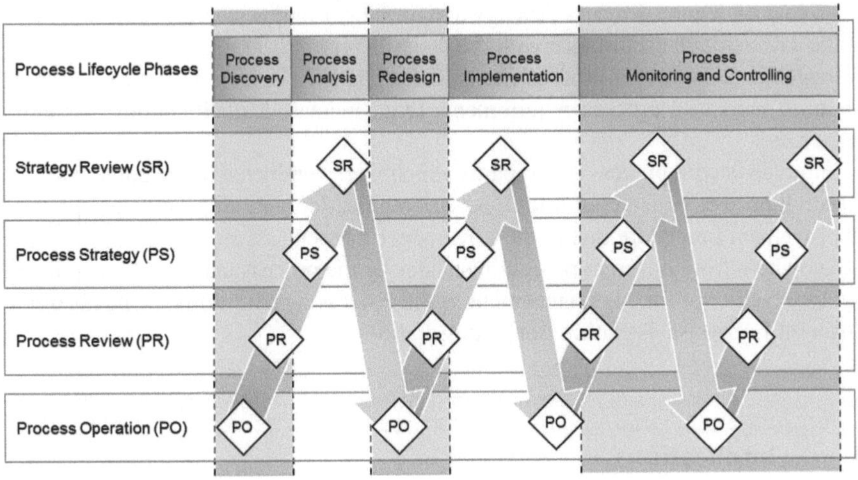

Fig. 5 Communication flows implemented according to process lifecycle cycle

The results of this survey are subsequently evaluated — in the context of the Process Operation meeting — by the Process Owner, the Process Architect, and Process Managers during a 2-day workshop. The result of this workshop is a proposal for improvement measures, which is at first discussed by the Process Owner and representatives of the Resource Responsibles in the Process Review meeting, and then aligned to the overall Process Domain Strategy meeting by Process Owner and Process Domain Owner in the Process Strategy meeting. Finally, the proposal is presented to the senior management and confirmed within the Strategy Review meeting.

Based on this proposal, the Process Architect starts to implement the measures in close cooperation with Process Managers. The degree of involvement of Process Managers varies from one measure to the other, according to the relevance for basic requirement changes within the process instances (i.e., in case of increased qualification requirements, a strong coordination with Process Managers is necessary, while in case of simple adjustments to the order of activities, an information to process managers will be sufficient).

Subsequently, the same cascade of Process Operation, Process Review, Process Strategy, and Strategy Review meetings is used to monitor and steer implementation of improvement measures and process operations until a new cycle is started.

The Process Operation meeting in particular is used to discuss process changes on an operational level by relying on the expertise of process managers. This supports the development of processes which will satisfy the requirements of the process instances.

The Process Review meeting supports the alignment of the process development to the needs of the organizational units and facilitates the acceptance of the upcoming changes by Resource Responsibles.

In case of dispute, Process Strategy and Strategy Review meetings can be used to make a decision in accordance with the overall corporate strategy and to ensure top management support for process changes, especially in case of necessary activities to fulfill increased process requirements (e.g., increased qualifications, capacity, resources).

Interviews with process participants which were conducted in the context of our research project indicate an improved communication and an accelerated process improvement procedure due to the governance concept. Especially the integration of knowhow from different process instances by the process managers was pointed out as a facilitator for an enhancement of the process which fulfills the needs of the different Lufthansa Technik Group subsidiaries.

4 Implications

Our approach provides a structured governance model according to Dumas et al.'s (2013) definition for continuous process improvement. FAR+ drives innovation in BPM "[by helping] to address the issues identified" (Dumas et al., 2013, p. 22). Clear assignment of tasks, accountabilities and responsibilities entails professionalism of the process experts' task execution. Thereby, especially the process architect can focus on driving process improvement and innovation.

In addition, improvement and innovations can be initiated by Process Responsibility as well as by Disciplinary Responsibility, which support alignment of process and business needs. FAR+ provides regular and structured communication whereby cross-domain knowledge as well as trust and respect can be fostered (Wagner & Weitzel, 2012).

Due to the fact that the approach provides both a top-down as well as a bottom-up procedure, typical challenges like management resistance or staff rejection (Laumer & Eckhardt, 2010; Münstermann, Möderer, & Weitzel, 2010) can be avoided. The process experts (i.e., process architects and process managers) are involved in every phase of the process lifecycle and they are very well connected with the employees performing the process. Thus, ideas and claims of the employees can be considered early and help to improve the process to fit the needs of the business. Furthermore, process improvement is closely connected to corporate strategy by the 'process strategy' and 'strategy review' communication flows, enabling top management support (Münstermann, Möderer, & Weitzel, 2010) as well as top management involvement (Wagner & Weitzel, 2012), which are both key success factors to raise employee motivation and avoid rejection on their part. Due to involvement of process experts and management at different levels, decisions are made at the right level and process improvement can be driven in a professional way (Kokkonen & Bandara, 2010).

5 Conclusion

In this chapter, we introduced a mode providing a role-based framework for precise assignment of process management responsibilities. With its corresponding roles and communication flows, it supports process operations as well as process improvement and innovation. In addition, we presented an exemplary application of the framework to a single process at Lufthansa Technik.

Although the importance of BPM increases, there has as yet been no precise framework on how to successfully manage and improve business processes (Spanyi, 2010). FAR+ addresses this research gap and provides a valuable and robust framework for researchers and practitioners. It is a structured approach and to be considered for successful BPM implementation and operation. Due to the combination of different governance mechanisms (Markus & Jacobson, 2010), clear accountabilities and responsibilities for process definition, improvement, and coordination as well as accomplishment can be effectively established. As a consequence, specific roles can be assigned to specialized persons with corresponding capacity and adequate qualification. Due to clearly defined contact persons, process changes can be coordinated fast and, in case of a dispute, structured escalation ensures quick decision making.

References

Braganza, A., & Lambert, R. (2000). Strategic integration: Developing a process-governance framework. *Knowledge and Process Management, 7*(3), 177–186.

Davenport, T. H. (1993). *Process innovation: Reengineering work through information technology*. Boston, MA: Harvard Business School Press.

De Bruin, T. (2009). *Business process management: Theory on progression and maturity*. Doctoral thesis, Queensland University of Technology, Brisbane.

Doebeli, G., Fisher, R., Gapp, R., & Sanzogni, L. (2011). Using BPM governance to align systems and practice. *Business Process Management Journal, 17*(2), 184–202.

Dumas, M., La Rosa, M., Mendling, J., & Reijers, H. A. (2013). *Fundamentals of business process management*. Berlin: Springer.

Kokkonen, A., & Bandara, W. (2010). Expertise in business process management. In J. vom Brocke & M. Rosemann (Eds.), *Handbook of business process management* (Vol. 2, pp. 401–421). Heidelberg: Springer.

Laumer, S., & Eckhardt, A. (2010). *Why do people reject technologies? – Towards an understanding of resistance to it-induced organizational change*. Paper presented at the 31st International Conference on Information Systems (ICIS), St. Louis.

Loshin, D. (2008). *Master data management*. Burlington: Morgan Kaufmann.

Markus, M. L., & Jacobson, D. D. (2010). Business process governance. In J. vom Brocke & M. Rosemann (Eds.), *Handbook on business process management* (Vol. 2). Heidelberg: Springer.

McPhee, I. (2008). *Public sector governance – Showing the way*. Paper presented at the Public Sector Governance Forum, Canberra.

Münstermann, B., Möderer, P., & Weitzel, T. (2010). *Setting up and managing business process standardization: Insights from a case study with a multinational e-commerce firm*. Paper presented at the 43rd Hawaii International Conference on System Science Manoa, Hawaii.

Nesheim, T. (2011). Balancing process ownership and line management in a matrix-like organization. *Knowledge and Process Management, 18*(2), 109–119.

Oliveira, C. A. L., Lima, R. M. F., & Reijers, H. A. (2015). Strategy-aware business process management. In J. vom Brocke & T. Schmiedel (Eds.), *Business process management: Driving innovation in a digital world.* Berlin: Springer.

Osterloh, M., & Frost, J. (2006). *Prozessmanagement als Kernkompetenz* (Process management as core competence) (5 ed.). Wiesbaden: Gabler.

Rosemann, M., & De Bruin, T. (2005). *Towards a business process management maturity model.* Paper presented at the 13th European Conference on Information Systems, Regensburg, Germany.

Sackmann, S., & Kittel, K. (2015). Flexible workflows and compliance: A solvable contradiction?! In J. vom Brocke & T. Schmiedel (Eds.), *Business process management: Driving innovation in a digital world.* Berlin: Springer.

Schmiedel, T., & vom Brocke, J. (2015). Business process management: Potentials and challenges of driving innovation. In J. vom Brocke & T. Schmiedel (Eds.), *Business process management: Driving innovation in a digital world.* Berlin: Springer.

Spanyi, A. (2010). Business process management governance. In J. vom Brocke & M. Rosemann (Eds.), *Handbook on business process management* (Vol. 2). Heidelberg: Springer.

Spender, J.-C., & Kessler, E. H. (1995). Managing the uncertainties of innovation: Extending Thompson. *Human Relations, 43*, 35 ff.

Wagner, H.-T., & Weitzel, T. (2012). How to achieve operational business-IT alignment: Insights from a global aerospace firm. *MIS Quarterly Executive, 11*(1), 25–36.

Weill, P., & Ross, J. W. (2004). *IT governance: How top performers manage IT decision rights for superior results.* Cambridge, MT: HBR Press.

Curricula Vitae

Wil van der Aalst

Eindhoven University of Technology, The Netherlands

Wil van der Aalst is a Full Professor of Information Systems at the Technische Universiteit Eindhoven (TU/e). He is the Academic Supervisor of the International Laboratory of Process-Aware Information Systems of the National Research University in Moscow. Since 2003 he has a part-time appointment at Queensland University of Technology. His research interests include workflow management, process mining, Petri nets, BPM, process modeling, and process analysis. He published more than 175 journal papers, 17 books, 400 refereed conference and workshop publications, and 50 book chapters. His work is highly cited (highest H-index among European computer scientists, 115 according to Google Scholar). In 2012, he received the doctor honoris causa from Hasselt University, Belgium. In 2013, he was appointed as Distinguished University Professor of TU/e. He is also a member of the Royal Netherlands Academy of Arts and Sciences (Koninklijke Nederlandse Akademie van Wetenschappen), Royal Holland Society of Sciences and Humanities (Koninklijke Hollandsche Maatschappij der Wetenschappen) and the Academy of Europe (Academia Europaea).

J. vom Brocke, T. Schmiedel (eds.), *BPM – Driving Innovation in a Digital World*, Management for Professionals, DOI 10.1007/978-3-319-14430-6

Peyman Ardalani

Saarland University, Germany

Peyman Ardalani has been doing his academical research as a Ph.D. student since 2012 at the Institute for Information Systems (IWi) at the German Research Institute for Artificial Intelligence (DFKI). Earlier he has completed two Bachelor degrees in the fields of Software Engineering and Economics pursuing his Master of Science degree in the field of Information Technology Engineering. His research activities mainly focus on practical solutions for integrating business process models, analyzing the similarity of business process models and developing reference models. In his earlier careers he has been involved in project management and designing software architecture and developing Content Management Systems (CMS) for more than 10 years.

Jörg Becker

University of Münster, Germany

Jörg Becker is Full Professor and head of the Department of Information Systems at the University of Münster. He is the Academic Director of the European Research Center for Information Systems (ERCIS). He is Editor in Chief of the journal Information Systems and e-Business Management and serves on various editorial boards. His work has appeared in several journals (e.g., Communications of the AIS, Information Systems Journal, and Business Process Management Journal) and was presented on international conferences (e.g. ICIS, AMCIS, and ECIS). His research interests include BPM, retail IS, e-Government, and strategic IT-management. He is Honorary Professor of the National Research University Higher School of Economics Moscow. Also, Jörg is partner of two university spin-offs on BPM consulting for retail and e-Government.

Daniel Beimborn

Frankfurt School of Finance & Management, Germany

Daniel Beimborn is Full Professor for Information Systems at the Frankfurt School of Finance & Management, Germany. He received his Ph.D. from Goethe University in Frankfurt, and afterwards held a PostDoc position at the University of Bamberg. His current research activities cover the management of outsourcing and nearshoring relationships, IT governance and business/IT alignment, business process standardization, BPO and shared services in the financial industry, the business value of Service Oriented Architectures (SOA), and the role of IT in innovation processes. He has published articles in renowned IS journals, such as MIS Quarterly, Journal of Management Information Systems, Journal of IT, and he is member of the Editorial Review Board of the Journal of the AIS.

Marlon Dumas

University of Tartu, Estonia

Marlon Dumas is Professor of Software Engineering at University of Tartu, Estonia. He is also Strategic Area Leader at STACC, a collaborative research center that gathers ten Estonian IT organizations with the aim of conducting industry-driven research in service engineering and data mining. From 2000 to 2007, he worked in the BPM group at Queensland University of Technology in Australia. He has been recipient of best paper awards at the ETAPS'2006, BPM'2010, and BPM'2013 conferences and recipient of the 10-year most influential paper award at MODELS'2011 conference. He is co-author of the textbook "Fundamentals of Business Process Management" (Springer).

Peter Fettke

Saarland University, Germany

Peter Fettke obtained a master's degree in Information Systems from the University of Münster, Germany, a Ph.D. Degree in Information Systems from the Johannes Gutenberg-University Mainz, Germany, and a Habilitation Degree in Information Systems from the Saarland University, Germany. Currently, he is the deputy chair of the Institute for Information Systems (IWi) at the German Research Center for Artificial Intelligence (DFKI), Saarbrücken. In 2013 he became a DFKI Research Fellow. Peter has taught and researched previously at the Technical University of Chemnitz and the University Mainz, Germany. His research interests include Reference Modeling, Business Engineering, Applications, and Philosophy of Information Systems. He uses both design-oriented and experimental research methods.

Shengnan Han

Stockholm University, Sweden

Shengnan Han is a senior lecturer and associated professor at Stockholm University, Sweden. She obtained her D.Sc. (Economics) in information systems at Åbo Akademi University, Finland in 2005. Since 2001, she started her research and practice in mobile services. She worked in the large projects carried out with Duodecim (the Finnish Medical Society), Pfizer Finland Ltd, Nokia Ventures, Nokia Mobile phones, etc. She is an expert on issues of user acceptance and evaluation of mobile services. Her research interests include social/mobile services, business process management, business-IT alignment, IT Governance, e-government, and technology-enhanced learning.

Peter Händel

Uppsala University, Sweden

Peter Händel received the Ph.D. degree from Uppsala University, Uppsala, Sweden, in 1993. From 1987 to 1993, he was with Uppsala University. From 1993 to 1997, he was with Ericsson AB, Kista, Sweden. From 1996 to 1997, he was a Visiting Scholar with the Tampere University of Technology, Tampere, Finland. Since 1997, he has been with the Royal Institute of Technology KTH, Stockholm, Sweden, where he is currently a Professor of Signal Processing and Head of the Department of Signal Processing. From 2000 to 2006, he held an adjunct position at the Swedish Defence Research Agency. He has been a Guest Professor at the Indian Institute of Science (IISc), Bangalore, India, and at the University of Gävle, Sweden. Since 2011 he has an adjunct position at Movelo AB. His research interests include disruptive sensor based technologies like insurance telematics.

Sandra Haraldson

Viktoria Swedish ICT, Sweden

Industrial researcher Sandra Haraldson is with the Sustainable Business group at Viktoria Swedish ICT. She holds a Licentiate Degree in Information Systems Development from Linköping University. She has a professional background from IT-consultancy related to different sectors. Her work focus Business Process Modelling on Multi-Organizational foundations. Sandra has experience from ICT-related transport and logistics from third-party logistics and mail-order settings. She was a key researcher in the Future Airports endeavour and had a core role in applying BPM-related research leading to tangible results. Today she is substantially engaged in the EU-project MONALISA 2.0 that has the goal to introduce a sea traffic management system for sustainable maritime transports.

Sandy Kemsley

Kemsley Design LTD., Canada

Sandy Kemsley is an independent analyst and application architect specializing in business process management and the social enterprise. During her career of more than 25 years, she founded and ran product and service companies in the area of content management, process management and e-commerce, and held the position of BPM evangelist for a major BPM vendor. Currently, she practices as a BPM industry analyst and process architect, performing engagements for end-user organizations and BPM vendors. She writes the popular "Column 2" BPM blog at www.column2.com and is a featured conference speaker on BPM.

Janina Kettenbohrer

University of Bamberg, Germany

Janina is Graduate Research Assistant at University of Bamberg, Department of Information Systems and Services. She studied Information Systems at University of Bamberg and she holds a Master of Science. Her Ph.D. topic covers the human side of business process standardization whereby her research focuses on business process standardization, and business process governance. Besides her research, she works as an external consultant at Lufthansa Technik AG.

Kai Kittel

Baur Fulfillment Solutions GmbH, Germany

Kai Kittel is a business process specialist at Baur Fulfillment Solutions GmbH. He has a background in business economics und computer science and has obtained his economic doctorate degree from the Martin-Luther-University Halle-Wittenberg in 2013. Kai's research interests are topics related to the use and management of information systems and information technology in business. His main interest is in business process management, compliance and system integration of business rules and workflow management systems. He has published over 12 fully refereed articles in internationally recognized journals and conferences.

Mirko Kloppenburg

Lufthansa Technik AG, Germany

Mirko Kloppenburg is project manager at Lufthansa Technik AG and is responsible for the implementation of measures to improve the company's process management system. Before, he held various positions in the context of process management within Lufthansa Group. He holds a diploma in Business Information Systems from the University of Cooperative Education Mannheim, Germany, and a Master of Business Administration from University of Louisville, USA. Mirko is co-founder of the Process Management Alliance e.V. which facilitates the identification of Best Practices in Process Management (BPinPM.net) and the transfer of BPM knowledge to the social and education sector.

Monika Klun

University of Ljubljana, Slovenia

Monika Klun is a full-time researcher and Ph.D. student at the Faculty of Economics of the University of Ljubljana, Slovenia. Before starting her Ph.D. studies in October 2013 she worked at a multinational electronics company in Austria. In the Ph.D. thesis she will research how to improve employee involvement in business process management ('BPM'), focusing on the conceptual behaviour of employees during BPM projects as well as the possibilities (tools) that increase involvement and collaboration of employees within organizations.

Ricardo Massa F. Lima

Federal University of Pernambuco, Brazil

Ricardo Massa F. Lima received the Ph.D. degree in computer science from Federal University of Pernambuco (UFPE), Recife, Brazil, in 2000. He was a Postdoc with the Formal Methods Group, Chalmers University of Technology, Göteborg, Sweden, in 2001. He is currently an Associate Professor with UFPE. He is the Vice-Coordinator of UFPE's computer science postgraduate program. His main research interests include compiler construction and optimization, and performance evaluation of discrete-event dynamic systems using Petri nets, with projects sponsored by the Brazilian Petroleum Industry (Petrobras), São Francisco's Hydroelectric Company (Chesf), and National Council for Scientific and Technological Development (CNPq). Dr. Lima is a member of the ACM and the Brazilian Computer Society.

Mikael Lind

Viktoria Swedish ICT and Chalmers University of Technology, Sweden

Associate Professor Mikael Lind is with the Viktoria Swedish ICT and Chalmers University of Technology. He is the research manager of the sustainable transports group at Viktoria Swedish ICT (www.viktoria.se) and heads and/or has initiated several open innovation initiatives related to ICT for sustainable transports of people and goods, as, e.g., cross-industrial design of intelligent infrastructure for electric vehicles, ICT-enabled innovation for sustainable everyday travel, and future airports focusing sustainable passenger flows based on ICT enabled multi-organizational collaboration throughout the door-to-door process. The research takes a pragmatic stance oriented towards open digital innovation, multi-organizational business innovation, and business process management. He is also one of the initiators of Maritime Informatics for applied research of digitalization in the maritime sector.

Peter Loos

Saarland University, Germany

Peter Loos is Director of the Institute for Information Systems (IWi) at the German Research Center for Artificial Intelligence (DFKI) and is Professor of Information Systems at Saarland University. His research activities include business process management, information modelling, enterprise systems as well as implementation of information systems. Peter graduated from Saarland University (Dipl.-Kfm.). He received his Ph.D. (Dr. rer. pol.) and his venia legendi also from Saarland University. He held positions as professor at Chemnitz University of Technology and at Johannes Gutenberg University Mainz. Before he pursued a career in academics he worked for 6 years as software development manager. Peter wrote several books, contributed to 40 books, and published more than 100 papers in journals and proceedings.

Fabrizio Maggi

University of Tartu, Estonia

Fabrizio Maggi is Senior Research Fellow at University of Tartu. Prior to this appointment, he was postdoctoral researcher in the Architecture of Information Systems group at Eindhoven University of Technology. His research interests are business process mining, declarative business process modeling and information systems monitoring. He has published close to 50 journal and conference articles in these fields. He is also the main developer of a number of plugins for automated discovery of declarative process models available in the ProM open-source process mining toolset. He received a Ph.D. in Computer Science in 2010 from University of Bari.

Monika Malinova

Vienna University of Economics and Business, Austria

Monika Malinova is a teaching and research associate and a doctoral candidate at the Institute for Information Business at the Vienna University of Economics and Business, Austria. She completed her Master studies in Information Systems at the Humboldt Universität zu Berlin, Germany. Her research focuses on process architectures and the design of process maps. In particular, she is interested in how process maps enable an understanding of an organization's operations. Besides process architectures, her other research interests include the adoption of business process management and enterprise architectures.

Jan Mendling

Vienna University of Economics and Business, Austria

Jan Mendling is a Full Professor and head of the Institute for Information Business at WU Vienna. His research areas include BPM, Conceptual Modelling and Enterprise Systems. He studied at University of Trier (Germany) and UFSIA Antwerpen (Belgium), and received a Ph.D. degree from WU Vienna (Austria). He was a postdoc with QUT Brisbane (Australia) and a junior professor at HU Berlin (Germany). He has published more than 200 research papers, a.o. in ACM Transactions on Software Engineering and Methodology, IEEE Transaction on Software Engineering, Information Systems, Data & Knowledge Engineering, and Decision Support Systems. He is in the editorial board of three international journals, one of the founders of the Berlin BPM Community of Practice, and board member of the Austrian Society for BPM.

Charles Møller

Aalborg University, Denmark

Charles Møller (born 1962) is professor in business process innovation at the Department of Business and Management, Aalborg University in Denmark. Charles is researching topics like supply chain management, enterprise systems management and business process management. Charles Møller is the director of the Center for Industrial Production (CIP) at Aalborg University. CIP is serving as a national competence center for industrial manufacturing.

Jens Ohlsson

Stockholm University, Sweden

Jens Ohlsson received the MSc in Computer and Systems Sciences, Stockholm University, 1999. In 2004, he obtained an additional BSc in Communications-Pedagogics, Stockholm University. Between 1999 and 2011, Mr Ohlsson worked with business development at companies like SAP, Aptus Consulting, and IDS Scheer. In March 2011, he joined Movelo AB as CEO. Since 2011, he also holds a position at the Department of Computer and System Sciences, Stockholm University. His research interests include disruptive technologies and business model innovations.

César Augusto L. Oliveira

University of Pernambuco, Brazil

César Augusto L. Oliveira received the M.Sc. degree in computer engineering from the Computing Systems Department, University of Pernambuco (Recife, Brazil) in 2008 and his Ph.D. degree in computer science from the Center for Informatics, Federal University of Pernambuco (Recife, Brazil), in 2014. He has participated in several research and development projects in the manufacturing and energy industries. His main research area is business process management, with a focus on the alignment between business and IT. He has also worked as a Consultant for the Inter-American Development Bank and the United Nations Development Program on the subjects of strategic monitoring and business intelligence.

Jan Recker

Queensland University of Technology, Australia

Jan Recker is the Woolworths Chair of Retail Innovation, Alexander-von-Humboldt Fellow and a Full Professor for Information Systems at Queensland University of Technology. His research focuses on organizational innovation, process management in organizational practice, and IT-enabled business transformations. Jan has written over 130 journal articles and conference papers on these and other topics and published 3 books on process management and research. His work has received funding in excess of $2 million, from government and several large organizations, including SAP, Woolworths, Hargreaves, Suncorp, IP Australia, Australian Federal Police, Ergon, Stanwell, Federal and State Government, and others.

Hajo Reijers

Eindhoven University of Technology, The Netherlands

Hajo Reijers is a Full Professor in Information Systems at Eindhoven University of Technology as well as the head of BPM research at Perceptive Software. He received a Ph.D. in Computer Science (2002), a M.Sc. in Computer Science (1994), and a M.Sc. in Technology and Society (1994), all from TU/e. Hajo wrote his Ph.D. thesis on the topic of BPM for the service industry while he was a manager with Deloitte. By now, he published over 150 scientific papers, chapters in edited books, and articles in professional journals. He is the managing director of the European BPM Round Table initiative.

Michael Rosemann

Queensland University of Technology, Australia

Dr. Michael Rosemann is Professor and Head of the Information Systems School at Queensland University of Technology, where he established a number of industry-funded Chairs in the domain of innovation management. His main areas of interest are business process management, corporate innovation and research management.

Dr. Rosemann is the author/editor of seven books, more than 230 refereed papers, Editorial Board member of ten international journals and co-inventor of US patents. His publications have been translated into Russian, Mandarin, German and Portuguese. His research projects received funding from industry partners such as Accenture, Australia Post, Brisbane Airport Corporation, Infosys, Rio Tinto, SAP and Woolworths. Michael is a frequent, global keynote speaker and regularly provides advice to organisations. He is a Visiting Professor at Viktoria Swedish ICT, Gothenburg.

Stefan Sackmann

University of Halle-Wittenberg, Germany

Stefan Sackmann is full professor and holds the Chair of Information Management at the University of Halle-Wittenberg, Germany. After studying political economics at the University of Freiburg, he received a doctorate in 2003 and a professorship in information systems and business economics (Habilitation) in 2010. His main research interests are compliance in flexible workflows, economics of controls, risk management, and IT-support for disaster response management.

Bernd Schenk

University of Liechtenstein, Liechtenstein

Bernd Schenk is senior lecturer for Information Systems at the University of Liechtenstein. He holds a Ph.D. in Information Systems from the Vienna University of Economics and Business and a MSc from the University of Innsbruck, Austria. His core research interests are Enterprise Resource Planning systems (ERP systems), Serviceoriented Architectures (SOA), and Business Process Management (BPM). Bernd has worked as a consultant for different companies in the area of ERP systems and E-commerce. Furthermore, he has taught at different universities, including the University of Barcelona, Spain and the Tongji University, Shanghai, China. He served as global edition reviewer for the textbook "Management Information Systems" (Laudon/Laudon).

Theresa Schmiedel

University of Liechtenstein, Liechtenstein

Theresa Schmiedel is an Assistant Professor at the Hilti Chair of Business Process Management at the University of Liechtenstein. She holds a Ph.D. in business economics from the University of Liechtenstein and a Diploma in economics from the University of Hohenheim, Stuttgart, Germany, which she conducted partially at York University, Toronto, Canada. She worked as a Research Assistant at the Department for Sociology and Empirical Social Research, University of Hohenheim, and the Center for Cultural and General Studies, University of Karlsruhe, Germany. Her research focuses on social aspects in information systems research, particularly on the interconnection of culture and business process management (www.bpm-culture.org). Her research has been published in journals, including Information & Management, Enterprise Information Systems, and Business Process Management Journal, as well as in academic books and conference proceedings.

Tom Thaler

Saarland University, Germany

Tom Thaler is researcher at the Institute for Information Systems (IWi) at the German Research Center for Artificial Intelligence (DFKI) and research project lead at Saarland University. His research activities include business process management, process mining, software development as well as implementation of information systems. After his study he worked as a Business Intelligence Consultant at SAP. Since 2012, he coordinates the information systems study at Saarland University and supervises several classes at Saarland University, Göttingen University and VGU School of Business Informatics. He is sponsored by the German Federal Ministry of Education and Research (BMBF) and currently works on his Ph.D. thesis.

Peter Trkman

University of Ljubljana, Slovenia

Peter Trkman is Associate Professor at the Faculty of Economics of the University of Ljubljana. His research interests encompass business models and various aspects of business process, supply chain and operations management. He participated in several projects and published over 70 papers including papers in journals like Decision Support Systems, IEEE Transactions on Engineering Management, International Journal of Information Management, International Journal of Production Economics, Journal of Strategic Information Systems, Long Range Planning and Wirtschaftsinformatik. He won several research awards and has been cited over 1,000 times.

Amy Van Looy

Ghent University, Belgium

Amy Van Looy holds a Ph.D. in applied economics. She is Assistant Professor at the Faculty of Economics and Business Administration of Ghent University. Before entering academia, Amy worked as an IT consultant (i.e., mainly business and functional analyst) for large e-government projects. Her research focuses on business process maturity and capabilities in public and private organizations, by considering the traditional process lifecycle as well as the organizational culture and structure. Other research interests include business process integration and business process modelling. Her research is published in scientific outlets such as Total Quality Management & Business Excellence, Enterprise Information Systems, and Information & Management.

Jan vom Brocke

University of Liechtenstein, Liechtenstein

Jan vom Brocke is Head of the BPM group in Liechtenstein. He is Professor of Information Systems, the Hilti Chair of Business Process Management, and Director of the Institute of Information Systems. He is Founder and Co-Director of the international Master Program in "IT and Business Process Management" and Director of the Ph.D. program in "Information and Process Management" at the University of Liechtenstein (www.bpm-eduction.org). Since 2012 he has been appointed Vice-President of the University of Liechtenstein responsible for research and innovation. Jan has over 15 years of experience in IT and BPM projects and he has published more than 300 papers in renowned outlets, including MIS Quarterly (MISQ), the Journal of Management Information Systems (JMIS), and the Business Process Management Journal (BPMJ). He has authored and edited 22 books, including "Green BPM—Towards the Sustainable Enterprise", and the "International Handbook on Business Process Management". Jan is an invited speaker and trusted advisor on BPM serving many organizations around the world.

Jürgen Walter

Saarland University, Germany

Jürgen Walter studied computer science at the Brandenburg University of Technology (BTU). His research activities include business process management, software development and graph theory. He reviewed several scientific project proposals as well as papers of established IS conferences like ICIS, ECIS, AMCIS, HICCS and EMISA and produced own publications, especially focusing structural and semantic aspects of EPCs.

Richard Welch

Concord Group Insurance Companies, USA

Richard Welch is presently serving as VP—Corporate Planning for the Concord Group Insurance Companies in the USA. He is the former President and CEO of the Premier Insurance Company of Massachusetts where he served 20 years as a senior executive. Welch is also the bformer principal of REW Insurance Consulting Services, where he provided services in strategic planning, product management & pricing, underwriting strategy, and usage based insurance strategies to Property-Casualty insurance companies, agencies, and service providers. Welch has co-authored or contributed to several publications regarding usage based insurance.

Richard J. Welke

Georgia State University, USA

Dr. Welke is director of the Center for Process Innovation, professor and previous chair of the CIS department at the Robinson College of Business at Georgia State University. Prior appointments include professorships at TU-Delft, Erasmus University and McMaster University. He is a co-founder of ICIS, AIS, TIMS College on IS, and IFIP WG 8.2. He has held C-level positions at a number of companies in the US and Canada. His 100+ papers are published in various books, refereed journals and conference proceedings. Dr. Welke's scholarly contributions are in the areas of methodology engineering, meta-modeling, business process management, service innovation BAM/CEP, compliance business rules, SOA and mobile application uptake.

Index

J. vom Brocke, T. Schmiedel (eds.), *BPM – Driving Innovation in a Digital World*, Management for Professionals, DOI 10.1007/978-3-319-14430-6

M

N

O

P

MIX
Papier aus verantwortungsvollen Quellen
Paper from responsible sources
FSC® C105338

If you have any concerns about our products,
you can contact us on
ProductSafety@springernature.com

In case Publisher is established outside the EU,
the EU authorized representative is:
Springer Nature Customer Service Center GmbH
Europaplatz 3, 69115 Heidelberg, Germany

Printed by Libri Plureos GmbH
in Hamburg, Germany